Random House Webster's

BUILD YOUR
POWER VOCABULARY

RANDOM HOUSE
NEW YORK

Random House Webster's Build Your Power Vocabulary

Copyright © 1998 by Random House, Inc.

Some of the material in this work appeared in slightly different form in *The Random House Power Vocabulary Builder,* published in 1996.

Trademarks

This book is available for special purchases in bulk by organizations and institutions, not for resale, at special discounts. Please direct your inquiries to the Random House Special Sales Department, toll-free 888-591-1200 or fax 212-572-4961.

Please address inquiries about electronic licensing of reference products, for use on a network or on software or on CD-ROM, to the Subsidiary Rights Department, Random House Reference & Information Publishing, fax 212-940-7370.

Library of Congress Cataloging-in-Publication Data
Random House Webster's build your power vocabulary.
    p. cm.
  ISBN 0-375-70247-4
   1. Vocabulary—Problems, exercises, etc. I. Random House (Firm)
PE1449.R338   1998
428.2'4—dc21   98-7914
                                          CIP

Visit the Random House Reference & Information Publishing web site at www.randomwords.com

Typeset and printed in the United States of America on acid-free paper

0 9 8 7 6 5 4 3
January 2000

ISBN 0-375-70247-4

New York   Toronto   London   Sydney   Auckland

Contents

Project Editors: Carol G. Braham, Enid Pearsons, Jesse
Sheidlower
Contributing Editor: Carole Cook
Managing Editor: Andrew Ambraziejus
Database Manager: Constance A. Baboukis

Production Director: Patricia W. Ehresmann
Editorial Director: Wendalyn Nichols
Publisher: Charles M. Levine

Foreword

Self-expression is a basic human activity. Words, whether spoken or written, embody what we are thinking and what we wish to get across. A larger vocabulary can help you to express your thoughts more vividly and precisely. Along with teaching you new words, *Random House Webster's Build Your Power Vocabulary* gives you the tools to continue to expand your means of expressing your thoughts.

Random House Webster's Build Your Power Vocabulary explains the building blocks of the English language (roots, prefixes, suffixes, borrowed words); offers tips for proper expression (spelling, pronunciation, usage); and takes a look at language's ever-changing aspects (special words, sensitivity in language, and new words).

The English language is one of the richest in the world, with influences from all over the globe. There are, however, some core influences that reflect its largely European origins: primarily Latin, Greek, and French. A multitude of English words stem from these languages, and the greater part of this book is designed to teach you these word origins, thereby helping you build a broader and more versatile vocabulary. It also takes into account the contributions that a number of other languages—Italian, Spanish, German, Yiddish, and Japanese—have made to English vocabulary.

To further help you excel in English usage, this book provides quizzes and puzzles to reinforce what you will learn in the coming chapters. And to maintain this new knowledge, be sure to write and speak the words in complete sentences, thus incorporating and registering them in your growing, more powerful vocabulary.

Pronunciation Key

a	act, bat	m	my, him	u	up, love
ā	able, cape	n	now, on	ûr	urge, burn
âr	air, dare	ng	sing, England	v	voice, live
ä	art, calm	o	box, hot	w	west, away
b	back, rub	ō	over, no	y	yes, young
ch	chief, beach	ô	order, ball	z	zeal, lazy, those
d	do, bed	oi	oil, joy	zh	vision, measure
e	ebb, set	o͝o	book, put	ə	occurs only in
ē	equal, bee	o͞o	ooze, rule		unaccented
f	fit, puff	ou	out, loud		syllables and
g	give, beg	p	page, stop		indicates the
h	hit, hear	r	read, cry		sound of a *in*
i	if, big	s	see, miss		alone e *in*
ī	ice, bite	sh	shoe, push		system i *in*
j	just, edge	t	ten, bit		easily o *in*
k	kept, make	th	thin, path		gallop u *in*
l	low, all	t͟h	that, other		circus

Introduction

Words are the building blocks of thought. They are the means by which we understand the ideas of others and express our own opinions. It is only logical that people who know how to use words concisely and accurately find it easier to achieve their aims.

In fact, formal education has less relationship to vocabulary achievement than you might expect; people *can* improve their word power on their own. This section will show you how to expand and improve your vocabulary in *just fifteen minutes a day!*

Each of the following lessons is designed to take *fifteen* minutes to complete. Do one lesson a day. Work from beginning to end because the lessons build on each other. Follow these three easy steps:

Step 1: Time

Begin by setting aside a block of fifteen minutes a day. Don't split your time into three five-minute segments—set aside one fifteen-minute period every day. Consider using fifteen minutes in the early morning before you begin your regular activities. Or you might want to use fifteen minutes on the bus, subway, or train or fifteen minutes during a work break. Maybe right after dinner is a convenient time for you. Whatever time you select, make it *your* time—carve it in granite! To make your work even easier, try to set aside the same time every day. You'll be surprised at how quickly your vocabulary builds.

Step 2: Place

Now, find a place where you can work undisturbed. If you know that you have difficulty tuning out the distractions of public transportation or the office lunchroom, try to study at home. Perhaps you have the ability to completely ignore extraneous chatter or music and so can concentrate in the middle of the family room or in a crowded cafeteria. Wherever you decide to study, try to settle in the same place every day. In this way, you'll set to work more quickly, concentrate better, and succeed sooner.

Step 3: Method

Fifteen minutes a day is all it takes to build a powerful vocabulary. To help you get into the rhythm of working in fifteen-minute segments, set your alarm or kitchen timer for fifteen minutes. When you hear the buzzer, you'll know that you've spent fifteen minutes on your vocabulary. Soon you'll be able to pace yourself without the timer.

Test Your Vocabulary

To see how your vocabulary measures up to that of other people, take the following quizzes. As you go through each one, put a check mark next to any word you don't know. After you complete each quiz, check the answers on page xi to see which of your choices proved correct. Then take a minute to look up the words you missed in a good dictionary.

Quiz 1: Grading Your Word Power

The first quiz consists of twenty-five phrases, each containing an italicized word. Circle the correct response. This quiz has no time limit.

1. a *lenient* supervisor
   a. short   b. not strict   c. inflexible   d. shrewd
2. an *audacious* endeavor
   a. foolish   b. serious   c. expensive   d. bold
3. a *latent* talent
   a. apparent   b. valuable   c. present but not apparent   d. useless
4. a *gaudy* dress
   a. expensive   b. deep green   c. flattering   d. showy
5. a *disheveled* person
   a. useless   b. untidy   c. miserable   d. vicious
6. *feign* illness
   a. suffer   b. pretend   c. die from   d. enjoy
7. an *agile* child
   a. intelligent   b. nimble   c. neglected   d. annoying
8. a *somber* night
   a. dismal   b. expensive   c. lively   d. disastrous
9. a *prosaic* event
   a. extraordinary   b. irregular   c. commonplace   d. pretty
10. a *vivacious* person
    a. annoying   b. dismal   c. vicious   d. spirited

11. a *baffling* situation
    a. puzzling   b. obvious   c. easy   d. old
12. a *hiatus* in the schedule
    a. continuation   b. uniformity   c. gap   d. beginning
13. a *lackluster* report
    a. enthusiastic   b. praiseworthy   c. dull   d. wordy
14. a *prevalent* condition
    a. adult   b. widespread   c. previous   d. fatal
15. a *loquacious* person
    a. talkative   b. cutthroat   c. laconic   d. enthusiastic
16. an *anonymous* victim
    a. willing   b. known   c. not known or named   d. foreign
17. a *vicarious* thrill
    a. incomplete   b. triumphant   c. spoiled   d. indirect
18. a *languid* feeling
    a. nervous   b. energetic   c. fatigued   d. robust
19. *vernacular* language
    a. ordinary   b. elevated   c. formal   d. informal
20. a religious *icon*
    a. gesture   b. picture   c. ritual   d. structure
21. *inclement* weather
    a. fair   b. unexpected   c. foul   d. disturbing
22. a *cavalier* attitude
    a. pleasant   b. dramatic   c. considerate   d. arrogant
23. a *caustic* remark
    a. wise   b. biting   c. prudent   d. complimentary
24. a timely *caveat*
    a. bargain   b. purchase   c. warning   d. movement
25. an *ominous* situation
    a. pleasant   b. rigid   c. obvious   d. threatening

Use the following chart to score your results:

0–6	correct	Below average
7–13	correct	Average
14–20	correct	Above average
21–25	correct	Superior

The following three quizzes evaluate whether you have an average, good, or excellent vocabulary. The quizzes have no time limit.

Quiz 2: Test for an Average Vocabulary

If you have an average vocabulary, you should be able to match the two columns below correctly. Write your answer in the space

provided. Nearly three quarters of the adults tested knew all these
words.

1. **imminent**	a. cleanse	_____
2. **fluster**	b. flashy	_____
3. **rigid**	c. confuse	_____
4. **purge**	d. restore	_____
5. **rehabilitate**	e. hinder	_____
6. **latent**	f. pretend	_____
7. **gaudy**	g. stiff	_____
8. **feign**	h. coax	_____
9. **cajole**	i. hidden	_____
10. **impede**	j. at hand	_____

Quiz 3: Test for a Good Vocabulary

Only half the adults tested got all of the following words correct.
See how well *you* can do! Write S if the word in the second column
is similar in meaning to the word in the first column or O if it is
opposite.

S or O

1. **myriad**	few	_____
2. **panacea**	cure-all	_____
3. **opulent**	spare	_____
4. **eschew**	shun	_____
5. **nefarious**	wicked	_____
6. **incarcerate**	imprison	_____
7. **ameliorate**	make worse	_____
8. **candor**	hypocrisy	_____
9. **taciturn**	talkative	_____
10. **verbose**	wordy	_____

Quiz 4: Test for an Excellent Vocabulary

Fewer than one-quarter of the adults tested got all of the following words correct. In the space provided, write T if the sentence is
true or F if it is false.

T or F

1. *Obsequiousness* is a sign of pride. _____
2. *Parsimonious* people are extravagant. _____
3. Recycling is an *exigency* of the moment. _____
4. The hawk is a *predatory* bird. _____
5. An *aquiline* nose is straight. _____

6. A *covert* plan is out in the open. _____
7. It is hard to explain things to an *obtuse* person. _____
8. Someone with *catholic* views is narrow-minded. _____
9. A large debt *obviates* financial worries. _____
10. *Erudite* people are well-read. _____

Answers to Tests

Answers to Quiz 1

1. b 2. d 3. c 4. d 5. b 6. b 7. b 8. a 9. c 10. d 11. a 12. c 13. c 14. b 15. a
16. c 17. d 18. c 19. a 20. b 21. c 22. d 23. b 24. c 25. d

Answers to Quiz 2

1. j 2. c 3. g 4. a 5. d 6. i 7. b 8. f 9. h 10. c

Answers to Quiz 3

1. O 2. S 3. O 4. S 5. S 6. S 7. O 8. O 9. O 10. S

Answers to Quiz 4

1. F 2. F 3. T 4. T 5. F 6. F 7. T 8. F 9. F 10. T

Improve Your Pronunciation

Most people feel comfortable enough among their friends and family to use informal speech patterns. We tend, in these relaxed circumstances, not to think about how we sound and whether we are pronouncing words correctly. But we are not always surrounded by people we know well. There are times when it is necessary to make a good impression. That impression is based in great part not only on the way we look but on what we say and how well we say it.

The fact is that different environments call for appropriate adjustments in language just as they call for appropriate changes in clothing. The idea is to be able to make informed, deliberate choices. But not only are there issues concerning how to say certain words, some of these words are even the subject of continuing controversy.

For example: Have you ever argued at the dinner table about how to pronounce a word? ("It's CAR-ib-**BE**-an!" "No, it's Ca-**RIB**-be-an!" The answer, by the way, is that it's either.) Have you ever felt a little vulnerable about your pronunciation during a job interview? ("I'll be able to start the first of *February.*") Or are you simply curious about how to say a word you have just read for the first time?

If you answered yes to any of these questions, you will find the pronunciation notes in desk dictionaries to be remarkably useful. They provide balanced, reassuring guidance, indicating which pronunciations some people might be critical of and whether that criticism is justifiable or not. With their help, you will be able to make conscious pronunciation choices as part of your larger concern about how you want to sound to other people in various circumstances.

Here is a sampling of pronunciation notes, taken from the *Random House Webster's College Dictionary,* about some words that are known to give people trouble:

athlete   *Athlete, athletic,* and *athletics,* normally pronounced (ath′lēt), (ath let′ik), and (ath let′iks), are heard frequently with an extra schwa, an intrusive unstressed vowel inserted between the first and second syllables: (ath′ə lēt′), (ath′ə let′ik), and (ath′ə let′iks). The pronunciations containing the extra syllable are usually considered nonstandard, in spite of their widespread use on radio and television. Pronunciations with similarly intrusive vowels are also heard, though less frequently, for other words, as (fil′əm) for *film,* (el′əm) for *elm,* and (är′thə rī′tis) for *arthritis,* rather than the standard (film), (elm), and (är thrī′tis).

covert   *Covert,* related to cover, has historically been pronounced (kuv′ərt), with (u), the same stressed vowel found in cover. This (u) is the traditional and unchallenged vowel in many other English words spelled with stressed *o* followed by *v,* voiced *th,* or a nasal in the same syllable, words of high frequency like *love* and *above, mother* and *other, some* and *honey.* The adjective *covert,* however, by analogy with *overt* (ō vûrt′, ō′vərt), its opposite in meaning, has developed the pronunciation (kō′vərt), perhaps because of the frequent pairing of the two terms in the news media. This is now the more common pronunciation for the adjective in American English, though not in British English, which retains the historical pronunciation. For the noun senses, less likely to appear in the news or to be contrasted with *overt* and its (ō) sound, the older (kuv′ərt) remains the more frequent pronunciation.

either   The pronunciations (ē′thər) and (nē′thər), with the vowel (ē) of *see,* are the usual ones in American English for the words *either* and *neither.* The pronunciations (ī′thər) and (nī′thər), with the (ī) vowel of *bite,* occur occasionally for these words, chiefly in the speech of the educated and in the network standard English of radio and television. Both the (ē) and (ī) pronunciations existed in British English, and in the nineteenth century the (ī) came to predominate in standard British speech. In American English, therefore, it reflects a recent borrowing from British speech rather than a survival from the time of early settlement, influenced as well by the *ei* spelling, which is pronounced as (ī) in such words as *height* and *stein.*

February   The pronunciation (feb′yōō er′ē), with the first (r) replaced by (y), results both from *dissimilation,* the tendency of sounds that are alike to become unlike when they follow each other closely, and from analogy with *January.* Although sometimes criticized, this dissimilated pronunciation of *February* is used by educated speakers. Therefore, both (feb′rōō er′ē) and (feb′yōō er′ē) are considered standard.

forte   In the sense of a person's strong point *(He draws well, but sculpture is his forte),* the older and historical pronunciation of *forte* is the one-syllable (fôrt) or (fōrt). The word is derived from the French word *fort* "strong." A two-syllable pronunciation (fôr′tā) is increasingly heard, especially from younger educated speakers, perhaps owing to confusion with the musical term *forte,* pronounced in English as (fôr′tā) and in Italian as (fôʀ′te). Both the one- and two-syllable pronunciations of *forte* are now considered standard.

harass   *Harass,* a seventeenth-century French borrowing, has traditionally been pronounced (har′əs), with stress on the first syllable. A newer pronunciation, (hə ras′), has developed in North American (but not British) English. While this newer pronunciation is sometimes criticized by older educated speakers, it has become the more common one in the United States, especially among younger educated speakers, some of whom have little, if any, familiarity with the older form.

Ms.   *Ms.* is pronounced (miz), a pronunciation that is identical with one standard South Midland and Southern U.S. pronunciation of *Mrs.*

nuclear   The second and third syllables of (nu·cle·ar) are commonly pronounced as (-klē ər), which can be shown more broadly as (-klə yər). The somewhat controversial pronunciation of these two syllables as (-kyə lər), prominent in recent years, results from a process in which the sounds (1) and (y) change places. This pronunciation, reinforced by analogy with words like *molecular,* is disapproved of by many, although it occurs among such highly educated speakers as scientists, professors, and high government officials.

process   The word *process,* an early fourteenth-century French borrowing, has a regularly formed plural that adds *-es* to the singular. This plural, as in similar words like *recesses* and *successes,* has traditionally been pronounced (-iz): (pros'es iz, prō'ses-) or (pros'ə siz, prō'sə-). Recent years have seen the increasing popularity of an (-ēz') pronunciation for *processes,* perhaps by mistaken analogy with such plurals as *theses* and *hypotheses,* with which it has no connection. This newer pronunciation is common among younger educated speakers.

British vs. American Pronunciation

All languages exist in a variety of forms, called dialects. These are reflected, for example, in choices in vocabulary *(hero sandwich* vs. *hoagie),* in grammar *(he doesn't* vs. *he don't),* and in pronunciation. English is no exception.

Perhaps the dialect difference most noticeable to the vast majority of Americans is that between standard British and so-called standard American speech. Certain kinds of sounds are consistently different in these two dialects. British speakers do not pronounce the (r) after a final vowel or between a vowel and a consonant in words like *car* (*Amer.* kär; *Brit.* kä) and *cart* (*Amer.* kärt; *Brit.* kät). British speakers who speak the dialect recorded in their dictionaries also tend to use a "broad a" in words like *half* (häf), *dance* (däns), and *rather* (rä'ᵗħər). Most Americans use a "flat a": (haf), (dans), and (ratħ'ər).

However, some words are spoken in the two countries with even more radically different pronunciations. Here are a few words that sound strikingly different in Britain and America. Notice which words display differences in stress patterns, vowels, and—occasionally—consonants.

	American	*British*
ate	(āt)	(et)
charade	(shə rād')	(shə räd')
clerk	(klûrk)	(kläk)
leisure	(lē'zhər)	(lezh'ər)
laboratory	(lab'rə tôr'ē)	(lə bor'ə tri)
lieutenant	(lo͞o ten'ənt)	(lef ten'ənt)
missile	(mis'əl)	(mis'īl)
privacy	(prī'və sē)	(priv'ə si)
schedule	(skej'o͞ol)	(shej'o͞ol)
"z"	(zē)	(zed)

American Dialects

Though the English of England (Standard British English) and the English of America (Standard American English) have many differences, there are dialect differences within American English as well. In America, the main dialect regions are the North (which stretches all of the way across the country), the South (which chiefly refers to the coastal regions from Maryland and Virginia down, and over to eastern Texas), the Midlands (in between the North and the coastal South, going over to Iowa and Missouri), and the West. The defining characteristics and precise boundaries of these regions—and their many sub-regions—are debated by experts, but they are sufficient as broad categories.

As with the national dialects, these regional American dialects can vary in several ways. Carbonated beverages can be called *soda* in the Northeast, *pop* in the Midwest and West, *tonic* in the Boston area, and *dope* in the South. The South, and the southern parts of the Midlands, can have "double modal" verbs, with sentences such as "He might could do it" or "They used to could." In the North, the words *all the* can be used with comparatives, such as "That's all the farther I can go." And in the Midwest, the word *anymore* can be used in positive sentences, meaning "nowadays," such as "I'm spending less time reading anymore"—a use that appears to be spreading around the country.

The main thing that distinguishes dialects, however, is pronunciation. The differences among the American dialects are not as great as those between American English and British English, but they still exist and are often quite striking, which is why we speak of the "Southern drawl" or the "New England twang." What you do with the vowels in *cot* and *caught* (are they the same or different?) or in *Mary, marry,* and *merry* (again, are they the same or different?); whether you pronounce the final *r* of *door,* or add an *r* to *idea;* whether you pronounce *air* or *mirror* with one syllable or two—these are the kinds of factors that determine the boundaries of dialect areas.

There is no true single variety of American English that can be considered "General American." It is likely that these regional dialects will become more distinct over time, and that they will not be replaced by a uniform national variety of English.

How American Dictionaries Handle Dialects

Only a few American dialects are shown in most American desk dictionaries—that is, the "college" dictionaries familiar to most users. For the most part, the dictionaries do not designate the particular regions where these dialects are common. That is not the purpose of ordinary dictionary pronunciations. Detailed information about dialects belongs in more specialized works: pronunciation dictionaries, dialect atlases, and other books intended for scholars.

A Conflict of Symbol Systems: IPA vs. Diacritical Systems

The specialized works mentioned above have as their primary audience students, teachers, dictionary editors, and other professionals in fields like linguistics, dialectology, and phonology. These scholars often study small variations in pronunciation that the average person would not even notice. For their purposes, a system for transcribing sounds must not only render those sounds exactly, it must also be common to scholars in many parts of the world, easily crossing language and dialect barriers.

Such a system has evolved in the International Phonetic Alphabet, commonly referred to as IPA, which offers a wealth of symbols that can show a wide range, from very "broad," general pronunciations to "narrow," specific ones. IPA can therefore make extremely fine distinctions. Its sets of symbols, as related to the sound system of each individual language or dialect being studied, can convey information accurately and with precision. Training in IPA is therefore mandatory for anyone planning to enter one of these fields. IPA is also used in other fields, such as theater or opera, where performers must learn accurate pronunciations of other languages.

However, most Americans do not study IPA in the normal course of their education, and they are not likely to consult a dictionary to find out how many dialect pronunciations there are for a given word. Thus, the general aim of dictionary pronunciations is more simple and direct. They exist to provide confidence. They enable the average user to say words—especially unfamiliar ones—in ways that are perfectly acceptable in the workplace, at school, and in various social circumstances. Therefore, compilers of American dictionaries tend to use pronunciation systems that are both (1) accurate enough to convey just the amount of information needed, and (2) simple enough for an average reader, with no special training, to understand.

Most American dictionaries rely on variations of a familiar system, based on English spellings, that uses diacritical marks over vowels to represent differences in vowel quality. It features well-known conventions: For example, "long a" (ā) as in *fate,* "short a" (a) as in *fat,* and "broad a" (ä) as in the first syllable of *father* are all vowel sounds represented by a printed *a.* The symbols for these three sounds remain "kinds of *a*" in a diacritical system. In IPA, by contrast, the vowel in *fate* would be /e/ or /ei/, the vowel of *fat* /æ/, and the first vowel of *father* /ɒ/.

In other words, a diacritical system is able to make efficient use of the knowledge that a native speaker of English has about the language. The stressed vowels of *divine* and *divinity,* for example, are both spelled with the letter *i.* The dictionary-style pronunciation symbols for these two sounds, (ī) and (i) respectively, are also forms of *i,* reflecting the relationship between the two words. Once again, IPA, which is based not on English but on European languages derived from Latin, would show very different looking symbols: /ai/ and /ɪ/.

Diacritical systems are also known as "key-word systems." That is because the symbols used, while guiding the reader to correct choices, do not represent precise, unvarying sounds. Instead, any individual reader looking at a pronunciation key (usually included in the front matter of a dictionary) should, in effect, say: "This symbol represents the sound *I* make when *I* say the following key words." Therefore, although speakers from Boston, New York, Seattle, Savannah, and Baltimore all pronounce the (ou) of *plow, out, loud,* and *cow* quite differently, the (ou) symbol they find in other pronunciations they look up will accurately reflect their individual dialects and lead them to use an appropriate pronunciation in the new word that is consistent with the way they normally speak.

What Kinds of Dialects Are Shown?

Because American dialects vary in the number of fine distinctions they make, it is also common for speakers in some parts of the country to "collapse" certain differences. In much of the Midwest, for example, no perceptible difference exists between the pronunciations of the word *dawn* and the name *Don.* Yet most dictionaries show the first as (dôn) and the second as (don), in order to accommodate those sections of the country where the two vowel sounds are distinguished. Those who do not have this distinction, and who may even have difficulty hearing it, can still use a key-word system; they will merely pronounce the vowels in the key words for both (ô) and (o) in the same way.

Here is a short list of words that the *Random House Webster's College Dictionary* shows with two pronunciations. Which ones are closer to your own?

dog (dôg, dog)
fore (fôr, fōr)
half (haf, häf)
huge (hyo͞oj, yo͞oj)
sure (sho͝or, shûr)
tune (to͞on, tyo͞on)
when (hwen, wen)

r-*dropping*

One dialect that most American dictionaries do *not* show is *r*-dropping. (It is interesting to note that linguists tend to write about this dialect phenomenon from the perspective of whatever is common in their own countries. American linguists refer to the standard British dialect, as reflected in British dictionaries, as "*r*-less," while British linguists designate the standard American dialect, as shown in American dictionaries, as "*r*-full.")

In an *r*-less dialect, not all *r* sounds are dropped. The ones that are left out in continuous speech are those that occur after a vowel, as at the end of an utterance or before a consonant. (Note the use of "utterance" rather than "word.") Typically, the preceding vowel is lengthened or a faint neutral vowel (a schwa) is inserted, to compensate for the missing sound. Some examples are:

far (fä)
fear (fēə)
cart (kät)

The *r*-sound in this dialect is present before a vowel, as in *row* and *throw,* as well as between vowels, as in *barrel* (bar′əl). But some interesting things sometimes occur. Notably, when a word that ends in vowel-plus-*r* is followed in an utterance by a word that starts with a vowel, the *r*, which is then between vowels, is therefore restored and pronounced! Thus the isolated word *here* is pronounced as (hēə), but the utterance *here is* is pronounced as (hēr iz). Consequently, many speakers of *r*-less dialects insert an *r*-sound in analogous utterances *even when* there is no spelled r *to begin* with! For example, certain residents of Massachusetts would put an *r*-sound in the phrase *the idea of.* Can you figure out where it would appear? You're right. You'd hear it between the words *idea* and *of:* (t͟hē ī dēr′ uv).

Lesson 1. Test Your Pronunciation Skills

Let's see how you pronounce some fairly difficult words. As you work through each quiz, put a check mark next to any word whose pronunciation you don't know. After you finish each quiz, go back and see which of your choices were right. (Some words have alternate pronunciations.) Finally, take a few minutes to study the words you missed.

Each of the following quizzes contains twenty words. See how many you can pronounce correctly. There is no time limit.

Quiz 1: Pronunciation

1. badinage
2. salubrious
3. apocryphal
4. putsch
5. effeminacy
6. effusive
7. mandible
8. raison d'être
9. amblyopia
10. dacha
11. exegesis
12. dishabille
13. élan
14. febrile
15. gamut
16. obsequious
17. jejune
18. ribald
19. apothegm
20. wizened

Answers:

To satisfy your curiosity, here are the definitions as well as the pronunciations. To rank yourself against others, refer to the chart at the end of this quiz.

If you are not familiar with the pronunciation symbols, refer to the pronunciation key at the end of this section.

1. **badinage** (bad′n āzh′, bad′n ij) light, playful talk; banter.
2. **salubrious** (sə lo͞o′brē əs) favorable to or promoting health; healthful.

3. **apocryphal** (ə pok′rə fəl) of doubtful authenticity; false.
4. **putsch** (poŏch) a plot to overthrow a government.
5. **effeminacy** (i fem′ə nə sē) the quality of being soft or delicate to an unmanly degree in traits, tastes, habits, etc.
6. **effusive** (i fyoō′siv) unduly demonstrative; lacking reserve.
7. **mandible** (man′də bəl) the bone of the lower jaw.
8. **raison d'être** (rā′zōn de′trə) reason or justification for being or existing.
9. **amblyopia** (am′blē ō′pē ə) dimness of sight, without an apparent organic cause.
10. **dacha** (dä′chə) a Russian country house or villa.
11. **exegesis** (ek′si jē′sis) a critical explanation or interpretation, especially of Scripture.
12. **dishabille** (dis′ə bēl′) the state of being carelessly or partly dressed; a state of disarray or disorder.
13. **élan** (ā län′) dash; impetuous ardor.
14. **febrile** (fē′brəl, feb′rəl) feverish.
15. **gamut** (gam′ət) the entire scale or range.
16. **obsequious** (əb sē′kwē əs) servile, compliant, or deferential.
17. **jejune** (ji joōn′) not interesting; childish; deficient or lacking in nutritive value.
18. **ribald** (rib′əld) vulgar or indecent in speech; coarsely mocking.
19. **apothegm** (ap′ə them′) a short, pithy saying; aphorism.
20. **wizened** (wiz′ənd) withered; shriveled.

Use the following chart to score your results:

0–5	correct	Below average
6–10	correct	Average
11–15	correct	Above average
16–20	correct	Superior

Want to try again? See how many of these twenty words you can pronounce correctly. The quiz has no time limit.

Quiz 2: Pronunciation

1. vignette
2. bailiwick
3. juvenilia
4. baroque
5. flaccid
6. cupidity
7. turgid
8. sententious
9. zealous
10. ragout
11. blasé
12. cabochon
13. loath
14. quotidian
15. obdurate
16. cache
17. jocund
18. schism
19. escutcheon
20. satyr

Answers:

To rank yourself against others, refer to the scoring chart at the end of this test section.

1. **vignette** (vin yet′) a short, graceful literary sketch; a decorative design or small illustration used on the title page of a book or at the beginning or end of a chapter.
2. **bailiwick** (bā′lə wik′) a person's area of skill, knowledge, or training; the district within which a bailiff has jurisdiction.
3. **juvenilia** (jōō′və nil′ē ə) works, especially writings, produced in youth.
4. **baroque** (bə rōk′) extravagantly ornamented; ornate; designating a style of art or music of the seventeenth to eighteenth century.
5. **flaccid** (flak′sid) soft and limp; flabby.
6. **cupidity** (kyōō pid′i tē) eager or excessive desire, especially for wealth; greed or avarice.
7. **turgid** (tûr′jid) swollen or distended; pompous; bombastic.
8. **sententious** (sen ten′shəs) given to excessive moralizing; self-righteous; abounding in pithy aphorisms or maxims, as a book.
9. **zealous** (zel′əs) ardently active or devoted.
10. **ragout** (ra gōō′) a highly seasoned stew of meat or fish.
11. **blasé** (blä zā′) indifferent to or bored with life or a particular activity.
12. **cabochon** (kab′ə shon′) a precious stone of convex hemispherical or oval form, polished but not cut into facets.
13. **loath** (lōth, lōth) unwilling; reluctant.
14. **quotidian** (kwō tid′ē ən) daily; everyday; ordinary.
15. **obdurate** (ob′dōō rit, -dyōō-) unmoved by persuasion, pity, or tender feelings; unyielding.
16. **cache** (kash) a hiding place.
17. **jocund** (jok′ənd) cheerful; merry.
18. **schism** (siz′əm, skiz′-) division; disunion.
19. **escutcheon** (i skuch′ən) a shield or shieldlike surface on which a coat of arms is depicted.
20. **satyr** (sā′tər) in Greek myths, a woodland deity.

Use the following chart to score your results:

0–5	correct	Below average
6–10	correct	Average
11–15	correct	Above average
16–20	correct	Superior

Lesson 2.

Here are two more pronunciation quizzes to provide you with additional practice.

Quiz 3: Pronunciation

1. dybbuk
2. hauteur
3. nacre
4. sidle
5. toque
6. viscid
7. lingua franca
8. phlegmatic
9. guano
10. apropos

11. insouciance
12. folderol
13. cavil
14. macabre
15. elision
16. denouement
17. parvenu
18. pince-nez
19. alopecia
20. chicanery

Answers:

1. **dybbuk** (dib′ək) in Jewish folklore, a demon or the soul of a dead person that enters the body of a living person and controls him or her.
2. **hauteur** (hō tûr′) a haughty manner or spirit.
3. **nacre** (nā′kər) mother-of-pearl.
4. **sidle** (sīd′l) to move sideways.
5. **toque** (tōk) a soft, brimless, close-fitting hat for women; a chef's hat; a velvet hat with a narrow, turned-up brim, a full crown, and a plume, worn especially in the sixteenth century.
6. **viscid** (vis′id) having a glutinous consistency; sticky.
7. **lingua franca** (ling′gwə frang′kə) a language widely used as a means of communication among speakers of different languages.
8. **phlegmatic** (fleg mat′ik) not easily excited; calm or apathetic in temperament.
9. **guano** (gwä′nō) a natural manure composed chiefly of the excrement of sea birds, found especially on islands near the Peruvian coast; bird lime.
10. **apropos** (ap′rə pō′) appropriate; timely; to the purpose; opportunely; with reference or regard.
11. **insouciance** (in sōō′sē əns) lack of care or concern; indifference.
12. **folderol** (fol′də rol′) mere nonsense; foolish talk or ideas.
13. **cavil** (kav′əl) to quibble; an irritating or trivial objection.
14. **macabre** (mə kä′brə) gruesome; horrible; grim.

15. **elision** (i lizh′ən) the omission of a vowel, consonant, or syllable in pronunciation.
16. **denouement** (dā′noo mäN′) the final resolution of a plot, as of a drama or novel; outcome.
17. **parvenu** (pär′və noo′, -nyoo′) a person who has suddenly acquired wealth or importance but lacks the proper social qualifications; upstart.
18. **pince-nez** (pans′nā′, pins′-) a pair of eyeglasses held on the face by a spring that pinches the nose.
19. **alopecia** (al′ə pē′shē ə, -sē ə) baldness.
20. **chicanery** (shi kā′nə rē, chi-) trickery or deception by the use of cunning or clever tricks.

Quiz 4: Pronunciation

1. façade
2. obeisance
3. gnome
4. diva
5. liaison
6. mauve
7. fiat
8. kiosk
9. chassis
10. omniscient
11. defalcation
12. contumacious
13. heinous
14. emollient
15. gibe
16. ewer
17. hirsute
18. ogle
19. ennui
20. canard

Answers:

1. **façade** (fə säd′) the front of a building, especially an imposing or decorative one; a superficial appearance or illusion of something.
2. **obeisance** (ō bā′səns, ō bē′-) a movement of the body expressing deep respect or deferential courtesy, as before a superior; a deep bow.
3. **gnome** (nōm) one of a legendary species of very small creatures, usually described as shriveled little old men, who inhabit the interior of the earth and act as guardians of its treasure; troll; dwarf.
4. **diva** (dē′və, -vä) a distinguished female singer; prima donna.
5. **liaison** (lē ā′zən, lē′ā zôN′, lē′ə zon′) a contact maintained between units to ensure concerted action; an illicit sexual relationship.
6. **mauve** (mōv, môv) pale bluish purple.
7. **fiat** (fē′ät, -at; fī′ət, -at) an authoritative decree, sanction, or order.

8. **kiosk** (kē′osk, kē osk′) a kind of open pavilion or summerhouse common in Turkey and Iran; a similar structure used as a bandstand, newsstand, etc.
9. **chassis** (chas′ē, -is, shas′ē) the frame, wheels, and machinery of a motor vehicle, on which the body is supported.
10. **omniscient** (om nish′ənt) having complete or infinite knowledge, awareness, or understanding; perceiving all things; all-knowing.
11. **defalcation** (dē′fal kā′shən, -fôl-) the misappropriation of money held by an official, trustee, or other fiduciary.
12. **contumacious** (kon′to͞o mā′shəs, -tyo͞o-) stubbornly perverse or rebellious; obstinately disobedient.
13. **heinous** (hā′nəs) hateful or evil.
14. **emollient** (i mol′yənt) something that softens or soothes the skin, as a lotion or medicine.
15. **gibe** (jīb) to mock or jeer; a caustic remark.
16. **ewer** (yo͞o′ər) a pitcher with a wide spout.
17. **hirsute** (hûr′so͞ot, hûr so͞ot′) hairy; shaggy.
18. **ogle** (ō′gəl) to look at amorously, flirtatiously, or impertinently.
19. **ennui** (än wē′) weariness and discontent resulting from satiety or lack of interest; boredom.
20. **canard** (kə närd′) a false story, report, or rumor, usually derogatory.

Words Often Mispronounced

The following is a list of words that are often considered difficult because their pronunciation is not obvious. You will find the correct pronunciation in parentheses next to each of these words. The pronunciation key appears at the end of the list. A great way to remember these words is by testing yourself, repeatedly uttering the correct pronunciations.

abdomen	(ab′də mən)	cello	(chel′ō)
aborigine	(ab′ə rij′ə nē)	cerebral	(sə rē′brəl, ser′ə-)
agile	(aj′əl)		
albino	(al bī′nō)	chaise longue	(shāz′ lông′)
apropos	(ap′rə pō′)	chamois	(sham′ē)
avoirdupois	(av′ər də poiz′)	chantey	(shan′tē)
		chauffeur	(shō′fər, shō fûr′)
balk	(bôk)		
baroque	(bə rōk′)	chic	(shēk)
bayou	(bī′o͞o)	cholera	(kol′ər ə)
brooch	(brōch)	cinchona	(sing kō′nə)
buoy	(bo͞o′ē, boi)	clandestine	(klan des′tin)

clapboard	(klab′ərd)	glazier	(glā′zhər)
clique	(klēk)	glower	(glou′ər)
colonel	(kûr′nl)	gnu	(nōō)
compote	(kom′pōt)	gourmet	(gŏŏr mā′,
conduit	(kon′dwit)		gŏŏr′mā)
consommé	(kon′sə mā′)	granary	(gran′ə rē)
corps	(kôr, kōr)	guerrilla	(gə ril′ə)
corpuscle	(kôr′pə səl)	guillotine	(gil′ə tēn′)
cortege	(kôr tezh′)	gunwale	(gun′l)
cotillion	(kə til′yən)		
coup	(kōō)	habitué	(hə bich′ōō ā′)
coxswain	(kok′sən)	harbinger	(här′bin jər)
crosier	(krō′zhər)	heifer	(hef′ər)
crouton	(krōō′ton)	heinous	(hā′nəs)
cuisine	(kwi zēn′)	hirsute	(hûr′sōōt)
		holocaust	(hol′ə kôst′)
dachshund	(däks′hŏŏnt′,	hosiery	(hō′zhə rē)
	-hŏŏnd′, dash′-)		
debris	(də brē′, dā′brē)	iguana	(i gwä′nə)
debut	(dā byōō′)	imbroglio	(im brōl′yō)
devotee	(dev′ə tē′)	inchoate	(in kō′it)
dinghy	(ding′gē)	incognito	(in′kog nē′tō,
diphtheria	(dif thēr′ē ə)		in kog′ni tō′)
diphthong	(dif′thəng)	indigenous	(in dij′ə nəs)
discern	(di sûrn′)	interstice	(in tûr′stis)
draught	(draft)	inure	(in yŏŏr′)
drought	(drout)	irascible	(i ras′ə bəl)
duodenum	(dōō′ə dē′nəm)	isosceles	(ī sos′ə lēz′)
dyspepsia	(dis pep′shə,-sē ə)	isthmus	(is′məs)
edifice	(ed′ə fis)	jodhpurs	(jod′pərz)
egregious	(i grē′jəs)	joust	(joust)
emu	(ē′myōō)		
entree	(än′trā)	khaki	(kak′ē)
		kohlrabi	(kōl rä′bē)
façade	(fə säd′)		
facile	(fas′il)	labyrinth	(lab′ə rinth)
fiancé	(fē′än sā′,	lascivious	(lə siv′ē əs)
	fēän′sā)	legerdemain	(lej′ər də mān′)
frigate	(frig′it)	leisure	(lē′zhər)
fuchsia	(fyōō′shə)	lemur	(lē′mər)
fuselage	(fyōō′sə läzh′)	liaison	(lē ā′zən,
fusillade	(fyōō′sə läd′,		lē′ə zon′)
	-läd′)	lien	(lēn)
		lieu	(lōō)
gendarme	(zhän′därm)	lineage	(lin′ē ij)
gentian	(jen′shən)	lingerie	(län′zhə rā′)
gestation	(jes tā′shən)	liturgy	(lit′ər jē)
gibber	(jib′ər)	llama	(lä′mə)
gladiolus	(glad′ē ō′ləs)	locale	(lō kal′)

logy	(lō′gē)
lorgnette	(lôrn yet′)
louver	(lo͞o′vər)
lucid	(lo͞o′sid)
lucre	(lo͞o′kər)
machete	(mə shet′ē)
machination	(mak′ə nā′shən)
mademoiselle	(mad′əm ə zel′, mad′mwə-)
maestro	(mīs′trō)
mannequin	(man′i kin)
marijuana	(mar′ə wä′nə)
marquis	(mär′kwis, mär kē′)
matinee	(mat′n ā′)
mauve	(mōv, môv)
meliorate	(mēl′yə rāt′)
mesa	(mā′sə)
mien	(mēn)
modiste	(mō dēst′)
motif	(mō tēf′)
murrain	(mûr′in)
myrrh	(mûr)
naïve	(nä ēv′)
naphtha	(nap′thə, naf′-)
niche	(nich)
nihilism	(nī′ə liz′əm)
nirvana	(nir vä′nə)
nom de plume	(nom′ də plo͞om′)
nonpareil	(non′pə rel′)
nougat	(no͞o′gət)
nuance	(no͞o′äns, nyo͞o′-)
oblique	(ə blēk′)
ocher	(ō′kər)
omniscient	(om nish′ənt)
onerous	(on′ər əs)
onus	(ō′nəs)
opiate	(ō′pē it)
pachyderm	(pak′i dûrm′)
palsy	(pôl′zē)
paprika	(pa prē′kə)
parfait	(pär fā′)
parquet	(pär kā′)

paschal	(pas′kəl)
pecan	(pi kän′, kan′)
pellagra	(pə lag′rə)
petit	(pet′ē)
philistine	(fil′ə stēn′)
pimiento	(pi myen′tō)
plebeian	(plə bē′ən)
pneumatic	(no͞o mat′ik, nyo͞o-)
poignant	(poin′yənt)
posthumous	(pos′chə məs)
precipice	(pres′ə pis)
premier	(pri mēr′)
pristine	(pri stēn′)
protégé	(prō′tə zhā′)
pueblo	(pweb′lō)
purulent	(pyo͞or′ə lənt)
quaff	(kwof)
qualm	(kwäm)
quay	(kē)
ragout	(ra go͞o′)
regime	(rā zhēm′)
renege	(ri nig′, -neg′)
reveille	(rev′ə lē)
ricochet	(rik′ə shā′)
rudiment	(ro͞o′də mənt)
savoir-faire	(sav′wär fär′)
short-lived	(shôrt′līvd′)
sleazy	(slē′zē)
soufflé	(so͞o flā′)
specious	(spē′shəs)
suave	(swäv)
subpoena	(sə pē′nə)
tarpaulin	(tär pô′lin, tär′pə lin)
thyme	(tīm)
travail	(trə vāl′)
usury	(yo͞o′zhə rē)
valance	(vā′ləns)
worsted	(wo͞os′tid, wûr′stid)

Pronunciation Key

a	act, bat	m	my, him	u	up, love
ā	able, cape	n	now, on	ûr	urge, burn
âr	air, dare	ng	sing, England	v	voice, live
ä	art, calm	o	box, hot	w	west, away
b	back, rub	ō	over, no	y	yes, young
ch	chief, beach	ô	order, ball	z	zeal, lazy, those
d	do, bed	oi	oil, joy	zh	vision, measure
e	ebb, set	o͝o	book, put	ə	occurs only in
ē	equal, bee	o͞o	ooze, rule		unaccented
f	fit, puff	ou	out, loud		syllables and
g	give, beg	p	page, stop		indicates the
h	hit, hear	r	read, cry		sound of a *in*
i	if, big	s	see, miss		alone e *in*
ī	ice, bite	sh	shoe, push		system i *in*
j	just, edge	t	ten, bit		easily o *in*
k	kept, make	th	thin, path		gallop u *in*
l	low, all	t͟h	that, other		circus

Improve Your Spelling

An important part of improving your vocabulary is learning to spell correctly and confidently. English spellings present some difficulties because so many words are not spelled the way they sound. Most of these words come from other languages. For example, the word *bouillon,* meaning a kind of broth, came into English from French, and its common English pronunciations, (bŏŏl′yon) and (bŏŏl′yən), are very much like its pronunciation in French (bōō yôN′).

English spellings can also create confusion because certain words do not sound the way they look. For example, *cough* and *though,* although spelled similarly, are pronounced quite differently. The first is pronounced (kôf), to rhyme with *off,* and the second is (thō), to rhyme with *go* (see also the pronunciation guide toward the end of this chapter).

But these words are exceptions, and most English spelling is not as difficult as some people would have you believe. There are ways to make it all easier, and the objective of this chapter is to remove some of the confusion and to give a clearer concept of English spelling.

The classic criticism of the difficulties of English spelling is the one attributed to George Bernard Shaw, in which he claims that our spelling is so irregular (and so absurd!) that the common word *fish* could as well be spelled in English as *ghoti.* The idea is as follows

> *gh* in cou*gh* equals the sound of *f*
> *o* in w*o*men equals the sound of *i*
> *ti* in na*ti*on equals the sound of *sh*

The trouble with this analysis, amusing though it may be, is that it does not take into account what might be called "the rules of the game." Without denying that in the English language we can have more than one sound for each spelling and more than one spelling for each sound, we can point to certain regularities regarding sound-spelling correspondences, among them rules of position. Taking these into account, we can see that Shaw's suggested spelling of *ghoti* for *fish* falls apart; *gh* NEVER equals the sound of *f* at the beginning of a word, only at the end, as in *rough, cough,* or *laugh*. The use of the letter *o* to represent the "short" *i* sound is even more restricted, appearing ONLY in the word *women*. Finally, *ti* produces the *sh* sound ONLY medially, typically in suffixes like *-tion* and *-tious*.

There are reasons for the sound-spelling irregularities in English; its history warrants them. For one thing, the number of sounds in the language is greater than the number of symbols available in our alphabet; some of these symbols must do double duty (as with "hard" and "soft" *c* and *g*) or must combine with other symbols in order to account for all the sounds. For another, English has borrowed heavily from other languages, retaining traces of their pronunciations with their spellings. In addition, spelling in general is conservative—it changes less readily than pronunciation. Modern English retains spellings that do not reflect the many changes in pronunciation that have occurred over the years, particularly during the fifteenth century.

Nor can any single set of spellings reflect the diversity of English dialects. English is a varied language that flourishes not only throughout North America and England, but over the entire globe. Add to this the fact that early printers were inconsistent and idiosyncratic in their spelling, and some of their misspellings have survived. All of these factors have led to the kinds of spelling irregularities that make the English language both frustrating and fascinating.

Nevertheless, for all its difficulties, English spelling is not entirely irrational. We return to "the rules of the game." If certain letter combinations occur predominantly in certain portions of words, a growing familiarity with these patterns can increase your confidence in using and working with the English language. And it can help to resolve an age-old problem.

Finding Spellings When You Know the Sounds

The Problem

Traditionally, there has been a fundamental difficulty with making efficient use of dictionaries and other reference books: How can you look up a word if you don't know how to spell it? Where do you look? In what part of the alphabet?

The Solution

Although no complete solution exists, a "Table of Sound-Spelling Correspondences" like the one that follows can help. By listing alternative spellings for each of the sounds of English, and tying these sounds and spellings together, the table allows you to relate what you already know about a word—how to SAY it—with what you are trying to find out about the word—how to SPELL it.

Understanding the Table
of Sound-Spelling Correspondences

Contexts for Given Spelling Patterns

Tables showing the relationship between sounds and spellings can be found in most unabridged and desk dictionaries. The table that follows not only shows spelling patterns and the sounds they represent, but indicates which part of a word (beginning, middle, or end) is likely to contain these patterns. For example, "-ag(m)," as in "diaphragm," is shown with a preceding hyphen and with parentheses around the m, as one of the patterns representing the "short" a sound. This means that when the letters ag precede an m and the agm ends a word or syllable, ag is pronounced as a vowel, as if the g were not there. In fact, when an agm combination is split between syllables, as in the word "syn·tag·mat·ic," so that the g ends one syllable and the m starts the next one, the g is NOT silent.

From this example, you can see that parenthesized letters in the table indicate a CONTEXT for a given spelling pattern. Similarly, hyphens show where in a word or syllable that pattern is most likely to occur. A spelling pattern shown without any hyphens can occur in various parts of a word; some of these, like air, are also found as entire words.

Key-Word Patterns

For each sound shown along the left margin, the table shows a boldface **spelling,** followed by a word (or words) in which that spelling typically occurs. This key word allows you to fix the sound in your mind.

Following the bold spellings is a list of other spellings for the same sound and the words in which those spellings are used. Notice that you may pronounce some of the spellings in the lists differently from the bold spellings. Such spellings are probably repeated following the sounds more appropriate for your dialect. Tables of this sort usually include unusual sound-spelling associations: some that are simply rare, like the *u* in *busy* or *business* for the short *i* sound, and others that are derived from languages other than English. French spellings standing for the "long" *o* sound, for example, might include *-eau, -eaux,* and *-ot.* Long lists of such spelling patterns, with no indication of which ones are frequent enough to be useful, can indeed be overwhelming. To simplify our table, we have marked the common spelling patterns for each sound with an asterisk.

Note that the combination of a vowel plus an ellipsis (three dots) and an *e* stands for any spelling in which that vowel and the *e* are separated by a single consonant. As a general rule, this "discontinuous vowel" pattern represents the long sound of that vowel. (Long *i*, for example, is frequently spelled with *i . . . e*, as in *ice.*) But a discontinuous vowel can stand for other than long vowel sounds. In the word *have,* the *a . . . e* stands for a short *a* sound, and in the word *love, o . . . e* stands for the sound of short *u*.

Table of Sound-Spelling Correspondences

This table is useful for finding a word in the dictionary when you know the pronunciation but not the spelling. To find a word, first sound it out and then try various spelling equivalents. For example, the spellings of *pursue* and *persuade* (with first syllables that sound alike but are spelled differently) can be found by checking the spellings listed for the (ər) sound and then looking in the dictionary under *per-, pir-, pur-,* etc.

Vowels and Diphthongs

(a) *a-, -a- as in at, hat ("short" a)

-a'a-	ma'am
-ach(m)	drachm
-ag(m)	diaphragm
-ah-	dahlia
-ai-	plaid
-al-	half
-au-	laugh
-ua-	guarantor
-ui-	guimpe
i(n)-, -i(n)-	ingenue, lingerie
-i(m)-	timbre

(ā) *a . . . e, -a . . . e as in ate, hate ("long" a)

-ae-	Gaelic
-ag(n)	champagne
*-ai-	rain
-aigh-	straight
-aig(n)	arraign
-ao-	gaol
-au-	gauge
-a(g)ue	vague
*-ay	ray
*é-, -é	étude, exposé
-e . . . e	suede
*-ea-	steak
-ee	matinee
eh	eh
*-ei-	veil
*-eig(n)	feign
*eigh-, -eigh-, -eigh	eight, weight, weigh
-eilles	Marseilles
-er	dossier
-es(ne)	demesne
-et	beret
*-ey	obey

(âr) *air as in chair

*-aire	doctrinaire
*-ar-	chary
*-are	dare
-ayer	prayer
*-ear	wear
-eer	Mynheer
e'er	ne'er

*-eir	their
-er	mal de mer
*-ere	there
-ey're	they're

(ä) *ah as in hurrah ("broad" a)

*-a-	father
à	à la mode
-aa-	bazaar
*-al(f)	half
*-al(m)	calm
-as	faux pas
-at	éclat
-au	laugh
-e(r)-	sergeant
*-ea(r)-	hearth
-oi-	reservoir
-ua-	guard
i(n)-, -i(n)-	ingenue, lingerie

(e) *e as in ebb ("short" e)

a-, -a-,	any, many
ae-	aesthete
-ai-	said
-ay-	says
*-ea-	leather
-eg(m)	phlegm
-ei-	heifer
-eo-	jeopardy
-ie-	friend
-oe-	foetid

(ē) *ee as in keep ("long" e)

ae-, -ae-	Aesop, Caesar
-ay	quay
*-e-, -e-	equal, secret
-e	strophe
*-ea-, -ea-, -ea	each, team, tea
*-ea(g)ue	league
e'e-	e'en
*-e . . . e	precede
*-ei-	receive
-eip(t)	receipt
-eo-	people
*-ey	key
-i	rani
*i . . . e	machine
*-ie-	field

-is	debr*is*
*-i(g)ue	intr*igue*
*-i(q)ue	ant*ique*
-oe-	am*o*eba
-uay	q*uay*
*-y	cit*y*

(i) *i as in if ("short" i)

*-a-	dam*a*ge
-ae-	an*a*esthetic
e-	*E*ngland
-ee-	b*ee*n
*-ei-	counterf*ei*t
-ia-	carr*ia*ge
-ie-	s*ie*ve
-o-	w*o*men
(b)u(s)-	b*u*siness
-ui(l)-	b*ui*ld, g*ui*lt
*-y-	s*y*mpathetic

(ī) *i . . . e as in ice ("long" i)

*-ai-	f*ai*lle
ais-	*ai*sle
-ay-	k*ay*ak
aye	*aye*
*-ei-	st*ei*n
-eigh-	h*eigh*t
eye	*eye*
*-ie	p*ie*
*-igh	h*igh*
is-	*i*sland
*-uy	b*uy*
*-y-, -y	c*y*cle, sk*y*
*-ye	l*ye*

(o) *o as in box

*(w)a-	w*a*nder
*-(u)a-	qu*a*drant
-ach-	y*a*cht
-au-	astron*au*t
-eau-	bur*eau*cracy
-ou-	c*ou*gh
*ho-	*h*onor

(ō) *o as in lo

*-au-	m*au*ve
-aut	h*au*tboy
-aux	f*au*x pas
-eau	b*eau*

-eaux	Bord*eaux*
-eo-	y*eo*man
-ew	s*ew*
*o . . . e	r*o*te
*-oa-	r*oa*d
*-oe	t*oe*
oh	*oh*
*-ol-	yo*l*k
-oo-	br*oo*ch
-ot	dep*ot*
*-ou-	s*ou*l
*-ow	fl*ow*
*-owe	*owe*

(ô) *-aw as in paw

*-a-	t*a*ll
*(w)a(r)-	w*a*rrant
-ah	Ut*ah*
*-al-	w*a*lk
-as	Arkans*as*
*au-, -au-	*au*thor, v*au*lt
*-augh-	c*augh*t
*-o-	alcoh*o*l
*-oa-	br*oa*d
-oo-	fl*oo*r
*-ough-	s*ough*t

(oi) *-oy as in boy

-awy-	l*aw*yer
-eu-	Fr*eu*d
*-oi-	*oi*l
-ois	Iroqu*ois*
-uoy	b*uoy*

(o͝o) *-oo- as in look

-o-	w*o*lf
*-oul-	w*ou*ld
*-u-	p*u*ll

(o͞o) *oo-, *-oo-, *-oo as in ooze, mood, ahchoo

-eu-	man*eu*ver
*-ew	gr*ew*
-iew	l*ieu*
-o	wh*o*
o . . . e	m*o*ve
-oe	can*oe*
-oeu-	man*oeu*vre
*-ou-	tr*ou*p

*u . . . e	r*u*le
*-ue	fl*ue*
-ug(n)	imp*u*gn
*-ui-	s*ui*t

(ou) *-ow as in brow	
au-	*Au*f Wiedersehen
-au	land*au*
*ou-, *-ou-	*ou*t, sh*ou*t
*-ough	b*ough*

(u) *u-, -u- as in up, pup	
o-, *-o-	*o*ther, s*o*n
-oe-	d*oe*s
*o . . . e	l*o*ve
-oo-	bl*oo*d
-ou(ble)	tr*ou*ble

(ûr) *ur-, *-ur- as in urn, turn	
*ear-, -ear-	*ear*n, l*ear*n
*er-, -er-	*er*mine, t*er*m
err	*err*
-eur	pos*eur*
her-	*her*b
*-ir-, -ir	th*ir*sty, f*ir*
(w)or-	w*or*k
-our-	sc*our*ge
-urr	p*urr*
-yr-	m*yr*tle

(yo͞o) *u-, -u as in utility, future	
-eau-	b*eau*ty
-eu-	f*eu*d
*-ew	f*ew*
*hu-	*hu*man

hu . . . e	*hu*ge
-ieu	purl*ieu*
-iew	v*iew*
*u . . . e	*u*se
*-ue	c*ue*
-ueue	q*ueue*
yew	*yew*
you	*you*
yu-	*Yu*kon
yu . . . e	*yu*le

(ə) *a as in alone	
*-e-	syst*e*m
*-i-	eas*i*ly
*-o-	gall*o*p
*-u-	circ*u*s
a	tête-*a*-tête
-ai(n)	mount*ai*n
-ei(n)	mull*ei*n
-eo(n)	dung*eo*n
-ia-	parl*ia*ment
-io-	leg*io*n
-oi-	porp*oi*se
*-ou-	cur*iou*s
-y-	mart*y*r

(ər) *-er as in father	
*-ar	li*ar*
*-ir	elix*ir*
*-or	lab*or*
*-our	lab*our*
*-ur	aug*ur*
*-ure	fut*ure*
-yr	mart*yr*

Consonants

(Note that consonant spelling patterns such as -*bb*-, shown with hyphens on either side, are frequently part of two adjacent syllables in a word, with part of the combination in one syllable and the rest in the next.)

(b) *b-, *-b-, *-b as in bed, amber, rub	
*-bb-, *bb-	ho*bb*y, e*bb*
*-be	lo*be*
bh-	*bh*eesty

(ch) *ch-, -ch-, *-ch as in chief, ahchoo, rich	
c-	*c*ello
*-che	ni*che*
*-tch-, *-tch	ha*tch*et, ca*tch*

-te-	righ*te*ous
*-ti-	ques*ti*on
*-tu-	na*tu*ral

(d) *d-, *-d-, *-d as in do, odor, red

*-'d	we*'d*
*-dd-, *-dd	la*dd*er, o*dd*
*-de	fa*de*
dh-	*dh*urrie
*-ed	pull*ed*
*-ld	shou*ld*

(f) *f-, *-f-, as in feed, safer

*-fe	li*fe*
*-ff-, *-ff	mu*ff*in, o*ff*
*-ft-	so*f*ten
*-gh	tou*gh*
*-lf	cal*f*
pf-	*pf*ennig
*ph-, -ph-, -ph	*ph*ysics, sta*ph*ylococcus, sta*ph*

(g) *g-, *-g-, *-g as in give, agate, fog

*-gg	e*gg*
*gh-	*gh*ost
*gu-	*gu*ard
*-gue	pla*gue*

(h) *h-, *-h- *as in* h*it,* a*h*oy

wh-	*wh*o

(hw) *wh- *as in* where

(hyōō) *hu- *as in* huge

(j) *j- *as in* just

-ch	Greenwi*ch*
*-d(u)	gra*d*uate
*-dg-	ju*dg*ment
*-dge	bri*dge*
*-di-	sol*di*er
*-ge	sa*ge*
-gg-	exa*gg*erate
*g(e)-, *-g(e)-	*g*em, a*g*ent
*g(i)-, *-g(i)-	*g*in, a*g*ile
-jj-	Ha*jj*i

(k) *k-, *-k- as in keep, making

*c-, *-c-	*c*ar, be*c*ome

*-cc-	a*cc*ount
-cch-	ba*cch*anal
*ch-	*ch*aracter
*-ck	ba*ck*
-cq-	a*cq*uaint
-cqu-	la*cqu*er
-cque	sa*cque*
cu-	bis*cu*it
-gh	lou*gh*
*-ke	ra*ke*
-kh	Si*kh*
-lk	wa*lk*
q-	*q*adi
-q	Ira*q*
-qu-	li*qu*or
-que	pla*que*

(l) *l-, *-l-, *-l as in live, alive, sail

*-le	mi*le*
*-ll	ca*ll*
-lle	fai*lle*
-sl-	li*sl*e
-sle	ai*sle*

(m) *m-, *-m-, *-m as in more, amount, ham

-chm	dra*chm*
-gm	paradi*gm*
*-lm	ca*lm*
*-mb	li*mb*
*-me	ho*me*
mh-	*mh*o
*-mm-	ha*mm*er
-mn	hy*mn*

(n) *n-, *-n-, *-n as in not, center, can

*gn-	*gn*at
*kn-	*kn*ife
mn-	*mn*emonic
*-ne	do*ne*
*-nn-	ru*nn*er
*pn(eu)-	*pn*eumatic

(ng) *-ng-, *-ng as in ringing, ring

*-n(k)	pi*n*k
-ngg	mahjo*ngg*
-ngue	to*ngue*

(p) *p-, *-p-, *-p as in pen, super, stop

*-pe	ho*pe*

*-pp-	su*pp*er
-ppe	lagnia*ppe*

> **(r) *r-, *-r-, *-r** as in **r**ed, a**r**ise, fou**r**

*-re	pu*re*
*rh-	*rh*ythm
*-rr-	ca*rr*ot
-rrh	cata*rrh*
*wr-	*wr*ong

> **(s) *s-, *-s-, *-s** as in **s**ee, be**s**ide, ala**s**

*c(e)-, *-c(e)-,	*c*enter, ra*c*er
*c(i)-, *-c(i)-	*c*ity, a*c*id
*-ce	mi*ce*
*ps-	*ps*ychology
*sc-	*sc*ene
sch-	*sch*ism
*-se	mou*se*
*-ss-, *-ss	me*ss*enger, lo*ss*

> **(sh) *sh-, *-sh-, *-sh** as in **sh**ip, a**sh**amed, wa**sh**

-ce-	o*ce*an
ch-, *-ch-	*ch*aise, ma*ch*ine
-chs-	fu*chs*ia
*-ci-	spe*ci*al
psh-	*psh*aw
s(u)-	*s*ugar
sch-	*sch*ist
*-sci-	con*sci*ence
-se-	nau*se*ous
*-si-	man*si*on
*-ss-	ti*ss*ue
*-ssi-	mi*ssi*on
*-ti-	cap*ti*on

> **(t) *t-, *-t-, *-t** as in **t**oe, a**t**om, ha**t**

-bt	dou*bt*
-cht	ya*cht*
ct-	*ct*enophore
*-ed	talk*ed*
*-ght	bou*ght*
phth-	*phth*isic

't-	'*t*was
*-te	bi*te*
th-	*th*yme
*-tt-	bo*tt*om
tw-	*tw*o

> **(th) *th-, *-th-, *-th** as in **th**in, e**th**er, pa**th**

chth-	*chth*onian

> **(th) *th-, *-th-, -th** as in **th**en, o**th**er, smoo**th**

*-the	ba*the*

> **(v) *v-, *-v-, -v** as in **v**isit, o**v**er, lu**v**

-f	o*f*
-ph-	Step*h*en
*-ve	ha*ve*
-vv-	fli*vv*er

> **(w) *w-, *-w-** as in **w**ell, a**w**ay

-ju-	mari*ju*ana
-o(i)-	ch*o*ir
ou(i)-	*ou*ija
(q)u-	q*u*iet
*wh-	*wh*ere

> **(y) *y-** as in **y**et

*-i-	un*i*on
-j-	hallelu*j*ah
-ll-	torti*ll*a

> **(z) *z-, -z-** as in **z**one, Bi**z**et

*-s	ha*s*
-sc-	di*sc*ern
*-se	ri*se*
x-	*x*ylem
-ze	fu*ze*
*-zz-, *-zz	bu*zz*ard, fu*zz*

> **(zh) -zi-** as in bra**zi**er (like *zh*)

*-ge	gara*ge*
*-s(u)-	mea*s*ure
*-si	divi*si*on
*-z(u)-	a*z*ure

Rules of Spelling

No spelling rule should be followed blindly, because every rule has exceptions.

1. Silent E Dropped. Silent *e* at the end of a word is usually dropped before a suffix beginning with a vowel: *abide, abiding; recite, recital.*

   Exceptions: Words ending in *ce* or *ge* retain the *e* before a suffix beginning with *a* or *o* to keep the soft sound of the consonant: *notice, noticeable; courage, courageous.*

2. Silent E Kept. A silent *e* following a consonant (or another *e*) is usually retained before a suffix beginning with a consonant: *late, lateness; spite, spiteful.*

   Exceptions: *fledgling, acknowledgment, judgment, wholly,* and a few similar words.

3. Final Consonant Doubled. A final consonant following a single vowel in one-syllable words, or in a syllable that will take the main accent when combined with a suffix, is doubled before a suffix beginning with a vowel: *begin, beginning; occur, occurred; bat, batted.*

   Exceptions: *h* and *x* in final position; *transferable, gaseous,* and a few others.

4. Final Consonant Single. A final consonant following another consonant, a double vowel or diphthong, or that is not in a stressed syllable, is not doubled before a suffix beginning with a vowel: *part, parting; remark, remarkable.*

   Exceptions: an unaccented syllable does not prevent doubling of the final consonant, especially in British usage: *traveller* for *traveler.*

5. Double Consonants Remain. Double consonants are usually retained before a suffix except when a final *l* is to be followed by *ly* or *less.* To avoid a triple *lll,* one *l* is usually dropped: *full, fully.*

   Exceptions: Usage is divided, with some preferring *skilful* over *skillful, instalment* over *installment,* etc.

6. Final Y. If the *y* follows a consonant, change *y* to *i* before all endings except *ing.* Do not change it before *ing* or if it follows a vowel: *bury, buried, burying; try, tries;* but *attorney, attorneys.*

   Exceptions: *day, daily, gay, gaily; lay, laid; say, said.*

7. Final IE to Y. Words ending in *ie* change to *y* before *ing: die, dying, lie, lying*

8. Double and Triple E Reduced. Words ending in double *e* drop one *e* before an ending beginning in *e,* to avoid a triple *e.* Words ending in silent *e* usually drop the *e* before endings beginning in *e* to avoid forming a syllable. Other words ending in a vowel sound commonly retain the letters indicating the sound. *Free + ed = freed.*

9. EI or IE. Words having the sound of *ē* are commonly spelled *ie* following all letters but *c;* with a preceding *c,* the common spelling is *ei.* Examples: *believe, achieve, besiege;* but *conceit, ceiling, receive, con-*

ceive. When the sound is *ā* the common spelling is *ei* regardless of the preceding letter. Examples: *eight, weight, deign.*

Exceptions: *either, neither, seize, financier;* some words in which *e* and *i* are pronounced separately, such as *notoriety.*

10. Words Ending in C. Before an ending beginning with *e, i,* or *y,* words ending in *c* commonly add *k* to keep the *c* hard: *panic, panicky.*
11. Compounds. Some compounds written as a unit bring together unusual combinations of letters. They are seldom changed on this account: *bookkeeper, roommate.*

Exceptions: A few words are regularly clipped when compounded, such as *full* in *awful, cupful,* etc.

Using a Spell Checker

A spell checker is a computer program that checks or verifies the spelling of words in an electronic document. While it can be a valuable tool for writers, it cannot be relied upon to catch all types of spelling errors. It is most useful in finding misspellings that produce "nonwords"—words with transposed, wrong, or missing letters. For example, it will reject *ther* (for *there*) and *teh* (for *the*). However, it cannot distinguish between words that sound or look alike but differ in meaning. It will accept *to* or *too* regardless of whether the context is correct, and it will accept typos such as *on* (for *of*) or *form* (for *from*). It is important, therefore, not to rely too heavily on spell checkers, and to go over your writing carefully to avoid such mistakes.

Words Commonly Confused

Often two or more words with different meanings are confused because they are pronounced alike or almost alike. Confusion can also arise if the words have identical or very similar spellings. Many of these soundalikes and lookalikes are listed in Chapter 3, along with an explanation of how they differ in meaning. Here are a few examples:

affect/effect
canvas/canvass
desert/dessert
elicit/illicit
gibe/jibe/jive

Rules of Word Division

1. Do not divide a one-syllable word. This includes past tenses like *walked* and *dreamed,* which should never be split before the *-ed* ending.
2. Do not divide a word so that a single letter is left at the end of a line, as in *a·bout,* or so that a single letter starts the following line, as in *cit·y.*
3. Hyphenated compounds should preferably be divided only after the hyphen. If the first portion of the compound is a single letter, however, as in *D-day,* the word should not be divided.
4. Word segments like *-ceous, -scious, -sial, -tion, -tious* should not be divided.
5. The portion of a word left at the end of a line should not encourage a misleading pronunciation, as would be the case if *acetate,* a three-syllable word, were divided after the first *e.*

Words Most Often Misspelled

We have listed here some of the words that have traditionally proved difficult to spell. The list includes not only exceptions, words that defy common spelling rules, but some that pose problems even while adhering to these conventions.

aberrant	across	always	appropriate
abscess	address	amateur	approximate
absence	adequate	analysis	apropos
absorption	adherent	analytical	arctic
abundance	adjourn	analyze	arguing
accede	admittance	anesthetic	argument
acceptance	adolescence	annual	arouse
accessible	adolescent	anoint	arrangement
accidentally	advantageous	anonymous	arthritis
accommodate	advertisement	answer	article
according	affidavit	antarctic	artificial
accordion	against	antecedent	asinine
accumulate	aggravate	anticipation	asked
accustom	aggression	antihistamine	assassin
achievement	aging	anxiety	assess
acknowledge	aisle	aperitif	asthma
acknowledgment	all right	apocryphal	athlete
acoustics	alien	apostasy	athletic
acquaintance	allegiance	apparent	attorneys
acquiesce	almost	appearance	author
acquire	already	appetite	authoritative
acquittal	although	appreciate	auxiliary

bachelor
balance
bankruptcy
barbiturate
barrette
basically
basis
beggar
beginning
belief
believable
believe
beneficial
beneficiary
benefit
benefited
blizzard
bludgeon
bologna
bookkeeping
bouillon
boundaries
braggadocio
breathe
brief
brilliant
broccoli
bronchial
brutality
bulletin
buoy
buoyant
bureau
bureaucracy
burglary
business

cafeteria
caffeine
calisthenics
camaraderie
camouflage
campaign
cancel
cancellation
candidate
cantaloupe
capacity
cappuccino

carburetor
career
careful
carriage
carrying
casserole
category
caterpillar
cavalry
ceiling
cellar
cemetery
census
certain
challenge
chandelier
changeable
changing
characteristic
chief
choir
choose
cinnamon
circuit
civilized
clothes
codeine
collateral
colloquial
colonel
colossal
column
coming
commemorate
commission
commitment
committed
committee
comparative
comparison
competition
competitive
complaint
concede
conceivable
conceive
condemn
condescend
conferred

confidential
congratulate
conscience
conscientious
conscious
consensus
consequently
consistent
consummate
continuous
control
controlled
controversy
convalesce
convenience
coolly
copyright
cornucopia
corollary
corporation
correlate
correspondence
correspondent
counselor
counterfeit
courageous
courteous
crisis
criticism
criticize
culinary
curiosity
curriculum
cylinder

debt
debtor
deceive
decide
decision
decisive
defendant
definite
definitely
dependent
de rigueur
descend
descendant
description

desiccate
desirable
despair
desperate
destroy
develop
development
diabetes
diaphragm
different
dilemma
dining
diocese
diphtheria
disappear
disappearance
disappoint
disastrous
discipline
disease
dissatisfied
dissident
dissipate
distinguish
divide
divine
doesn't
dormitory
duly
dumbbell
during

easier
easily
ecstasy
effervescent
efficacy
efficiency
efficient
eighth
eightieth
electrician
eligibility
eligible
eliminate
ellipsis
embarrass
encouraging
endurance

energetic
enforceable
enthusiasm
environment
equipped
erroneous
especially
esteemed
exacerbate
exaggerate
exceed
excel
excellent
except
exceptionally
excessive
executive
exercise
exhibition
exhilarate
existence
expense
experience
experiment
explanation
exquisite
extemporaneous
extraordinary
extremely

facilities
fallacy
familiar
fascinate
fascism
feasible
February
fictitious
fiend
fierce
fiftieth
finagle
finally
financial
fluorine
foliage
forcible
forehead
foreign

forfeit
formally
forte
fortieth
fortunately
forty
fourth
friend
frieze
fundamental
furniture

galoshes
gauge
genealogy
generally
gnash
government
governor
graffiti
grammar
grateful
grievance
grievous
guarantee
guard
guidance

handkerchief
haphazard
harass
harebrained
hazard
height
hemorrhage
hemorrhoid
hereditary
heroes
hierarchy
hindrance
hoping
hors d'oeuvres
huge
humorous
hundredth
hurrying
hydraulic
hygiene

hygienist
hypocrisy

icicle
identification
idiosyncrasy
imaginary
immediately
immense
impresario
impostor
inalienable
incident
incidentally
inconvenience
incredible
indelible
independent
indestructible
indictment
indigestible
indispensable
inevitable
inferred
influential
initial
initiative
innocuous
innuendo
inoculation
inscrutable
installation
instantaneous
intellectual
intelligence
intercede
interest
interfere
intermittent
intimate
inveigle
irrelevant
irresistible
island

jealous
jeopardize
journal

judgment
judicial

khaki
kindergarten
knowledge

laboratory
laid
larynx
leery
leisure
length
liable
liaison
libel
library
license
lieutenant
lightning
likelihood
liquefy
liqueur
literature
livelihood
loneliness
losing
lovable

magazine
maintenance
manageable
management
maneuver
manufacturer
maraschino
marital
marriage
marriageable
mathematics
mayonnaise
meant
medicine
medieval
memento
mileage
millennium
miniature
minuet

miscellaneous
mischievous
misspell
mistletoe
moccasin
molasses
molecule
monotonous
mortgage
murmur
muscle
mutual
mysterious

naive
naturally
necessarily
necessary
necessity
neighbor
neither
nickel
niece
ninetieth
ninety
ninth
noticeable
notoriety
nuptial

obbligato
occasion
occasionally
occurred
occurrence
offense
official
omission
omit
omitted
oneself
ophthalmology
opinion
opportunity
optimism
optimist
ordinarily
origin

original
outrageous

paean
pageant
paid
pamphlet
paradise
parakeet
parallel
paralysis
paralyze
paraphernalia
parimutuel
parliament
partial
participate
particularly
pasteurize
pastime
pavilion
peaceable
peasant
peculiar
penicillin
perceive
perform
performance
peril
permanent
permissible
perpendicular
perseverance
persistent
personnel
perspiration
persuade
persuasion
persuasive
petition
philosophy
physician
piccolo
plaited
plateau
plausible
playwright
pleasant
plebeian

pneumonia
poinsettia
politician
pomegranate
possess
possession
possibility
possible
practically
practice
precede
precedence
precisely
predecessor
preference
preferred
prejudice
preparatory
prescription
prevalent
primitive
prior
privilege
probability
probably
procedure
proceed
professor
proffer
pronounce
pronunciation
propagate
protégé(e)
psychiatry
psychology
pursuant
pursue
pursuit
putrefy

quantity
questionnaire
queue

rarefy
recede
receipt
receivable

receive
recipe
reciprocal
recognize
recommend
reference
referred
reign
relegate
relevant
relieve
religious
remembrance
reminisce
remiss
remittance
rendezvous
repetition
replaceable
representative
requisition
resistance
responsibility
restaurant
restaurateur
resuscitate
reticence
reveille
rhyme
rhythm
riddance
ridiculous
rococo
roommate

sacrifice
sacrilegious
safety
salary
sandwich
sarsaparilla
sassafras
satisfaction
scarcity
scene
scenery
schedule
scheme

scholarly	specimen	tariff	using
scissors	speech	temperament	usually
secede	sponsor	temperature	utilize
secrecy	spontaneous	temporarily	
secretary	statistics	tendency	vacancy
seize	statute	tentative	vacuum
seizure	stevedore	terrestrial	vague
separate	stiletto	therefore	valuable
separately	stopped	thirtieth	variety
sergeant	stopping	thorough	vegetable
serviceable	strength	thought	veil
seventieth	strictly	thousandth	vengeance
several	studying	through	vermilion
sheik	stupefy	till	veterinarian
shepherd	submitted	titillate	vichyssoise
sheriff	substantial	together	village
shining	subtle	tonight	villain
shoulder	subtly	tournament	
shrapnel	succeed	tourniquet	warrant
siege	successful	tragedy	Wednesday
sieve	succession	tragically	weird
significance	successive	transferred	wherever
silhouette	sufficient	transient	whim
similar	superintendent	tries	wholly
simultaneity	supersede	truly	whose
simultaneous	supplement	twelfth	wield
sincerely	suppress	twentieth	woolen
sixtieth	surprise	typical	wretched
skiing	surveillance	tyranny	writing
socially	susceptible		written
society	suspicion	unanimous	wrote
solemn	sustenance	undoubtedly	wrought
soliloquy	syllable	unique	
sophomore	symmetrical	unison	xylophone
sorority	sympathize	unmanageable	
sovereign	sympathy	unnecessary	yacht
spaghetti	synchronous	until	yield
spatial	synonym	upholsterer	
special	syphilis	usable	zealous
specifically	systematically	usage	zucchini

Words Commonly Confused

Words are often confused if they have similar or identical forms or sounds. You may have the correct meaning in mind, but choosing the wrong word will change your intended meaning. An *ingenuous* person is not the same as an *ingenious* person. Similarly, you may be using a word that is correct in a different context but does not express your intended meaning. To *infer* something is not the same as to *imply* it.

Use of the wrong word is often the result of confusing words that are identical or very similar in pronunciation but different in spelling. An example of a pair of words with the same pronunciation is "compliment, complement." The confusion may arise from a small difference in spelling, as the pair "canvas, canvass"; or the soundalikes may be spelled quite differently, as the pairs "manor, manner" and "brake, break." An example of a pair of words with similar but not identical pronunciation is "accept, except"; they are very different in usage and grammatical function.

Words may also be confused if they are spelled the same way but differ in meaning or in meaning and pronunciation, as the soundalikes *bear* "animal" and *bear* "carry, support" or the lookalikes *row* (rō) "line" and *row* (rou) "fight."

Errors in word choice may also result if word groups overlap in meaning or usage. In informal contexts, *aggravate* may be used to mean "annoy" and *mad* may be used to mean "angry." *Leave* and *let* are interchangeable when followed by the word "alone" in the sense "to stop annoying or interfering with someone."

The following glossary lists words that are commonly confused and discusses their meanings and proper usage. Chapter 4 provides further guidance on matters of usage.

accept/except *Accept* is a verb meaning "to receive": *Please accept a gift. Except* is usually a preposition or a conjunction meaning "other than" or "but for": *He was willing to accept an apology from everyone except me.* When *except* is used as a verb, it means "to leave out": *He was excepted from the new regulations.*

accidentally/accidently The correct adverb is *accidentally,* from the root word *accidental,* not *accident* (*Russell accidentally slipped on the icy sidewalk*). *Accidently* is a misspelling.

adoptive/adopted *Adoptive* refers to the parent: *He resembles his adoptive father. Adopted* refers to the child: *Their adopted daughter wants to adopt a child herself.*

adverse/averse Both words are adjectives, and both mean "opposed" or "hostile." *Averse,* however, is used to describe a subject's opposition to something (*The minister was averse to the new trends developing in the country*), whereas *adverse* describes something opposed to the subject (*The adverse comments affected his self-esteem*).

advice/advise *Advice,* a noun, means "suggestion or suggestions": *Here's some good advice. Advise,* a verb, means "to offer ideas or suggestions": *Act as we advise you.*

affect/effect Most often, *affect* is a verb, meaning "to influence," and *effect* is a noun meaning "the result of an action": *His speech affected my mother very deeply, but had no effect on my sister at all. Affect* is also used as a noun in psychology and psychiatry to mean "emotion": *We can learn much about affect from performance.* In this usage, it is pronounced with the stress on the first syllable. *Effect* is also used as a verb meaning "to bring about": *His letter effected a change in their relationship.*

aggravate/annoy In informal speech and writing, *aggravate* can be used as a synonym for *annoy.* However, in formal discourse the words mean different things and should be used in this way: *Her back condition was aggravated by lifting the child, but the child's crying annoyed her more than the pain.*

agree to/agree with *Agree to* means "to consent to, to accept" (usually a plan or idea). *Agree with* means "to be in accord with" (usually a person or group): *I can't believe they will agree to start a business together when they don't agree with each other on anything.*

aisle/isle *Aisle* means "a passageway between sections of seats": *It was impossible to pass through the airplane aisle during the meal service. Isle* means "island": *I would like to be on a desert isle on such a dreary morning.*

all ready/already *All ready,* a pronoun and an adjective, means "entirely prepared"; *already,* an adverb, means "so soon" or "previously": *I was all ready to leave when I noticed that it was already dinnertime.*

allusion/illusion An *allusion* is a reference or hint: *He made an allusion to the past.* An *illusion* is a deceptive appearance: *The canals on Mars are an illusion.*

a lot/alot/allot *A lot* is always written as two words. It is used informally to mean "many": *The unrelenting heat frustrated a lot of people. Allot* is a verb meaning "to divide" or "to set aside": *We alloted a portion of the yard for a garden. Alot* is not a word.

altogether/all together *Altogether* means "completely" or "totally"; *all together* means "all at one time" or "gathered together": *It is altogether proper that we recite the Pledge all together.*

allude/elude Both words are verbs. *Allude* means "to mention briefly or accidentally": *During our conversation, he alluded to his vacation plans. Elude* means "to avoid or escape": *The thief has successfully eluded capture for six months.*

altar/alter *Altar* is a noun meaning "a sacred place or platform": *The couple approached the altar for the wedding ceremony. Alter* is a verb meaning "to make different; to change": *He altered his appearance by losing fifty pounds, growing a beard, and getting a new wardrobe.*

amount/number *Amount* refers to quantity that cannot be counted: *The amount of work accomplished before a major holiday is always negligible. Number,* in contrast, refers to things that can be counted: *He has held a number of jobs in the past five months.* But some concepts, like time, can use either *amount* or *number,* depending how the elements are identified in the specific sentence: *We were surprised by the amount of time it took us to settle into our new surroundings. The number of hours it took to repair the sink pleased us.*

ante-/anti- The prefix *ante-* means "before" *(antecedent, antechamber, antediluvian);* the prefix *anti-* means against *(antigravity, antifreeze). Anti-* takes a hyphen before an *i* or a capital letter: *anti-Marxist, anti-inflationary.*

anxious/eager Traditionally, *anxious* means "nervous" or "worried" and consequently describes negative feelings. In addition, it is usually followed by the word "about": *I'm anxious about my exam. Eager* means "looking forward" or "anticipating enthusiastically" and consequently describes positive feelings. It is usually followed by "to": *I'm eager to get it over with.* Today, however, it is standard usage for *anxious* to mean "eager": *They are anxious to see their new home.*

anybody, any body/anyone, any one *Anybody* and *anyone* are pronouns; *any body* is a noun modified by "any" and *any one* is a pronoun or adjective modified by "any." They are used as follows: *Was anybody able to find any body in the debris? Will anyone help me? I have more cleaning than any one person can ever do.*

any more/anymore *Any more* means "no more"; *anymore,* an adverb, means "nowadays" or "any longer": *We don't want any more trouble. We won't go there anymore.*

apt/likely *Apt* is standard in all speech and writing as a synonym for "likely" in suggesting chance without inclination: *They are apt to call any moment now. Likely,* meaning "probably," is frequently preceded by a qualifying word: *The new school budget will very likely raise taxes.* However, *likely* without the qualifying word is standard in all varieties of English: *The new school budget will likely raise taxes.*

ascent/assent *Ascent* is a noun that means "a move upward or a climb": *Their ascent up Mount Rainier was especially dangerous because of the recent rock slides. Assent* can be a noun or a verb. As a verb, *assent* means "to concur, to express agreement": *The union representative assented to the agreement.* As a noun, *assent* means "an agreement": *The assent was not reached peacefully.*

assistance/assistants *Assistance* is a noun that means "help, support": *Please give us your assistance here for a moment. Assistants* is a plural noun that means "helpers": *Since the assistants were late, we found ourselves running behind schedule.*

assure, ensure, insure *Assure* is a verb that means "to promise": *The plumber assured us that the sink would not clog again.* *Ensure* and *insure* are both verbs that mean "to make certain," although some writers use *insure* solely for legal and financial writing and *ensure* for more widespread usage: *Since it is hard to insure yourself against mudslide, we did not buy the house on the hill. We left late to ensure that we would not get caught in traffic.*

bare/bear *Bare* is an adjective or a verb. As an adjective, *bare* means "naked, unadorned": *The wall looked bare without the picture.* As a verb, *bare* means "to reveal": *He bared his soul.* *Bear* is a noun or a verb. As a noun, *bear* refers to the animal: *The teddy bear was named after Theodore Roosevelt.* As a verb, *bear* means to carry: *He bears a heavy burden.*

before/prior to *Prior to* is used most often in a legal sense: *Prior to settling the claim, the Smiths spent a week calling the attorney general's office.* Use *before* in almost all other cases: *Before we go grocery shopping, we sort the coupons we have clipped from the newspaper.*

beside/besides Although both words can function as prepositions, they have different shades of meaning: *beside* means "next to"; *besides* means "in addition to" or "except": *Besides, Richard would prefer not to sit beside the dog. There is no one here besides John and me.* *Besides* is also an adverb meaning "in addition": *Other people besides you feel the same way about the dog.*

bias/prejudice Generally, a distinction is made between *bias* and *prejudice.* Although both words imply "a preconceived opinion" or a "subjective point of view" in favor of something or against it, *prejudice* is generally used to express unfavorable feelings.

blonde/blond A *blonde* indicates a woman or girl with fair hair and skin. *Blond,* as an adjective, refers to either sex *(I have three blond children. He is a cute blond boy),* but *blonde,* as an adjective, still applies to women: *The blonde actress and her companion made the front page of the tabloid.*

borrow/lend *Borrow* means "to take with the intention of returning": *The book you borrow from the library today is due back in seven days.* *Lend* means "to give with the intention of getting back": *I will lend you the rake, but I need it back by Saturday.* The two terms are not interchangeable.

brake/break The most common meaning of *brake* as a noun is a device for slowing a vehicle: *The car's new brakes held on the steep incline.* *Brake* can also mean "a thicket" or "a species of fern." *Break,* a verb, means "to crack or make useless": *Please be especially careful that you don't break that vase.*

breath/breathe *Breath,* a noun, is the air taken in during respiration: *Her breath looked like fog in the frosty morning air.* *Breathe,* a verb, refers to the process of inhaling and exhaling air: *"Please breathe deeply," the doctor said to the patient.*

bring/take *Bring* is to carry toward the speaker: *She brings it to me.* *Take* is to carry away from the speaker: *She takes it away.*

buy/by *Buy,* a verb, means "to acquire goods at a price": *We have to buy a new dresser.* *By* can be a preposition, an adverb, or an adjective. As a preposition, *by* means "next to": *I pass by the office building every day.* As an adverb, *by* means "near, at hand": *The office is close by.* As an adjective, *by* means "situated to one side": *They came down on a by passage.*

canvas/canvass *Canvas,* a noun, refers to a heavy cloth: *The boat's sails are made of canvas. Canvass,* a verb, means "to solicit votes": *The candidate's representatives canvass the neighborhood seeking support.*

capital/Capitol *Capital* is the city or town that is the seat of government: *Paris is the capital of France. Capitol* refers to the building in Washington, D.C., in which the U.S. Congress meets: *When I was a child, we went for a visit to the Capitol.* When used with a lowercase letter, *capitol* is the building of a state legislature. *Capital* also means "a sum of money": *After the sale of their home, they had a great deal of capital.* As an adjective, *capital* means "foremost" or "first-rate": *He was a capital fellow.*

censor/censure Although both words are verbs, they have different meanings. To *censor* is to remove something from public view on moral or other grounds, and to *censure* is to give a formal reprimand: *The committee censored the offending passages from the book and censured the librarian for placing it on the shelves.*

cite/sight/site To *cite* means to "quote a passage": *The scholar often cited passages from noted authorities to back up his opinions. Sight* is a noun that means "vision": *With her new glasses, her sight was once again perfect. Site* is a noun that means "place or location": *They picked out a beautiful site overlooking a lake for their new home.*

climatic/climactic The word *climatic* comes from the word "climate" and refers to weather: *This summer's brutal heat may indicate a climatic change. Climactic,* in contrast, comes from the word "climax" and refers to a point of high drama: *In the climactic last scene the hideous creature takes over the world.*

clothes/cloths *Clothes* are garments: *For his birthday, John got some handsome new clothes. Cloths* are pieces of fabric: *Use these cloths to clean the car.*

coarse/course *Coarse,* an adjective, means "rough or common": *The horsehair fabric was too coarse to be made into a pillow. Although he's a little coarse around the edges, he has a heart of gold. Course,* a noun, means "a path" or "a prescribed number of classes": *They followed the bicycle course through the woods. My courses include English, math, and science.*

complement/compliment Both words can function as either a noun or a verb. The noun *complement* means "that which completes or makes perfect": *The rich chocolate mousse was a perfect complement to the light meal.* The verb *complement* means "to complete": *The oak door complemented the new siding and windows.* The noun *compliment* means "an expression of praise or admiration": *The mayor paid the visiting officials the compliment of escorting them around town personally.* The verb *compliment* means "to pay a compliment to": *Everyone complimented her after the presentation.*

complementary/complimentary *Complementary* is an adjective that means "forming a complement, completing": *The complementary colors suited the mood of the room. Complimentary* is an adjective that means "expressing a compliment": *The complimentary reviews ensured the play a long run. Complimentary* also means "free": *We thanked them for the complimentary tickets.*

continual/continuous Use *continual* to mean "intermittent, repeated often" and *continuous* to mean "uninterrupted, without stopping": *We suffered continual losses of electricity during the hurricane. They had continuous phone service during the hurricane. Continuous* and *continual* are never interchangeable with regard to spatial relationships, *a continuous series of passages.*

corps/corpse Both words are nouns. A *corps* is a group of people acting together; the word is often used in a military context: *The officers' corps assembled before dawn for the drill.* A *corpse* is a dead body: *The corpse was in the morgue.*

counsel/council *Counsel* is a verb meaning "to give advice": *They counsel recovering gamblers. Council* is a noun meaning "a group of advisers": *The trade union council meets in Ward Hall every Thursday.*

credible/creditable/credulous These three adjectives are often confused. *Credible* means "believable": *The tale is unusual, but seems credible to us. Creditable* means "worthy": *Sandra sang a creditable version of the song. Credulous* means "gullible": *The credulous Marsha believed that the movie was true.*

descent/dissent *Descent,* a noun, means "downward movement": *Much to their surprise, their descent down the mountain was harder than their ascent had been. Dissent,* a verb, means "to disagree": *The town council strongly dissented with the proposed measure. Dissent* as a noun means "difference in sentiment or opinion": *Dissent over the new proposal caused a rift between colleagues.*

desert/dessert *Desert* as a verb means to abandon; as a noun, an arid region: *People deserted in the desert rarely survive. Dessert,* a noun, refers to the sweet served as the final course of a meal: *My sister's favorite dessert is strawberry shortcake.*

device/devise *Device* is a noun meaning "invention or contrivance": *Do you think that device will really save us time? Devise* is a verb meaning "to contrive or plan": *Did he devise some device for repairing the ancient pump assembly?*

die/dye *Die,* as a verb, means "to cease to live": *The frog will die if released from the aquarium into the pond. Dye* as a verb means "to color or stain something": *I dye the drapes to cover the stains.*

discreet/discrete *Discreet* means "tactful;" *discrete,* "separate." For example: *Do you have a discreet way of refusing the invitation? The mosaic is made of hundreds of discrete pieces of tile.*

disinterested/uninterested *Disinterested* is used to mean "without prejudice, impartial" *(He is a disinterested judge)* and *uninterested* to mean "bored" or "lacking interest." *(They are completely uninterested in sports).*

dominant/dominate *Dominant,* an adjective, means "ruling, controlling": *Social scientists have long argued over the dominant motives for human behavior. Dominate,* a verb, means "to control": *Advice columnists often preach that no one can dominate you unless you allow them to.*

elicit/illicit *Elicit,* a verb, means "call forth;" *illicit,* an adjective, means "against the law": *The assault elicited a protest against illicit handguns.*

emigrate/immigrate *Emigrate* means "to leave one's own country to settle in another": *She emigrated from France. Immigrate* means "to enter a different country and settle there": *My father immigrated to America when he was nine years old.*

eminent/imminent *Eminent* means "distinguished": *Marie Curie was an eminent scientist in the final years of her life. Imminent* means "about to happen": *The thundershower seemed imminent.*

envelop/envelope *Envelop* is a verb that means "to surround": *The music envelops him in a soothing atmosphere. Envelope,* a noun, is a flat paper container, usually for a letter: *Be sure to put a stamp on the envelope before you mail that letter.*

especially/specially The two words are not interchangeable: *especially* means "particularly," *specially* means "for a specific reason." For example: *I especially value my wedding ring; it was made specially for me.*

ever so often/every so often *Ever so often* means happening very often and *every so often* means happening occasionally.

everyday/every day *Everyday* is an adjective that means "used daily, typical, ordinary"; *every day* is made up of a noun modified by the adjective "every" and means "each day": *Every day they had to deal with the everyday business of life.*

exam/examination *Exam* should be reserved for everyday speech and *examination* for formal writing: *The College Board examinations are scheduled for this Saturday morning at 9:00.*

explicit/implicit *Explicit* means "stated plainly;" *implicit* means "understood," "implied": *You know we have an implicit understanding that you are not allowed to watch any television shows that contain explicit sex.*

fair/fare *Fair* as an adjective means "free from bias," "ample," "unblemished," "of light hue," or "attractive." As an adverb, it means "favorably." It is used informally to mean "honest." *Fare* as a noun means "the price charged for transporting a person" or "food."

farther/further Traditionally, *farther* is used to indicate physical distance *(Is it much farther to the hotel?)* and *further* is used to refer to additional time, amount, or abstract ideas *(Your mother does not want to talk about this any further).*

flaunt/flout *Flaunt* means "to show off"; *flout,* "to ignore or treat with disdain." For example: *They flouted convention when they flaunted their wealth.*

flounder/founder *Flounder* means "to struggle with clumsy movements": *We floundered in the mud. Founder* means "to sink": *The ship foundered.*

formally/formerly Both words are adverbs. *Formally* means "in a formal manner": *The minister addressed the king and queen formally. Formerly* means "previously": *Formerly, he worked as a chauffeur; now, he is employed as a guard.*

forth/fourth *Forth* is an adverb meaning "going forward or away": *From that day forth, they lived happily ever after. Fourth* is most often used as an adjective that means "next after the third": *Mitchell was the fourth in line.*

gibe/jibe/jive The word *gibe* means "to taunt; deride; jeer." The word *jibe* means "to be in agreement with; accord; correspond": *The facts of the case didn't jibe.* The word *jive* is slang, and means "to tease; fool; kid."

healthy/healthful *Healthy* means "possessing health;" *healthful* means "bringing about health": *They believed that they were healthy people because they ate healthful food.*

historic/historical The word *historic* means "important in history": *a historic speech; a historic battlefield.* The word *historical* means "being a part of, or inspired by, history": *historical records; a historical novel.*

home in/hone in The expression *home in* means "to approach or focus on (an objective)." It comes from the language of guided missiles, where *homing in* refers to locking onto a target. The expression *hone in* is an error.

human/humane Both words are adjectives. *Human* means "pertaining to humanity": *The subject of the documentary is the human race.* *Humane* means "tender, compassionate, or sympathetic": *Many of her patients believed that her humane care speeded their recovery.*

idea/ideal *Idea* means "thought," while *ideal* means "a model of perfection" or "goal." The two words are not interchangeable. They should be used as follows: *The idea behind the blood drive is that our ideals often move us to help others.*

imply/infer *Imply* means "to suggest without stating": *The message on Karen's postcard implies that her vacation has not turned out as she wished.* *Infer* means "to reach a conclusion based on understood evidence": *From her message I infer that she wishes she had stayed home.* When used in this manner, the two words describe two sides of the same process.

incredible/incredulous *Incredible* means "cannot be believed;" *incredulous* means "unbelieving": *The teacher was incredulous when she heard the pupil's incredible story about the fate of his term project.*

individual/person/party *Individual* should be used to stress uniqueness or to refer to a single human being as contrasted to a group of people: *The rights of the individual should not supersede the rights of a group.* *Person* is the preferred word in other contexts. *What person wouldn't want to have a chance to sail around the world?* *Party* is used to refer to a group: *Send the party of five this way, please.* *Party* is also used to refer to an individual mentioned in a legal document.

ingenious/ingenuous *Ingenious* means "resourceful, clever": *My sister is ingenious when it comes to turning leftovers into something delicious.* *Ingenuous* means "frank, artless": *The child's ingenuous manner is surprising considering her fame.*

later/latter *Later* is used to refer to time; *latter,* the second of two items named: *It is later than you think. Of the two shirts I just purchased, I prefer the latter.*

lay/lie *Lay* is a transitive verb that means "to put down" or "to place." It takes a direct object: *Please lay the soup spoon next to the teaspoon. Lie* is an intransitive verb that means "to be in a horizontal position" or "be situated." It does not take a direct object: *The puppy lies down where the old dog had always lain. The hotel lies on the outskirts of town.* The confusion arises over *lay,* which is the present tense of the verb *lay* and the past tense of the verb *lie.*

To lie (recline)
Present: *Spot lies (is lying) down.*
Future: *Spot will lie down.*
Past: *Spot lay down.*
Perfect: *Spot has (had, will have) lain down.*

To lay (put down)
Present: *He lays (is laying) his dice down.*
Future: *He will lay his dice down.*
Past: *He laid his dice down.*
Perfect: *He has (had, will have) laid his dice down.*

Although *lie* and *lay* tend to be used interchangeably in all but the most careful, formal speech, the following phrases are generally considered nonstandard and are avoided in written English: *Lay down, dears. The dog laid in the sun. Abandoned cars were laying in the junkyard. The reports have laid in the mailbox for a week.*

lead/led *Lead* as a verb means "to take or conduct on the way": *I plan to lead a quiet afternoon. Led* is the past tense: *He led his followers through the dangerous underbrush. Lead,* as a noun, means "a type of metal": *Pipes are made of lead.*

learn/teach *Learn* is to acquire knowledge: *He learned fast. Teach* is to impart knowledge: *She taught well.*

leave/let *Leave* and *let* are interchangeable only when followed by the word "alone": *Leave him alone. Let him alone.* In other instances, *leave* means "to depart" or "permit to remain in the same place": *If you leave, please turn off the copier. Leave the extra paper on the shelf. Let* means "to allow": *Let him work with the assistant, if he wants.*

lessen/lesson *Lessen* is a verb meaning "to decrease": *To lessen the pain of a burn, apply ice to the injured area. Lesson* is most often used as a noun meaning "material assigned for study": *Today, the lesson will be on electricity.*

lightening/lightning *Lightening* is a form of the verb that means "to brighten": *The cheerful new drapes and bunches of flowers went a long way in lightening the room's somber mood. Lightning* is most often used as a noun to mean "flashes of light generated during a storm": *The thunder and lightning frightened the child.*

loose/lose *Loose* as an adjective meaning "free and unattached": *The dog was loose again. Loose* can also be a verb meaning "let loose": *The hunters loose the dogs as soon as the ducks fall. Lose* is a verb meaning "to part with unintentionally": *He will lose his keys if he leaves them on the countertop.*

mad/angry Traditionally, *mad* has been used to mean "insane"; *angry* has been used to mean "full of ire." While *mad* can be used to mean "enraged, angry," in informal usage, you should replace *mad* with *angry* in formal discourse: *The president is angry at Congress for overriding his veto.*

maybe/may be *Maybe,* an adverb, means "perhaps": *Maybe the newspapers can be recycled with the plastic and glass. May be,* a verb, means "could be": *It may be too difficult, however.*

moral/morale As a noun, *moral* means "ethical lesson": *Each of Aesop's fables has a clear moral. Morale* means "state of mind" or "spirit": *Her morale was lifted by her colleague's good wishes.*

orient/orientate The two words both mean "to adjust to or familiarize with new surroundings; place in a particular position." There is no reason to prefer or reject either word, although sometimes people object to *orientate*.

passed/past *Passed* is a form of the verb meaning "to go by": *Bernie passed the same buildings on his way to work each day. Past* can function as a noun, adjective, adverb, or preposition. As a noun, *past* means "the history of a nation, person, etc.": *The lessons of the past should not be forgotten.* As an adjective, *past* means "gone by or elapsed in time": *John is worried about his past deeds.* As an adverb, *past* means "so as to pass by": *The fire engine raced past the parked cars.* As a preposition, *past* means "beyond in time": *It's past noon already.*

patience/patients *Patience,* a noun, means "endurance": *Chrissy's patience makes her an ideal baby-sitter. Patients* are people under medical treatment: *The patients must remain in the hospital for another week.*

peace/piece *Peace* is "freedom from discord": *The negotiators hoped that the new treaty would bring about lasting peace. Piece* is "a portion of a whole" or "a short musical arrangement": *I would like just a small piece of cake, please. The piece in E flat is especially beautiful.*

percent/percentage *Percent* is used with a number, *percentage* with a modifier. *Percentage* is used most often after an adjective: *A high percentage of your earnings this year is tax deductible.*

personal/personnel *Personal* means "private": *The lock on her journal showed that it was clearly personal. Personnel* refers to employees: *Attention all personnel!* The use of *personnel* as a plural has become standard in business and government: *The personnel were dispatched to the Chicago office.*

plain/plane *Plain* as an adjective means "easily understood," "undistinguished," or "unadorned": *His meaning was plain to all. The plain dress suited the gravity of the occasion.* As an adverb, *plain* means "clearly and simply": *She's just plain foolish.* As a noun, *plain* is a flat area of land: *The vast plain seemed to go on forever.* As a noun, *plane* has a number of different meanings. It most commonly refers to an airplane, but is also used in mathematics and fine arts and as a tool used to shave wood.

practicable/practical *Practicable* means "capable of being done": *My decorating plans were too difficult to be practicable. Practical* means "pertaining to practice or action": *It was just and practical to paint the floor white.*

precede/proceed Although both words are verbs, they have different meanings. *Precede* means "to go before": *Morning precedes afternoon. Proceed* means "to move forward": *Proceed to the exit in an orderly fashion.*

presence/presents *Presence* is used chiefly to mean "attendance, close proximity": *Your presence at the ceremony will be greatly appreciated. Presents* are gifts. *Thank you for giving us such generous presents.*

principal/principle *Principal* can be a noun or an adjective. As a noun, *principal* means "chief or head official" (*The principal decided to close school early on Tuesday*) or "sum of capital" (*Invest only the interest, never the principal*). As an adjective, *principal* means "first or highest": *The principal ingredient is sugar. Principle* is a noun only, meaning "rule" or "general truth": *Regardless of what others said, she stood by her principles.*

quiet/quite *Quiet,* as an adjective, means "free from noise": *When the master of ceremonies spoke, the room became quiet. Quite,* an adverb, means "completely, wholly": *By the late afternoon, the children were quite exhausted.*

quotation/quote *Quotation,* a noun, means "a passage quoted from a speech or book": *The speaker read a quotation of twenty-five lines to the audience. Quote,* a verb, means "to repeat a passage from a speech, etc.": *Marci often quotes from popular novels. Quote* and *quotation* are often used interchangeably in speech; in formal writing, however, a distinction is still observed between the two words.

rain/reign/rein As a noun, *rain* means "water that falls from the atmosphere to earth." As a verb, *rain* means "to send down, to give abundantly": *The crushed piñata rained candy on the eager children.* As a noun, *reign* means "royal rule," as a verb, "to have supreme control": *The monarch's reign was marked by social unrest.* As a noun, *rein* means "a leather strap used to guide an animal," as a verb, "to control or guide": *He used the rein to control the frisky colt.*

raise/rise/raze *Raise,* a transitive verb, means "to elevate": *How can I raise the cost of my house? Rise,* an intransitive verb, means "to go up, to get up": *Will housing costs rise this year? Raze* is a transitive verb meaning "to tear down, demolish": *The wrecking crew was ready to raze the condemned building.*

respectful/respective *Respectful* means "showing (or full of) respect": *If you are respectful toward others, they will treat you with consideration as well. Respective* means "in the order given": *The respective remarks were made by executive board members Joshua Whittles, Kevin McCarthy, and Warren Richmond.*

reverend/reverent As an adjective (usually capitalized). *Reverend* is an epithet of respect given to a member of the clergy: *The Reverend Mr. Jones gave the sermon.* As a noun, a *reverend* is "a member of the clergy": *In our church, the reverend opens the service with a prayer. Reverent* is an adjective meaning "showing deep respect": *The speaker began his remarks with a reverent greeting.*

right/rite/write *Right* as an adjective means "proper, correct" and "as opposed to left," as a noun it means "claims or titles," as an adverb it means "in a straight line, directly," as a verb it means "to restore to an upright position." *Rite* is a noun meaning "a solemn ritual": *The religious leader performed the necessary rites. Write* is a verb meaning "to form characters on a surface": *The child liked to write her name over and over.*

sensual/sensuous *Sensual* carries sexual overtones: *The massage was a sensual experience. Sensuous* means "pertaining to the senses": *The sensuous aroma of freshly baked bread wafted through the house.*

set/sit *Set,* a transitive verb, describes something a person does to an object: *She* *set the book down on the table. Sit,* an intransitive verb, describes a person resting: *Marvin sits on the straight-backed chair.*

somebody/some body *Somebody* is an indefinite pronoun: *Somebody recommended this restaurant. Some body* is a noun modified by an adjective: *I have a new spray that will give my limp hair some body.*

someone/some one *Someone* is an indefinite pronoun: *Someone who ate here said the pasta was delicious. Some one* is a pronoun adjective modified by "some": *Please pick some one magazine that you would like to read.*

sometime/sometimes/some time Traditionally, these three words have carried different meanings. *Sometime* means "at an unspecified time in the future": *Why not plan to visit Niagara Falls sometime? Sometimes* means "occasionally": *I visit my former college roommate sometimes. Some time* means "a span of time": *I need some time to make up my mind about what you have said.*

stationary/stationery Although these two words sound alike, they have very different meanings. *Stationary* means "staying in one place": *From this distance, the satellite appeared to be stationary. Stationery* means "writing paper": *A hotel often provides stationery with its name preprinted.*

straight/strait *Straight* is most often used as an adjective meaning "unbending": *The path cut straight through the woods. Strait,* a noun, is "a narrow passage of water connecting two large bodies of water" or "distress, dilemma": *He was in dire financial straits.*

subsequently/consequently *Subsequently* means "occurring later, afterward": *We went to a new French restaurant for dinner; subsequently, we heard that everyone who had eaten the Caesar salad became ill. Consequently* means "therefore, as a result": *The temperature was above 90 degrees for a week; consequently all the tomatoes burst on the vine.*

taught/taut *Taught* is the past tense of "to teach": *My English teachers taught especially well. Taut* is "tightly drawn": *Pull the knot taut or it will not hold.*

than/then *Than,* a conjunction, is used in comparisons: *Robert is taller than Michael. Then,* an adverb, is used to indicate time: *We knew then that there was little to be gained by further discussion.*

their/there/they're Although these three words sound alike, they have very different meanings. *Their,* the possessive form of "they," means "belonging to them": *Their house is new. There* can point out place *(There is the picture I was telling you about)* or call attention to someone or something *(There is a mouse behind you!). They're* is a contraction for "they are": *They're not at home right now.*

threw/thru/through *Threw,* the past tense of the verb "throw," means "to hurl an object": *He threw the ball at the batter. Through* means "from one end to the other" or "by way of": *They walked through the museum all afternoon. Through* should be used in formal writing in place of *thru,* an informal spelling.

to/too/two Although the words sound alike, they are different parts of speech and have different meanings. *To* is a preposition indicating direction or part of an infinitive; *too* is an adverb meaning "also" or "in extreme"; and *two* is a number: *I have to go to the store to buy two items. Do you want to come too?*

track/tract *Track,* as a noun, is a path or course: *The railroad track in the Omaha* *station has recently been electrified. Track,* as a verb, is "to follow": *Sophisticated guidance control systems are used to track the space shuttles. Tract* is "an expanse of land" or "a brief treatise": *Jonathan Swift wrote many tracts on the political problems of his day.*

unexceptional/unexceptionable Although both *unexceptional* and *unexceptionable* are adjectives, they have different meanings and are not interchangeable. *Unexceptional* means "commonplace, ordinary": *Despite the glowing reviews the new restaurant had received, we found it offered unexceptional meals and services. Unexceptionable* means "not offering any basis for exception or objection, beyond criticism": *We could not dispute his argument because it was unexceptionable.*

usage/use *Usage* is a noun that refers to the generally accepted way of doing something. The word refers especially to the conventions of language: *"Most unique"* is considered incorrect usage. *Use* can be either a noun or a verb. As a noun, use means "the act of employing or putting into service": *In the adult education course, I learned the correct use of tools. Usage* is often misused in place of the noun *use: Effective use (not "usage") of your time results in greater personal satisfaction.*

use/utilize/utilization *Utilize* means "to make use of": *They should utilize the new profit-sharing plan to decrease taxable income. Utilization* is the noun form of utilize. In most instances, however, *use* is preferred to either *utilize* or *utilization* as less overly formal and stilted: *They should use the new profit-sharing plan to decrease taxable income.*

which/witch *Which* is a pronoun meaning "what one": *Which desk is yours? Witch* is a noun meaning "a person who practices magic": *The superstitious villagers accused her of being a witch.*

who's/whose *Who's* is the contraction for "who is" or "who has": *Who's the person in charge here? Who's got the money? Whose* is the possessive form of "who": *Whose book is this?*

your/you're *Your* is the possessive form of "you": *Your book is overdue at the library. You're* is the contraction of "you are": *You're just the person we need for this job.*

4

Usage Basics

Language and the way it is used change constantly. This glossary provides a concise guide to contemporary English usage. It will show you how certain words and phrases are used and why certain usage is unacceptable.

"Informal" indicates that a word or phrase is often used in everyday speech but should generally be avoided in formal discourse. "Nonstandard" means that the word or phrase is not suitable for everyday speech and writing or in formal discourse.

a/an In both spoken and written English, *an* is used before words beginning with a vowel sound *(He carried an umbrella. The Nobel is an honor)* and when the consonants *f, h, l, m, n, r, s,* and *x* are pronounced by name *(The renovations created an L-shaped room. Miles received an F in physics).* Use *a* before words beginning with a consonant sound *(What a fish! I bought a computer)* and words that start with vowels but are pronounced as consonants. *(A union can be dissolved. They live in a one-room apartment).* Also use *a* with words that start with consonant letters not listed above and with the vowel *u (She earned a C in French. He made a U-turn).*

For words that begin with *h,* if the initial *h* is not pronounced, the word is preceded by *an (It will take an hour).* Adjectives such as *historic, historical, heroic,* and *habitual* are commonly preceded by *an,* especially in British English, but the use of *a* is common in both writing and speech *(She read a historical novel).* When the *h* is strongly pronounced, as in a stressed first syllable, the word is preceded by *a (I bought a history of Long Island).*

above *Above* can be used as an adjective *(The above entry is incomplete)* or as a noun *(First, please read the above)* in referring to what has been previously mentioned in a passage. Both uses are standard in formal writing.

ain't The term is nonstandard for "am not," "isn't," or "aren't." It is used in informal speech and writing for humorous effect or for emphasis, usually in dialogue.

all right/alright *All right* is always written as two words: *alright* is a misspelling: *Betsy said that it was all right to use her car that afternoon.*

almost/most *Almost,* an adverb, means "nearly"; *most,* an adjective, means "the greatest part of" something. *Most* is not synonymous with *almost,* as the following example shows: *During our vacation we shop at that store almost every day and buy most of the available snack foods.*

In informal speech, *most* (as a shortened form of *almost*) is used as an adverb. It occurs before such pronouns as *all, anyone, anybody, everyone,* and *everybody;* the adjectives *all, any,* and *every;* and the adverbs *anywhere* and *everywhere.* For example: *Most everyone around here is related.* The use of *most* as an adverb is nonstandard and is uncommon in formal writing except when used to represent speech.

A.M., P.M./a.m., p.m. These abbreviations for time are most frequently restricted to use with figures: *The ceremony begins at 10:00 a.m.* (not *"ten thirty a.m."*)

among/between *Among* is used to indicate relationships involving more than two people or things, while *between* is used to show relationships involving two people or things, or to compare one thing to a group to which it belongs: *The three quarreled among themselves because she had to choose between two of them. Between* is also used to express relationships of persons or things considered individually, no matter how many: *Between holding public office, teaching, and raising a family, she has little free time.*

and etc. Since *etc.* means "and all the rest," *and etc.* is redundant; the "and" is not needed. Many prefer to use "and so forth" or "and the like" as a substitute for the abbreviation.

and/or The combination *and/or* is used mainly in legal and business writing. Its use should be avoided in general writing, as in *He spends his weekends watching television and/or snacking.* In such writing, either one or the other word is sufficient. If you mean "either," use *or;* if you mean "both," use *and.* To make a greater distinction, revise the phrasing: *He spends his weekends watching television, snacking, or both.*

and which/and who "And" is unnecessary when "which" or "who" is used to open a relative clause. Use *and which* or *and who* only to open a second clause starting with the same relative pronoun: *Elizabeth is my neighbor who goes shopping every morning and who calls me every afternoon to tell me about the sales.*

a number/the number As a subject, *a number* is most often plural and the *number* is singular. *A number of choices are available. The number of choices is limited.* As with many agreement questions, this guideline is followed more often in formal discourse than in speech and informal writing.

anyplace *Anyplace* is an informal expression for "anywhere." It occurs in speech and informal writing but is best avoided in formal prose.

anyways/anyway; anywheres/anywhere *Anyways* is nonstandard for *anyway; anywheres* is nonstandard for *anywhere.*

as Do not use *as* in place of *whether: We're not sure whether* (not *"as"*) *you should do that.* Also avoid using *as* as a substitute for *because, since, while, whether, or who,* where its use may create confusion. In the following sentence, for example, *as* may mean "while" or "because": *As they were driving to California they decided to see the Grand Canyon.*

as/because/since While all three words can function as subordinating conjunctions, they carry slightly different shades of meaning. *As* establishes a time relationship and can be used interchangeably with "when" or "while." *Because* and *since,* in contrast, describe causes and effects: *As we brought out the food, it began to drizzle. Because (since) Nancy goes skiing infrequently, she prefers to rent skis.*

as/like When *as* functions as a preposition, the distinction between *as* and *like* depends on meaning: *As* suggests that the subject is equivalent to the description: *He was employed as a teacher. Like,* in contrast, suggests similarity but not equivalence: *Speakers like her excel in front of large groups.*

at Avoid using *at* after "where": *Where are you seeing her (not "at")?* Whether used as an adverb or as a preposition, "where" contains the preposition "at" in its definition.

at this point in time Although the term *at this point in time* is widely used (especially in politics), many consider it verbose and stuffy. Instead, use "now" or "at this time": *We are not now ready to discuss the new budget.*

awful/awfully Avoid using *awful* or *awfully* to mean "very" in formal discourse: *We had an awfully busy time at the amusement park.* Although the use of *awful* to mean "terrible" (rather than "inspiring awe") has permeated all levels of writing and speech, consider using in its place a word that more closely matches your intended meaning: *We had an unpleasant (not "awful") time because the park was hot, noisy, and crowded.*

awhile/a while *Awhile* is an adverb and is always spelled as one word: *We visited awhile. A while* is a noun phrase (an article and a noun) and is used after a preposition: *We rested for a while.*

backward/backwards In formal discourse, *backward* is preferred: *This stroke is easier if you use a backward motion* (adjective). *Counting backward from 100 can be an effective way to induce sleep* (adverb).

bad/badly *Bad,* an adjective, is used to describe a noun or pronoun. *Badly,* an adverb, is used to describe a verb, adjective, or another adverb. Thus: *She felt bad because her broken leg throbbed badly.*

because/due to the fact that/since *Because* or *since* are preferred over the wordy phrase *due to the fact* that: *He wrote the report longhand because (not "due to the fact") his computer was broken.*

being as/being that Avoid both *being as* and *being that* in formal writing. Instead, use "since" or "because." For example: *Since you asked, I'll be glad to help.*

better/had better The verb "had" is necessary in the phrase *had better* and should be retained. *She had better return the lawn mower today.*

between you and I Pronouns that function as objects of prepositions are traditionally used in the objective case. *Please keep this between you and me. I would appreciate it if you could keep this between her and them.*

bi- Many words that refer to periods of time through the prefix *bi-* are potentially confusing. Ambiguity is avoided by using the prefix *semi-,* meaning "twice each" *(semiweekly, semimonthly, semiannual)* or by using the appropriate phrases *(twice a week, twice each month, every two months; every two years).*

borrow off/borrow from *Borrow off,* considered informal, is not used in formal speech and writing; *borrow from* is the preferred expression.

bottom line This overworked term is frequently used as a synonym for "outcome" or "the final result": *The bottom line is that we have to reduce inventory* *to maintain profits.* Careful writers and speakers avoid it for less shopworn descriptions.

bunch Use the noun *bunch* in formal writing only to refer to clusters of things grouped together, such as grapes or bananas: *That bunch of grapes looks better than the other one.* In formal writing, use *group* or *crowd* to refer to gatherings of people; *bunch* is used to refer to groups of people or items only in speech and informal writing.

burst, bursted/bust, busted *Burst* is a verb meaning "to come apart suddenly." The word *bursted* is not acceptable in either speech or writing. The verb *bust* and adjective *busted* are both informal or slang terms; as such, they should not be used in formal writing.

but however/but yet There is no reason to combine *but* with another conjunction: *She said she was leaving, yet (not "but yet") she poured another cup of coffee.*

but that/but what As with the previous example, there is no reason to add the word *but* to either *that* or *what: We don't doubt that (not "but that") you will win this hand.*

calculate/figure/reckon None of these words is an acceptable substitute for *expect* or *imagine* in formal writing, although they are used in speech and informal prose.

can/may Traditionally, *may* is used in formal writing to convey permission; *can,* ability or capacity. In speech, however, the terms are used interchangeably to mean permission: *Can (May) I borrow your hedge clippers? Can* and *may* are frequently but not always interchangeable when used to mean possibility: *A blizzard can (or may) occur any time during February.* In negative constructions, *can't* is more common than *mayn't,* the latter being rare. *You can't eat that taco in the den.*

cannot/can not *Cannot* is occasionally spelled *can not.* The one-word spelling is by far the more common. The contraction *can't* is used mainly in speech and informal writing.

can't help but *Can't help but,* as in: *You can't help but like her,* is a double negative. This idiom can be replaced by the informal *can't help* or the formal *cannot but* where each is appropriate: *She can't help wishing that it was spring. I cannot but wish things had turned out differently.* While *can't help but* is common in all types of speech, avoid using it in formal writing.

cause of . . . on account of/due to The phrases *on account of* and *due to* are unnecessary with *cause of.* Omit the phrases or revise the entire sentence: *One cause of physical and psychological problems is due to too much stress.* Change the sentence to: *Too much stress causes physical and psychological problems.*

center around/center on Although both phrases are often criticized for being illogical, they have been used in writing for more than a hundred years to express the notion of collecting or gathering as if around a center point. The phrase *revolve around* is often suggested as an alternative, and the prepositions *at, in,* and *on* are considered acceptable with *center* in the following sense: *Their problems centered on their lack of expertise.*

chair/chairperson *Chairperson* is used widely in academic and governmental circles as an alternative to "chairman" or "chairwoman." While some reject the term *chairperson* as clumsy and unnecessary and use the term *chair* for any presiding officer, regardless of sex, *chairperson* is still standard in all types of writing and speech.

choose/chose *Choose* is a verb that means "to select one thing in preference to another": *Why choose tomatoes when they are out of season? Chose* is the past tense of "to choose": *I chose tomatoes over cucumbers at the salad bar.*

conformity to/conformity with Although the word *conformity* can be followed by either "to" or "with," *conformity to* is generally used when the idea of obedience is implied. *The new commissioner issued a demand for conformity to health regulations. Conformity with* is used to imply agreement or correspondence: *This is an idea in conformity with previous planning.*

consensus/consensus of The expression *consensus of (consensus of opinion)* is considered redundant, and the preferred usage is the single noun *consensus,* meaning "general agreement or concord": *Since the consensus was overwhelming the city planners moved ahead with the proposal.* The phrase *general consensus* is also considered redundant. Increasingly, the word *consensus* is widely used attributively, as in the phrase *consensus politics.*

contact The word is both a verb and a noun. As a verb, it is frequently used unprecisely to mean "to communicate" when a more exact word *(telephone, write to, consult)* would better communicate the idea. *Contact* as a noun meaning "a person through whom one can obtain information" is now standard usage: *He is my contact in the state department.*

couple/couple of Both phrases are informally used to mean "two" or "several": *I need a couple more cans of paint. I took a couple of aspirins for my headache.* The expression *a couple of* is used in standard English, especially in referring to distance, money, or time: *He is a couple of feet away. I have a couple of thousand dollars in the bank. The store will open in a couple of weeks. Couple* may be treated as either a singular or plural noun.

criteria/criterion *Criteria* is the plural of *criterion* (a standard for judgment). For example: *Of all their criteria for evaluating job performance, customer satisfaction was the most important criterion.*

data/datum *Data* is the plural of *datum* (fact). Although *data* is often used as a singular, it should still be treated as plural in formal speech and writing: *The data pertain (not "pertains") to the first half of the experiment.* To avoid awkward constructions, most writers prefer to use a more commonplace term such as "fact" or "figure" in place of *datum.*

decimate The word *decimate* comes from a Latin term that meant "to select by lot and kill one person in ten of (a rebellious military unit)." The usual use of the word in English is "to destroy a large amount or proportion of": *Disease decimated the population.* Some people claim that *decimate* should only be used to mean "to destroy a tenth of," but in fact the word has never been used this way in English. There is nothing wrong with the sense "to destroy a large amount or proportion of."

differ from/differ with *Differ from* means "to be unlike"; *differ with* means "to disagree with": *The sisters differ from each other in appearance. We differ with you on this matter.*

different from/different than Although *different from* is the preferred usage *(His attitude is different from mine)*, *different than* is widely accepted when a clause follows, especially when the word "from" would create an awkward sentence. Example: *The stream followed a different course than the map showed.*

don't/does not *Don't* is the contraction for "do not," not for *does not,* as in *I don't care, she doesn't (not don't) care.*

done Using *done* as an adjective to mean "through, finished" is standard. Originally, *done* was used attributively *(The pact between them was a done thing)*, but it has become more common as a compliment: *Are your pictures done yet? When we were done with the power saw, we removed the blade.*

double negatives Although the use of double negatives *(They never paid no dues)* was standard for many years in English, today certain uses of the double negative are universally considered unacceptable: *He didn't have nothing to do,* for example. In educated speech and writing, "anything" would be used in place of "nothing."

doubt that/doubt whether/doubt if *Doubt that* is used to express conviction *(I doubt that they intended to hurt your feelings)*; *doubt whether* and *doubt if* are used to indicate uncertainty: *I doubt whether (or if) anyone really listened to the speaker.*

due to In formal discourse, *due to* is acceptable only after a form of the verb "to be": *Her aching back was due to poor posture. Due to* is not acceptable as a preposition meaning "because of" or "owing to": *Because of (not "due to") the poor weather, the bus was late.*

each When *each* is used as a pronoun, it takes a singular verb *(Each was born in Europe)*, although plurals are increasingly used in formal speech and writing in an attempt to avoid using "he" or "his" for sentences that include females or do not specify sex *(Each of them had their (rather than "his") own agenda).* More and more, the same pattern of pronoun agreement is being used with the singular pronouns *anyone, anybody, everyone, everybody, no one, someone* and *somebody.* When the pronoun *each* is followed by an "of" phrase containing a plural noun or pronoun, usage guides suggest that the verb be singular, but the plural is used often even in formal writing: *Each of the children has (or "have") had a school physical.*

When the adjective *each* follows a plural subject, the verb agrees with the subject: *The rooms each have separate thermostats.*

each and every Use "each" or "every" in place of the phrase *each and every,* generally considered wordy: *Each of us enjoyed the concert. Every one of us stayed until the end of the performance.*

each other/one another *Each other* is traditionally used to indicate two members; *one another* for three or more: *The two children trade lunches with each other. The guests greeted one another fondly.* In standard practice, though, these distinctions are not observed in either speech or writing.

eminent/imminent *Eminent* means "distinguished": *Marie Curie was an eminent scientist in the final years of her life. Imminent* means "about to happen": *The thundershower seemed imminent.*

enormity The word *enormity* means "outrageousness; atrociousness; monstrousness": *the enormity of his crime.* It is often used to mean "great size; enormousness": *The enormity of the task overwhelmed her.* Though this use is common, many people consider it to be an error.

enthused/enthusiastic The word *enthused* is used informally to mean "showing enthusiasm." For formal writing and speech, use the adjective *enthusiastic: The team was enthusiastic about the quarterback's winning play.*

-ess/-or/-er The suffix *-ess* has often been used to denote feminine nouns. While many such words are still in use, English is moving increasingly toward nouns that do not denote sex differences. The most widely observed guideline today is that if the sex of the performer is not relevant to the performance of the task or function, the neutral ending *-or* or *-er* should be used in place of *-ess.* Thus, words such as *ambassadress, ancestress, authoress, poetess, proprietress, sculptress* are no longer used, and the airlines, for example, have replaced both *steward* and *stewardess* with *flight attendant.*

et al. *Et al.,* the Latin abbreviation for "and other people," is fully standard for use in a citation to refer to works with more than three authors: *Harris et al.*

etc. Since *etc.* (et cetera) is the Latin abbreviation for "and other things," it should not be used to refer to people. In general, it should be avoided in formal writing as imprecise. In its place, provide the entire list of items or use "and so on."

-ette English nouns whose *-ette* ending signifies a feminine role or identity are passing out of usage. *Suffragette* and *usherette,* for example, have been replaced by *suffragist* and *usher,* respectively.

everybody, every body/everyone, every one *Everybody* and *everyone* are indefinite pronouns: *Everybody likes William, and everyone enjoys his company. Every body* is a noun modified by "every" and *every one* is a pronoun modified by "every"; both refer to a person in a specific group and are usually followed by "of": *Every body of water in our area is polluted; every one of our ponds is covered in debris.*

everywheres/everywhere *Everywheres* is a nonstandard term for *everywhere* and should be avoided in speech and writing.

except for the fact that/except that Use *except that* in place of the verbose phrase *except for the fact that: Except that (not "except for the fact that") the button is missing, this is a lovely skirt.*

fewer/less Traditionally, *fewer,* a plural noun, has most often been used to refer to individual units that can be counted: *There are fewer buttons on this shirt. No fewer than forty of the fifty voters supported the measure. Less,* a singular noun, is used to refer to uncountable quantities: *She eats less every day. I have less patience than I used to.*

Standard English does not usually reflect these distinctions, however. When followed by "than," *less* is used as often as *fewer* to indicate plural nouns that refer to items that can be counted. *There were no less than eight million people. No less than forty of the fifty voters supported the measure.*

figuratively/literally *Figuratively,* meaning "involving a figure of speech," usually implies that the statement is not true. *Literally,* meaning "actually, without exaggeration," implies that the statement is true: *The poet Robert Frost once fig-*

uratively described writing poetry without regular meter and rhyme as playing tennis with the net down. My sister literally passed out when she saw what had happened to her new car.

Literally is commonly used as an intensifier meaning "in effect, virtually": *The state representative was literally buried alive in the caucus.* This usage should be avoided in formal discourse.

fix The verb *fix,* meaning "to repair," is fully accepted in all areas of speech and writing. The noun *fix,* meaning "repair" or "adjustment," is used informally.

fixing to/intend to Use *intend to* in place of the informal or dialectal term *fixing to: The community intends to (not "is fixing to") raise money to help the victims of the recent fire.*

flunk/fail Use the standard term *fail* in speech and writing; *flunk* is an informal substitute.

former/latter *Former* is used to refer to the first of two items; *latter,* the second: *We enjoy both gardening and painting, the former during the summer and the latter during the winter.* When dealing with three or more items, use "first" and "last" rather than *former* and *latter: We enjoy gardening, painting, and skiing, but the last is very costly.*

fortuitous *Fortuitous* means "happening accidentally": *A fortuitous meeting with a former acquaintance led to a change in plans.* It is also used sometimes as a synonym for "lucky" or "fortunate."

from whence Although the phrase *from whence* is sometimes criticized on the grounds that "from" is redundant because it is included in the meaning of "whence," the idiom is nonetheless standard in both speech and writing: *She finally moved to Kansas, from whence she began to build a new life.*

fulsome Originally, *fulsome* meant "abundant," but for hundreds of years the word has been used to mean "offensive, disgusting, or excessively lavish." While the word still maintains the connotations of "excessive" or "offensive," it has also come to be used in the original sense as well: *Compare the severe furniture of the living room to the fulsome decorations in the den.*

fun *Fun* should not be used as an adjective in formal writing. Instead, substitute a word such as "happy," "pleasant," or "entertaining": *They had a pleasant (not "fun") afternoon at the park.*

gentleman Once used only to refer to men of high social rank, the term *gentleman* now also specifies a man of courtesy and consideration: *He behaves like a gentleman.* It is also used as a term of polite reference and address in the singular and plural: *This gentleman is waiting to be served. Are we ready to begin, gentlemen?*

get The verb *get* is used in many slang and informal phrases as a substitute for forms of "to be." For example: *They won't get accepted with that attitude.* In American English, an alternative past participle is *gotten,* especially in the sense of "received" and "acquired": *I have gotten (or "got") all I ever wanted.*

Both *have* and *has got* (meaning "must") are occasionally criticized as being redundant, but are nonetheless fully standard in all varieties of speech and writing: *You have got to carry your driver's license at all times.*

good/well *Good,* an adjective, should be used to describe someone or something: *Joe is a good student. Well,* when used as an adverb, should describe an action: *She and Laura play well together on the swing set. Well,* when used as an adjective after "look," "feel" or other linking verbs, often refers to good health: *You're looking well.*

good and/very Avoid using *good and* as a substitute for *very: I was very (not "good and") hungry.*

graduate The passive form, once considered the only correct usage, is seldom used today: *I was graduated from the Merchant Marine Academy last May.* Although some critics condemn the use of *graduate* as a verb meaning "to receive a degree or diploma (from)" its use is common in both speech and writing: *She graduated from elementary school in Cleveland.*

great The word *great* has been overused in informal writing and speech as a synonym for "enthusiastic," "good," or "clever": *She was really great at making people feel at home.*

had drank/had drunk According to some authorities, *had drank* is acceptable usage: *I had drank a gallon of milk. Had drunk,* though, is fully standard and the preferred usage.

has/have; has got/have got The word "got" is unnecessary; simply use *has* or *have: Jessica has a mild case of chicken pox.*

had ought/ought *Had ought* is considered wordy; the preferred usage is *ought: She ought (not "had ought") to heed her mother's advice.*

half/a half a/a half Use either *half* or *a half; a half a* is considered wordy: *Please give me a half (not "a half a") piece. I'd like half that slice, please.*

hanged/hung Although both words are past-tense forms of "to hang," *hanged* is used to refer to executions: *(Billy Budd was hanged)* and *hung* is used for all other meanings: *The stockings were hung by the chimney with care.*

have/of Use *have* rather than *of* after helping verbs like "could," "should," "would," "may," and "might": *They should have (not "of") let me know of their decision earlier.*

he, she; he/she The pronouns *he* and *she* refer to male and female antecedents, respectively. Traditionally, when an antecedent in singular form could be either female or male, "he" was always used to refer to either sex: *A child is often apprehensive when he first begins school.* Today, however, various approaches have been developed to avoid the all-purpose "he." Many people find the construction *he/she* (or *he or she*) awkward: *A child is often apprehensive when he/she first begins school.* The blended form *s/he* has not been widely adopted, probably because of confusion over pronunciation. Most people now favor either rephrasing the sentence entirely to omit the pronoun or reconstructing the sentence in the third-person plural: *Children are often apprehensive when they first begin school.*

hopefully *Hopefully* originally meant "in a hopeful manner": *The beggar looked up hopefully.* It is now usually used to mean "it is to be hoped; I hope; let us hope": *Hopefully, we'll get there on time.* Although this sense is common and standard, many people consider it incorrect.

how come/why *How come* is used informally in speech to substitute for *why.*

if/whether Use *whether* rather than *if* to begin a subordinate clause when the clause states a choice: *I don't know whether (not "if") I should stay until the end or leave right after the opening ceremony.*

impact Both the noun and verb *impact* are used to indicate forceful contact: *I cannot overstate the impact of the new policy on productivity.* Some speakers and writers avoid using *impact* as a verb to mean "to have an effect," as in *Our work here impacts on every division in the firm.*

in Several phrases beginning with *in* are verbose and should be avoided in formal writing. Refer to the following chart.

Replace the phrase
in this day and age
With
now

Replace the phrase
in spite of the fact that
With
although or *even though*

Replace the phrase
in the neighborhood of
With
approximately or *about*

Replace the phrase
in the event that
With . . .
if

The following phrases can be omitted entirely: *in a very real sense, in number, in nature, in reality, in terms of,* and *in the case of.*

in/into *In* is used to indicate condition or location, "positioned within": *She was in labor. The raccoon was in the woodpile. Into,* in contrast, indicates movement or a change in condition "from the outside to the inside": *The raccoon went into the shed. He went into cardiac arrest. Into* is also used as a slang expression for "involved with" or "interested in": *They are really into health foods.*

inferior than *Inferior to* and *worse than* are the generally preferred forms: *This wine is inferior to (not "inferior than") the burgundy we had last night.*

in regards to/with regards to Both terms are considered nonstandard terms for "regarding," "in regard to," "with regard to," and "as regards:" *As regards (not "in regards to") your request of April 1, we have traced your shipment and it will be delivered tomorrow.*

inside/outside; inside of/outside of When the words *inside* and *outside* are used as prepositions, the word *of* is not included: *Stay inside the house. The authorization is outside my department. Inside of* is used informally to refer to time *(I'll be there inside of an hour)* but in formal speech or writing *within* is the preferred usage: *The dump was cleaned up within a month.*

insignia *Insignia* was originally the plural of the Latin word "insigne." The plural term *insignias* has been standard usage since the eighteenth century.

irregardless/regardless *Regardless* is the standard term; avoid *irregardless* in both speech and writing.

is when/is where Both phrases are unacceptable and are to be avoided.

its/it's/its' *Its* is the possessive form of *it: The shrub is losing its blossoms. It's* is the contraction for *it is: It's a nice day.* The two are often confused because possessives are most frequently formed with -*'s. Its'* is nonstandard usage.

It's me/It's I The traditional rule is that personal pronouns after the verb "to be" take the nominative case *(I, she, he, we, they).* Today, however, such usage as *it's me, that's him, it must be them* is almost universal in informal speech. The objective forms have also replaced the nominative forms in informal speech in such constructions as *me neither* and *who, them?* In formal discourse, however, the nominative forms are still used: *it's I, that is he.*

-ize/-wise Use the suffix -*ize* to change a noun or adjective into a verb: *categorize.* Use the suffix -*wise* to change a noun or adjective into an adverb: *otherwise.*

kind of/sort of/type of Avoid using either *kind of, sort of,* or *type of* as synonyms for "somewhat" in formal speech and writing. Instead, use "rather": *She was rather (not "kind of") slender.* It is acceptable to use the three terms only when the word *kind, sort,* or *type* is stressed: *This kind of cheese is hard to digest.* Do not add "a": *I don't know what kind of (not "kind of a") cheese that is.* When the word *kind, sort,* or *type* is not stressed, omit the phrase entirely: *That's an unusual (not "unusual kind of") car. She's a pleasant (not "pleasant sort of a") person.*

lead/led *Lead* as a verb means "to take or conduct on the way": *I plan to lead a quiet afternoon. Led* is the past tense: *He led his followers through the dangerous underbrush. Lead,* as a noun, means "a type of metal": *Pipes are made of lead.*

let's *Let's* is often used as a word in its own right rather than as the contraction of "let us." As such, it is often used in informal speech and writing with redundant or appositional pronouns: *Let's us take in a movie. Let's you and me go for a walk.* Usage guides suggest avoiding *let's us* in formal speech and writing, although both *let's you and me* and *let's you and I* occur in the everyday speech of educated speakers. While the former conforms to the traditional rules of grammar, the latter, nevertheless, occurs more frequently.

like/such as Use *like* to compare an example to the thing mentioned and *such as* to show that the example is representative of the thing mentioned: *Judy wants to be a famous clothing designer like John Weitz, Liz Claiborne, and Yves St. Laurent. Judy has samples of many fine articles such as evening dresses, suits, and jackets.*

Many writers favor not separating *such* and *as* with an intervening word: *samples of many fine articles such as* rather than *samples of such fine articles as.*

lots/lots of Both terms are used in informal speech and writing as a substitute for "a great many," "very many," or "much."

man The use of the term *man* as a synonym for "human being," both by itself and in compounds *(mankind),* is declining. Terms such as *human being(s), human* *race, humankind, humanity, people,* and, when necessary, *men and women* or *women and men* are widely accepted in formal usage.

-man/-person The use of the term *man* as the last element in compound words referring to a person of either sex who performs some function *(anchorman, chairman, spokesman)* has declined in recent years. Now such compound words are only widely used if the word refers to a male. The sex-neutral word person is otherwise substituted for man *(anchorperson, chairperson, spokesperson)*. In other instances, a form without a suffix *(anchor, chair)*, or a word that does not denote gender *(speaker)*, is used.

The compound words *freshman, lowerclassmen, underclassmen* are still generally used in schools, and *freshman* is used in the U.S. Congress as well. These terms are applied to members of both sexes. As a modifier, *freshman* is used with both singular and plural nouns: *freshman athlete, freshman legislators.* See also *chair/chairperson.*

me and *Me and* is considered nonstandard usage when part of a compound subject: *Bob and I (not "Me and Bob") decided to fly to Boston.*

media *Media,* the plural of *medium,* is used with a plural verb: *Increasingly, the radio and television media seem to be stressing sensational news.*

mighty *Mighty* is used informally for "very" or "extremely": *He is a mighty big fighter.*

more important/more importantly Both phrases are acceptable in standard English: *My donations of clothing were tax deductible; more important(ly), the clothes were given to homeless people.*

Ms. (or Ms) The title *Ms.* is widely used in business and professional circles as an alternative to "Mrs." and "Miss," both of which reveal a woman's marital status. Some women prefer "Mrs.," where appropriate, or the traditional "Miss," which is still fully standard for an unmarried woman or a woman whose marital status is unknown. Since *Ms.* is not an abbreviation, some sources spell it without a period, others use a period to parallel "Mr." It is correctly used before a woman's name but not before her husband's name: *Ms. Leslie Taubman* or *Ms. Taubman (not "Ms. Steven Taubman").*

much/many Use *many* rather than *much* to modify plural nouns: *They had many (not "much") dogs. There were too many (not "much") facts to absorb.*

Muslim/Moslem *Muslim* is now the preferred form for an adherent of Islam, though *Moslem,* the traditional form, is still in use.

mutual One current meaning of *mutual* is "reciprocal": *Employers and employees sometimes suffer from a mutual misunderstanding. Mutual* can also mean "held in common, shared": *Their mutual goal is clearly understood.*

myself; herself; himself; yourself The *-self* pronouns are intensive or reflexive, intensifying or referring to an antecedent: *Kerri herself said so. Mike and I did it ourselves.* Questions are raised when the *-self* forms are used instead of personal pronouns (I, me, etc.) as subjects, objects, or complements. This use of the *-self* forms is especially common in informal speech and writing: *Many came to welcome my wife and myself back from China.* All these forms are also used, alone or with other nouns or pronouns, after "as," "than," or "but" in all varieties of speech and writing: *Letters have arrived for everyone but the counselors and yourselves.* Although there is ample precedent in both British and American usage for the expanded uses of the *-self* constructions, the *-self* pronouns should be used in formal speech and writing only with the nouns and pronouns to which they refer: *No one except me (not "myself") saw the movie.*

nauseous/nauseated *Nauseated* is generally preferred in formal writing over *nauseous: The wild ride on the roller coaster made Wanda feel nauseated.*

neither . . . nor When used as a correlative, *neither* is almost always followed by *nor: neither Caitlyn nor her father* . . . The subjects connected by *neither . . . nor* take a singular verb when both subjects are singular *(Neither Caitlyn nor her father is going to watch the program)* and a plural verb when both are plural *(Neither the rabbits nor the sheep have been fed yet today).* When a singular and a plural subject are joined by these correlatives, the verb should agree with the nearer noun or pronoun: *Neither the mayor nor the council members have yielded. Neither the council members nor the mayor has yielded.*

nohow The word *nohow,* nonstandard usage for "in no way" or "in any way," should be avoided in speech and writing.

none *None* can be treated as either singular or plural depending on its meaning in a sentence. When the sense is "not any persons or things," the plural is more common: *The rescue party searched for survivors, but none were found.* When *none* is clearly intended to mean "not one" or "not any," it is followed by a singular verb: *Of all the ailments I have diagnosed during my career, none has been stranger than yours.*

no . . . nor/no . . . or Use *no . . . or* in compound phrases: *We had no milk or eggs in the house.*

nothing like, nowhere near Both phrases are used in informal speech and writing, but they should be avoided in formal discourse. Instead, use "not nearly": *The congealed pudding found in the back of the refrigerator is not nearly as old as the stale bread on the second shelf.*

nowheres/nowhere The word *nowheres,* nonstandard usage for *nowhere,* should be avoided in speech and writing.

of Avoid using *of* with descriptive adjectives after the adverbs "how" or "too" in formal speech and writing. This usage is largely restricted to informal discourse: *How long of a ride will it be? It's too cold of a day for swimming.*

off of/off *Off of* is redundant and awkward; use *off: The cat jumped off the sofa.*

OK/O.K./okay All three spellings are considered acceptable, but the phrases are generally reserved for informal speech and writing.

on account of/because of Since it is less wordy, *because of* is the preferred phrase: *Because of her headache they decided to go straight home.*

on the one hand/on the other hand These two transitions should be used together: *On the one hand, we hoped for fair weather. On the other hand, we knew the rain was needed for the crops.* This usage, though, can be wordy. Effective substitutes include "in contrast," "but," "however," and "yet": *We hoped for fair weather, yet we knew the rain was needed for the crops.*

only The placement of *only* as a modifier is more a matter of style and clarity than of grammatical rule. In strict formal usage, *only* should be placed as close as possible *before* the word it modifies. In the following sentence, for example, the placement of the word *only* suggests that no one but the children was examined: *The doctor examined only the children.* In the next sentence, the placement of *only* says that no one but the doctor did the examining: *Only the doctor examined the children.* Nonetheless, in all types of speech and writing, people often place *only* before the verb regardless of what it modifies. In spoken discourse, speakers may convey their intended meaning by stressing the word or construction to which only applies.

owing to the fact that "Because" is generally accepted as a less wordy substitute for *owing to the fact that.*

pair/pairs When modified by a number, the plural of *pair* is commonly *pairs,* especially when referring to persons: *The three pairs of costumed children led off Halloween parade.* The plural *pair* is used mainly in reference to inanimate objects or nonhumans: *There are four pair (or "pairs") of shoelaces. We have two pair (or "pairs") of rabbits.*

people/persons In formal usage, *people* is most often used to refer to a general group, emphasizing anonymity: *We the people of the United States . . .* Use *persons* to indicate any unnamed individuals within the group: *Will the persons who left their folders on the table please pick them up at their earliest convenience?* Except when individuals are being emphasized, *people* is generally used rather than *persons.*

per; a/an *Per,* meaning "for each," occurs mainly in technical or statistical contexts: *This new engine averages fifty miles per hour. Americans eat fifty pounds of chicken per person per year.* It is also frequently used in sports commentary: *He scored an average of two runs per game. A* or *an* is often considered more suitable in nontechnical use: *The silk costs ten dollars a yard. How many miles an hour can you walk?*

percent/per cent Percent comes from the English *per cent.,* an abbreviation of the Latin *per centum.* It almost always follows a number: *I made 12 percent interest by investing my money in that new account.* In formal writing, use the word rather than the symbol (%). The use of the two-word form *per cent* is diminishing.

phenomena Like words such as *criteria* and *media, phenomena* is a plural form (of "phenomenon"), meaning "an observable fact, occurrence, or circumstance": *The official explained that the disturbing phenomena we had seen for the past three evenings were nothing more than routine aircraft maneuvers.*

plenty As a noun, *plenty* is acceptable in standard usage: *I have plenty of money.* In informal speech and writing *plenty* is often a substitute for "very": *She was traveling plenty fast down the freeway.*

plus *Plus* is a preposition meaning "in addition to": *My salary plus overtime is enough to allow us a gracious lifestyle.* Recently, *plus* has been used as a conjunctive adverb in informal speech and writing: *It's safe, plus it's economical.* Many object to this use.

practically Use *practically* as a synonym for "in effect," or "virtually." It is also considered correct to use it in place of "nearly" in all varieties of speech and writing.

previous to/prior to "Before" is generally preferred in place of either expression: *Before (not "previous to" or "prior to") repairing the tire, you should check to see if there are any other leaks.*

providing/provided Both forms can serve as subordinating conjunctions meaning "on the condition that": *Provided (Providing) that we get the contract in time, we will be able to begin work by the first of the month.* While some critics feel that *provided* is more acceptable in formal discourse, both are correct.

question of whether/question as to whether Both phrases are wordy substitutes for "whether": *Whether (not "the question of whether" or "the question as to whether") it rains or not, we are planning to go on the hike.*

rarely ever/rarely/hardly The term *rarely ever* is used informally in speech and writing. For formal discourse, use either *rarely* or *hardly* in place of *rarely ever: She rarely calls her mother. She hardly calls her mother.*

real/really In formal usage, *real* (an adjective meaning "genuine") should not be used in place of *really* (an adverb meaning "actually"): *The platypus hardly looked real. How did it really happen?*

reason is because/reason is since Although both expressions are commonly used in informal speech and writing, formal usage requires a clause beginning with "that" after "reason is": *The reason the pool is empty is that (not "because" or "since") the town recently imposed a water restriction.* Another alternative is to recast the sentence: *The pool is empty because the town recently imposed a water restriction.*

regarding/in regard to/with regard to/relating to/relative to/with respect to/respecting All the above expressions are wordy substitutes for "about," "concerning," or "on": *Janet spoke about (not "relative to," etc.) the PTA's plans for the September fund drive.*

relate to The phrase *relate to* is used informally to mean "understand" or "respond in a favorable manner": *I don't relate to chemistry.* It is rarely used in formal writing or speech.

repeat it/repeat it again *Repeat it* is the expression to use to indicate someone should say something for a second time: *I did not hear your name; please repeat it. Repeat it again* indicates the answer is to be said a third time. In the majority of instances, *repeat it* is the desired phrase; *again,* an unnecessary addition.

says/said Use *said* rather than *says* after a verb in the past tense: *At the public meeting, he stood up and said (not "says"). "The bond issue cannot pass."*

seldom ever/seldom *Seldom* is the preferred form in formal discourse: *They seldom (not "seldom ever") visit the beach.*

shall/will Today, *shall* is used for first-person questions requesting consent or opinion. *Shall we go for a drive? Shall I buy this dress or that? Shall* can also be used in the first person to create an elevated tone: *We shall call on you at six o'clock.* It is sometimes used with the second or third person to state a speaker's resolution: *You shall obey me.*

Traditionally, *will* was used for the second and third persons: *Will you at-*

tend the party? Will he and she go as well? It is now widely used in speech and writing as the future-tense helping verb for all three persons: *I will drive, you will drive, they will drive.*

should/would Rules similar to those for choosing between "shall" and "will" have long been advanced for *should* and *would.* In current American usage, use of *would* far outweighs that of *should. Should* is chiefly used to state obligation: *I should repair the faucet. You should get the parts we need. Would,* in contrast, is used to express a hypothetical situation or a wish: *I would like to go. Would you?*

since *Since* is an adverb meaning "from then until now": *She was appointed in May and has been supervisor ever since.* It is also used as an adverb meaning "between a particular past time and the present, subsequently": *They had at first refused to cooperate, but have since agreed to volunteer.* As a preposition, *since* means "continuously from": *It has been rainy since June.* It is also used as a preposition meaning "between a past time or event and the present": *There have been many changes since the merger.* As a conjunction, *since* means "in the period following the time when": *He has called since he changed jobs. Since* is also used as a synonym for "because": *Since you're here early, let's begin.*

situation The word *situation* is often added unnecessarily to a sentence: *The situation is that we must get the painting done by the weekend.* In such instances, consider revisiting the sentence to pare excess words: *We must get the painting done by the weekend.*

slow/slowly Today *slow* is used chiefly in spoken imperative constructions with short verbs that express motion, such as "drive," "walk," "swim," and "run." For example: *Drive slow. Don't walk so slow. Slow* is also combined with present participles to form adjectives: *He was slow-moving. It was a slow-burning fire. Slowly* is found commonly in formal writing and is used in both speech and writing before a verb *(He slowly walked through the hills)* as well as after a verb *(He walked slowly through the hills).*

so Many writers object to *so* being used as an intensifier, noting that in such usage it is often vague: *They were so happy. So* followed by "that" and a clause usually eliminates the vagueness: *They were so happy that they had been invited to the exclusive party.*

so/so that *So that,* rather than *so,* is most often used in formal writing to avoid the possibility of ambiguity: *He visited Aunt Lucia so that he could help her clear the basement.*

some *Some* is often used in informal speech and writing as an adjective meaning "exceptional, unusual" and as an adverb meaning "somewhat." In more formal instances, use "somewhat" in place of *some* as an adverb or a more precise word such as "remarkable" in place of *some* as an adjective: *Those are unusual (not "some") shoes. My sister and brother-in-law are going to have to rush somewhat (not "some") to get here in time for dinner.*

someplace/somewhere *Someplace* should be used only in informal writing and speech; use *somewhere* for formal discourse.

somewheres *Somewheres* is not accepted in formal writing or speech; use the standard "somewhere": *She would like to go somewhere (not "somewheres") special to celebrate New Year's Eve.*

split infinitive There is a longstanding convention that prohibits placing a word between "to" and the verb: *To understand fully another culture, you have to live among its people for many years.* This convention is based on an analogy with Latin, in which an infinitive is only one word and therefore cannot be divided. Criticism of the split infinitive was especially strong when the modeling of English on Latin was especially popular, as it was in the nineteenth century. Today many note that a split infinitive sometimes creates a less awkward sentence: *Many American companies expect to more than double their overseas investments in the next decade.*

suppose to/supposed to; use to/used to Both *suppose to* and *use to* are incorrect. The preferred usage is *supposed to* or *used to: I was supposed to (*not *"suppose to") get up early this morning to go hiking in the mountains. I used to (*not *"use to") enjoy the seashore but now I prefer the mountains.*

sure/surely When used as an adverb meaning *surely, sure* is considered inappropriate for formal discourse. A qualifier like "certainly" should be used instead of *sure: My neighbors were certainly right about it.* It is widely used, however, in speech and informal writing: *They were sure right about that car.*

sure and/sure to; try and/try to *Sure to* and *try to* are the preferred forms for formal discourse: *Be sure to (*not *"sure and") come home early tonight. Try to (*not *"try and") avoid the traffic on the interstate.*

that The conjunction *that is* occasionally omitted, especially after verbs of thinking, saying, believing, and so forth: *She said (that) they would come by train.* The omission of the conjunction almost always occurs when the dependent clause begins with a personal pronoun or a proper name. The omission is most frequent in informal speech and writing.

that/which Traditionally, *that* is used to introduce a restrictive clause: *They should buy the cookies that the neighbor's child is selling. Which,* in contrast, is used to introduce nonrestrictive clauses: *The cookies, which are covered in chocolate, would make a nice evening snack.* This distinction is maintained far more often in formal writing than in everyday speech, where voice can often distinguish restrictive from nonrestrictive clauses.

that/which/who *That* is used to refer to animals, things, and people: *That's my dog. I like that pen. Is that your mother?* In accepted usage, *who* is used to refer only to people: *Who is the man over there? Which* is used to refer only to inanimate objects and animals: *Which pen do you prefer? Which dog is the one that you would like to buy?*

them/those *Them* is nonstandard when used as an adjective: *I enjoyed those (*not *"them") apples a great deal.*

they/their/them Although the word *they* is traditionally a third-person plural pronoun, many people now use it as a singular pronoun, in place of "he" or "she": *If anyone comes to the door, tell them I'm not at home.* Some people disapprove of this use, but it is becoming very common, especially in informal use. This is partly because there is no gender-neutral pronoun in English.

this here/these here/that there/them there Each of these phrases is nonstandard: *this here* for "this," *these here* for "these," *that there* for "that;" *them there* for "those."

thusly/thus *Thusly* is a pointless synonym for *thus.* Speakers and writers often use *thusly* only for a deliberately humorous effect.

till/until/'til *Till* and *until* are used interchangeably in speech and writing; *'til,* a shortened form of *until,* is rarely used.

time period The expression *time period* is redundant, since "period" is a period of time: *The local ambulance squad reported three emergency calls in a one-week period* (not *"time period"*).

too Be careful when using *too* as an intensifier in speech and writing: *The dog is too mean.* Adding an explanation of the excessive quality makes the sentence more logical: *The dog is too mean to trust alone with children.*

toward/towards The two words are used interchangeably in both formal and informal speech and writing.

try and/try to While *try to* is the preferred form for formal speech and writing, both phrases occur in all types of speech and writing.

type/type of In written English, *type of* is the preferred construction: *This is an unusual type of flower.* In informal speech and writing, it is acceptable to use *type* immediately before a noun: *I like this type car.*

used to could/used to be able to The phrase *used to could* is nonstandard for *used to be able to: I used to be able to* (not *"used to could"*) *touch my toes.*

very The adverb *very* is sometimes used unnecessarily, especially in modifying an absolute adjective: *It was a very unique experience.* In such instances, it clearly should be omitted. Further, *very* has become overworked and has lost much of its power. Use more precise modifiers such as "extremely" and "especially."

want in/want out Both phrases are informal: *want in* for "want to enter," *want out* for "want to leave": *The dog wants to enter* (not *"wants in"*). *The cat wants to leave* (not *"wants out"*).

way/ways *Way* is the preferred usage for formal speech and writing; *ways* is used informally: *They have a little way* (not *"ways"*) *to go before they reach the campground.*

when/where *Where* and *when* are not interchangeable: *Weekends are occasions when* (not *"where"*) *we have a chance to spend time with the family.*

where at/where to Both phrases are generally considered to be too informal to be acceptable in good writing and speech: *Where is John?* (not *"Where is John at?"*) *Where is Mike going?* (not *"Where is Mike going to?"*)

where/that *Where* and *that* are not interchangeable: *We see by the memo that* (not *"where"*) *overtime has been discontinued.*

who/whoever; whom/whomever Traditionally, *who/whoever* is used as a subject (the nominative case) and *whom/whomever* as an object (the objective case). In informal speech and writing, however, since *who* and *whom* often occur at the beginning of a sentence, people usually select *who,* regardless of grammatical function.

without/unless *Without* as a conjunction is a dialectical or regional use of *unless.*

with regards to/with regard to/as regards/regarding Use *with regard to, regarding,* or *as regards* in place of *with regards to* in formal speech and writing: *As re-*

gards your inquiry, we have asked our shipping department to hold the merchandise until Monday.

would have Do not use the phrase *would have* in place of had in clauses that begin with "if" and express a state contrary to fact: *If the driver had (*not *"would have") been wearing his seat belt, he would have escaped without injury.*

would of/could of There is no such expression as *would of* or *could of: He would have (*not *"would of") gone.* Also, "of" is not a substitute for " 've": *She would've (*not *"would of") left earlier.*

you was *You was* is nonstandard for *you were: You were (*not *"you was") late on Thursday.*

5

Learning How Words Are Built Using Prefixes and Suffixes

Prefixes

A prefix is a letter or group of letters placed at the beginning of a word to change its meaning and make a new word. In the following chapter, we will show you how a knowledge of Latin and Greek roots can help you figure out the meanings of many English words. Here we will begin by teaching you a few prefixes that can open the door to a more powerful vocabulary. The following, for example, is a sampling of words that derive from the Latin prefix "circum-," meaning *around*.

Circum- Words

circumambulate	to walk around
circumference	the outer boundary of something
circumfluent	flowing around; encompassing
circumfuse	to surround, as with fluid
circumjacent	lying around; surrounding
circumlocution	a roundabout way of speaking
circumlunar	rotating about the moon
circumnavigate	to sail around
circumpolar	around or near one of the earth's poles
circumrotate	to rotate like a wheel
circumscribe	to encircle; mark off or delimit; restrict

Lesson 1. Common Latin Prefixes

Below are ten common Latin prefixes and their variations. Study the chart and examples. Then, to help you remember them, complete the quizzes that follow.

Prefix	Meaning	Variations	Examples
1. ad-	to, toward		adjoin, adverb
		a-	ascribe
		ac-	accede
		af-	affix
		ag-	aggregate
		at-	attempt
2. com-	with, together		commotion
		co-	cohabit, coworker
		col-	collaborate
		con-	concede, conduct
		cor-	correlate, correspond
3. de-	down		depress, deform
4. dis-	away, apart, opposite of		disagree, dishonest
		di-	divert
		dif-	diffuse
5. ex-	out		exchange, excavate
		e-	elongate, evaporate
		ec-	eccentric
		ef-	effluent, effuse
6. in-	in, into		inscribe, inhabit
		il-	illuminate
		im-	import, impart
		ir-	irradiate
7. in-	not		inflexible, indecent
		ig-	ignoble
		il-	illiterate, illegal
		im-	immodest, impatient
		ir-	irregular
8. pre-	before		premature
9. pro-	forward		proclaim
10. re-	again, back		recover, return

Quiz 1: Synonyms

Each of the following phrases contains an italicized word. Based on the meaning of its prefix, select the closest synonym.

1. *adjudicate* the matter
   a. sit in judgment on   b. throw out   c. argue   d. adjust
2. an *illicit* affair
   a. public   b. external   c. unlawful   d. renewed
3. an important *confederation*
   a. visit   b. return   c. church   d. alliance
4. *prolong* a speech
   a. shorten   b. dictate   c. extend   d. preserve
5. an *accredited* school
   a. second-rate   b. authorized   c. undesirable   d. separated
6. valuable *collateral*
   a. security   b. comments   c. opinions   d. animals
7. *ascribe* the phrase to
   a. write   b. scrawl   c. scribble   d. credit
8. *imbibe* too freely
   a. speak   b. drink   c. travel   d. laugh
9. *precursor* of greater things
   a. banner   b. detractor   c. forerunner   d. hope
10. *compress* metal
    a. help   b. coat   c. squeeze   d. buff

Quiz 2: Defining Words

Based on the meaning of its prefix, define each of the following words.

1. accord _____

2. irradiate _____

3. predestination _____

4. reincarnation _____

5. convolution _____

6. invoke _____

7. cohabit _____

8. irrelevant _____

9. irreducible _____

10. excommunicate _____

Suggested Answers: 1. agreement 2. illuminate 3. fate; destiny 4. rebirth; resurrection 5. a rolled up or coiled condition 6. to request or call forth 7. to live together as husband and wife 8. not relevant 9. incapable of being reduced 10. to exclude from communion

Lesson 2. Common Greek Prefixes

Below are five common Greek prefixes and their variations. Study the chart and examples. Then, to help you remember the prefixes, complete the quizzes that follow.

Prefix	Meaning	Variations	Examples
1. a-	not, without		atypical, asexual
		an-	anarchy
2. apo-	off, away		apology, apostrophe
3. epi-	beside, upon		epigraph, epidermis
		ep-	epoch
4. para-	beside		paragraph, paraphrase
5. syn-	together, with		synthesis, synonym
		syl-	syllable, syllogism
		sym-	symbiosis, symphony

Quiz 3: Synonyms

Each of the following phrases contains an italicized word. Based on the meaning of its prefix, select the closest synonym.

Formed from:

1. a new *synagogue*
   a. combination
   b. sentence
   c. house of worship
   d. building

   Greek "syn-" + "agogos," *bringer, gatherer*

2. the true *apogee*
   a. limit of endurance
   b. insult
   c. closest point of an orbit
   d. farthest point of an orbit

   Greek "apo-" + "ge," *earth*

3. the fifth annual *synod*
   a. church council
   b. religious holiday
   c. house-cleaning
   d. painting

   Greek "syn-" + "hodos," *way*

4. the sad *episode*
   a. incident
   b. anecdote
   c. death
   d. accident

   Greek "epi-" + "hodos," *way*

5. the witty *epigram*
   a. television show
   b. radio broadcast
   c. saying
   d. song

   Greek "epi-" + "gramma," *something written*

6. guilty of *apostasy*
   a. murder   c. an unnamed crime   Greek "apo-" +
   b. desertion   d. abandonment of   "stasis," *standing*
                         religious faith

7. *aseptic* ointment
   a. free from germs   c. expensive   Greek "a-" +
   b. effective   d. greasy   "septos," *rotted*

8. clear and effective *syntax*
   a. treatment   c. speech   Greek "syn-" +
   b. word arrangement   d. magazine article   "taxis," *order*

9. injured *epidermis*
   a. leg ligament   c. skin   Greek "epi-" +
   b. elbow   d. shinbone   "dermis," *skin*

10. a cutting *epithet*
    a. weapon   c. knife   Greek "epi-" +
    b. funeral oration   d. descriptive word   "theton," *placed*

Quiz 4: Matching

Based on your knowledge of Greek prefixes, match each of the numbered words with the closest synonym. Write your answer in the space provided.

1. **syllogism**	a. running beside	_____
2. **paralegal**	b. climax; highest point	_____
3. **anonymous**	c. bottomless hole	_____
4. **anesthetic**	d. one sent out; messenger	_____
5. **apostle**	e. logical argument	_____
6. **parallel**	f. doubting God's existence	_____
7. **apocryphal**	g. attorney's assistant	_____
8. **apogee**	h. false; spurious	_____
9. **agnostic**	i. causing loss of feeling	_____
10. **abyss**	j. nameless	_____

Lesson 3. Old English Prefixes

Below are the five most common Old English prefixes and their variations. Study the chart and examples. Then, to help you remember the prefixes, complete the quizzes that follow.

Prefix	*Meaning*	*Examples*
a-	on, to, at, by	ablaze, afoot
be-	over, around	bespeak, besiege

mis-	wrong, badly	mistake, misspell
over-	beyond, above	overreach, overawe
un-	not	unwilling, unethical

Quiz 5: Synonyms

Each of the following phrases contains an italicized word. Based on the meaning of its prefix, select the closest synonym.

1. a *miscarriage* of justice
   a. instance b. hero c. failure d. example
2. *beseech* movingly
   a. implore b. search c. evoke d. refuse
3. walking two *abreast*
   a. together b. side by side c. back to back d. in tandem
4. *bestowed* on us
   a. hurled b. smashed c. dependent d. presented
5. an unfortunate *misalliance*
   a. treaty b. conversation c. bad deal d. improper marriage
6. an *overwrought* patient
   a. highly emotional b. extremely ill c. very restrained
   d. overmedicated
7. an *unkempt* look
   a. funny b. messy c. ugly d. pretty
8. an embarrassing *miscue*
   a. joke b. anecdote c. step d. error
9. *bedaub* with clay
   a. sculpt b. present c. smear d. create
10. *bemoan* his situation
    a. celebrate b. share c. lament d. hide

Quiz 6: Matching

Based on your knowledge of Old English prefixes, match each of the numbered words with the closest synonym. Write your answer in the space provided.

1. **unfeigned**	a. conquer	_____
2. **misbegotten**	b. right on the mark	_____
3. **beguile**	c. too fervent	_____
4. **miscarriage**	d. envy, resent	_____
5. **bemuse**	e. sincere, genuine	_____
6. **mishap**	f. accident	_____
7. **overcome**	g. illegitimate	_____
8. **begrudge**	h. mislead	_____

9. **unerring**   i. bewilder   _____
10. **overzealous**   j. spontaneous abortion   _____

Suffixes

A suffix is a letter or group of letters placed at the end of a word to change its grammatical function, tense, or meaning. Suffixes can be used to create a verb from a noun or adjective or an adjective from a verb, for example. They can change a word's tense as well; "-ed" can make a present-tense verb into a past participle, for instance. They can even change a word's meaning; the suffix "-ette," for example, can make a word into its diminutive: "kitchen" becomes "kitchenette."

Just as recognizing a small number of prefixes can help you figure out many unfamiliar words, so knowing a few common suffixes can help you build a more powerful vocabulary.

Lesson 4. Ten Powerful Suffixes

Below are ten useful suffixes. Read through the chart and examples. To reinforce your study, complete the quizzes that follow.

Suffix	Meaning	Variations	Examples
1. -ate	to make		alienate, regulate
	marked by		passionate, affectionate
2. -en	to make		weaken, moisten
3. -ism	the quality or practice of		absolutism, baptism
4. -ation	the act or condition of		allegation, affirmation
		-ition	recognition
		-tion	commotion
5. -ty	the state of		modesty
		-ity	security
6. -er	one that does or deals with		worker, teacher
		-ar	scholar
		-ier	furrier
		-or	bettor
7. -an	one that does or deals with		comedian, historian

8.	-al	resembling or pertaining to		natural, accidental
9.	-ous	full of		perilous
			-ious	gracious, vicious
10.	-able	capable of being		lovable, affordable
			-ible	reversible

Quiz 7: Synonyms

Each of the following phrases contains an italicized word. Based on the meaning of its suffix, select the closest synonym.

1. *combustible* rubbish
   a. unbreakable   b. able to burst   c. affordable   d. flammable
2. *pastoral* scenes
   a. clerical   b. attractive   c. rural   d. homely
3. a *partisan* of the rebellion
   a. flag   b. supporter   c. sign   d. result
4. a *palatial* home
   a. magnificent   b. modest   c. formal   d. enjoyable
5. the *collegiate* atmosphere
   a. churchlike   b. friendly   c. cooperative   d. academic
6. *assiduity* in studies
   a. alacrity   b. cleverness   c. diligence   d. laziness
7. a number of *pedestrians*
   a. scholars   b. walkers   c. shopkeepers   d. students
8. an *abstemious* eater
   a. aloof   b. idle   c. absent-minded   d. sparing
9. *perilous* practices
   a. commonplace   b. rare   c. dangerous   d. useless
10. *deleterious* effects
    a. good   b. neutral   c. bad   d. delightful

Quiz 8: Matching

Based on your knowledge of suffixes, match each of the numbered words with the closest synonym. If in doubt, refer to the root word that follows each numbered word. Write your answer in the space provided.

1. **culpable**   a. blameworthy   _____
   (Root word: Latin
   "culpa," *blame*)

2. **parity**
   (Root word: Latin
   "par," *equal*)

   b. injurious   _____

3. **amenable**
   (Root word: French
   "amener," *to lead to*)

   c. everlasting   _____

4. **mendacious**
   (Root word: Latin
   "mendax," *dishonest*)

   d. reversion to type   _____

5. **sempiternal**
   (Root word: Latin
   "semper," *always*)

   e. equality   _____

6. **nihilism**
   (Root word: Latin
   "nihil," *nothing*)

   f. to chastise; censure   _____

7. **atavism**
   (Root word: Latin
   "atavus," *remote*)

   g. willing   _____

8. **fealty**
   (Root word: French
   "fealté," *fidelity*)

   h. total rejection of law   _____

9. **castigate**
   (Root word: Latin
   "castus," *chaste*)

   i. lying; false   _____

10. **noxious**
    (Root word: Latin
    "noxa," *harm*)

    j. faithfulness   _____

Lesson 5. Ten Additional Powerful Suffixes

The following ten suffixes will help you understand countless additional words. After you read through the suffixes and their definitions, complete the two quizzes at the end of the lesson.

Suffix	Meaning	Examples
1. -esque	in the manner of; like	Lincolnesque
2. -aceous	resembling or having	carbonaceous
3. -ic	associated with	democratic
4. -age	act or process of; quantity or measure	marriage, coverage; footage
5. -itis	inflammation	tonsillitis
6. -ish	similar to; like a	foolish; babyish

7. -less	without	guiltless; helpless
8. -ship	occupation or skill; condition of being	authorship, penmanship; friendship
9. -ian	a person who is, does, or participates in	comedian
10. -ferous	bearing or conveying	odoriferous

Quiz 9: Matching

Based on your knowledge of suffixes, match each of the numbered words with its closest synonym. Write your answer in the space provided.

1. **waspish**	a. inattentive, sloppy	_____
2. **fellowship**	b. egotistic	_____
3. **angelic**	c. distance	_____
4. **mileage**	d. huge	_____
5. **picturesque**	e. eternal	_____
6. **curvaceous**	f. irritable	_____
7. **titanic**	g. voluptuous	_____
8. **careless**	h. companionship	_____
9. **selfish**	i. innocent	_____
10. **timeless**	j. colorful	_____

Quiz 10: Synonyms

Each of the following phrases contains an italicized word. Based on the meaning of its suffix, select the closest synonym. If in doubt, refer to the root word listed in the right-hand column.

Root Word

1. *auriferous* mineral
   a. containing gold   b. extremely hard   Latin "aurum," *gold*
   c. having an odor   d. very common
2. *conical* shape
   a. humorous; amusing   b. like a cone   Greek "konos," *cone*
   c. spherical   d. rigid
3. suffering from *carditis*
   a. eye infection   b. a tin ear   Greek "kardia,"*heart*
   c. inflammation of the heart   d. stiff joints
4. graceful *Romanesque*
   a. architectural style   b. departure   c. essay   d. apology
5. *olivaceous* color
   a. oily   b. deep green   c. faded   d. attractive

6. frightful *carnage*
   a. journey   b. slaughter   c. scene   Latin "carnis," *flesh*
   d. sensuality
7. *satanic* nature
   a. evil   b. cheerful   c. shiny   d. generous
8. admirable *craftsmanship*
   a. display   b. individual   c. shop   d. artfulness
9. *veracious* remarks
   a. vivid   b. vicious   c. windy   d. truthful   Latin "verus," *true*
10. painful *appendicitis*
    a. news   b. surgery   c. inflammation of the appendix
    d. removal of the appendix

Answers to Quizzes in Chapter 5

Answers to Quiz 1

1. a 2. c 3. d 4. c 5. b 6. a 7. d 8. b 9. c 10. c

Answers to Quiz 3

1. c 2. d 3. a 4. a 5. c 6. d 7. a 8. b 9. c 10. d

Answers to Quiz 4

1. e 2. g 3. j 4. i 5. d 6. a 7. h 8. b 9. f 10. c

Answers to Quiz 5

1. c 2. a 3. b 4. d 5. d 6. a 7. b 8. d 9. c 10. c

Answers to Quiz 6

1. e 2. g 3. h 4. j 5. i 6. f 7. a 8. d 9. b 10. c

Answers to Quiz 7

1. d 2. c 3. b 4. a 5. d 6. c 7. b 8. d 9. c 10. c

Answers to Quiz 8

1. a 2. e 3. g 4. i 5. c 6. h 7. d 8. j 9. f 10. b

Answers to Quiz 9

1. f 2. h 3. i 4. c 5. j 6. g 7. d 8. a 9. b 10. e

Answers to Quiz 10

1. a 2. b 3. c 4. a 5. b 6. b 7. a 8. d 9. d 10. c

6

Learning How Words Are Built from Their Roots

One of the quickest and most effective ways to improve your vocabulary is by learning to recognize the most common Latin and Greek roots, since any one of them can help you define a number of English words. Whenever you come upon an unfamiliar word, first check to see if it has a recognizable root. If you know that the Latin root "ami," for example, means *like* or *love,* you can easily figure out that "amiable" means *pleasant or friendly* and "amorous" means *loving.* Even if you cannot define a word exactly, recognizing the root will still give you a general idea of the word's meaning. Remembering that the Greek root "ge, geo" means *earth* would certainly help you define "geophysics" as *the physics of the earth,* but it also might help you figure out that "geocentric" has to do with the center of the earth or with the earth as a center. Begin by studying the following lists of common Latin and Greek roots and representative words. Then tackle the quizzes.

Lesson 1. Common Latin Roots

Root	*Meaning*	*Example*	*Definition*
ag	act	agent	representative
cad, cas	fall	cadence	rhythmic flow
cap, cept	take, hold	receptacle	container
ced, cess	go	recessive	tending to go back
cid, cis	kill, cut	incision	cut, gash
clud, clus	shut	seclusion	separation from others
cred	believe	credible	believable
cur(r), curs	run	concur	agree (i.e., run together)

fer	bear	odoriferous	yielding an odor
her, hes	cling	adhere	cling, stick
ject	throw	projection	jutting out, protrusion
leg, lect	read	legible	easily readable
pel(l), puls	drive	repulse	repel (i.e., drive back)
pon, posit	put	postpone	defer
port	carry	portable	movable
rupt	break	abrupt	sudden, quick
scrib, script	write	inscription	engraving, writing
sect	cut	dissect	cut apart
sent, sens	feel	sensitive	tender
sequ, secut	follow	sequel	result
spect	look	prospect	outlook, expectation
sta, stat	stand	stable	fixed, firm
tang, tact	touch	tactile	tangible
termin	end	terminate	abolish, end
tract	pull, draw	tractor	vehicle that pulls
ven, vent	come	convene	assemble (i.e., come together)
vert, vers	turn	invert	overturn
vid, vis	see	provident	having foresight
vinc, vict	conquer	invincible	unconquerable
volv, volut	roll, turn	evolve	develop

Quiz 1: Synonyms

Each of the following phrases contains an italicized word. Based on the meaning of the root, select the closest synonym.

1. a *captive* animal
   a. confined   b. wild   c. charming   d. domestic
2. an *inverted* glass
   a. broken   b. upside-down   c. returned   d. drunk from
3. an *abrupt* stop
   a. slow   b. bad   c. sudden   d. harmful
4. a disappointing *sequel*
   a. television show   b. beginning   c. movie   d. follow-up
5. *terminate* the relationship
   a. doubt   b. intensify   c. begin   d. finish
6. an *incredible* story
   a. outlandish   b. unbelievable   c. foolish   d. upsetting
7. a *recessive* trait
   a. dominant   b. receding   c. hurtful   d. missing
8. *illegible* writing
   a. unreadable   b. graceful   c. distinct   d. large

9. a thorough *dissection*
   a. cutting apart   b. conference   c. discussion   d. putting together
10. an *unstable* relationship
    a. new   b. unsteady   c. one-sided   d. unreliable
11. an *odoriferous* cheese
    a. commonplace   b. brightly colored   c. malodorous   d. faded
12. an *invincible* warrior
    a. huge   b. foreign   c. defeated   d. unbeatable
13. the *advent* of summer
    a. departure   b. middle   c. arrival   d. complaint
14. a *provident* move
    a. prosperous   b. injudicious   c. prudent   d. hurtful
15. the top-secret *projectile*
    a. missile   b. project   c. plan   d. meeting

Quiz 2: True/False

In the space provided, write T if the definition of the numbered word is true or F if it is false.

		T or F
1. **adhere**	cling	_____
2. **cadaver**	cavort	_____
3. **evolve**	develop	_____
4. **incision**	cut	_____
5. **concurrent**	disjointed	_____
6. **recluse**	vivacious person	_____
7. **inscription**	story	_____
8. **agent**	deputy	_____
9. **tactile**	tangible	_____
10. **repulse**	repel	_____

Lesson 2. Common Greek Roots

Root	*Meaning*	*Example*	*Definition*
aster, astro	star	asterisk	star-shaped mark
chrom	color	chromatic	pertaining to color
chron, chrono	time	synchronize	occur simultaneously
cosmo	world	cosmopolitan	citizen of the world
dem	people	democracy	government by the people
meter	measure	thermometer	instrument that measures temperature

onym	name, word	pseudonym	a fictitious name
path	feeling	apathy	absence of feeling
phob	fear	claustrophobia	fear of enclosed places
phon	sound	cacophony	harsh, discordant sound
psycho	mind	psychology	science of the mind
soph	wisdom	sophistry	subtle, tricky reasoning

Quiz 3: True/False

In the space provided, write T if the definition of the numbered word is true or F if it is false.

			T or F
1. **epidemic**	plague		_____
2. **homonym**	same-sounding name		_____
3. **claustrophobia**	fear of dogs		_____
4. **cacophony**	dissonance		_____
5. **apathy**	enthusiasm		_____
6. **accelerometer**	instrument for measuring acceleration		_____
7. **synchronize**	squabble		_____
8. **cosmopolitan**	international		_____
9. **sophism**	specious argument		_____
10. **chromatic**	crisp		_____

Quiz 4: Defining Words

Based on the meaning of its root, define each of the following words. If in doubt, check the suggested answers.

1. asteroid _____

2. chromatics _____

3. cosmos _____

4. anonymous _____

5. Anglophobia _____

6. cosmography _____

7. synchronous _____

8. pathetic _____

9. pedometer _____

10. democracy _____

11. phonograph _____

12. demographics _____

13. psychotic _____

14. sophisticated _____

15. cognition _____

Suggested Answers 1. a small mass that orbits the sun 2. the science of colors 3. universe 4. without any name acknowledged 5. fear of things English 6. the study of the structure of the universe 7. coinciding in time 8. evoking feelings of pity 9. an instrument that measures distance covered in walking 10. government by the people 11. a sound-reproducing machine. 12. the statistical data of a population 13. a person who is mentally ill 14. worldly-wise 15. act or fact of knowing

Lesson 3. "Other Places, Other Faces": *al, all, alter*

An "alibi" is a defense by an accused person who claims to have been elsewhere at the time the offense was committed. The word comes from the Latin root "al," meaning *other*. Outside of law, an alibi often means an excuse, especially to avoid blame.

The Latin roots "al" and "alter," as well as the related Greek root "all" or "allo," all mean *other* or *another,* and form the basis of a number of English words. Below are ten such words. After you study the definitions and practice the pronunciations, complete the quizzes.

1. **alien** (āl′yən, ā′lē ən) a person born in and owing allegiance to a country other than the one in which he or she lives; a nonterrestrial being; foreign or strange.

   Although my neighbor is not an American citizen, he has lived in this country so long he no longer thinks of himself as an alien.

2. **allegory** (al′ə gôr′ē) a representation of an abstract meaning through concrete or material forms; figurative treatment of one subject under the guise of another.

   Nathaniel Hawthorne's short story "Young Goodman Brown" can be read as an allegory of an average person's encounter with sin and temptation.

3. **alias** (ā′lē əs) a false or assumed name, especially as used by a criminal. From the Latin word meaning *otherwise.*

   Many criminals use an alias with the same initials as their real name. Clyde Griffith, for example, took as his alias "Chester Gillett."

4. **alienate** (āl′yə nāt′, ā′lē ə-) to make indifferent or hostile. From Latin "alienare," *to make another.*

   Unkempt yards alienate prospective home buyers.

5. **altruism** (al′trōoiz′əm) unselfish concern for the welfare of others.

   Devotion to the poor, sick, and unfortunate of the world shows a person's altruism.

6. **altercation** (ôl′tər kā′shən) a heated or angry dispute; noisy argument or controversy. From Latin "altercari," *to quarrel with another.*

   The collision resulted in an altercation between the two drivers.

7. **inalienable** (in āl′yə nə bəl, -ā′lē ə-) not transferable to another; incapable of being repudiated.

   Freedom of speech is the inalienable right of every American citizen.

8. **allograft** (al′ə graft′) tissue grafted or transplanted to another member of the same species.

   Allografts of vital organs have saved many lives.

9. **allogamy** (ə log′ə mē) cross-fertilization in plants. From "allo-," *other* + "-gamy," *pollination.*

   To ensure allogamy, the farmer set out many different plants close together.

10. **alter** ego (ôl′tər ē′gō) another self; an inseparable friend.

    Superman's alter ego, the mild-mannered Clark Kent, is a reporter for the *Daily Planet.*

Quiz 5: Matching

Match each of the numbered words with its closest synonym. Write your answer in the space provided.

1. **alien**	a. absolute	_____
2. **alias**	b. cross-fertilization	_____
3. **alter ego**	c. selflessness, kindness	_____
4. **allogamy**	d. best friend	_____
5. **allegory**	e. another name	_____
6. **inalienable**	f. transplant	_____
7. **altruism**	g. contention, quarrel	_____
8. **alienate**	h. symbolic narrative	_____
9. **allograft**	i. stranger, outcast	_____
10. **altercation**	j. turn away, estrange	_____

Quiz 6: True/False

In the space provided, write T if the definition of the numbered word is true or F if it is false.

			T or F
1.	alien	foreign	_____
2.	alias	excuse	_____
3.	alter ego	egotist	_____
4.	allogamy	multiple marriage	_____
5.	allegory	moral story	_____
6.	inalienable	without basis in fact	_____
7.	altruism	unselfishness	_____
8.	alienate	estrange	_____
9.	allograft	illegal money	_____
10.	altercation	dispute	_____

Lesson 4. "The Breath of Life": *anima*

Ancient peoples connected the soul with the breath. They saw that when people died they stopped breathing, and they believed that the soul left the body at the same time. They also believed that when people sneezed, the soul left the body for a moment, so they muttered a hasty blessing to ensure that the soul would return quickly to its rightful place. The Latin root for air or breath, "anima," also means *soul, spirit,* or *mind,* reflecting this belief in a connection between life and breathing. Many English words come from this root.

Below are ten words linked to "anima." After you study the definitions and practice the pronunciations, complete the quizzes.

1. **animation** (an′ə mā′shən) liveliness or vivacity; the act or an instance of animating or enlivening. From Latin "animare," *to give life to.*

   In speech class we learned how to talk with animation to make our presentations more interesting.
2. **animadversion** (an′ə mad vûr′zhən, -shən) criticism; censure. From Latin "animus," *mind, spirit* + "adversio," *attention, warning.*

   The critic's animadversion on the subject of TV shows revealed his bias against popular culture.
3. **animus** (an′ə məs) hostile feeling or attitude.

   The jury's animus toward the defendant was obvious from the jurors' stony faces and stiff posture.
4. **pusillanimous** (pyoo′sə lan′ə məs) lacking courage or resolution; cowardly. From Latin "pusillus," *very small* + "animus," *spirit.*

   He was so pusillanimous that he wouldn't even run away from a bully.

5. **unanimity** (yoo′ nə nim′i tē) the state or quality of being in complete agreement; undivided opinion or a consensus. From Latin "unus," *one* + "animus," *mind, spirit.*

   The school board's unanimity on the controversial issue of sex education was all the more surprising in light of their well-known individual differences.

6. **animate** (an′ə māt′) to give life or liveliness to; alive.

   Her presence animated the otherwise dull party.

7. **animalcule** (an′ə mal′kyool) a minute or microscopic organism. From Latin "animalis," *living, animal* + "-culum," *tiny thing.*

   The animalcule could not be seen with the naked eye.

8. **magnanimous** (mag nan′ə məs) generous in forgiving an insult or injury; free from petty resentfulness. From Latin "magnus," *large, great* + "animus," *soul.*

   The governor's magnanimous pardon of the offender showed his liberal nature.

9. **inanimate** (in an′ə mit) not alive or lively; lifeless.

   Pinocchio was inanimate, a puppet carved from a block of wood.

10. **animism** (an′ə miz′əm) the belief that natural objects, natural phenomena, and the universe itself possess souls or consciousness.

    Their belief in animism drew them to the woods, where they felt more in touch with nature's spirit.

Quiz 7: Matching

Match each of the numbered words with the closest synonym. Write your answer in the space provided.

1. **animadversion**	a. enliven	_____
2. **animus**	b. harmony	_____
3. **pusillanimous**	c. generous	_____
4. **unanimity**	d. cowardly	_____
5. **animate**	e. hostility	_____
6. **animalcule**	f. spirit, zest	_____
7. **magnanimous**	g. a censorious remark	_____
8. **inanimate**	h. a belief in spirits	_____
9. **animation**	i. a minute organism	_____
10. **animism**	j. insert	_____

Quiz 8: True/False

In the space provided, write T if the definition of the numbered word is true or F if it is false.

T or F

1. **animadversion**   praise   _____
2. **animus**   hostility   _____
3. **pusillanimous**   cowardly   _____
4. **unanimity**   total agreement   _____
5. **animate**   deaden   _____
6. **animalcule**   small soul   _____
7. **magnanimous**   generous   _____
8. **inanimate**   living   _____
9. **animation**   liveliness   _____
10. **animism**   love of animals   _____

Lesson 5. "The Year of Wonders": *ann, enn*

While certain years are celebrated for great wonders, the first year that was actually designated "The Year of Wonders," *Annus Mirabilis,* was 1666. The English poet, dramatist, and critic John Dryden (1631–1700) enshrined that year as "Annus Mirabilis" in his poem of the same name, which commemorated the English victory over the Dutch and the Great Fire of London. "Annus," meaning *year* comes from the Latin root "ann," a source of many useful English words. The same root is also written "enn" in the middle of a word.

Below are ten words drawn from this root. After you look over the definitions and practice the pronunciations, complete the quizzes that follow.

1. **per annum** (pər an′əm) by the year; yearly.
    The firm promised to bill the additional interest charges per annum, the invoice to arrive every January.
2. **annual** (an′yoo əl) of, for, or pertaining to a year; yearly.
    The annual enrollment in the high school has increased sharply since the new housing was built.
3. **anniversary** (an′ə v ûr′sə rē) the yearly recurrence of the date of a past event, especially the date of a wedding. From Latin "ann(i)," *year* + "vers(us)," *turned* + adjectival suffix "-ary."
    For their twenty-fifth wedding anniversary, the happy couple decided to have dinner at the restaurant where they first met.
4. **biennial** (bī en′ē əl) happening every two years; lasting for two years. From Latin "bi-," *two* + root "enn" + adjectival suffix "-ial."
    My flowering fig tree has a biennial cycle; it blooms every two years.

5. **triennial** (trī en′ē əl) occurring every three years; lasting three years. From Latin "tri-," *three* + root "enn" + adjectival suffix "-ial."

The university has set up a triennial cycle of promotions to review candidates for advancement.

6. **decennial** (di sen′ē əl) of or for ten years; occurring every ten years. From Latin "dec(em)," *ten* + root "enn" + adjectival suffix "-ial."

Every ten years, the PTA holds its decennial meeting in the state capital.

7. **centennial** (sen ten′ē əl) of or pertaining to a period of one hundred years; recurring once every hundred years. From Latin "cent(um)," *hundred* + root "enn" + adjectival suffix "-ial."

To celebrate the railroad's centennial anniversary, the town's historical society restored the run-down station so it looked exactly as it did when it was built a hundred years ago.

8. **bicentennial** (bī′sen ten′ē əl) pertaining to or in honor of a two-hundredth anniversary; consisting of or lasting two hundred years.

To advertise its bicentennial festivities next year, the town has adopted the slogan "Celebrating Two Hundred Years of Progress."

9. **millennium** (mi len′ē əm) a period of one thousand years. From Latin "mille," *thousand* + root "enn" + noun suffix "-ium."

Technology advances so rapidly now that we can scarcely imagine what life will be like in the next millennium.

10. **annuity** (ə no͞o′ i tē, ə nyo͞o′-) a specified income payable each year or at stated intervals in consideration of a premium paid. From Latin "ann(uus)," *yearly* + noun suffix "-ity."

The annuity from her late husband's life-insurance policy was barely adequate for the poor widow's needs.

Quiz 9: Matching

Select the best definition for each numbered word. Write your answer in the space provided.

1. **bicentennial**	a. every ten years	_____
2. **anniversary**	b. every two years	_____
3. **decennial**	c. every two hundred years	_____
4. **millennium**	d. every three years	_____
5. **per annum**	e. one thousand years	_____
6. **centennial**	f. fixed payment	_____
7. **annuity**	g. yearly recurrence of a date	_____
8. **triennial**	h. every hundred years	_____

9. **biennial**   i. by the year   _____
10. **annual**   j. yearly   _____

Quiz 10: True/False

In the space provided, write T if the definition of the numbered word is true or F if it is false.

			T or F
1.	**annuity**	every two hundred years	_____
2.	**bicentennial**	every other year	_____
3.	**millennium**	one thousand years	_____
4.	**annual**	fixed amount of money	_____
5.	**centennial**	every hundred years	_____
6.	**triennial**	every three years	_____
7.	**per annum**	by order	_____
8.	**biennial**	every third year	_____
9.	**decennial**	every thousand years	_____
10.	**anniversary**	yearly event	_____

Lesson 6. "Man of the World": *anthropo*

In the early twentieth century, Rudolph Steiner developed an esoteric system of knowledge he called "anthroposophy." Steiner developed the word from the Greek roots "anthropo," meaning *man* or *human,* and "soph," meaning *wisdom.* He defined his philosophy as "the knowledge of the spiritual human being . . . and of everything which the spirit man can perceive in the spiritual world."

We've taken several more words from "anthropo"; below are six of them. After you look over the definitions and practice the pronunciations, complete the quizzes that follow.

1. **anthropoid** (an'thrə poid') resembling humans.
   The child was fascinated by the anthropoid ape on display in the natural history museum.
2. **anthropomorphism** (an'thrə pə môr'fiz əm) the ascription of human form or attributes to a being or thing not human, such as a deity.
   To speak of the "cruel, crawling foam" is an example of anthropomorphism, for the sea is not cruel.
3. **misanthrope** (mis'ən thrōp', miz'-) a hater of humankind. From Greek "mis(o)," *hate* + "anthropos," *man.*

In *Gulliver's Travels,* the great misanthrope Jonathan Swift depicts human beings as monstrous savages.

4. **philanthropy** (fi lan'thrə pē) good works; affection for humankind, especially as manifested in donations, as of money, to needy persons or to socially useful purposes. From Greek "phil(o)," *loving* + "anthropos," *man.*

   Thanks to the philanthropy of a wealthy patron, the new hospital wing was fully stocked with the latest equipment.

5. **anthropology** (an'thrə pol'ə jē) the science that deals with the origins, physical and cultural development, racial characteristics, and social customs and beliefs of humankind.

   After the student completed the anthropology course, she visited some of the exotic cultures she had read about.

6. **anthropocentric** (an'thrə pō sen'trik) regarding humans as the central fact of the universe.

   Philosophy that views and interprets the universe in terms of human experience and values is anthropocentric.

Quiz 11: Matching

Select the best definition for each numbered word. Write your answer in the space provided

1. **anthropology**	a. believing that humans are the center of the universe _____
2. **philanthropy**	b. one who dislikes people _____
3. **anthropocentric**	c. science of humankind's origins, beliefs, and customs _____
4. **anthropoid**	d. personification of inanimate things _____
5. **anthropomorphism**	e. doing good for people _____
6. **misanthrope**	f. humanlike _____

Quiz 12: True/False

In the space provided, write T if the definition of the numbered word is true or F if it is false.

		T or F
1. **misanthrope**	cynic	_____
2. **philanthropy**	goodwill to humankind	_____
3. **anthropomorphism**	insecurity	_____
4. **anthropocentric**	unselfish	_____
5. **anthropology**	science of flowers	_____
6. **anthropoid**	resembling humans	_____

Lesson 7. "Know Thyself": *gno*

One of the fascinating things about the study of words is the discovery of close relationships between seemingly unrelated words. Because English draws its vocabulary from many sources, it often appropriates foreign words that ultimately derive from the same source as a native English word. A good example is our word "know," which has its exact equivalent in the Latin and Greek root "gno." Here are eight words from this root. First read through the pronunciations, definitions, and examples. Then complete the quizzes that follow.

1. **cognizant** (kog′nə zənt, kon′ə-) aware. From Latin "cognoscere," *to come to know* ("co-," *together* + "gnoscere," *to know*)
   He was fully cognizant of the difficulty of the mission.
2. **incognito** (in′kog nē′tō, in kog′ni tō′) with one's identity concealed, as under an assumed name. From Latin "incognitus," *not known* ("in-," *not* + "cognitus," *known*).
   The officer from naval intelligence always traveled incognito to avoid any problems with security.
3. **prognosticate** (prog nos′ti kāt′) to forecast from present indications. From Greek "prognostikos," *knowing beforehand* ("pro-," *before* + "(gi)gno(skein)," *to know*).
   The fortuneteller was able to prognosticate with the help of her tea leaves, crystal ball, and a good deal of inside information about her client.
4. **diagnostician** (dī′əg no stish′ən) an expert in determining the nature of diseases. From Greek "diagnosis," *determination* (of a disease) ("dia-," *through* + "(gi)gno(skein)," *to know*).
   The diagnostician was able to allay her patient's fears after the x-ray showed that he had suffered only a sprain, not a break.
5. **cognoscenti** (kon′yə shen′tē, kog′nə-) well-informed persons, especially in a particular field, as in the arts. From Italian, ultimately derived from Latin "co-," *together* + "gnoscere," *to know.*
   Although the exhibit had only been open one week, the cognoscenti were already proclaiming it the show of the decade.
6. **gnostic** (nos′tik) pertaining to knowledge, especially to the esoteric knowledge taught by an early Christian mystical sect. From Greek "gnostikos," *knowing,* from the root of "(gi)gno(skein)," *to know.*
   The gnostic view that everything is knowable is opposed by the agnostic view.
7. **ignoramus** (ig′nə rā′məs, -ram′əs) an extremely uninformed per-

son. From the Latin word meaning *we don't know,* derived from "ignorare," *to not know* ("i(-n-),*" *not* + the root of "gno(scere),*" *to come to know).*

Only an ignoramus would insist that the earth is flat.

8. **cognition** (kog nish′ən) the act or process of knowing; perception. From Latin "cognitio," derived from "cognoscere," *to come to know* ("co-," *together* + "gnoscere," *to know*)

Cognition is impaired by narcotic drugs.

Quiz 13: True/False

In the space provided, write T if the definition of the numbered word is true or F if it is false.

		T or F
1. **gnostic**	knowing	_____
2. **incognito**	disguised	_____
3. **prognosticate**	curse	_____
4. **ignoramus**	ignorant person	_____
5. **cognoscenti**	aromatic herb	_____
6. **cognition**	perception	_____
7. **diagnostician**	expert mechanic	_____
8. **cognizant**	conscious	_____

Quiz 14: Defining Words

Define each of the following words.

1. ignoramus _____

2. cognoscenti _____

3. cognition _____

4. incognito _____

5. gnostic _____

6. prognosticate _____

7. diagnostician _____

8. cognizant _____

Suggested Answers 1. unschooled person 2. those who have a superior knowledge 3. the act or process of knowing; perception 4. with one's identity concealed 5. pertaining to knowledge 6. to forecast 7. an expert in making diagnoses 8. aware

Lesson 8. "Rulers and Leaders": *arch*

In Christian theology, Michael is given the title of "archangel," principal angel and primary opponent of Satan and his horde.

The Greek root "arch," meaning *chief, first, rule* or *ruler,* is the basis of a number of important and useful words.

Below are ten words drawn from this root. Read the definitions and practice the pronunciations. Then study the sample sentences and see if you can use the words in sentences of your own.

1. **archenemy** (arch′en′ə mē) a chief enemy; Satan.
   In Christian theology, Satan is the archenemy.
2. **patriarch** (pā′trē ärk′) the male head of a family or tribe. From Greek "patria," *family* + "-arches," *head, chief.*
   When we gathered for Thanksgiving dinner, our great-grandfather, the family patriarch, always sat at the head of the table.
3. **anarchy** (an′ər kē) society without rule or government; lawlessness; disorder; confusion; chaos. From Greek "an-," *not* + "arch(os)," *rule, ruler.*
   The king's assassination led to anarchy throughout the country.
4. **hierarchy** (hī′ə rär′kē, hī′rär-) any system of persons or things ranked one above another; formerly, rule by church leaders, especially a high priest. From Greek "hieros," *sacred* + "arch(os)," *rule, ruler.*
   The new office hierarchy ranks assistant vice presidents over directors.
5. **monarchy** (mon′ər kē) rule or government by a king, queen, emperor, or empress. From Greek "mon(o)-," *one* + "arch(os)," *rule, ruler.*
   The French Revolution ended with the overthrow of the monarchy.
6. **oligarchy** (ol′i gär′kē) rule or government by a few persons. From Greek "oligos," *few* + "arch(os)," *rule, ruler.*
   After the revolution, an oligarchy of army officers ruled the newly liberated country.
7. **archbishop** (ärch′bish′əp) a bishop of the highest rank; chief bishop.
   The archbishop meets with the bishops from his area once a month to discuss their concerns.
8. **matriarch** (mā′trē ärk′) the female head of a family or tribe. From Greek "matri-," *mother* + "-arches," *head, chief.*
   The younger members of the clan usually seek out Grandma Josie, the family matriarch, for advice.
9. **archetype** (är′ki tīp′) the original pattern or model after which a thing is made; prototype. From Greek "arch(e)-," *first, original* + "typos," *mold, type.*
   Odysseus is the archetype for James Joyce's Leopold Bloom in his novel *Ulysses.*

10. **archaic** (är kā′ik) marked by the characteristics of an earlier period, antiquated. From Greek "arch(aios)," *old, early, first.*
    With the advent of the pocket calculator, the slide rule has become archaic.

Quiz 15: Synonyms

Select the best synonym for each of the italicized words.

1. the *archbishop* of Canterbury
   a. oldest bishop   b. youngest bishop   c. highest-ranking bishop
   d. recently appointed bishop
2. a strong *monarchy*
   a. government by a president   b. government by a consortium
   c. government by the proletariat   d. government by a king or queen
3. an *archaic* device
   a. old-fashioned   b. complicated   c. expensive   d. useful
4. a wise *patriarch*
   a. old woman   b. general   c. revolutionary   d. male family head
5. the literary and social *archetype*
   a. concern   b. exhibition   c. prototype   d. major problem
6. a state of *anarchy*
   a. hopefulness   b. lawlessness   c. strict order   d. female control
7. a brutal *archenemy*
   a. less powerful enemy   b. chief enemy   c. strict enemy
   d. Gabriel
8. the iron-handed *oligarchy*
   a. government by few   b. communist state   c. democracy
   d. unstable government
9. a highly respected *matriarch*
   a. confidant   b. duke   c. male leader   d. female family head
10. the strict governmental *hierarchy*
    a. leadership   b. promotions   c. system of ranking   d. discipline

Quiz 16: True/False

In the space provided, write T if the synonym or definition of the numbered word is true or F if it is false

		T or F
1. **patriarch**	male family head	_____
2. **archetype**	model	_____
3. **archenemy**	chief enemy	_____
4. **monarchy**	royal government	_____
5. **oligarchy**	chaos	_____
6. **archbishop**	church deacon	_____

7. **matriarch**	wife and mother	_____
8. **anarchy**	political lawlessness	_____
9. **hierarchy**	higher orders	_____
10. **archaic**	old-fashioned	_____

Lesson 9. "To Life!": *bio*

In 1763 the Scottish writer James Boswell was first introduced to the acclaimed English poet, literary critic, and dictionary-maker Samuel Johnson, setting the stage for the birth of modern biography. From 1772 until Johnson's death in 1784, the two men were closely associated, and Boswell devoted much of his time to compiling detailed records of Johnson's activities and conversations. Seven years after Johnson's death, Boswell published his masterpiece, the *Life of Samuel Johnson.* The word "biography," *a written account of another person's life,* comes from the Greek root "bio," meaning *life,* and "graphy," meaning *writing.* Besides *life,* "bio" can also mean *living, living thing,* or *biological.*

A number of other important words come from "bio." Here's a list of eight of them. Read through the definitions and practice the pronunciations, then go on to the quizzes.

1. **biodegradable** (bī′ō di grā′də bəl) capable of being decomposed by living organisms, as paper and kitchen scraps are, as opposed to metals, glass, and plastics, which do not decay.
    After a long campaign, the local residents persuaded the supermarkets to use biodegradable paper bags rather than nondegradable plastic.
2. **biofeedback** (bī′ō fēd′bak′) a method of learning to modify one's own bodily or physiological functions with the aid of a visual or auditory display of one's brain waves, blood pressure, or muscle tension.
    Desperate to quit smoking, she made an appointment to try biofeedback.
3. **bioengineering** (bī′ō en′jə nēr′ing) the application of engineering principles and techniques to problems in medicine and biology.
    In the last few decades, bioengineering has made important progress in the design of artificial limbs.
4. **biological clock** (bī′ə loj′i kəl klok′) an innate system in people, animals, and organisms that causes regular cycles of function or behavior.
    Recently the term "biological clock" has been used in refer-

ence to women in their late thirties and early forties who are concerned about having children before they are no longer able to reproduce.

5. **bionic** (bī on′ik) utilizing electronic devices and mechanical parts to assist humans in performing tasks, as by supplementing or duplicating parts of the body. Formed from "bio-" + "(electr)onic."

   The scientist used a bionic arm to examine the radioactive material.

6. **biopsy** (bī′op sē) the excision for diagnostic study of a piece of tissue from a living body. From "bio-" + Greek "opsis," *sight, view.*

   The doctor took a biopsy from the patient's lung to determine the nature of the infection.

7. **biota** (bī ō′tə) the plant and animal life of a region or period. From Greek "biote," *life,* from the root "bio."

   The biota from the cliffside proved more useful for conservation than the biologists had initially suspected.

8. **biohazard** (bī′ō haz′ərd) a disease-causing agent or organism, especially one produced by biological research; the health risk caused by such an agent or organism.

   Will new technology like gene splicing produce heretofore unknown biohazards to threaten the world's population?

Quiz 17: Definitions

Select the word that best fits the definition. Write your answer in the space provided.

_____ 1. the excision for diagnostic study of a piece of tissue from a living body
   a. biopsy   b. bioengineering   c. incision

_____ 2. utilizing electronic devices and mechanical parts to assist humans in performing tasks
   a. biota   b. bioengineering   c. bionic

_____ 3. capable of decaying and being absorbed by the environment
   a. biogenic   b. biodegradable   c. bionic

_____ 4. a method of learning to modify one's own bodily or physiological functions
   a. autobiography   b. biofeedback   c. biota

_____ 5. the application of engineering principles and techniques to problems in medicine and biology
   a. bioengineering   b. autobiography   c. biometry

_____   6. an innate system in people, animals, and organisms that
               causes regular cycles of function
               a. biota   b. bionic   c. biological clock

_____   7. the plant and animal life of a region
               a. biota   b. autobiography   c. biometry

_____   8. an agent or organism that causes a health risk
               a. biopsy   b. biohazard   c. biota

Quiz 18: *True/False*

In the space provided, write T if the definition of the numbered
word is true or F if it is false.

			T or F
1.	**biopsy**	tissue sample	_____
2.	**biota**	plants and animals	_____
3.	**biological clock**	perpetual clock	_____
4.	**biohazard**	health risk	_____
5.	**biodegradable**	capable of decomposing	_____
6.	**bionic**	superhero	_____
7.	**biofeedback**	culinary expertise	_____
8.	**bioengineering**	railroad supervision	_____

Lesson 10. "Speak!": *dict, dic*

The earliest known dictionaries were found in the library of the
Assyrian king at Nineveh. These clay tablets, inscribed with
cuneiform writing dating from the seventh century B.C., provide
important clues to our understanding of Mesopotamian culture.
The first English dictionary did not appear until 1440. Compiled
by the Dominican monk Galfridus Grammaticus, the *Storehouse
for Children or Clerics,* as the title translates, consists of Latin definitions of 10,000 English words. The word "dictionary" was first
used in English in 1526, in reference to a Latin dictionary by Peter
Berchorius. This was followed by a Latin-English dictionary published by Sir Thomas Elyot in 1538. The first monolingual English
dictionary was published by Thomas Cawdrey in 1604. All these
early efforts confined themselves to uncommon words and phrases
not generally known or understood, because the daily language
was not supposed to require explanation.

Today we understand the word "dictionary" to mean *a book
containing a selection of the words of a language, usually arranged*

alphabetically, giving information about their meanings, pronunciations, etymologies, etc.; a lexicon. The word comes from the Latin root "dictio," taken from "dicere," meaning *to say, state, declare, speak.* This root has given us scores of important English words. Below are eight for you to examine. After you read through their pronunciations and definitions, complete the quizzes.

1. **malediction** (mal'i dik'shən) a curse or the utterance of a curse. From Latin "male-," *evil* + "dictio," *speech, word.*

    After the witch delivered her malediction, the princess fell into a swoon.

2. **abdication** (ab'di kā'shən) the renunciation or relinquishment of something such as a throne, right, power, or claim, especially when formal.

    Following the abdication of Edward VIII for the woman he loved, his brother George VI assumed the throne of England.

3. **benediction** (ben'i dik'shən) the invocation of a blessing. From Latin "bene-," *well, good* + "dictio," *speech, word.*

    The chaplain delivered a benediction at the end of the service.

4. **edict** (ē'dikt) a decree issued by a sovereign or other authority; an authoritative proclamation or command.

    Herod's edict ordered the massacre of male infants throughout his realm.

5. **predicate** (pred'i kāt') to proclaim, declare, or affirm; base or found.

    Your acceptance into the training program is predicated upon a successful personal interview.

6. **jurisdiction** (jŏŏr'is dik'shən) the right, power, or authority to administer justice.

    The mayor's jurisdiction extends only to the area of the village itself, outside its limits, the jurisdiction passes to the town board.

7. **dictum** (dik'təm) an authoritative pronouncement; saying or maxim.

    The firm issued a dictum stating that smoking was forbidden on the premises.

8. **predictive** (pri dik'tiv) indicating the future or future conditions; predicting.

    Although the day was clear and balmy, the brisk wind was predictive of the approaching cold snap.

Quiz 19: Matching

Match each of the following numbered words with its closest synonym. Write your answer in the space provided.

1. predictive	a. assert	_____
2. edict	b. maxim	_____
3. predicate	c. indicating the future	_____
4. benediction	d. authority	_____
5. abdication	e. decree	_____
6. malediction	f. imprecation, curse	_____
7. dictum	g. blessing	_____
8. jurisdiction	h. renunciation	_____

Quiz 20: True/False

In the space provided, write T if the definition of the numbered word is true or F if it is false.

		T or F
1. predictive	indicative of the future	_____
2. predicate	declare	_____
3. edict	decree	_____
4. jurisdiction	authority	_____
5. dictum	blessing	_____
6. abdication	assumption	_____
7. malediction	machismo	_____
8. benediction	opening services	_____

Lesson 11. "Lead On, Macduff!": *duc, duct*

Aqueducts, artificial channels built to transport water, were used in ancient Mesopotamia, but the ones used to supply water to ancient Rome are the most famous. Nine aqueducts were built in all; eventually they provided Rome with about thirty-eight million gallons of water daily. Parts of several are still in use, supplying water to fountains in Rome. The word "aqueduct" comes from the Latin "aqua," meaning *water,* and "ductus," meaning *a leading* or *drawing off.*

A great number of powerful words are derived from the "duc, duct" root. Here are nine such words. Read through the definitions and practice the pronunciations. Try to use each word in a sentence of your own. Finally, work through the two quizzes at the end of the lesson to help fix the words in your memory.

1. **induce** (in dōōs′, -dyōōs′) to influence or persuade, as to some action.
   Try to induce her to stay at least a few hours longer.

2. **misconduct** (mis kon′dukt) improper conduct or behavior.
   Such repeated misconduct will result in a reprimand, if not an outright dismissal.
3. **abduct** (ab dukt′) to carry (a person) off or lead (a person) away illegally; kidnap.
   Jason's mother was so fearful that he might be abducted by a stranger that she refused even to let him walk to school alone.
4. **deduce** (di do͞os′, -dyo͞os′) to derive as a conclusion from something known or assumed.
   The detective was able to deduce from the facts gathered thus far that the murder took place in the early hours of the morning.
5. **viaduct** (vī′ə dukt′) a bridge for carrying a road or railroad over a valley, gorge, or the like, consisting of a number of short spans; overpass.
   The city government commissioned a firm of civil engineers to explore the possibility of building a viaduct over the river.
6. **reductive** (ri duk′tiv) pertaining to or producing reduction or abridgment. From Latin "reduct-, reducere," *to lead back.*
   There was an urgent need for reductive measures.
7. **seduce** (si do͞os′, -dyo͞os′) to lead astray, as from duty or principles.
   He was seduced by the prospect of gain.
8. **traduce** (trə do͞os′, -dyo͞os′) to speak maliciously and falsely of; slander. From Latin "traducere," *to transfer, lead across.*
   To traduce someone's character can do permanent harm to his or her reputation.
9. **ductile** (duk′tl) pliable or yielding.
   The new plastic is very ductile and can be molded into many forms.

Quiz 21: Matching

Match each of the numbered words with the closest synonym. Write your answer in the space provided.

1. **seduce**	a. overpass	_____
2. **viaduct**	b. minimizing	_____
3. **induce**	c. kidnap	_____
4. **reductive**	d. bad behavior	_____
5. **traduce**	e. infer	_____
6. **abduct**	f. entice	_____
7. **misconduct**	g. pliable	_____
8. **deduce**	h. defame	_____
9. **ductile**	i. persuade	_____

Quiz 22: True/False

In the space provided, write T if the definition of the numbered word is true or F if it is false.

			T or F
1.	**deduce**	infer	_____
2.	**ductile**	pliable	_____
3.	**seduce**	lead astray	_____
4.	**reductive**	magnifying	_____
5.	**traduce**	malign	_____
6.	**viaduct**	overpass	_____
7.	**abduct**	restore	_____
8.	**misconduct**	improper behavior	_____
9.	**induce**	persuade	_____

Lesson 12. "Just the Facts, Ma'am": *fac, fact, fect*

We have formed a great many important and useful words from the Latin "facere," *to make* or *do*. A "facsimile," for example, derives from the Latin phrase "fac simile," meaning *to make similar,* and has come to mean *an exact copy.* Since facsimile copiers and transmitters have become very common, "facsimile" is now generally shortened and changed in spelling to "fax."

Many potent words are derived from the "fac, fact, fect" root. Eight such words follow. Learn them by completing this lesson; then try to use the root to help you figure out other "fac, fact" words you encounter.

1. **factious** (fak'shəs) given to or marked by discord; dissenting. From Latin "factio," *act of doing or of making connections; group* or *clique,* derived from "facere," *to do* or *make.*
   Factious groups threatened to break up the alliance.
2. **factotum** (fak tō'təm) a person employed to do all kinds of work, as a personal secretary or the chief servant of a household.
   Jeeves was the model of a gentleman's gentleman—the indispensable factotum of the frivolous Bertie Wooster.
3. **factitious** (fak tish'əs) made artificially; contrived.
   The report was merely a factitious account, not factual at all.
4. **facile** (fas'il) moving or acting with ease; fluent. From Latin "facilis," *easy to do,* derived from "facere," *to do.*
   With his facile mind, he often thought of startlingly original solutions to old problems.

5. **artifact** (är'tə fakt') any object made by human skill or art. From the Latin phrase "arte factum," *(something) made with skill.*

   The archaeologists dug up many artifacts from the ancient Indian culture.

6. **facsimile** (fak sim'ə lē) an exact copy, as of a book, painting, or manuscript; a method of transmitting typed or printed material by means of radio or telegraph.

   If they could not obtain a facsimile of the document by noon, the deal would fall through.

7. **putrefaction** (pyōō'trə fak'shən) the decomposition of organic matter by bacteria and fungi. From Latin "putrere," *to rot* + "factio," *act of doing.*

   Once the putrefaction of the compost pile was complete, the gardener used the rotted material to enrich the soil.

8. **prefect** (prē'fekt) a person appointed to any of various positions of command, authority, or superintendence. From Latin "praefectus," formed from "prae," *ahead, surpassing* + "fectus," *doing* (from "facere," *to do*).

   The prefect was appointed to a term of three years.

Quiz 23: Definitions

Select the word that best fits the definition. Write your answer in the space provided.

_____ 1. the decomposition of organic matter by bacteria and fungi
   a. chemical analysis   b. hypothermia   c. putrefaction

_____ 2. not natural; artificial
   a. factious   b. facile   c. factitious

_____ 3. an exact copy, as of a book, painting, or manuscript
   a. factoid   b. facsimile   c. putrefaction

_____ 4. given to dissension or strife
   a. facile   b. factious   c. obsequious

_____ 5. an object made by humans
   a. artifact   b. factotum   c. factious

_____ 6. a person employed to do all kinds of work
   a. facile   b. factotum   c. faculty

_____ 7. moving or acting easily
   a. putrefaction   b. prefect   c. facile

_____ 8. someone appointed to any of various positions of command, authority, or superintendence
   a. prefect   b. facile   c. factotum

Quiz 24: True/False

In the space provided, write T if the definition of the numbered word is true or F if it is false.

		T or F
1. **factitious**	contrived	_____
2. **factotum**	carrier	_____
3. **putrefaction**	rotting	_____
4. **artifact**	machinery	_____
5. **facsimile**	instant transmission	_____
6. **prefect**	administrator	_____
7. **factious**	dissenting	_____
8. **facile**	fluent	_____

Lesson 13. "Always Faithful": *feder, fid, fide*

"Semper fidelis" is Latin for *always faithful.* The phrase is the motto of the United States Marine Corps and the title of an 1888 march by John Philip Sousa. This phrase, as with a number of useful words, comes from the Latin root "fid, fide," meaning *trust, faith.*

Below are seven words derived from this root. Read through the meanings, practice the pronunciations, and complete the quizzes that follow to help fix the words in your memory.

1. **fidelity** (fi del′i tē) faithfulness; loyalty.
   Dogs are legendary for their fidelity to their masters.
2. **fiduciary** (fi doo′shē er′ē, -dyoo′-) a person to whom property or power is entrusted for the benefit of another; trustee. From Latin "fiducia," *trust,* related to "fidere," *to trust.*
   The bank's fiduciary administers the children's trust funds.
3. **infidel** (in′fi dl, -del′) a person who does not accept a particular religious faith. From Latin "in," *not* + "fidelis," *faithful* (from "fide," *faith*).
   The ayatollah condemned Salman Rushdie as an infidel.
4. **perfidious** (pər fid′ē əs) deliberately faithless; treacherous. From Latin "perfidia" ("per-," *through* + "fide," *faith*).
   The perfidious lover missed no opportunity to be unfaithful.
5. **confide** (kən fīd′) to entrust one's secrets to another. From Latin "confidere" ("con-," *with* + "fidere," *to trust*).
   The two sisters confided in each other.
6. **bona fide** (bō′nə fīd′, bon′ə) genuine; real; in good faith.
   To their great astonishment, the offer of a free vacation was bona fide.

7. **affidavit** (af′i dā′vit) a written declaration upon oath made before an authorized official. From a Medieval Latin word meaning *(he) has declared on oath,* from Latin "affidare," *to pledge on faith.*

In the affidavit, they swore they had not been involved in the accident.

Quiz 25: Matching

Match each of the following numbered words with its closest synonym. Write your answer in the space provided.

1. **confide**	a. faithfulness		_____
2. **fidelity**	b. heathen		_____
3. **bona fide**	c. declaration		_____
4. **infidel**	d. entrust		_____
5. **affidavit**	e. trustee		_____
6. **perfidious**	f. genuine		_____
7. **fiduciary**	g. faithless		_____

Quiz 26: Definitions

Select the best definition for each numbered word. Write your answer in the space provided.

_____ 1. bona fide
   a. unauthorized   b. deboned   c. real   d. well-trained

_____ 2. perfidious
   a. irreligious   b. content   c. loyal   d. treacherous

_____ 3. fidelity
   a. loyalty   b. alliance   c. great affection   d. random motion

_____ 4. fiduciary
   a. bank teller   b. trustee   c. insurance   d. default

_____ 5. infidel
   a. warrior   b. intransigent   c. heathen   d. outsider

_____ 6. affidavit
   a. affright   b. declaration   c. loyalty   d. betrothal

_____ 7. confide
   a. combine   b. recline   c. entrust   d. convert

Lesson 14. "Flow Gently, Sweet Afton": *flu*

In 1998, the upper fifth of working Americans took home more money than the other four-fifths put together—the highest proportion of wealthy people since the end of World War II. One word to describe such wealthy people is "affluent," *prosperous.* The word comes from the Latin root "fluere," meaning *to flow.* As a river would flow freely, so the money of the affluent flows easily.

Seven of the most useful and important words formed from the "flu" root follow. Study the definitions and read through the pronunciations. Then do the quizzes.

1. **flume** (flo͞om) a deep, narrow channel containing a mountain stream or torrent; an amusement-park ride through a water-filled chute or slide.
    The adults steadfastly refused to try the log flume ride, but the children enjoyed it thoroughly.
2. **confluence** (kon′flo͞o əns) a flowing together of two or more streams; their place of junction.
    The confluence of the rivers is marked by a strong current.
3. **fluent** (flo͞o′ənt) spoken or written effortlessly; easy; graceful; flowing.
    Jennifer was such a fluent speaker that she was in great demand as a lecturer.
4. **fluctuation** (fluk′cho͞o ā′shən) continual change from one course, condition, etc., to another.
    The fluctuation in temperature was astonishing, considering it was still only February.
5. **fluvial** (flo͞o′vē əl) of or pertaining to a river; produced by or found in a river.
    The contours of the riverbank were altered over the years by fluvial deposits.
6. **influx** (in′fluks′) a flowing in.
    The unexpected influx of refugees severely strained the community's resources.
7. **flux** (fluks) a flowing or flow; continuous change.
    His political views are in constant flux.

Quiz 27: True/False

In the space provided, write T if the definition of the numbered word is true or F if it is false.

		T or F
1. **fluctuation**	change	_____
2. **fluvial**	deep crevasse	_____
3. **fluent**	flowing	_____
4. **flux**	flow	_____

5. **influx**   egress   ＿＿＿＿＿
6. **confluence**   diversion   ＿＿＿＿＿
7. **flume**   feather   ＿＿＿＿＿

Quiz 28: Matching

Select the best definition for each numbered word. Write your answer in the space provided.

1. **flux**   a. gorge   ＿＿＿＿＿
2. **confluence**   b. flowing easily   ＿＿＿＿＿
3. **flume**   c. continual shift ＿＿＿＿＿
4. **fluctuation**   d. an inflow   ＿＿＿＿＿
5. **fluent**   e. a flow   ＿＿＿＿＿
6. **influx**   f. riverine   ＿＿＿＿＿
7. **fluvial**   g. convergence   ＿＿＿＿＿

Lesson 15. "In The Beginning": *gen*

Genesis, the first book of the Old Testament, is an account of the beginning of the world. The English word "genesis" is taken from the Greek word for *origin* or *source*. From the root "gen," meaning *beget, bear, kind,* or *race,* a number of powerful vocabulary builders has evolved.

Here are ten "gen" words. Study the definitions and practice the pronunciations to help you learn the words. To accustom yourself to using these new terms in your daily speech and writing, work through the two quizzes at the end of the lesson.

1. **gene** (jēn) the unit of heredity in the chromosomes that controls the development of inherited traits. From Greek "-genes," *born, begotten.*
   The gene for color blindness is linked to the Y chromosome.
2. **engender** (en jen′dər) to produce, cause, or give rise to.
   Hatred engenders violence.
3. **gentility** (jen til′i tē) good breeding or refinement.
   Her obvious gentility marked her as a member of polite society.
4. **gentry** (jen′trē) wellborn and well-bred people; in England, the class under the nobility.
   In former times, the gentry lived on large estates with grand houses, lush grounds, and many servants.
5. **genus** (jē′nəs) the major subdivision of a family or subfamily in the classification of plants and animals, usually consisting of more than one species.

The biologist assigned the newly discovered plant to the appropriate genus.

6. **genial** (jēn′yəl, jē′nē əl) cordial; warmly and pleasantly cheerful; favorable for life, growth, or comfort.

   Under the genial conditions in the greenhouse, the plants grew and flourished.

7. **congenital** (kən jen′i tl) existing at or from one's birth.

   The child's congenital defect was easily corrected by surgery.

8. **eugenics** (yōō jen′iks) the science of improving the qualities of a breed or species, especially the human race, by the careful selection of parents.

   Through eugenics, scientists hope to engineer a superior race of human beings.

9. **genealogy** (jē′nē ol′ə jē) a record or account of the ancestry and descent of a person, family, group, etc.; the study of family ancestries.

   Genealogy shows that Franklin Delano Roosevelt was a cousin of Winston Churchill.

10. **congenial** (kən jēn′yəl) agreeable or pleasant; suited or adapted in disposition; compatible.

    The student enjoyed the congenial atmosphere of the library.

Quiz 29: Definitions

Select the word that best fits the definition. Write your answer in the space provided.

_____ 1. the major subdivision of a family or subfamily in the classification of plants and animals.
   a. gene   b. genus   c. genial   d. gentry

_____ 2. suited or adapted in disposition; agreeable.
   a. genial   b. congenial   c. genealogy   d. congenial

_____ 3. wellborn and well-bred people.
   a. gene   b. gentry   c. nobility   d. gentility

_____ 4. the science of improving the qualities of a breed or species.
   a. genetics   b. gentry   c. genealogy   d. eugenics

_____ 5. the unit of heredity transmitted in the chromosome.
   a. ancestry   b. DNA   c. gene   d. genus

_____ 6. cordial; favorable for life, growth, or comfort.
   a. genial   b. gentry   c. eugenics   d. hospitality

_____ 7. to produce, cause, or give rise to.
   a. gentility   b. engender   c. genealogy   d. genial

_____ 8. a record or account of the ancestry of a person, family, group, etc.
   a. gene   b. genealogy   c. glibness   d. gentry

_____   9. good breeding or refinement.
                    a. reductive   b. genus   c. gentility   d. eugenics
_____   10. existing at or from one's birth.
                    a. congenital   b. genus   c. congenial   d. gene

Quiz 30: True/False

In the space provided, write T if the definition of the numbered word is true or F if it is false.

T or F

1. **gentry**	peasants	_____
2. **congenital**	incurable	_____
3. **genial**	debased	_____
4. **gene**	genetic material	_____
5. **eugenics**	matricide	_____
6. **gentility**	viciousness	_____
7. **genealogy**	family history	_____
8. **congenial**	pleasant	_____
9. **genus**	subdivision	_____
10. **engender**	cease	_____

Lesson 16. "This Way to the Egress": *grad, gres, gress*

P.T. Barnum was a nineteenth-century American showman whose greatest undertaking was the circus he called "The Greatest Show on Earth." The circus, which included a menagerie featuring Jumbo the elephant and a museum of freaks, was famous all over the country. After its merger in 1881 with James Anthony Bailey's circus, the enterprise gained international renown. When Barnum's customers took too long to leave his famous exhibits, he posted a sign: "This way to the egress." Following the arrow in eager anticipation of a new oddity, the visitors were ushered through the egress—the exit.

Knowing that the root "grad, gres, gress" means *step, degree, or walk* might have given these suckers a few more minutes to enjoy the exhibits, and it can certainly help you figure out a number of powerful words. Here are nine words that use this Latin root. Study the definitions, practice the pronunciations, and work through the two quizzes.

1. **digress** (di gres', dī-) to wander away from the main topic. From Latin "digressus, digredi," *to walk away* ("di-," *away, apart* + "gressus, gredi," *to walk, step*)

   The manager cautioned her salespeople that they would fare better if they did not digress from their prepared sales talks.

2. **transgress** (trans gres', tranz-) to break or violate a law, command, moral code, etc. From Latin "transgressus, transgredi," *to step across.*

   Those who transgress the laws of their ancestors often feel guilty.

3. **retrograde** (re'trə grād') moving backward; having backward motion.

   Most of the townspeople regarded the new ordinance as a prime example of retrograde legislation.

4. **regression** (ri gresh'ən) the act of going or fact of having gone back to an earlier place or state.

   The child's regression could be seen in his thumbsucking.

5. **degrade** (di grād') to reduce the dignity of (someone); deprive (someone) of office, rank, or title; lower (someone or something) in quality or character.

   He felt they were degrading him by making him wash the dishes.

6. **Congress** (kong'gris) the national legislative body of the United States, consisting of the Senate and the House of Representatives; *(lower case)* a formal meeting of representatives.

   Congress held a special session to discuss the situation in the Middle East.

7. **gradation** (grā dā'shən) any process or change taking place through a series of stages, by degrees, or gradually. From Latin "gradatio," *series of steps,* derived from "gradus," *step, degree.*

   He decided to change his hair color by gradation rather than all at once.

8. **gradient** (grā'dē ənt) the degree of inclination, or the rate of ascent or descent, in a highway, railroad, etc.

   Although they liked the house very much, they were afraid that the driveway's steep gradient would make it hard to park a car there in the winter.

9. **progressive** (prə gres'iv) characterized by progress or reform; innovative; going forward, gradually increasing.

   The progressive legislation wiped out years of social inequity.

Quiz 31: Matching

Match each of the following numbered words with its closest synonym. Write your answer in the space provided.

1. **congress**	a. backward moving	_____
2. **regression**	b. depart from a subject	_____
3. **gradient**	c. disobey	_____
4. **progressive**	d. meeting	_____
5. **digress**	e. stage, degree	_____
6. **gradation**	f. reversion	_____
7. **retrograde**	g. humiliate	_____
8. **degrade**	h. innovative	_____
9. **transgress**	i. incline	_____

Quiz 32: Defining Words

Define each of the following words.

1. gradient _____

2. Congress _____

3. progressive _____

4. regression _____

5. retrograde _____

6. degrade _____

7. digress _____

8. gradation _____

9. transgress _____

Suggested Answers 1. the degree of inclination, or the rate of ascent or descent, in a high-way, etc. 2. the national legislative body of the United States; a meeting or assembly 3. characterized by reform; increasing gradually 4. the act of going back to an earlier place or state 5. moving backward; having backward motion 6. to reduce (someone) to a lower rank; deprive of office, rank, or title, to lower in quality or character 7. to wander away from the main topic 8. any process or change taking place through a series of stages, by degrees, or gradually 9. to break or violate a law, command, moral code, etc.

Lesson 17. "Splish, Splash, I Was Taking a Bath": *hydro, hydr*

According to mythology, the ancient Greeks were menaced by a monstrous nine-headed serpent with fatally poisonous breath. Killing it was no easy matter. When you lopped off one head, it grew two in its place, and the central head was immortal. Hercules, sent to destroy the serpent as the second of his twelve labors, was triumphant when he burned off the eight peripheral heads and buried the ninth under a huge rock. From its residence, the watery marsh, came the monster's name, "Hydra," from the Greek root "hydr(o)," meaning *water.*

Quite a few words are formed from the "hydro" or "hydr" root. Here are ten of them. Read through the definitions, practice the pronunciations, and then work through the two quizzes that follow.

1. **hydrostat** (hī′drə stat′) an electrical device for detecting the presence of water, as from an overflow or a leak.
   The plumber used a hydrostat to locate the source of the leak in the bathroom.
2. **dehydrate** (dē hī′drāt) to deprive of water; dry out.
   Aside from being tasty and nutritious, dehydrated fruits and vegetables are easy to store and carry.
3. **hydrophobia** (hī′drə fō′bē ə) rabies; fear of water.
   Sufferers from hydrophobia are unable to swallow water.
4. **hydroplane** (hī′drə plān′) a light, high-powered boat, especially one with hydrofoils or a stepped bottom, designed to travel at very high speeds.
   The shore police acquired a new hydroplane to help them apprehend boaters who misuse the waterways.
5. **hydroponics** (hī′drə pon′iks) the cultivation of plants by placing the roots in liquid nutrients rather than soil.
   Some scientists predict that in the future, as arable land becomes increasingly more scarce, most of our vegetables will be grown through hydroponics.
6. **hydropower** (hī′drə pou′ər) electricity generated by falling water or another hydraulic source.
   Hydropower is efficient, clean, and economical.
7. **hydrate** (hī′drāt) to combine with water.
   Lime is hydrated for use in plaster, mortar, and cement.
8. **hydrangea** (hī drān′jə) a showy shrub, cultivated for its large white, pink, or blue flower clusters, that typically requires deep watering. From Greek "hydr-," *water* + "angeion," *vessel.*
   Hydrangeas require a great deal of water to flourish.
9. **hydrotherapy** (hī′drə ther′əpē) the treatment of disease by the scientific application of water both internally and externally.
   To alleviate strained muscles, physical therapists often prescribe hydrotherapy.
10. **hydrosphere** (hī′drə sfēr′) the water on or surrounding the surface of the planet Earth, including the water of the oceans and the water in the atmosphere.
    Scientists are investigating whether the greenhouse effect is influencing the hydrosphere.

Quiz 33: Definitions

Select the word that best fits the definition. Write your answer in the space provided.

_____ 1. electricity generated by water
a. hydropower   b. hydrangea   c. hydrotherapy
d. electrolysis

_____ 2. the treatment of disease by the scientific application of water both internally and externally
a. hydrate   b. electrolysis   c. hydrotherapy
d. hydroponics

_____ 3. a light, high-powered boat, especially one with hydrofoils or a stepped bottom
a. hydropower   b. hydroplane   c. hydroelectric
d. hydroship

_____ 4. rabies; fear of water
a. hydrate   b. hydrotherapy   c. hydroponics
d. hydrophobia

_____ 5. the water on or surrounding the surface of the globe, including the water of the oceans and the water in the atmosphere
a. hydrosphere   b. hydrate   c. hydrofoil   d. hydrangea

_____ 6. to deprive of water
a. hydrate   b. dehydrate   c. hydrolyze
d. hydrotherapy

_____ 7. a showy shrub with large white, pink, or blue flower clusters
a. hydrate   b. hydrangea   c. hydroponics   d. hydrofoil

_____ 8. the cultivation of plants by placing the roots in liquid nutrient solutions rather than soil
a. hydrotherapy   b. hydrangea   c. hydroponics
d. hydrolyze

_____ 9. to combine with water
a. hydrostat   b. hydrosphere   c. hydrangea
d. hydrate

_____ 10. an electrical device for detecting the presence of water, as from an overflow or a leak
a. hydrosphere   b. hydrangea   c. hydroponics
d. hydrostat

Quiz 34: True/False

In the space provided, write T if the definition of the numbered word is true or F if it is false.

		T or F
1. **hydropower**	hydroelectric power	_____
2. **hydroplane**	boat	_____
3. **hydroponics**	gardening in water	_____
4. **hydrostat**	water power	_____
5. **hydrangea**	flowering plant	_____
6. **hydrotherapy**	water cure	_____
7. **hydrate**	lose water	_____
8. **hydrosphere**	bubble	_____
9. **dehydrate**	wash thoroughly	_____
10. **hydrophobia**	pneumonia	_____

Lesson 18. "After Me, The Deluge": *lav, lu*

The failure of Louis XV (1710–74) to provide strong leadership and badly needed reforms contributed to the crisis that brought about the French Revolution. Louis took only nominal interest in ruling his country and was frequently influenced by his mistresses. In the last years of his reign, he did cooperate with his chancellor to try to reform the government's unequal and inefficient system of taxation, but it was too late. His reported death-bed prophecy, "After me, the deluge," was fulfilled in the overthrow of the monarchy less than twenty years later. The word "deluge," meaning *flood,* comes from the Latin root "lu," *to wash.* As a flood, a deluge would indeed wash things clean.

A number of words were formed from the "lav, lu" root. Here are several examples. Study the definitions and practice the pronunciations. To help you remember the words, complete the two quizzes at the end of the lesson.

1. **dilute** (di lo͞ot′, dī-) to make thinner or weaker by adding water; to reduce the strength or effectiveness of (something). From Latin "dilutus, diluere," *to wash away.*
   The wine was too strong and had to be diluted.
2. **lavabo** (lə vā′bō, -vä′-) the ritual washing of the celebrant's hands after the offertory in the Mass; the passage recited with the ritual. From the Latin word meaning *I shall wash,* with which the passage begins.
   The priest intoned the Latin words of the lavabo.
3. **lavage** (lə väzh′) a washing, especially the cleansing of an organ, as the stomach, by irrigation.
   Lavage is a preferred method of preventing infection.

4. **diluvial** (di lo͞o′vē əl) pertaining to or caused by a flood or deluge.
   The diluvial aftermath was a bitter harvest of smashed gardens, stained siding, and missing yard furniture.
5. **alluvium** (ə lo͞o′vē əm) a deposit of sand, mud, etc., formed by flowing water.
   Geologists study alluvium for clues to the earth's history.
6. **ablution** (ə blo͞o′shən) a cleansing with water or other liquid, especially as a religious ritual; a washing of the hands, body, etc.
   He performed his morning ablutions with vigor.

Quiz 35: Matching

Select the best or closest synonym for each numbered word. Write your answer in the space provided.

_____ 1. lavage
    a. molten rock b. sewage c. washing
    d. religious ritual

_____ 2. alluvium
    a. great heat b. rain c. flood d. deposit of sand

_____ 3. lavabo
    a. religious cleansing b. volcano c. flooding
    d. lavatory

_____ 4. ablution
    a. cleansing with water b. absence c. sacrifice
    d. small font

_____ 5. dilute
    a. wash b. weaken c. cleanse d. liquefy

_____ 6. diluvial
    a. before the flood b. antedate c. monarchy
    d. of a flood

Quiz 36: True/False

In the space provided, write T if the definition of the numbered word is true or F if it is false.

		T or F
1. **dilute**	reduce strength	_____
2. **diluvial**	two-lipped	_____
3. **lavage**	security	_____
4. **alluvium**	molten rock	_____
5. **ablution**	washing	_____
6. **lavabo**	religious ritual	_____

Lesson 19. "Silver Tongue": *loqui, loqu, locu*

For many years, the ventriloquist Edgar Bergen amused audiences as he tried to outwit his monocled wooden dummy, Charlie McCarthy. Among the most popular entertainers of his age, Bergen astonished audiences with his mastery of ventriloquism, the art of speaking so that projected sound seems to originate elsewhere, as from a hand-manipulated dummy. This ancient skill sounds easier than it is, since it requires modifying the voice through slow exhalation, minimizing movement of the tongue and lips, and maintaining an impassive expression to help shift viewers' attention to the illusory source of the voice.

The word "ventriloquism" comes from Latin "ventri-," *abdomen, stomach,* and the root "loqui," *to speak* (because it was believed that the ventriloquist produced sounds from his stomach). Many useful and important words were formed from the "loqui, loqu" root. Below are seven you should find especially helpful. Study the definitions and practice the pronunciations. To reinforce your learning, work through the two quizzes.

1. **obloquy** (ob′lə kwē) blame, censure, or abusive language.
    The vicious obloquy surprised even those who knew of the enmity between the political rivals.
2. **colloquial** (kə lō′kwē əl) characteristic of or appropriate to ordinary or familiar conversation rather than formal speech or writing.
    In standard American English, "He hasn't got any" is colloquial, while "He has none" is formal.
3. **soliloquy** (sə lil′ə kwē) the act of talking while or as if alone.
    A soliloquy is often used as a device in a drama to disclose a character's innermost thoughts.
4. **eloquent** (el′ə kwənt) having or exercising the power of fluent, forceful, and appropriate speech; movingly expressive.
    William Jennings Bryan was an eloquent orator famous for his "Cross of Gold" speech.
5. **interlocution** (in′tər lō kyōō′shən) conversation; dialogue.
    The interlocutions disclosed at the Watergate hearings riveted the American public to their TV sets.
6. **loquacious** (lō kwā′shəs) talking much or freely; talkative; wordy.
    After the sherry, the dinner guests became loquacious.
7. **elocution** (el′ə kyōō′shən) a person's manner of speaking or reading aloud; the study and practice of public speaking.

After completing the course in public speaking, the pupils were skilled at elocution.

Quiz 37: Matching

Match each of the numbered words with its closest synonym. Write your answer in the space provided.

1. **loquacious**	a. censure	_____
2. **interlocution**	b. informal	_____
3. **elocution**	c. monologue	_____
4. **colloquial**	d. talkative	_____
5. **soliloquy**	e. conversation	_____
6. **obloquy**	f. fluent	_____
7. **eloquent**	g. public speaking	_____

Quiz 38: Definitions

Select the word that best fits the definition. Write your answer in the space provided.

_____ 1. a person's manner of speaking or reading aloud; the study and practice of public speaking
a. obloquy   b. soliloquy   c. prologue   d. elocution

_____ 2. conversation; dialogue
a. colloquial   b. interlocution   c. monologue   d. elocution

_____ 3. tending to talk; garrulous
a. eloquent   b. colloquial   c. loquacious   d. elocutionary

_____ 4. characteristic of or appropriate to ordinary or familiar conversation rather than formal speech or writing
a. colloquial   b. eloquent   c. prologue   d. dialogue

_____ 5. the act of talking while or as if alone
a. circumlocution   b. dialogue   c. soliloquy   d. obloquy

_____ 6. having or exercising the power of fluent, forceful, and appropriate speech; movingly expressive
a. interlocution   b. eloquent   c. colloquial   d. loquacious

_____ 7. censure; abusive language
a. interlocution   b. soliloquy   c. obloquy   d. dialogue

Lesson 20. "Star Light, Star Bright": *luc, lux, lum*

Before he was driven out of heaven for the sin of pride, Satan was called "Lucifer," which translates as *bringer of light.* In his epic retelling of the Bible, *Paradise Lost,* John Milton used the name "Lucifer" for the demon of sinful pride, and we call the planet Venus "Lucifer" when it appears as the morning star. "Lucifer" comes from the root "luc, lux" meaning *light.*

A number of powerful words derive from "luc" and its variations. We trust that you'll find the following seven *light* words "enlightening"! Study the definitions and practice the pronunciations. Then complete the two quizzes at the end of the lesson.

1. **pellucid** (pə lo͞o′sid) allowing the maximum passage of light; clear.
   The pellucid waters of the Caribbean allowed us to see the tropical fish clearly.
2. **lucid** (lo͞o′sid) shining or bright; clearly understood.
   Stephen Hawking's lucid explanation of astrophysics became a bestseller.
3. **translucent** (trans lo͞o′sənt, tranz-) permitting light to pass through but diffusing it so that persons, objects, etc., on the opposite side are not clearly visible.
   Frosted window glass is translucent.
4. **elucidate** (i lo͞o′si dāt′) to make light or clear; explain.
   Once my math teacher elucidated the mysteries of geometry, I had no further difficulty solving the problems.
5. **lucubrate** (lo͞o′kyo͞o brāt′) to work, write, or study laboriously, especially at night. From Latin "lucubrare," *to work by artificial light.*
   The scholar lucubrated for many long nights in an attempt to complete his thesis.
6. **luminary** (lo͞o′mə ner′ē) an eminent person; an object that gives light.
   Certain that the elegant woman emerging from the limousine had to be a theatrical luminary, the crowd surged forward to get a closer look.
7. **luminous** (lo͞o′mə nəs) radiating or emitting light; brilliant.
   The luminous paint emitted an eerie glow—not at all what the designer had envisioned.

Quiz 39: True/False

In the space provided, write T if the definition of the numbered word is true or F if it is false.

		T or F
1. **lucid**	comprehensible	_____
2. **elucidate**	explain	_____
3. **lucubrate**	lubricate	_____
4. **pellucid**	limpid, clear	_____
5. **luminous**	reflective	_____
6. **luminary**	lightning	_____
7. **translucent**	opaque	_____

Quiz 40: Matching

Select the best definition for each numbered word. Write your answer in the space provided

1. **luminous**	a. study hard	_____
2. **elucidate**	b. prominent person	_____
3. **pellucid**	c. brilliant	_____
4. **lucubrate**	d. permitting but diffusing light	_____
5. **lucid**	e. clearly understood	_____
6. **luminary**	f. allowing the passage of maximum light	_____
7. **translucent**	g. clarify	_____

Lesson 21. "Evil Be to Him Who Does Evil": male, mal

"Malnutrition" is defined as *a lack of the proper type and amount of nutrients required for good health.* It is estimated that more than ten million American children suffer from malnutrition; the World Health Organization reports that over 600 million people suffer from malnutrition in the emerging countries alone. Malnourished people endure a variety of side effects, including a failure to grow; increased susceptibility to infection; anemia; diarrhea; and lethargy.

The root "mal" in the word "malnourished" means *bad, evil,* and words formed around this root invariably carry negative overtones. In Latin, the root is spelled "male"; in French, it's "mal," but regardless of the spelling, the root means *evil.* Study the definitions and pronunciations of the following "mal" words until you become comfortable with them. Then work through the two quizzes.

1. **maladjusted** (mal′ə jus′tid) badly adjusted.

   Despite attempts by the psychologist to ease him into his environment, the child remained maladjusted.

2. **malefactor** (mal′ə fak′tər) a person who violates the law; a criminal.

   The police issued an all-points bulletin for the apprehension of the malefactor.

3. **maladroit** (mal′ə droit′) unskillful; awkward; clumsy.

   With his large hands and thick fingers, the young man was maladroit at fine needlework.

4. **malevolent** (mə lev′ə lənt) wishing evil to another or others; showing ill will.

   Her malevolent uncle robbed the heiress of her estate and made her a virtual prisoner.

5. **malapropism** (mal′ə prop iz′əm) a confused use of words, especially one in which one word is replaced by another of similar sound but ludicrously inappropriate meaning: an instance of such a use. The word comes from Mrs. Malaprop, a character in Sheridan's comedy *The Rivals* (1775), noted for her misapplication of words. Sheridan coined the character's name from the English word "malapropos," meaning *inappropriate,* derived from the French phrase "mal à propos," *badly (suited) to the purpose.*

   "Lead the way and we'll precede" is a malapropism.

6. **malicious** (mə lish′əs) full of or characterized by evil intention.

   The malicious gossip hurt the young couple's reputation.

7. **malfeasance** (mal fē′zəns) the performance by a public official of an act that is legally unjustified, harmful, or contrary to law.

   Convicted of malfeasance, the mayor was sentenced to six months in jail.

8. **malignant** (mə lig′nənt) disposed to cause harm, suffering, or distress; tending to produce death, as a disease or tumor.

   The patient was greatly relieved when the pathologist reported that the tumor was not malignant.

9. **malign** (mə līn′) to speak harmful untruths about; slander.

   "If you malign me again," the actor threatened the tabloid reporter, "I will not hesitate to sue."

Quiz 41: Matching

Match each of the numbered words with its closest synonym. Write your answer in the space provided.

1. maladroit	a. wishing others evil	_____
2. malicious	b. harmful; fatal	_____
3. malapropism	c. official misconduct	_____
4. malfeasance	d. bungling, tactless	_____
5. malign	e. badly adjusted	_____
6. malignant	f. spiteful	_____
7. malefactor	g. criminal	_____
8. malevolent	h. revile, defame	_____
9. maladjusted	i. confused use of words	_____

Quiz 42: True/False

In the space provided, write T if the definition of the numbered word is true or F if it is false.

		T or F
1. malefactor	ranger	_____
2. malapropism	faulty stage equipment	_____
3. malfeasance	food poisoning	_____
4. malicious	spiteful	_____
5. maladjusted	poorly adjusted	_____
6. malignant	benign	_____
7. maladroit	clumsy	_____
8. malevolent	bad winds	_____
9. malign	defame	_____

Lesson 22. "I Do!": *mater, matr*

The word "matrimony," meaning *marriage,* derives from the Latin root "mater," *mother,* because the union of a couple was established through motherhood. Most of us accept without question the idea of matrimony based on romantic love, but this is a relatively new belief. Only recently, following the rise of the middle class and the growth of democracy, has there been a tolerance of romantic marriages based on the free choice of the partners involved. Arranged marriages, accepted almost everywhere throughout history, eventually ceased to prevail in the West, although they persist in aristocratic circles to the present. The most extreme application of the custom of arranged marriages occurred in pre-revolutionary China, where the bride and groom often met for the first time only on their wedding day.

We've inherited and created a number of significant words from the "mater, matr" root. Below are eight such words to help make your vocabulary more powerful and precise. Study the definitions and pronunciations; then complete the two quizzes.

1. **maternal** (mə tûr′nl) having the qualities of a mother; related through a mother.
   On his maternal side, he is related to Abigail and John Adams.
2. **matron** (mā′trən) a married woman, especially one with children, or one who has an established social position.
   The matrons got together every Thursday to play bridge or mahjong.
3. **mater** (mā′tər) informal or humorous British usage for "mother."
   "Mater is off to London again," said Giles snidely.
4. **matrix** (mā′triks) that which gives origin or form to a thing, or which serves to enclose it.
   Rome was the matrix of Western civilization.
5. **alma mater** (äl′mə mä′tər, al′-) a school, college, or university where a person has studied, and, usually, from which he or she has graduated. From the Latin phrase meaning *nourishing mother.*
   Ellen's alma mater is Queens College.
6. **matrilineal** (ma′trə lin′ē əl, mā′-) inheriting or determining descent through the female line.
   In a matrilineal culture, the children are usually part of the mother's family.
7. **matronymic** (ma′trə nim′ik) derived from the name of the mother or another female ancestor; named after one's mother. The word is also spelled "metronymic" (mē′trə nim′ik, me′-).
   Some men have matronymic middle names.
8. **matriculate** (mə trik′yə lāt′) to enroll or cause to enroll as a student, especially in a college or university.
   She intends to matriculate at City College in the fall.

Quiz 43: Definitions

Select the word that best fits the definition. Write your answer in the space provided.

_____ 1. that which gives origin or form to a thing, or which serves to enclose it
   a. matrix   b. matrimonial   c. mater   d. alma mater

_____ 2. a school, college, or university at which a person has studied, and, usually, from which he or she has graduated
   a. maternal   b. alma mater   c. maternity   d. matrimony

_____   3. inheriting or determining descent through the female line
a. femaleness   b. matrix   c. matrilineal   d. lineage

_____   4. derived from the name of the mother or another female ancestor; named after one's mother
a. matriarch   b. matrilocal   c. alma mater
d. matronymic

_____   5. having the qualities of a mother
a. alma mater   b. matrilineal   c. maternal   d. matrix

_____   6. a married woman, especially one with children, or one who has an established social position
a. matrix   b. matron   c. alma mater   d. homemaker

_____   7. to enroll or cause to enroll as a student, especially in a college or university
a. matriculate   b. graduate   c. matrix   d. alma mater

_____   8. informal British usage for "mother"
a. mater   b. matriarch   c. matron   d. ma

Quiz 44: True/False

In the space provided, write T if the definition of the numbered word is true or F if it is false.

		T or F
1. **matrix**	outer edges	_____
2. **alma mater**	stepmother	_____
3. **matrilineal**	grandmotherly	_____
4. **matriculate**	study for a degree	_____
5. **mater**	mother	_____
6. **maternal**	motherly	_____
7. **matronymic**	from the mother's name	_____
8. **matron**	single woman	_____

Lesson 23. "Birth and Rebirth": *nasc, nat*

The Renaissance (also spelled Renascence) occurred between 1300 and 1600, when the feudal society of the Middle Ages became an increasingly urban, commercial economy with a central political institution. The term "Renaissance," or *rebirth,* was first applied in the mid-nineteenth century by a French historian to what has been characterized as nothing less than the birth of modern humanity and consciousness. The word goes back to Latin "renasci," *to be reborn,* from "re-," *again* + "nasci," *to be born.*

Many significant words evolved from the "nasc, nat" root. Here are eight such words for your consideration. First, read through the pronunciations, definitions, and sentences. Then, to reinforce your reading, complete the two quizzes.

1. **natal** (nāt'l) of or pertaining to one's birth.
   The astrologer cast a natal chart for his client.
2. **nativity** (nə tiv'i tē, nā-) birth; the birth of Christ.
   The wanderer returned to the place of his nativity.
3. **nativism** (nā'ti viz'əm) the policy of protecting the interests of native inhabitants against those of immigrants.
   The supporters of nativism staged a protest to draw attention to their demands for protection against the newcomers.
4. **innate** (i nāt') existing from birth; inborn.
   The art lessons brought out her innate talent.
5. **nascent** (nas'ənt, nā'sənt) beginning to exist or develop.
   The nascent republic petitioned for membership in the United Nations.
6. **nationalism** (nash'ə nl iz'əm, nash'nə liz'-) national spirit or aspirations; devotion to the interests of one's own nation. From Latin "natio," *nation, race,* derived from "nasci," *to be born.*
   Many Americans feel a stirring of nationalism when they see the flag or hear the national anthem.
7. **naturalize** (nach'ər ə līz', nach'rə-) to invest (an alien) with the rights and privileges of a citizen. From Latin "natura," *birth, nature,* derived from "nasci," *to be born.*
   To become naturalized American citizens, immigrants have to study the Constitution of their adopted country.
8. **nee** (nā) born. The word is placed after the name of a married woman to introduce her maiden name. From French "nee," going back to Latin "nata," *born,* from "nasci," *to be born.*
   Madame de Staël, nee Necker, was the central figure in a brilliant salon.

Quiz 45: True/False

In the space provided, write T if the definition of the numbered word is true or F if it is false.

		T or F
1. **nativism**	protectionism	_____
2. **naturalize**	admit to citizenship	_____
3. **nee**	foreign wife	_____
4. **natal**	pertaining to birth	_____
5. **nationalism**	immigration	_____

6. **nativity**   rebirth   _____
7. **nascent**   native-born   _____
8. **innate**   inborn   _____

Quiz 46: Matching

Select the best definition for each numbered word. Write your answer in the space provided.

1. **innate**   a. admit to citizenship   _____
2. **nationalism**   b. relating to birth   _____
3. **naturalize**   c. beginning to exist   _____
4. **nee**   d. birth   _____
5. **natal**   e. protection of native
                        inhabitants   _____
6. **nascent**   f. inborn   _____
7. **nativism**   g. indicating maiden name   _____
8. **nativity**   h. patriotism   _____

Lesson 24. "A Rose by Any Other Name": *nomin, nomen*

The differences between the nominative and objective cases have baffled countless generations of English-speaking students. Is it I or me? Who or whom? The nominative case is so named because it *names* the subject, the doer of the action, whereas the objective case refers to the object, as of a verb or preposition. Here are eight words formed from the Latin root "nomin, nomen," *name*.

1. **nominee** (nom'ə nē') a person named, as to run for elective office or to fill a particular post.
    In order to qualify for consideration, the nominee was required to present a petition with three hundred verifiable signatures.
2. **misnomer** (mis nō'mər) a misapplied name or designation; an error in naming a person or thing.
    "Expert" was a misnomer; "genius" was a far more accurate description of the young chess player.
3. **nomenclature** (nō'mən klā'chər) a set or system of names or terms, as those used in a particular science or art.
    The scientific nomenclature devised by Linnaeus was a great innovation.
4. **ignominious** (ig'nə min'ē əs) disgracing one's name; humiliating; discreditable; contemptible.
    The army suffered an ignominious defeat.

5. **nominal** (nom'ə nl) being such in name only; so-called.

   The silent partner is the nominal head of the firm.

6. **nominate** (nom'ə nāt') to name (someone) for appointment or election to office.

   The delegate from Vermont was pleased to nominate a favorite son for President at the Democratic convention.

Quiz 47: True/False

In the space provided, write T if the definition of the numbered word is true or F if it is false.

		T or F
1. **ignominious**	foolish, ignorant	_____
2. **nominate**	name as a candidate	_____
3. **nomenclature**	clamp	_____
4. **nominee**	candidate	_____
5. **nominal**	so-called	_____
6. **misnomer**	faux pas	_____

Quiz 48: Synonyms

Select the best synonym for each numbered word. Write your answer in the space provided.

_____ 1. ignominious
   a. ignorant   b. enormous   c. disgraceful   d. successful

_____ 2. nomenclature
   a. biology   b. classification   c. torture device
   d. international transport

_____ 3. nominee
   a. elected official   b. hereditary title   c. candidate
   d. assumed name

_____ 4. misnomer
   a. misapplied name   b. married name   c. wrong road
   d. misapplied remedy

_____ 5. nominal
   a. a lot   b. allot   c. so-called   d. summons

_____ 6. nominate
   a. apply   b. designate   c. reject   d. elect

Lesson 25. "Oh My Papa": *pater, patr*

To sociologists and anthropologists, patriarchy is a system of social organization in which descent is traced through the male line and all offspring have the father's name or belong to his people. Often, the system is connected to inheritance and social prerogatives, as in primogeniture, in which the eldest son is the sole heir. The ancient Greeks and Hebrews were a patriarchal society, as were the Europeans during the Middle Ages. While many aspects of patriarchy, such as the inheritance of the family name through the male line, persist in Western society, the exclusive male inheritance of property and other patriarchal customs are dying out.

From the Latin root "pater, patr," meaning *father,* we have formed many useful words. Eight of them follow. Go through the pronunciations, definitions, and sentences to help you make the words part of your daily speech and writing. Then complete the two quizzes.

1. **patrician** (pə trish′ən) a member of the original senatorial aristocracy in ancient Rome; any person of noble or high rank.
    You could tell she was a patrician from her elegant manner.
2. **expatriate** (*v.* eks pā′trē āt′; *n.* eks pā′trē it) to banish (a person) from his or her native country; one who has left his or her native country.
    Among the most famous American expatriates in the 1920s were the writers F. Scott Fitzgerald, Ernest Hemingway, and Gertrude Stein.
3. **patronage** (pā′trə nij, pa′-) the financial support or business afforded to a store, hotel, or the like, by customers, clients, or paying guests; the encouragement or support of an artist by a patron; the control of appointments to government jobs, especially on a basis other than merit alone. From Latin "patronus," *patron, protector, advocate,* derived from "pater," father.
    To show its appreciation for its clients' patronage, the beauty shop offered a half-price haircut to all regular customers for the month of January.
4. **paternalism** (pə tûr′nl iz′əm) the system, principle, or practice of managing or governing individuals, businesses, nations, etc., in the manner of a father dealing benevolently and often intrusively with his children.
    The employees chafed under their manager's paternalism.
5. **paternoster** (pā′tər nos′tər, pä′-, pat′ər-) the Lord's Prayer, especially in the Latin form. The term is often capitalized.
    The term "paternoster" is a translation of the first two words of the prayer in the Vulgate version, "our Father."

6. **paterfamilias** (pā'tər fə mil'ē əs, pä'-, pat'ər-) the male head of a household or family.

   The paterfamilias gathered his children about him.

7. **patronymic** (pa'trə nim'ik) (a name) derived from the name of a father or ancestor, especially by the addition of a suffix or prefix indicating descent; family name or surname.

   Their patronymic was Williamson, meaning "son of William."

8. **patrimony** (pa'trə mō'nē) an estate inherited from one's father or ancestors; heritage.

   For his share of the patrimony, John inherited the family mansion at Newport.

Quiz 49: Definitions

Select the word that best fits the definition. Write your answer in the space provided.

_____   1. the Lord's Prayer
   a. patrician   b. paternoster   c. paternalism
   d. expatriate

_____   2. derived from the name of a father or ancestor; family name or surname
   a. paterfamilias   b. patronage   c. pater
   d. patronymic

_____   3. the male head of a household or family
   a. paterfamilias   b. patronymic   c. patrician
   d. patrimony

_____   4. any person of noble or high rank
   a. patricide   b. patrician   c. expatriate   d. patriot

_____   5. the system, principle, or practice of managing or governing in the manner of a father dealing with his children
   a. paterfamilias   b. expatriate   c. paternalism
   d. patronymic

_____   6. to banish someone from his or her native country; one who has left his or her native country
   a. repatriate   b. patronize   c. paternalize   d. expatriate

_____   7. an estate inherited from one's father or ancestors; heritage
   a. patrimony   b. patricide   c. paternoster
   d. patronage

_____   8. the financial support or business afforded to a store by its clients; the support of a patron; control of appointments to government jobs
   a. patronymic   b. pater   c. patronage
   d. paterfamilias

Quiz 50: Matching

Match each of the numbered words with its closest synonym.
Write your answer in the space provided.

1. **paternoster**	a. financial backing	_____
2. **patronymic**	b. exile	_____
3. **paterfamilias**	c. male head of a family	_____
4. **patrimony**	d. fatherly management	_____
5. **patronage**	e. the Lord's Prayer	_____
6. **paternalism**	f. aristocrat	_____
7. **patrician**	g. surname	_____
8. **expatriate**	h. inheritance	_____

Lesson 26. "Keep On Truckin' ": *ped, pod*

From the Latin root "ped" and the related Greek root "pod," both
meaning *foot,* we have derived many words relating to movement
by foot. The English word "foot" is itself a Germanic cousin of
the Latin and Greek forms. One curious aberration is "peddler"
(also spelled "pedlar," "pedler"), for it is *not* from the root "ped,"
as we would expect. The word may be derived from "pedde," a
Middle English word for a lidless hamper or basket in which fish
and other items were carried as they were sold in the streets,
though it is generally thought to be of unknown origin.

The following eight words, however, all come from the "ped,
pod" roots. Practice the pronunciations, study the definitions, and
read the sentences. Then, to help set the words in your mind, complete the two quizzes that follow.

1. **quadruped** (kwod′roo ped′) any animal, especially a mammal,
   having four feet.
   Horses, dogs, and cats are all classified as quadrupeds.
2. **podiatrist** (pə dī′ə trist′) a person who treats foot disorders. From
   Greek "pod-," *foot* + "-iatros," *physician.*
   Podiatrists were formerly known as chiropodists.
3. **chiropodist** (ki rop′ə dist′, kī-) a podiatrist. From Greek "cheir,"
   hand + "podos," *foot.*
   A chiropodist treats minor problems of the feet, including corns
   and bunions.
4. **biped** (bī′ped) a two-footed animal.
   Humans are bipeds.
5. **expedient** (ik spē′dē ənt) tending to promote some desired object;

fit or suitable under the circumstances. From Latin "expedire," *to make ready,* literally *to free the feet.*

It was expedient for them to prepare all the envelopes at the same time.

6. **pseudopod** (soo′də pod′) an organ of propulsion on a protozoan.

Amebas use pseudopods, literally "false feet," as a means of locomotion.

7. **pedigree** (ped′i grē′) an ancestral line; lineage. From the French phrase "pied de grue," *foot of a crane* (from the claw-shaped mark used in family trees to show lineage); "pied," *foot,* going back to the Latin root "ped."

The dog's pedigree could be traced six generations.

8. **pedometer** (pə dom′i tər) an instrument that measures distance covered in walking by recording the number of steps taken.

The race walker used a pedometer to keep track of how much distance she could cover in an hour.

Quiz 51: Definitions

Select the best definition for each numbered word. Write your answer in the space provided.

_____   1. pedigree
a. dog training   b. lineage   c. horse racing
d. nature walking

_____   2. biped
a. false feet   b. horses   c. two-footed animal
d. winged creature

_____   3. pedometer
a. race walking   b. jogger's injury   c. foot care
d. measuring device

_____   4. expedient
a. advantageous   b. extra careful   c. unnecessary
d. walking swiftly

_____   5. quadruped
a. four-footed animal   b. four-wheeled vehicle
c. racehorse   d. four animals

_____   6. chiropodist
a. orthopedic surgeon   b. chiropractor   c. podiatrist
d. physician's assistant

_____   7. podiatrist
a. children's doctor   b. foot doctor   c. chiropractor
d. skin doctor

_____   8. pseudopod
          a. false seed pod   b. widow's peak   c. bad seed
          d. organ of propulsion

Quiz 52: True/False

In the space provided, write T if the definition of the numbered word is true or F if it is false.

		T or F
1. **chiropodist**	foot doctor	_____
2. **pedigree**	lineage	_____
3. **expedient**	advantageous	_____
4. **podiatrist**	foot doctor	_____
5. **quadruped**	four-footed animal	_____
6. **pedometer**	scale	_____
7. **pseudopod**	cocoon	_____
8. **biped**	stereo	_____

Lesson 27: "It's My Pleasure": *plac*

"S'il vous plait" is what the French say to be polite. "Plait" derives from "plaire," *to please* which goes back to the Latin "placere." Thus the "plac" root, meaning *please,* forms the basis of the French expression for *if you please.* Many other words, including adjectives, nouns, and verbs, also derive from this root. Below are six "pleasing" words to add to your vocabulary. Look over the pronunciations, definitions, and sentences. Then to reinforce your memory, complete the two quizzes.

1. **placid** (plas´id) pleasantly peaceful or calm.
    The placid lake shimmered in the early morning sun.
2. **complacent** (kəm plā´sənt) pleased, especially with oneself or one's merits, advantages, situation, etc., often without awareness of some potential danger, defect, or the like.
    She stopped being so complacent after she lost her job.
3. **placebo** (plə sē´bō) a substance having no pharmacological effect but given to a patient or subject of an experiment who supposes it to be a medicine. From the Latin word meaning *I shall please.*
    In the pharmaceutical company's latest study, one group was given the medicine; the other, a placebo.
4. **placate** (plā´kāt) to appease or pacify.

To placate an outraged citizenry, the Board of Education decided to schedule a special meeting.

5. **implacable** (im plak′ə bəl, -plā′kə-) incapable of being appeased or pacified; inexorable.

Despite concessions made by the allies, the dictator was implacable.

6. **complaisant** (kəm plā′sənt, -zənt, kom′plə zant′) inclined or disposed to please; obliging; gracious. From "plaisant," the French word for *pleasing,* derived ultimately from Latin "complacere," *to be very pleasing.*

Jill's complaisant manner belied her reputation as a martinet.

Quiz 53: Synonyms

Select the best synonym for each numbered word. Write your answer in the space provided.

_____ 1. complaisant
   a. self-satisfied   b. fake   c. agreeable   d. successful
_____ 2. implacable
   a. obliging   b. foolish   c. calm   d. inexorable
_____ 3. placid
   a. lake   b. tranquil   c. wintery   d. nature-loving
_____ 4. complacent
   a. smug   b. wretched   c. contemplative
   d. obsessively neat
_____ 5. placebo
   a. strong medicine   b. harmless drug   c. sugar cube
   d. cure
_____ 6. placate
   a. offend   b. advertise   c. cause   d. appease

Quiz 54: Matching

Match each of the numbered words with its closest synonym. Write your answer in the space provided.

1. **placebo**	a. self-satisfied	_____
2. **complaisant**	b. serene	_____
3. **implacable**	c. harmless substance	_____
4. **complacent**	d. incapable of being appeased	_____
5. **placate**	e. pacify	_____
6. **placid**	f. obliging	_____

Lesson 28. "The City of Brotherly Love": *phil, philo*

The site of the future city of Philadelphia was settled in the mid-seventeenth century by Swedish immigrants. Later the prominent English Quaker William Penn (1644–1718) determined to establish a New World colony where religious and political freedom would be guaranteed. He first obtained from Charles II a charter for Pennsylvania (which was actually named by the king). In 1682 he surveyed the land and laid out the plan for the "City of Brotherly Love," Philadelphia. The settlement flourished from the time of its foundation, growing into a thriving center of trade and manufacturing.

The Greek root "phil, philo," meaning *love,* has given us many other words besides "Philadelphia." Here are ten of them to add to your vocabulary.

1. **philanthropy** (fi lan'thrə pē) affection for humankind, especially as manifested in donations of money, property, or work to needy persons or for socially useful purposes. From Greek "philanthropia," *love of humanity.*
   Millions of people have benefited from Andrew Carnegie's works of philanthropy.
2. **philanderer** (fi lan'dər ər) a man who makes love without serious intentions, especially one who carries on flirtations.
   When she discovered that her husband was a philanderer, she sued for divorce.
3. **bibliophile** (bib'lē ə f īl', -fil) a person who loves or collects books, especially as examples of fine or unusual printing, binding, or the like. From Greek "biblion," *book* + "philos," *loving.*
   The bibliophile was excited by the prospect of acquiring a first edition of Mark Twain's *Life on the Mississippi.*
4. **philharmonic** (fil'här mon'ik) a symphony orchestra.
   The philharmonic is presenting a concert this week.
5. **philately** (fi lat'l ē) the collection and study of postage stamps. From Greek "phil-," *loving* + "ateleia," *exemption from charges* (due to a sender's prepayment shown by a postage stamp).
   To pursue his hobby of philately, the collector attended stamp exhibitions as often as possible.
6. **philhellene** (fil hel'ēn) a friend and supporter of the Greeks.
   George was a philhellene whose greatest passion was ancient Greek sculpture.
7. **philter** (fil'tər) a potion or drug that is supposed to induce a person to fall in love with someone.

He so desperately wanted her love that he resorted to dropping a philter into her drink.

8. **Anglophile** (ang'glə fīl', -fil) a person who greatly admires England or anything English.

A devoted Anglophile, Barry visits England at least twice a year.

9. **philodendron** (fil'ə den'drən) an ornamental tropical plant.

The word "philodendron," meaning *fond of trees,* refers to the plant's climbing habit.

10. **philology** (fi lol'ə jē) the study of written records, their authenticity and original form, and the determination of their meaning; in earlier use, linguistics. From Greek "philo-," *loving* + "logos," *word, speech, reason.*

The subject of philology, in its broadest sense, is culture and literature.

Quiz 55: Definitions

Select the word that best fits the definition. Write your answer in the space provided.

_____ 1. a person who greatly admires England or anything English
   a. Anglophile   b. philhellene   c. bibliophile
   d. philanderer

_____ 2. an ornamental tropical plant
   a. philanthropy   b. philodendron   c. philately
   d. Anglophile

_____ 3. a love potion
   a. philhellene   b. philology   c. philter   d. bibliophile

_____ 4. the collection and study of stamps
   a. philanthropy   b. philology   c. philharmonic
   d. philately

_____ 5. a symphony orchestra
   a. philodendron   b. philter   c. philharmonic
   d. philately

_____ 6. a friend and supporter of the Greeks
   a. philanderer   b. philhellene   c. Anglophile
   d. bibliophile

_____ 7. linguistics
   a. philter   b. philately   c. philosophy   d. philology

_____ 8. a person who loves books
   a. philanderer   b. philter   c. Anglophile
   d. bibliophile

_____ 9. concern for humanity
            a. philanthropy   b. philodendron   c. philology
            d. philter
_____ 10. a man who makes love without serious intentions, especially one who carries on flirtations
            a. bibliographer   b. philanderer   c. bibliophile
            d. Anglophile

Quiz 56: True/False

In the space provided, write T if the definition of the numbered word is true or F if it is false.

			T or F
1.	**philately**	fondness for stamps	_____
2.	**philhellene**	supporter of Greek culture	_____
3.	**bibliophile**	lover of books	_____
4.	**philanderer**	womanizer	_____
5.	**philodendron**	plant	_____
6.	**philology**	study of geography	_____
7.	**philter**	filtration	_____
8.	**philanthropy**	stinginess	_____
9.	**philharmonic**	fond of books	_____
10.	**Anglophile**	stamp collector	_____

Lesson 29. "Hang In There, Baby!": *pend*

The word "appendix" has two meanings. First, it is an organ located in the lower right side of the abdomen. It is believed to be a vestigial organ that has no function in humans. Second, it refers to the supplementary material found at the back of a book. The two meanings can be surmised from their root, "pendere," *to hang or weigh.* The appendix (vermiform appendix, strictly speaking) "hangs" in the abdomen, as the appendix "hangs" at the end of a text.

Awareness of the "pend" root can help you figure out the meanings of other words as well. Below are eight such words to help you hone your language skills.

1. **append** (ə pend') to add as a supplement or accessory.
       My supervisor asked me to append this material to the report we completed yesterday.
2. **appendage** (ə pen'dij) a subordinate part attached to something; a person in a subordinate or dependent position.

The little boy had been hanging on his mother's leg for so long that she felt he was a permanent appendage.

3. **compendium** (kəm pen′dē əm) a brief treatment or account of a subject, especially an extensive subject.

The medical editors put together a compendium of modern medicine.

4. **stipend** (stī′pend) fixed or regular pay; any periodic payment, especially a scholarship allowance. From Latin "stips," *a coin* + "pendere," *to weigh, pay out.*

The graduate students found their stipends inadequate to cover the cost of living in a big city.

5. **pendulous** (pen′jə ləs, pend′yə-) hanging down loosely; swinging freely.

She had pendulous jowls.

6. **pendant** (pen′dənt) a hanging ornament.

She wore a gold necklace with a ruby pendant.

7. **impending** (im pen′ding) about to happen; imminent.

The impending storm filled them with dread.

8. **perpendicular** (pûr′pən dik′yə lər) vertical; upright.

They set the posts perpendicular to the ground.

Quiz 57: Matching

Match each of the numbered words with its closest synonym. Write your answer in the space provided.

1. **appendage**	a. upright	_____
2. **compendium**	b. salary	_____
3. **impending**	c. hanging	_____
4. **pendulous**	d. adjunct	_____
5. **perpendicular**	e. ornament	_____
6. **append**	f. summary	_____
7. **pendant**	g. attach	_____
8. **stipend**	h. imminently menacing	_____

Quiz 58: True/False

In the space provided, write T if the definition of the numbered word is true or F if it is false.

		T or F
1. **pendulous**	swinging freely	_____
2. **perpendicular**	curved	_____
3. **pendant**	hanging ornament	_____
4. **stipend**	fasten	_____

5. **append**	add	_____
6. **compendium**	excised section	_____
7. **appendage**	adjunct	_____
8. **impending**	imminent	_____

Lesson 30. "Oh God!": *the, theo*

Atheism is the doctrine that denies the existence of a supreme deity. Many people have been incorrectly labeled atheists because they rejected some popular belief in divinity. The Romans, for example, felt the early Christians were atheists because they did not worship the pagan gods. Buddhists and Jains have been called atheistic because they deny a personal God. The word "atheism" comes from the Greek prefix "a-," *without,* and the root "the, theo," meaning *god.*

Many words derive from this root. The following section provides just a few useful examples.

1. **theology** (thē ol′ə jē) the field of study that deals with God or a deity.
   Modern theology is chiefly concerned with the relationship between humanity and God.
2. **theism** (thē′iz′ əm) the belief in the existence of a God or deity as the creator and ruler of the universe.
   The religious seminary taught its students the philosophy of theism.
3. **monotheism** (mon′ə thē iz′əm) the doctrine or belief that there is only one God.
   Judaism and Christianity preach monotheism.
4. **theocracy** (thē ok′rə sē) a form of government in which God or a deity is recognized as the supreme ruler.
   Puritan New England was a theocracy, with ministers as governors and the Bible as its constitution.
5. **pantheism** (pan′thē iz′əm) the doctrine that God is the transcendent reality of which the material universe and human beings are only manifestations.
   The New England philosophy of Transcendentalism that flourished in the mid-nineteenth century included elements of pantheism.
6. **apotheosis** (ə poth′ē ō′sis, ap′ə thē′ə sis) the exaltation of a person to the rank of a god; ideal example; epitome.
   This poem is the apotheosis of the Romantic spirit.

7. **theogony** (thē og′ə nē) an account of the origin of the gods.
Hesiod wrote a theogony of the Greek gods.

Quiz 59: Defining Words

Define each of the following words.

1. pantheism _____

2. theology _____

3. theogony _____

4. theism _____

5. apotheosis _____

6. theocracy _____

7. monotheism _____

Suggested Answers 1. the doctrine that God is the transcendent reality of which the material universe and human beings are only manifestations. 2. the field of study that treats of the deity, its attributes, and its relation to the universe. 3. an account of the origin of the gods. 4. the belief in one God as the creator and ruler of the universe. 5. the exaltation of a person to the rank of a god; the glorification of a person, act, principle, etc., as an ideal. 6. a form of government in which God or a deity is recognized as the supreme civil ruler. 7. the doctrine or belief that there is only one God.

Quiz 60: True/False

In the space provided, write T if the definition of the numbered word is true or F if it is false.

		T or F
1. **apotheosis**	epitome	_____
2. **theogony**	account of the origin of the gods	_____
3. **theocracy**	religious government	_____
4. **theism**	belief in rebirth	_____
5. **monotheism**	viral illness	_____
6. **pantheism**	rejected beliefs	_____
7. **theology**	study of divine things	_____

Lesson 31. "Call Out!": *voc*

The voice box (more properly called the "larynx") is the muscular and cartilaginous structure in which the vocal cords are located. The vibration of the vocal cords by air passing out of the lungs causes the formation of sounds that are then amplified by the resonating nature of the oral and nasal cavities. The root "voc," meaning *call* or *voice,* is the basis of words like "vocal," as well as a host of other powerful words. Now study the following ten "vocal" words.

1. **avocation** (av′ə kā′shən) a minor or occasional occupation; hobby. From Latin "avocatio," *distraction,* derived from "avocare," *to call away.*
   His avocation is bird-watching.
2. **vocable** (vō′kə bəl) a word, especially one considered without regard to meaning. From Latin "vocabulum," derived from "vocare," *to call,* from "voc-, vox," *voice.*
   Lewis Carroll coined many nonsense vocables, such as *jabberwocky* and *bandersnatch.*
3. **vociferous** (vō sif′ər əs) crying out noisily; clamorous; characterized by noise or vehemence.
   She was vociferous in her support of reform legislation.
4. **advocate** (ad′və kāt′) to plead in favor of; support.
   The citizens' committee advocated a return to the previous plan.
5. **convoke** (kən vōk′) to summon to meet. From Latin "convocare" ("con-," *with together* + "vocare," *to call*).
   They will convoke the members for a noon meeting.
6. **evoke** (i vōk′) to call up, as memories or feelings. From Latin "evocare."
   The music evoked the mood of spring.
7. **revoke** (ri vōk′) to take back or withdraw; cancel. From Latin "revocare," *to call again, recall.*
   The king revoked his earlier decree.
8. **invoke** (in vōk′) to call forth or pray for; appeal to or petition; declare to be in effect. From Latin "invocare."
   The defendant invoked the Fifth Amendment so as not to incriminate himself.
9. **equivocal** (i kwiv′ə kəl) of uncertain significance; not determined; dubious. From Latin "aequivocus" ("aequus," *equal* + "vox," *voice*).
   Despite his demands for a clear-cut decision, she would give only an equivocal response.
10. **irrevocable** (i rev′ə kə bəl) incapable of being revoked or recalled; unable to be repealed or annulled.
    Once Caesar crossed the Rubicon, his decision to begin the civil war against Pompey was irrevocable.

Quiz 61: Matching

Match each of the numbered words with its closest synonym. Write your answer in the space provided.

1. convoke	a. word	_____
2. advocate	b. hobby	_____
3. revoke	c. uncertain	_____
4. equivocal	d. permanent	_____
5. invoke	e. summon	_____
6. vocable	f. pray for	_____
7. evoke	g. support	_____
8. vociferous	h. loud	_____
9. irrevocable	i. cancel	_____
10. avocation	j. call up; produce	_____

Quiz 62: True/False

In the space provided, write T if the definition of the numbered word is true or F if it is false.

		T or F
1. revoke	restore	_____
2. avocation	profession	_____
3. vociferous	quiet	_____
4. advocate	oppose	_____
5. evoke	stifle	_____
6. equivocal	unambiguous	_____
7. invoke	suppress	_____
8. irrevocable	changeable	_____
9. convoke	summon	_____
10. vocable	word	_____

Answers to Quizzes in Chapter 6

Answers to Quiz 1

1. a 2. b 3. c 4. d 5. d 6. b 7. b 8. a 9. a 10. b 11. c 12. d 13. c 14. c 15. a

Answers to Quiz 2

1. T 2. F 3. T 4. T 5. F 6. F 7. F 8. T 9. T 10. T

Answers to Quiz 3

1. T 2. T 3. F 4. T 5. F 6. T 7. F 8. T 9. T 10. F

Answers to Quiz 5

1. i 2. e 3. d 4. b 5. h 6. a 7. c 8. j 9. f 10. g

Answers to Quiz 6

1. T 2. F 3. F 4. F 5. T 6. F 7. T 8. T 9. F 10. T

Answers to Quiz 7

1. g 2. e 3. d 4. b 5. a 6. i 7. c 8. j 9. f 10. h

Answers to Quiz 8

1. F 2. T 3. T 4. T 5. F 6. F 7. T 8. F 9. T 10. F

Answers to Quiz 9

1. c 2. g 3. a 4. c 5. i 6. h 7. f 8. d 9. b 10. j

Answers to Quiz 10

1. F 2. F 3. T 4. F 5. T 6. T 7. F 8. F 9. F 10. T

Answers to Quiz 11

1. c 2. e 3. a 4. f 5. d 6. b

Answers to Quiz 12

1. F 2. T 3. F 4. F 5. F 6. T

Answers to Quiz 13

1. F 2. T 3. F 4. T 5. F 6. T 7. F 8. T

Answers to Quiz 15

1. c 2. d 3. a 4. d 5. c 6. b 7. b 8. a 9. d 10. c

Answers to Quiz 16

1. T 2. T 3. T 4. T 5. F 6. F 7. F 8. T 9. F 10. T

Answers to Quiz 17

1. a 2. c 3. b 4. b 5. a 6. c 7. a 8. b

Answers to Quiz 18

1. T 2. T 3. F 4. T 5. T 6. F 7. F 8. F

Answers to Quiz 19

1. c 2. e 3. a 4. g 5. h 6. f 7. b 8. d

Answers to Quiz 20

1. T 2. T 3. T 4. T 5. F 6. F 7. F 8. F

Answers to Quiz 21

1. f 2. a 3. i 4. b 5. h 6. c 7. d 8. e 9. g

Answers to Quiz 22

1. T 2. T 3. T 4. F 5. T 6. T 7. F 8. T 9. T

Answers to Quiz 23

1. c 2. c 3. b 4. b 5. a 6. b 7. c 8. a

Answers to Quiz 24

1. T 2. F 3. T 4. F 5. F 6. T 7. T 8. T

Answers to Quiz 25

1. d 2. a 3. f 4. b 5. c 6. g 7. e

Answers to Quiz 26

1. c 2. d 3. a 4. b 5. c 6. b 7. c

Answers to Quiz 27

1. T 2. F 3. T 4. T 5. F 6. F 7. F

Answers to Quiz 28

1. e 2. g 3. a 4. c 5. b 6. d 7. f

Answers to Quiz 29

1. b 2. d 3. b 4. d 5. c 6. a 7. b 8. b 9. c 10. a

Answers to Quiz 30

1. F 2. F 3. F 4. T 5. F 6. F 7. T 8. T 9. T 10. F

Answers to Quiz 31

1. d 2. f 3. i 4. h 5. b 6. e 7. a 8. g 9. c

Answers to Quiz 33

1. a 2. c 3. b 4. d 5. a 6. b 7. b 8. c 9. d 10. d

Answers to Quiz 34

1. T 2. T 3. T 4. F 5. T 6. T 7. F 8. F 9. F 10. F

Answers to Quiz 35

1. c 2. d 3. a 4. a 5. b 6. d

Answers to Quiz 36

1. T 2. F 3. F 4. F 5. T 6. T

Answers to Quiz 37

1. d 2. e 3. g 4. b 5. c 6. a 7. f

Answers to Quiz 38

1. d 2. b 3. c 4. a 5. c 6. b 7. c

Answers to Quiz 39

1. T 2. T 3. F 4. T 5. F 6. F 7. F

Answers to Quiz 40

1. c 2. g 3. f 4. a 5. e 6. b 7. d

Answers to Quiz 41

1. d 2. f 3. i 4. c 5. h 6. b 7. g 8. a 9. e

Answers to Quiz 42

1. F 2. F 3. F 4. T 5. T 6. F 7. T 8. F 9. T

Answers to Quiz 43

1. a 2. b 3. c 4. d 5. c 6. b 7. a 8. a

Answers to Quiz 44

1. F 2. F 3. F 4. T 5. T 6. T 7. T 8. F

Answers to Quiz 45

1. T 2. T 3. F 4. T 5. F 6. F 7. F 8. T

Answers to Quiz 46

1. f 2. h 3. a 4. g 5. b 6. c 7. e 8. d

Answers to Quiz 47

1. F 2. T 3. F 4. T 5. T 6. F

Answers to Quiz 48

1. c 2. b 3. c 4. a 5. c 6. b

Answers to Quiz 49

1. b 2. d 3. a 4. b 5. c 6. d 7. a 8. c

Answers to Quiz 50

1. e 2. g 3. c 4. h 5. a 6. d 7. f 8. b

Answers to Quiz 51

1. b 2. c 3. d 4. a 5. a 6. c 7. b 8. d

Answers to Quiz 52

1. T 2. T 3. T 4. T 5. T 6. F 7. F 8. F

Answers to Quiz 53

1. c 2. d 3. b 4. a 5. b 6. d

Answers to Quiz 54

1. c 2. f 3. d 4. a 5. c 6. b

Answers to Quiz 55

1. a 2. b 3. c 4. d 5. c 6. b 7. d 8. d 9. a 10. b

Answers to Quiz 56

1. T 2. T 3. T 4. T 5. T 6. F 7. F 8. F 9. F 10. F

Answers to Quiz 57

1. d 2. f 3. h 4. c 5. a 6. g 7. e 8. b

Answers to Quiz 58

1. T 2. F 3. T 4. F 5. T 6. F 7. T 8. T

Answers to Quiz 60

1. T 2. T 3. F 4. F 5. F 6. F 7. T

Answers to Quiz 61

1. e 2. g 3. i 4. c 5. f 6. a 7. j 8. h 9. d 10. b

Answers to Quiz 62

1. F 2. F 3. F 4. F 5. F 6. F 7. F 8. F 9. T 10. T

7

Learning Words from Their Histories

However helpful it is to learn how to figure out the meanings of words from their prefixes, suffixes, and roots, you may sometimes encounter an unusual or exotic word that resists the universal formula. Don't be discouraged. Some words can only be understood by puzzling through their histories, and that is just part of the fun of exploring the complex nature of English. Often the most powerful words come to us through mythology or biblical stories, historical events or literary works, obscure languages or twisted etymologies.

Keep in mind that none of these unusual words would have found its way into our vocabulary if it was not especially expressive and worthwhile, so these words are always deserving of the extra detective work it takes to understand them. Each one is a prize to add to your growing stockpile of new and potent vocabulary words.

To encourage you in this adventure into the more exotic reaches of English and help you to overcome your fear of strange and perplexing words, we have compiled a list of intriguing word histories. By the time you finish this chapter, you may be disappointed to remember that there are relatively few such words in the English lexicon—the prefix, suffix, and root method of word analysis remains the mainstay of vocabulary acquisition.

Lesson 1

Words, like people, have a past, and as with people, some words have more interesting stories than others. Knowing a word's history can help you remember it and incorporate it into your daily speech. The following ten words have especially intriguing backgrounds. Read through their histories, then complete the quizzes that follow.

1. **bootlegger** (boot'leg'ər) Originally, a "bootlegger" was a person who smuggled outlawed alcoholic liquor in the tops of his tall boots. The term was more common during the Prohibition era of the early twentieth century, but it is still used to mean *someone who unlawfully makes, sells, or transports alcoholic beverages without registration or payment of taxes.*

2. **bugbear** (bug'bâr') The word refers to *a source of fears, often groundless.* It comes from a Welsh legend about a goblin in the shape of a bear that ate up naughty children.

3. **fiasco** (fē as'kō) "Fiasco" is the Italian word for *flask* or *bottle.* How it came to mean *a complete and ignominious failure* is obscure. One theory suggests that Venetian glassblowers set aside fine glass with flaws to make into common bottles.

4. **jackanapes** (jak'ə nāps') Today the word is used to describe *an impertinent, presumptuous young man; a whippersnapper.* Although its precise origin is uncertain, we know that the term was first used as an uncomplimentary nickname for William de la Pole, Duke of Suffolk, who was murdered in 1450. His badge was an ape's clog and chain. In a poem of the time, Suffolk was called "the Apeclogge," and later referred to as an ape called "Jack Napes."

5. **jeroboam** (jer'ə bō'əm) We now use the term "jeroboam" to refer to *a wine bottle having a capacity of about three liters.* Historically, Jeroboam was the first king of the Biblical kingdom of Israel, described in I Kings 11:28 as "a mighty man of valor," who, three verses later, "made Israel to sin." Some authorities trace the origin of today's usage to the king, reasoning that since an oversized bottle of wine can cause sin, it too is a jeroboam.

6. **nonplus** (non plus', non'plus') The word "nonplus" means *to make utterly perplexed; to puzzle completely.* The original Latin phrase was "non plus ultra," meaning *no more beyond,* allegedly inscribed on the Pillars of Hercules, beyond which no ship could safely sail.

7. **quisling** (kwiz'ling) This term refers to *a traitor,* a person who betrays his or her own country by aiding an enemy and often serving later in a puppet government. It is directly derived from the name of Vidkun Quisling (1887–1945), a Norwegian army officer turned fascist who collaborated with the Nazis early in World War II.

8. **bowdlerize** (bōd′lə rīz′, boud′-) In 1818, Scottish physician Dr. Thomas Bowdler published a new edition of Shakespeare's works. The value of his edition, he stated, lay in the fact that he had edited it so that all "words and expressions are omitted which cannot with propriety be read aloud to the family." Good intentions aside, he found himself being held up to ridicule. From his name is derived the word "bowdlerize," meaning *to expurgate a literary text in a prudish manner.*

9. **boycott** (boi′kot) In an attempt to break the stranglehold of Ireland's absentee landlords, Charles Stewart Parnell advocated in 1880 that anyone who took over land from which a tenant had been evicted for nonpayment of rent should be punished "by isolating him from his kind as if he was a leper of old." The most famous application of Parnell's words occurred soon after on the estate of the Earl of Erne. Unable to pay their rents, the earl's tenants suggested a lower scale, but the manager of the estate, Captain Charles Cunningham Boycott, would not accept the reduction. In retaliation, the tenants applied the measures proposed by Parnell, not only refusing to gather crops and run the estate, but also intercepting Boycott's mail and food, humiliating him in the street, and threatening his life. Their treatment of Boycott became so famous that within a few months the newspapers were using his name to identify any such nonviolent coercive practices. Today "boycott" means *to join together in abstaining from, or preventing dealings with, as a protest.*

10. **chauvinism** (shō′və niz′əm) One of Napoleon's most dedicated soldiers, Nicolas Chauvin, was wounded seventeen times fighting for his emperor. After he retired from the army, he spoke so incessantly of the majestic glory of his leader and the greatness of France that he became a laughingstock. In 1831, his name was used for a character in a play who was an almost idolatrous worshiper of Napoleon. The word "chauvin" became associated with this type of extreme hero worship and exaggerated patriotism. Today we use the term "chauvinism" to refer to *zealous and belligerent nationalism.*

Quiz 1: Matching

Match each of the numbered words with its closest synonym. Write your answer in the space provided.

1. **bootlegger**	a. fanatical patriotism	_____
2. **bugbear**	b. total failure	_____
3. **fiasco**	c. expurgate	_____

4. **jackanapes**   d. groundless fear   _____
5. **jeroboam**   e. oversized wine bottle _____
6. **nonplus**   f. unlawful producer of
                            alcohol   _____
7. **quisling**   g. rude fellow   _____
8. **bowdlerize**   h. perplex   _____
9. **boycott**   i. traitor   _____
10. **chauvinism**   j. strike   _____

Quiz 2: True/False

In the space provided, write T if the definition of the numbered word is true or F if it is false.

		T or F
1. **bowdlerize**	expurgate	_____
2. **boycott**	male child	_____
3. **bootlegger**	petty thief	_____
4. **fiasco**	celebration	_____
5. **chauvinism**	fanatical patriotism	_____
6. **jackanapes**	jack-of-all-trades	_____
7. **quisling**	turncoat	_____
8. **bugbear**	baseless fear	_____
9. **jeroboam**	ancient queen	_____
10. **nonplus**	certain	_____

Lesson 2

The origins of the following words can be traced to Latin. Read through the histories, then complete the quizzes.

1. **aberration** (ab′ə rā′shən) This word comes from the Latin verb "aberrare," *to wander away from.* A person with a psychological "aberration" exhibits behavior that strays from the accepted path; hence the word means *deviation from what is common, normal, or right.*

2. **abominate** (ə bom′ə nāt′) "Abominate" is from the Latin "abominor," meaning *I pray that the event predicted by the omen may be averted.* The Romans murmured the word to keep away the evil spirits whenever anyone said something unlucky. Today we use it to mean *to regard with intense aversion or loathing; abhor.*

3. **impeccable** (im pek′ə bəl) The word comes from the Latin "impeccabilis," *without sin.* The religious meaning has been only

slightly extended over the years. Today an "impeccable" reputation is *faultless, flawless, irreproachable.*

4. **recalcitrant** (ri kal'si trənt) The word was formed from the Latin prefix "re-," *back,* and "calcitrare," *to kick.* Thus, a "recalcitrant" person is one who kicks back, resisting authority or control.

5. **ebullient** (i bul'yənt, i bool'-) This word derives from the Latin "ebullire," *to boil over.* A person who is "ebullient" is *overflowing with fervor, enthusiasm, or excitement.*

6. **enclave** (en'klāv, än'-) The word "enclave" refers to *a country or territory entirely or mostly surrounded by another country.* More generally, it means *a group enclosed or isolated within a larger one.* The word comes ultimately from Latin "inclavare," *to lock in.*

7. **expedite** (ek'spi dīt') The word "expedite" means *to speed up the progress of something.* It comes from the Latin "expedire," *to set the feet free.*

8. **expunge** (ik spunj') To indicate that a soldier had retired from service, the ancient Romans wrote a series of dots or points beneath his name on the service lists. The Latin "expungere" thus meant both *to prick through* and *to mark off on a list.* Similarly, the English word "expunge" means *to strike or blot out; to erase.*

9. **inchoate** (in kō'it, -āt) "Inchoate" comes from the Latin "inchoare," *to begin.* Thus, an "inchoate" plan is *not yet fully developed,* or *rudimentary.*

10. **prevaricate** (pri var'i kāt') Today "prevaricate" means *to speak falsely or misleadingly with deliberate intent; to lie.* It has its origin in a physical act. The Latin verb "praevaricare" means *to spread apart.* The plowman who "prevaricated," then, made crooked ridges, deviating from straight furrows in the field.

Quiz 3: True/False

In the space provided, write T if the definition of the numbered word is true or F if it is false.

		T or F
1. **enclave**	rendezvous	_____
2. **abominate**	detest	_____
3. **recalcitrant**	easygoing	_____
4. **expunge**	erase	_____
5. **prevaricate**	preplan	_____
6. **inchoate**	illogical	_____
7. **aberration**	fidelity	_____
8. **expedite**	slow down	_____

9. **impeccable**   perfect   _____
10. **ebullient**   enthusiastic   _____

Quiz 4: Matching

Match each of the following numbered words with its closest synonym. Write your answer in the space provided.

1. **recalcitrant**   a. dispatch   _____
2. **enclave**   b. divergence   _____
3. **inchoate**   c. balky   _____
4. **abominate**   d. obliterate   _____
5. **aberration**   e. misstate   _____
6. **impeccable**   f. enclosure   _____
7. **expunge**   g. detest   _____
8. **expedite**   h. without fault   _____
9. **ebullient**   i. incipient   _____
10. **prevaricate**   j. high-spirited   _____

Lesson 3

Some of the most disarming words have their beginnings in historical events, myths and legends, and special terminology. Here are ten more powerful words with interesting or unusual histories. Read through their backgrounds, then complete the quizzes that follow.

1. **abracadabra** (ab′rə kə dab′rə) This intriguing-sounding word was first used as a charm in the second century. The Romans believed that the word had the ability to cure toothaches and other illnesses. Patients seeking relief wrote the letters in the form of a triangle on a piece of parchment and wore it around their necks on a length of thread. Today "abracadabra" is used as a pretend conjuring word. It also means *meaningless talk, nonsense.*

2. **ambrosia** (am brō′zhə) Originally, "ambrosia" was the food of the Olympian gods (as "nectar" was their drink). The word comes from the Greek "a," *not,* and "brostos," *mortal,* hence, eating ambrosia conferred immortality. Today the word means *an especially delicious food,* with the implication that the concoction is savory enough to be fit for the gods. A popular dessert by this name contains shredded coconut, sliced fruits, and cream.

3. **gerrymander** (jer′i man′dər, ger′-) In 1812, Massachusetts governor Elbridge Gerry conspired with party members in order to

change the boundaries of voting districts to enhance their own political clout. Noticing that one such district resembled a salamander, a newspaper editor coined the term "gerrymander" to describe *the practice of dividing a state, county, etc., into election districts so as to give one political party a majority while concentrating the voting strength of the other party into as few districts as possible.*

4. **mesmerize** (mez′mə rīz′, mes′-) The Austrian doctor Friedrich Anton Mesmer first publicly demonstrated the technique of hypnotism in 1775. Today the term "mesmerize" is still used as a synonym for *hypnotize,* but it has broadened to also mean *spellbind* or *fascinate.*

5. **quintessence** (kwin tes′əns) The word comes from the medieval Latin term "quinta essentia," *the fifth essence.* This fifth primary element was thought to be ether, supposedly the constituent matter of the heavenly bodies, the other four elements being air, fire, earth, and water. The medieval alchemists tried to isolate ether through distillation. These experiments gave us the contemporary meaning of "quintessence": *the pure and concentrated essence of a substance; the most perfect embodiment of something.*

6. **desultory** (des′əl tôr′ē) Some Roman soldiers went into battle with two horses, so that when one steed wearied, the soldier could vault onto the second horse striding along parallel to the first without losing any time. The same skill was employed by circus performers, especially charioteers, who could leap between two chariots riding abreast. Such a skilled horseman was called a "desultor," *a leaper.* Perhaps because these equestrians stayed only briefly on their mounts, the word "desultory" acquired its present meaning: *lacking in consistency, constancy, or visible order.*

7. **aegis** (ē′jis) When Zeus emerged victorious from his rebellion against the Titans, he attributed his success in part to his shield, which bore at its center the head of one of the Gorgons. The shield was reputedly made of goatskin, and hence its name, "aigis," was said to derive from the Greek "aig-," the stem of "aix," *goat.* Our present use of the word to mean *protection* or *sponsorship* evolved from the notion of eighteenth-century English writers who assumed that the "egis" of Zeus or Athena— or their Roman counterparts Jove and Minerva—protected all those who came under its influence. Today the preferred spelling of the word is "aegis."

8. **utopia** (yo͞o tō′pē ə) Sir Thomas More (1478–1535) was one of the great humanists of the Renaissance era in England. More

held important government offices under Henry VIII, but as a devout Roman Catholic, he refused to accept the Act of Supremacy, which made the king the head of the English Church. He was imprisoned in the Tower of London and ultimately beheaded under a charge of treason. His *Utopia* (1516) is an account of an ideal state founded entirely on reason. More derived the title of his masterpiece from the Greek for "not a place." The popularity of this specific work has transformed the word "utopia" into a generic term meaning *any ideal place or state; a visionary system of social or political perfection.*

9. **aloof** (ə lŌŌf′) This was originally a sailor's term, "a loof," *to the luff or windward direction,* perhaps from the Dutch "te loef," *to windward.* Etymologists believe that our use of the word to mean *at a distance, especially in feeling or interest,* comes from the idea of keeping a ship's head to the wind, and thus clear of the lee shore toward which it might drift.

10. **bluestocking** (blŌŌ′stok′ing) A "bluestocking" is *a woman with considerable scholarly, literary, or intellectual ability or interest.* The word originated in connection with intellectual gatherings held in London about 1750 in the homes of women bored by the more frivolous pastimes of their age. Lavish evening dress was not required at these affairs; in fact, to put at ease visitors who could not afford expensive clothing, the women themselves dressed simply. One of the male guests went so far as to wear his everyday blue worsted stockings rather than the black silk ones usually worn at evening social gatherings. In response to their interests and dress, the English naval officer Admiral Edward Boscawen (1711–61) is said to have sarcastically called these gatherings "the Blue Stocking Society."

Quiz 5: Definitions

Select the best definition for each numbered word. Write your answer in the space provided.

1. mesmerize   _____
   a. attack   b. burst forth   c. fascinate
2. desultory   _____
   a. aggressive   b. fitful   c. nasty
3. aloof   _____
   a. remote   b. sailing   c. windy
4. aegis   _____
   a. intense interest   b. goat   c. sponsorship

5. gerrymander   _____
   a. medieval gargoyle   b. combine for historical sense
   c. redistrict for political advantage
6. abracadabra   _____
   a. beauty   b. hocus pocus   c. boredom
7. utopia   _____
   a. paradise   b. hell   c. delicious food
8. ambrosia   _____
   a. suppository   b. flower   c. delicious food
9. quintessence   _____
   a. pith   b. fruit   c. oil
10. bluestocking   _____
   a. chic woman   b. intellectual woman   c. poor man

Quiz 6: Matching

Select the best synonym for each numbered word. Write your answer in the space provided.

1. **utopia**	a. delicious food	_____
2. **aloof**	b. inconsistent; random	_____
3. **gerrymander**	c. distant; remote	_____
4. **ambrosia**	d. ideal state	_____
5. **abracadabra**	e. sponsorship	_____
6. **bluestocking**	f. enthrall	_____
7. **desultory**	g. mumbo-jumbo	_____
8. **aegis**	h. concentrated essence	_____
9. **mesmerize**	i. divide a political district	_____
10. **quintessence**	j. a well-read woman	_____

Lesson 4

The following words are all based on Greek myths and legends. Read through their histories, then complete the quizzes.

1. **amazon** (am′ə zon′) The word comes ultimately from the Greek, but the origin of the Greek word is uncertain. "Amazon" refers to *a tall, powerful, aggressive woman.* The Amazons of legend were female warriors who were allied with the Trojans against the Greeks.
2. **herculean** (hûr′ kyə lē′ ən) Hercules, who was by far the most popular of all Greek heroes, is often portrayed as a muscular he-man wearing a lion skin and bearing a huge club. As an infant, he strangled two serpents in his cradle. Later, he per-

formed the prodigious twelve labors, slaying one monster after another and cleansing the Augean stables to gain immortality among the gods. Sophocles, Euripides, and Seneca all celebrated his exploits in their plays. We use the word "herculean" to mean *of enormous power, size, or courage,* or to describe a task *requiring extraordinary strength or exertion.*

3. **cornucopia** (kôr′nə kō′pē ə, -nyə-) According to Greek mythology, to save the infant Zeus from being swallowed by his father Cronus, his mother, Rhea, hid her son in a cave and tricked Cronus into swallowing a stone wrapped in a cloth. The infant was then entrusted to the care of the nymph Amaltheia, who fed him on goat's milk. One day she filled a goat's horn with fresh fruit and herbs. The horn was thereafter magically refilled, no matter how much the child ate. To the Greeks, this boundless source was the horn of Amaltheia; to the Romans, it was the "cornu copiae," from "cornu," *horn,* and "copia," *plenty.* We know a "cornucopia" as *a horn containing food or drink in endless supply* or *horn of plenty.* It is often used as a symbol of abundance.

4. **diadem** (dī′ə dem′) In his quest to create a vast, unified empire with Babylon as its capital, the Macedonian hero Alexander the Great adopted a number of Persian and Oriental customs. He began to wear a blue-edged white headband with two ends trailing to the shoulders, a Persian symbol of royalty. The Greeks called this headpiece a "diadema," literally *a binding over.* The headpiece was adopted by other monarchs down through the ages and further embellished with gold and gems, eventually evolving into a rich crown. Today a "diadem" is *a crown* or *a headband worn as a symbol of royalty.*

5. **epicure** (ep′i kyŏor′) Epicurus was a Greek philosopher who lived from 342 to 270 B.C. He believed that pleasure, attained mainly through pure and noble thoughts, constituted the highest happiness. After his death, his disciples spread his views. Their critics argued that Epicurus's theory was little more than an excuse for debauchery. From this argument we derive the present-day meaning of "epicure," *a person with luxurious tastes or habits, especially in eating or drinking.*

6. **esoteric** (es′ə ter′ik) From the Greek "esoterikos," *inner,* the word was used to describe the secret doctrines taught by the philosopher Pythagoras to a select few of his disciples. Hence "esoteric" means *understood by or meant only for those who have special knowledge or interest: recondite.*

7. **labyrinth** (lab′ə rinth′) According to the Greek myth, King

Minos of Crete ordered Daedalus to build a prison for the Minotaur, a half-bull, half-human monster. Daedalus succeeded by creating a series of twisting passageways that kept the monster imprisoned. Today a "labyrinth" is *a devious arrangement of linear patterns forming a design; a maze.*

8. **lethargy** (leth′ər jē) The Greeks believed in an afterlife. In their mythology, the dead crossed the river Lethe, which flowed through Hades, the underground realm. Anyone who drank its water forgot the past. The Greek word "lethargia" derives from "lethe," *forgetfulness.* Hence our English word "lethargy," *drowsiness* or *sluggishness.*

9. **mentor** (men′tôr, -tər) In the *Odyssey* of Homer, Mentor is Odysseus's friend and tutor to his son Telemachus. Today the word "mentor" means *trusted teacher or guide.*

10. **nemesis** (nem′ə sis) Nemesis was the Greek goddess of vengeance, whose task it was to punish the proud and the insolent. Today a "nemesis" is *an agent or act of retribution or punishment,* or *something that a person cannot conquer or achieve.*

Quiz 7: True/False

In the space provided, write T if the definition of the numbered word is true or F if it is false.

		T or F
1. **diadem**	crown	_____
2. **labyrinth**	lazy	_____
3. **mentor**	mendacious	_____
4. **amazon**	female warrior	_____
5. **herculean**	puny	_____
6. **esoteric**	arcane	_____
7. **lethargy**	lassitude	_____
8. **nemesis**	downfall	_____
9. **cornucopia**	foot ailment	_____
10. **epicure**	hidden	_____

Quiz 8: Defining Words

Define each of the following words.

1. diadem _____

2. esoteric _____

3. mentor _____

4. nemesis _____

5. amazon _____

6. epicure _____

7. herculean _____

8. cornucopia _____

9. labyrinth _____

10. lethargy _____

Suggested Answers   1. crown 2. meant only for the select few with special knowledge or interest 3. trusted teacher or guide 4. act of retribution, or that which a person cannot conquer or achieve 5. female warrior 6. a person with luxurious tastes or habits, especially in eating or drinking 7. strong; powerful; courageous; mighty; difficult 8. boundless source 9. maze 10. sluggishness; weariness

Lesson 5

Now study the curious origins of these ten words and work through the two quizzes that follow.

1. **ostracize** (os′trə sīz′) The word "ostracize" comes originally from the Greek "ostrakon," *tile, potsherd, shell.* It refers to the ancient Greek practice of banishing a man by writing his name on a shell or a bit of earthen tile. Anyone considered dangerous to the state was sent into exile for ten years. The judges cast their votes by writing on the shells or pottery shards and dropping them into an urn. The word "ostracize" still retains the same sense, *to exclude, by general consent, from society.*

2. **sycophant** (sik′ə fənt, -fant′) The word "sycophant" now means *a self-seeking, servile flatterer.* Originally, it was used to refer to an informer or slanderer. Curiously, it comes from Greek "sykon," *fig,* and "-phantes," *one who shows;* thus, *a fig-shower.* One explanation for this odd coinage is that in ancient Greece a sycophant was an informer against merchants engaged in the unlawful exportation of figs.

3. **cynosure** (sī′nə shŏŏr′, sin′ə-) According to the myth, Zeus chose to honor the nymph who cared for him in his infancy by placing her in the sky as a constellation. One of her stars was so brilliant and stationary that all the other stars seemed to revolve around it. To the practical-minded ancient mariners, however, the bottom three stars of the constellation looked like a dog's tail. They named the entire constellation "Cynosura," *dog's tail.* From its name we get our word "cynosure," *something that at-*

tracts attention by its brilliance or interest. By the way, we now call the constellation "Ursa Minor," *Little Bear,* and the bright star "Polaris," *Pole Star* or *North Star.*

4. **Hobson's choice** (hob′sənz) Thomas Hobson (1544–1631) was a stable owner in Cambridge, England, who gave his name to this very useful, pithy phrase meaning *the choice of taking that which is offered or nothing at all; the lack of a real alternative.* Hobson gave his customers only one choice of a mount: that of the horse nearest the stable door. In a charming 1954 film of this title directed by David Lean, Charles Laughton hams it up as a prosperous but dipsomaniacal bootmaker hoist by his own petard when he banishes his oldest spinster daughter after she marries his best cobbler. When Hobson (the bootmaker) refuses to deal fairly with their demands for more equitable treatment as the mainstays of the business, the young couple set up in a nearby shop of their own that steals away his former customers. In the end, Hobson's choice is unavoidable and non-negotiable: He is forced to turn over his shop to the clever couple and retire from business.

5. **tantalize** (tan′tl īz′) For his transgressions against the Greek god Zeus, Tantalus was condemned to Tartarus, where he stood in a pool with his chin level with the water, eternally parched with thirst. When he bowed his head to drink, the water ebbed away. Above his head were trees laden with juicy fruits, but when he tried to seize them, the wind swept them out of his reach. From this hellish dilemma, we derive the word "tantalize," *to torment with the sight of something desired but out of reach; tease by arousing expectations.*

6. **eldorado** (el′də rä′dō, -rä′-) The word comes from Spanish legends of an incredibly wealthy city in South America, so rich that its streets were paved with gold. Many adventurers set off to find this elusive city; in 1595 Sir Walter Raleigh ventured into Guiana in a vain attempt to locate it. Among the Spaniards, the king of this fabulous land came to be called "El Dorado," *the Golden One.* Today "eldorado" is used generally to mean *any fabulously wealthy place.*

7. **mercurial** (mər kyoor′ē əl) Even schoolchildren are familiar with the character of the Mad Hatter from Lewis Carroll's account of *Alice's Adventures in Wonderland* and the concomitant phrase "as mad as a hatter," but few people are aware that the phrase had a basis in reality: Many hat-makers indeed were known to go mad as a result of the use of mercury, a poisonous substance, in their work. The celebrated English physicist and

mathematician Sir Isaac Newton (1642–1727) was also known to behave somewhat strangely at times following his scientific experiments with mercury. Today we use the word "mercurial" to mean *changeable; fickle; flighty; erratic* or sometimes *animated; lively.*

8. **filibuster** (fil′ə bus′tər) In the seventeenth century, English seamen who attacked Spanish ships and brought back wealth from New Spain were called "buccaneers." In Holland, they were known as "vrijbuiters," *free robbers.* In French, the word became first "fribustier" and then "flibuster." In Spain, the term was "filibustero." Then, when the nineteenth-century American soldier of fortune William Walker tried to capture Sonora, Mexico, the Mexicans promptly dubbed him a "filibuster." Today the term refers to *the use of irregular or disruptive tactics, such as exceptionally long speeches, by a member of a legislative assembly.* The current use of the word may have arisen through a comparison of a legislator's determination to block a bill with the tactics used by William Walker to evade the law.

9. **sophistry** (sof′ə strē) In the fifth century B.C.E., the Sophists were peripatetic Greek teachers paid to instruct the sons of the upper class who sought political and legal careers in pragmatic rhetorical skills. They sought knowledge primarily as a source of intellectual amusement, power, and social prominence. Thus, they were noted more for their ingenuity and speciousness in argumentation than their desire to discover the truth or establish moral principles. Some of them even boasted that they could "make the worst appear the better reason." Gorgias, one of the leading lights of the Sophist school, argued that nothing exists and nothing is knowable, since reality is entirely relative to the subjective experience of the individual. Not surprisingly, Socrates, who would accept no payment for his teaching, regarded their influence as pernicious. The current meaning of "sophistry," therefore, is *a subtle, tricky, superficially plausible but generally fallacious method of reasoning; a false argument or fallacy.*

10. **galvanize** (gal′və nīz′) In the mid-eighteenth century, Luigi Galvani, a professor of anatomy at the University of Bologna, concluded that the nerves are a source of electricity. Although Volta later proved his theory incorrect, Galvani's pioneering work inspired other scientists to produce electricity by chemical means. From the old-fashioned term "galvanism," *electricity,* which honors Galvani, we have derived the word "galvanize," *to stimulate; startle into activity.*

Quiz 9: Definitions

Each of the following phrases contains an italicized word. See how many you can define correctly. Write your answer in the space provided.

_____   1. accept a *Hobson's choice*
      a. firm offer   b. victory   c. nonnegotiable demand
      d. hobbled horse

_____   2. *ostracized* from society
      a. banished   b. beaten   c. walked   d. welcomed

_____   3. a shameless *sycophant*
      a. dreamer   b. alcoholic   c. romantic   d. toady

_____   4. clever *sophistry*
      a. embroidery   b. truth   c. teaching   d. fallacy

_____   5. seek *eldorado*
      a. physical comfort   b. delicious food   c. wealthy place
      d. death

_____   6. a *mercurial* disposition
      a. erratic   b. happy   c. sour   d. steady

_____   7. *tantalize* with promises
      a. frighten   b. tease   c. emboldon   d. discourage

_____   8. a lengthy *filibuster*
      a. entertainment   b. obstructive tactics   c. childhood
      d. voyage

_____   9. *galvanize* the crowd
      a. stir up   b. silence   c. insult   d. bore

_____   10. the *cynosure* of all eyes
      a. defect   b. attraction   c. sky-blue color
      d. cynicism

Quiz 10: True/False

In the space provided, write T if the definition of the numbered word is true or F if it is false.

		T or F
1. **Hobson's choice**	lack of alternative	_____
2. **tantalize**	tempt	_____
3. **mercurial**	unpredictable	_____
4. **ostracize**	exclude	_____
5. **filibuster**	obstruction	_____
6. **sophistry**	specious reasoning	_____
7. **cynosure**	sarcasm	_____
8. **eldorado**	Spain	_____

9. **galvanize**   pulverize   _____
10. **sycophant**   flatterer   _____

Lesson 6

Exotic words not only impress your listeners and readers; they also help to stretch your own imagination. Here are ten new ones to add to your growing vocabulary. Read through the etymologies and complete the two quizzes that follow.

1. **juggernaut** (jug′ər nôt′, -not′) Our modern word "juggernaut" comes from the Hindi name for a huge image of the god Vishnu, "Jagannath," at Puri, a city in Orissa, India. Each summer, the statue is moved to a new location a little less than a mile away from the old one. Early tourists to India brought back strange stories of worshipers throwing themselves under the wheels of the wagon carrying the idol. Since any shedding of blood in the presence of the god is sacrilege, what these travelers probably witnessed was a weary pilgrim being accidentally crushed to death. Thus, thanks to exaggeration and ignorance, "juggernaut" came to mean *blind and relentless self-sacrifice.* More often it is used to mean *any large, overpowering, or destructive force.*

2. **iconoclast** (ī kon′ə klast′) An "iconoclast" is *a person who attacks cherished beliefs or traditional institutions.* It is from the Greek "eikon," *image,* and "klastes," *breaker.* Although the contemporary usage is figurative, the word was originally used in a literal sense to describe the great controversy within the Christian church in the eighth century over religious images. One camp held that all visual representations should be destroyed because they encouraged idol worship; the other, that such artworks simply inspired the viewers to feel more religious. By the mid-eighth century, untold numbers of relics and images had been destroyed. The issue was not settled for nearly a century, when the images were restored to the church in Constantinople.

3. **laconic** (lə kon′ik) In Sparta, the capital of the ancient Greek region of Laconia, the children were trained in endurance, cunning, modesty, and self-restraint. From the terse style of speech and writing of the Laconians we derive the English word "laconic." Today the word retains this meaning, *expressing much in few words.*

4. **gamut** (gam′ət) Guido of Arezzo, one of the greatest musicians of medieval times, is credited with being first to use the lines of

the staff and the spaces between them. He used the Greek letter "gamma" for the lowest tone in the scale. This note was called "gamma ut." Contracted to "gamut," it then designated the entire scale. The word quickly took on a figurative as well as a literal sense. Today "gamut" is defined as *the entire scale or range*, as in the phrase "to run the gamut."

5. **guillotine** (gil′ə tēn′, gē′ə-) After the outbreak of the French Revolution, Dr. Joseph Ignace Guillotin became a member of the National Assembly. During an early debate, he proposed that future executions in France be conducted by a humane beheading machine that he had seen in operation in another country. His suggestion was received favorably; in 1791, after Dr. Guillotin had retired from public service, the machine that bears his name was designed by Antoine Louis and built by a German named Schmidt. The guillotine was first used in 1792 to behead a thief. At that time, the device was called a "Louisette" after its designer; but the public began calling it after Dr. Guillotin, the man who had first advocated its use. The device proved so popular among the masses, it seemed to demand more victims to satisfy their blood lust. During the subsequent Reign of Terror, more than 17,000 people were guillotined, including Robespierre, the author of the Terror.

6. **horde** (hôrd) Upon the death of Genghis Khan, his grandson Batu Khan led the Mongol invasion of Europe, cutting a merciless swath from Moscow to Hungary. At each post, Batu erected a sumptuous tent made of silk and leather. His followers called it the "sira ordu," *the silken camp.* In Czech and Polish the Turkic "ordu" was changed to "horda." The name came to be applied not only to Batu's tent but also to his entire Mongol army. Because of the terror they inspired across the land, "horde" eventually referred to any Tartar tribe. Today, it means *any large crowd; swarm.*

7. **lyceum** (lī sē′əm) The Lyceum was the shrine dedicated to Apollo by the Athenians. The name came from the Greek "Lykeion," meaning *Wolf Slayer,* a nickname of Apollo. The shrine was a favorite haunt of the Athenian philosophers, especially Aristotle, who taught his disciples while walking along its paths. Thus, the word "lyceum" came to mean *an institute for popular education, providing discussions, lectures, concerts, and so forth.* The term is most popular in New England, and is often used as a proper name for theaters.

8. **macabre** (mə kä′brə, -kä′bər) In modern usage, "macabre" means *gruesome and horrible; pertaining to death.* Its history is uncertain. However, most etymologists believe that the word's

use in the French phrase "Danse Macabre," *dance of Macabre,* a translation of Medieval Latin "chorea Macchabeorum," connects the word with the Maccabees, the leaders of the Jewish rebellion against Syria about 165 B.C., whose death as martyrs is vividly described in the Book of Maccabees (a part of the Apocrypha).

9. **gargantuan** (gär gan'choo ən) The sixteenth-century French writer François Rabelais created a giant he named "Gargantua" after a legendary giant of the Middle Ages. To fuel his enormous bulk—Gargantua rode on a horse as large as six elephants—he had to consume prodigious amounts of food and drink. Today we use the word "gargantuan" to mean *gigantic, enormous.*

10. **libertine** (lib'ər tēn') In ancient Rome, "libertinus" referred to a freed slave. Since those freed from slavery were unlikely to be strict observers of the laws that had enslaved them in the first place, "libertine" came to designate *a person who is morally or sexually unrestrained.*

Quiz 11: Matching

Match each of the numbered words with its closest synonym. Write your answer in the space provided.

1. **lyceum**	a. skeptic	_____
2. **libertine**	b. academy	_____
3. **iconoclast**	c. overpowering force	_____
4. **horde**	d. terse	_____
5. **gargantuan**	e. gruesome	_____
6. **laconic**	f. dissolute person	_____
7. **guillotine**	g. beheading machine	_____
8. **juggernaut**	h. entire range	_____
9. **gamut**	i. huge	_____
10. **macabre**	j. crowd	_____

Quiz 12: Defining Words

Define each of the following words

1. iconoclast _____

2. libertine _____

3. gamut _____

4. macabre _____

5. guillotine _____

6. laconic _____

7. gargantuan _____

8. lyceum _____

9. horde _____

10. juggernaut _____

Suggested Answers 1. a person who attacks cherished beliefs or traditional institutions 2. a rake 3. the entire scale or range 4. horrible, gruesome 5. a machine used to behead criminals 6. terse 7. enormous, colossal 8. institute for popular education 9. large group 10. an overpowering force

Lesson 7

The English language has adopted a prodigious number of words from unexpected sources, including literary works. Read through the histories of the ten unusual words that follow and then complete the quizzes.

1. **imp** (imp) In Old English, an "imp" was originally a young plant or seedling. Eventually, the term came to be used figuratively to indicate a descendant of a royal house, usually a male. Probably because of the behavior of such children, the word became synonymous with a young demon. Since the sixteenth century, the original meaning of "imp" as *scion* has been completely dropped, and the word is now used exclusively to mean *a little devil or demon, an evil spirit,* or *an urchin.*

2. **kaleidoscope** (kə līˊdə skōpˊ) Invented in 1816 by Scottish physicist Sir David Brewster, the "kaleidoscope" is a scientific toy constructed of a series of mirrors within a tube. When the tube is turned by hand, symmetrical, ever-changing patterns can be viewed through the eyepiece. Brewster named his toy from the Greek "kalos," *beautiful;* "eidos," *form;* and "skopos," *watcher.* In general, we use the term to mean *a continually shifting pattern or scene.*

3. **knave** (nāv) In Old English, the word "knave" (then spelled "cnafa") referred to *a male child, a boy.* It was later applied to *a boy or man employed as a servant.* Many of these boys had to be wily to survive their hard lot; thus the word gradually evolved to mean *a rogue* or *rascal.*

4. **Machiavellian** (makˊē ə velˊē ən) The Florentine political philosopher Nicolò Machiavelli (1469–1527) was a fervent supporter of a united Italy. Unfortunately, his methods for achieving his goals placed political expediency over morality. His masterpiece, *The Prince* (1513), advocated deception and hypocrisy

on the grounds that the end justifies the means. Therefore, the adjective "Machiavellian" means *unscrupulous, cunning,* and *deceptive in the pursuit of power.*

5. **indolence** (in′dl əns) Originally, "indolence" meant *indifference.* The word was used in that sense until the sixteenth century. Probably because indifference is frequently accompanied by an unwillingness to bestir oneself, the term has now come to mean *lazy* or *slothful.*

6. **incubus/succubus** (in′kyə bəs, ing′-; suk′yə bəs) In the Middle Ages, women were thought to give birth to witches after being visited in their sleep by an "incubus," or *evil male spirit.* The female version of this spirit, said to be the cause of nightmares, was a "succubus." Because the evil spirit pressed upon the sleeper's body and soul, the term "incubus" also means *something that oppresses like a nightmare.*

7. **hoyden** (hoid′n) A "hoyden" is *a boisterous, ill-bred girl; a tomboy.* The word is usually linked to the Dutch "heyden," meaning *a rustic person* or *rude peasant,* originally *a heathen* or *pagan,* and is related to the English word "heathen." At first in English the word meant *a rude, boorish man,* but beginning in the 1600s it was applied to girls in the sense of *a tomboy.* How the change came about is uncertain.

8. **Faustian** (fou′stē ən) The story of Dr. Faustus, a medieval alchemist or magician who sold his soul to the devil in exchange for knowledge and power, has its roots in German legend. Its most famous interpretations are to be found in the works of the English dramatist Christopher Marlowe (c. 1558) and the German poet Goethe (1770 and 1831), but the theme has proved so enduring that it found a new popularity in the mid-twentieth-century Broadway musical *Damn Yankees,* about a ballplayer willing to trade his soul for a pennant win over the then-indomitable New York Yankees. A "Faustian" bargain, therefore, is one *sacrificing spiritual values for power, knowledge, or material gain.* The word may also mean *characterized by spiritual dissatisfaction or torment,* or *obsessed with a hunger for knowledge or mastery.*

9. **macadam** (mə kad′əm) While experimenting with methods of improving road construction, John McAdam, a Scotsman, concluded that the prevailing practice of placing a base of large stones under a layer of small stones was unnecessary. As surveyor-general for the roads of Bristol, England, in the early nineteenth century, McAdam built roads using only six to ten inches of small crushed stones, thereby eliminating the cost of

constructing the base. Not only were the results impressive, the savings were so remarkable that his idea soon spread to other countries. McAdam's experiments led to our use of the term "macadam" for *a road or pavement* of compacted crushed stones, usually bound with asphalt or tar.

10. **albatross** (al′bə trôs′) Generations of students have enjoyed "The Rime of the Ancient Mariner" by Samuel Taylor Coleridge (1772–1834). One of the seminal works of the Romantic movement in England, this haunting, dreamlike poem tells the tale of a sailor forced by his shipmates to wear suspended from his neck the corpse of the albatross, or frigate bird, that he carelessly shot down with his cross-bow. Since seamen traditionally regarded the bird as a lucky omen, they attributed the many disasters that befell the ship thereafter to the man who killed it. The poem is so famous and beloved that the word "albatross" has come to mean *a seemingly inescapable moral or emotional burden, as of guilt or responsibility; a burden that impedes action or progress.*

Quiz 13: True/False

In the space provided, write T if the definition of the numbered word is true or F if it is false.

			T or F
1.	**incubus**	evil spirit	_____
2.	**hoyden**	howl	_____
3.	**Faustian**	swift	_____
4.	**macadam**	raincoat	_____
5.	**albatross**	reward	_____
6.	**imp**	male servant	_____
7.	**Machiavellian**	principled	_____
8.	**kaleidoscope**	optical toy	_____
9.	**indolence**	laziness	_____
10.	**knave**	dishonest fellow	_____

Quiz 14: Matching

Select the best definition for each numbered word. Write your answer in the space provided.

1.	**macadam**	a. burden	_____
2.	**hoyden**	b. little mischiefmaker	_____
3.	**Faustian**	c. laziness	_____
4.	**albatross**	d. optical toy	_____

5. Machiavellian   e. pavement   _____
6. imp   f. rogue   _____
7. kaleidoscope   g. evil spirit   _____
8. knave   h. materialistic   _____
9. indolence   i. sly and crafty   _____
10. incubus   j. tomboy   _____

Lesson 8

Our language is not only a record of our past; it is also a living organism that morphs over time to accommodate new usages. Follow the evolution of these ten words by studying their histories; then complete the quizzes that follow.

1. **maelstrom** (mâl'strəm) The word's figurative meaning, *a restless, disordered state of affairs,* is derived from its literal one. Today's meaning comes from "Maelstrom," the name of a strong tidal current off the coast of Norway. The current creates a powerful whirlpool because of its configuration. According to legend, the current was once so strong that it could sink any vessel that ventured near it.

2. **insolent** (in'sə lənt) The word comes from the Latin "insolentem," which literally meant *not according to custom.* Since those who violate custom are likely to offend, "insolent" evolved to imply that the person was also vain and conceited. From this meaning we derive our present usage, *contemptuously rude or impertinent in speech or behavior.*

3. **interloper** (in'tər lō'pər) The word "interloper" was used in the late sixteenth century to describe Spanish traders who carved out for themselves a piece of the successful trade the British had established with the Russians. The word was formed on the analogy of "landloper," meaning *one who trespasses on another's land,* from a Dutch word literally meaning *land runner.* Although the dispute over the Spanish intrusion was settled within a few years, the word remained in use to mean *a person who intrudes into some region or field of trade without a proper license; one who thrusts himself or herself into the affairs of others.*

4. **halcyon** (hal'sē ən) According to classical mythology, the demigod Halcyone threw herself into the sea when she saw the drowned body of her beloved mortal husband. After her tragic death, the gods changed Halcyone and her husband into birds, which they called "halcyons," our present-day kingfishers. The Greeks believed the sea calmed as the birds built their nests

and hatched their eggs upon its waves during the seven days before and after the winter solstice. This period came to be known as "halcyon days." The adjective is now used to mean *calm, peaceful, prosperous,* or *joyful.*

5. **hector** (hek′tər) Hector was a great Trojan hero, son of King Priam. As Homer recounts in the *Iliad,* Hector took advantage of his enemy Achilles's departure from the Greek camp to drive the Greeks back to their ships and slay Achilles's dearest friend, Patroclus. To the Romans, who regarded themselves as descendants of the Trojans, Hector was a symbol of courage. But in the seventeenth century, the name was applied to the gangs of bullies who terrorized anyone who ventured into the back streets of London. It is to their transgressions that we owe the present use of "hector," *to harass or persecute.*

6. **helpmeet** (help′mēt′) This synonym for *helpmate, companion, wife,* or *husband* is the result of a misunderstanding. The word comes from Genesis 2:18, "And the Lord God said, It is not good that the man should be alone; I will make him an help meet for him." In this passage, "meet" means *proper* or *appropriate,* but the two words came to be read as one, resulting in the word's current spelling.

7. **hermetic** (hûr met′ik) The Greeks linked the Egyptian god Thoth with Hermes, calling him "Hermes Trismegistus," Hermes Three-Times Greatest. He was accepted as the author of the books that made up the sum of Egyptian learning, called the "Hermetic Books." Since these forty-two works largely concerned the occult sciences, "hermetic" came to mean *secret,* and in a later usage, *made airtight by fusion or sealing.*

8. **intransigent** (in tran′si jənt) When Amadeus, the son of Victor Emmanuel II of Italy, was forced to abdicate the throne of Spain in 1873, those favoring a republic attempted to establish a political party. This group was called in Spanish "los intransigentes" (from "in," *not* and "transigente," *compromising*) because they could not come to terms with the other political parties. The term passed into English as "intransigent." Today the word retains the same meaning: *uncompromising* or *inflexible.*

9. **jitney** (jit′nē) The origin of this term has long baffled etymologists. The word first appeared in American usage in the first decade of the twentieth century as a slang term for a nickel. It then became associated with the public motor vehicles whose fare was five cents. Some authorities have theorized that the term is a corruption of "jeton," the French word for *token.*

Today a "jitney" is *a small passenger bus following a regular route at varying hours.*

10. **junket** (jung'kit) At first, the word referred to a basket of woven reeds used for carrying fish; it is ultimately derived from Latin "juncus," *reed.* Then the basket was used to prepare cheese, which in turn came to be called "junket." Since the basket also suggested the food it could carry, "junket" later evolved to mean *a great feast.* Today we use the term in closely related meanings: *a sweet custard-like food* or *flavored milk curdled with rennet* or *a pleasure excursion.*

Quiz 15: Matching

Match each numbered word with its closest synonym. Write your answer in the space provided.

1. **halcyon**	a. tightly sealed	_____
2. **intransigent**	b. intruder	_____
3. **jitney**	c. impertinent	_____
4. **maelstrom**	d. peaceful	_____
5. **junket**	e. inflexible	_____
6. **hector**	f. small bus	_____
7. **insolent**	g. companion	_____
8. **hermetic**	h. pleasure trip	_____
9. **interloper**	i. harass	_____
10. **helpmeet**	j. disorder	_____

Quiz 16: True/False

In the space provided, write T if the definition of the numbered word is true or F if it is false.

		T or F
1. **halcyon**	calm	_____
2. **jitney**	juggler	_____
3. **maelstrom**	masculine	_____
4. **intransigent**	uncompromising	_____
5. **insolent**	rude	_____
6. **interloper**	welcome guest	_____
7. **junket**	refuse	_____
8. **hector**	helper	_____
9. **hermetic**	airtight	_____
10. **helpmeet**	newcomer	_____

Lesson 9

Once you know the origins of these ten words, it should be easier to remember their current meanings. Complete the quizzes to reinforce your memory.

1. **Olympian** (ə lim'pē ən) In Greek mythology, the snow-topped summit of Olympus, a mountain range in northern Greece, eclipsed from the sight of mortal humans by a perpetual cloud cover, was the dwelling place of the gods. The divine family of twelve deities was headed by the all-powerful Zeus and his queen Hera. Poseidon ruled the sea and Hades the underworld. Ares, Hermes, Apollo, Hephaestus, Athena, Aphrodite, Artemis, and Dionysus occupied the lower echelons of the pantheon. Our word "Olympian," meaning *majestic; aloof; disdainful; haughty,* reflects the remote grandeur of the far-removed mountain abode of these immortal beings.

2. **Pollyanna** (pol'ē an'ə) Pollyanna, the child heroine created by the U.S. writer Eleanor Porter (1868–1920), was immortalized on the silver screen in 1960 by the young Hayley Mills. An orphan who comes to live with her strict, dour but very rich and influential aunt, the high-spirited girl gradually wins over the unhappy townspeople and even her mean old aunt with her ingenuous charm and cheerful outlook. Since many adult readers tend to find the story somewhat treacly, a "Pollyanna" now means *an excessively or blindly optimistic person.*

3. **garret** (gar'it) Originally, the French word "garite" referred to a watchtower from which a sentry could look out for approaching enemies. Among the linguistic innovations the Normans brought when they conquered England was the word "garite." In England the word came to mean a *loft* or *attic,* and its spelling was altered to "garret."

4. **lilliputian** (lil'i pyoo'shən) *Gulliver's Travels,* the enduring masterpiece by Jonathan Swift (1667–1745), is a scathing satire on politics and society that purports to be an account of the voyages of a naive traveler named Lemuel Gulliver to Brobdinag, a land of giants, and Lilliput, a country inhabited by people who measure around six inches tall. In honor of this Swiftian work, we use the word "lilliputian" to refer first of all to a person or thing that is *extremely small* but also one that is *narrow; petty; trivial.*

5. **gazette** (gə zet') In the beginning of the sixteenth century, Venetians circulated a small tin coin of little value they called a

"gazzetta," a diminutive of the word "gaza," magpie. Soon after, the government began to print official bulletins with news of battles, elections, and so forth. Because the cost of the newspaper was one gazzetta, the leaflet itself eventually came to be called a "gazzetta." By the end of the century, the term was used in England as well. The present spelling is the result of French influence. Today a "gazette" refers to *a newspaper* or *official government journal.*

6. **martinet** (mär'tn et', mär'tn et') In a move to improve his army, in 1660 Louis XIV hired Colonel Jean Martinet, a successful infantry leader, to devise a drill for France's soldiers. Martinet drilled his soldiers to such exacting standards that his name came to be applied to any officer intent on maintaining military discipline or precision. Thus, in English, a "martinet" is *a strict disciplinarian, especially a military one.* Interestingly, in France, Martinet's name acquired no such negative connotation.

7. **gorgon** (gôr'gən) The name comes from the Greek myth of the three monstrous sisters who inhabited the region of Night. Together they were known as the Gorgons; their individual names were Stheno, Euryale, and Medusa. Little has been written about the first two. Medusa was the most hideous and dangerous; her appearance, with her head of writhing serpents, was so ghastly that anyone who looked directly at her was turned to stone. Therefore, the current meaning of "gorgon" is *a mean or repulsive woman.*

8. **maudlin** (môd'lin) This word, meaning *tearfully or weakly emotional,* comes from the miracle plays of the Middle Ages. Although these plays depicted many of the Biblical miracles, the most popular theme was the life of Mary Magdalene. The English pronounced her name "maudlin," and since most of the scenes in which she appeared were tearful, this pronunciation of her name became associated with mawkish sentimentality.

9. **meander** (mē an'dər) In ancient times, the Menderes River in western Turkey was so remarkable for its twisting path that its Greek name, "Maiandros," came to mean *a winding.* In Latin this word was spelled "maeander," hence English "meander," used mainly as a verb and meaning *to proceed by a winding or indirect course.*

10. **gossamer** (gos'ə mər) In early times, November was a time of feasting and merrymaking in Germany. The time-honored meal was roast goose. So many geese were eaten that the month came to be called "Gänsemonat," *goose month.* The term traveled to England but in the course of migration, it became associated

with the period of unseasonably warm autumn weather we now call "Indian summer." During the warm spell, large cobwebs are found draped in the grass or suspended in the air. These delicate, airy webs, which we call "gossamer," are generally believed to have taken their name from "goose summer," when their appearance was most noticeable. We now define "gossamer" as *something fine, filmy, or light*. It also means *thin and light*.

Quiz 17: Sentence Completion

Complete each sentence with the appropriate word from the following list.

gossamer   gorgon   maudlin
Pollyanna   garret   meander
lilliputian   Olympian   gazette
martinet

1. It is pleasant to _____ slowly down picturesque country roads on crisp autumn afternoons.
2. The movie was so _____ that I was still crying when the closing credits began to roll.
3. The teacher was such a _____ that his students soon rebelled fiercely against his strict regulations.
4. She was charmed by the _____ furnishings of the dollhouse.
5. Even in the worst of times, he remained a _____.
6. Many budding artists have romantic fantasies about living in a wretched _____ and starving for the sake of their art.
7. His _____ manner intimidated the other actors.
8. The _____ cobwebs shredded at the slightest touch.
9. Since the daily _____ has excellent coverage of local sports, cultural events, and regional news, we tend to overlook its weak coverage of international events.
10. The gossip columnist was so mean and ugly that her victims referred to her as a _____.

Quiz 18: Definitions

Select the correct definition for each numbered word. Write your answer in the space provided.

_____   1. Olympian
            a. majestic   b. athletic   c. mountainous   d. abject
_____   2. meander
            a. moan   b. ramble   c. strike back   d. starve

_____   3. gorgon
    a. misunderstood person   b. foregone conclusion
    c. hideous monster   d. midget

_____   4. Pollyanna
    a. doll   b. traitor   c. pessimist   d. optimist

_____   5. lilliputian
    a. flowering plant   b. giant   c. great thinker
    d. pygmy

_____   6. garret
    a. basement   b. attic   c. garage   d. unsuccessful artist

_____   7. maudlin
    a. warlike   b. married   c. mawkish   d. intense

_____   8. martinet
    a. strict disciplinarian   b. facile problem   c. hawk
    d. musical instrument

_____   9. gazette
    a. journal   b. gazebo   c. silver coin   d. book of maps

_____   10. gossamer
    a. variety of goose   b. grasp   c. flimsy material
    d. idle talk

Lesson 10

Learning the backgrounds of the following ten words will give you an edge in recalling their meanings and using them in your conversation or writing. When you are finished reading, complete the two quizzes that follow.

1. **meerschaum** (mēr′shəm, -shôm) Since it is white and soft and often found along seashores, ancient people believed this white claylike mineral was foam from the ocean turned into stone. As a result, in all languages it was called "sea foam." It was of little use until German artisans began to carve it into pipes. As it absorbs the nicotine from the tobacco, it acquires a deep honey color. Because the Germans were the first to find a use for it, the German name stuck: "meer," *sea;* "schaum," *foam.* In English "meerschaum" often means *a tobacco pipe with a bowl made of meerschaum* (the mineral).

2. **toady** (tō′dē) In the seventeenth century, people believed that toads were poisonous, and anyone who mistakenly ate a toad's leg instead of a frog's leg would die. Rather than swear off frogs' legs, people sought a cure for the fatal food poisoning. Charlatans would sometimes hire an accomplice who would

pretend to eat a toad, at which point his employer would whip out his instant remedy and "save" his helper's life. For his duties, the helper came to be called a "toad-eater." Since anyone who would consume anything as disgusting as a toad must be completely under his master's thumb, "toad-eater" or "toady" became the term for *an obsequious sycophant; a fawning flatterer.*

3. **gregarious** (gri gâr'ē əs) The Latin term for a herd of animals is "grex." Because a group of people banded together in military formation resembles a herd of animals, the word "grex" was applied to people as well as animals. The way the people grouped together was called "gregarius," *like a herd.* The word has come down to us as "gregarious," meaning *friendly* or *fond of the company of others.*

4. **miscreant** (mis'krē ənt) The word's source, the Old French "mes," *wrongly,* and "creant," *believing,* tells us that "miscreant" was originally used to describe a heretic. The word has evolved over the centuries, however, to refer to *a base, villainous, or depraved person.*

5. **sinecure** (sī'ni kyo͝or', sin'i-) "Sinecure," a word meaning *an office or position requiring little or no work, especially one yielding profitable returns,* originally began as a church term, from the Latin "beneficium sine cura," *a benefice without care.* It referred to the practice of rewarding a church rector by giving him a parish for which he had no actual responsibilities. The real work was carried on by a vicar, but his absent superior received the higher recompense. Although the church practice was abolished in the mid-nineteenth century, the term is often used today in a political context.

6. **mecca** (mek'ə) The prophet Muhammad (570?–632), the founder and great lawgiver of Islam, was born to a wealthy family in the city of Mecca, in Saudi Arabia, long a center of pagan religious sects. At the age of forty, he was selected by Allah to be the Arabian prophet of true religion and the successor of Jesus Christ; many of his revelations were later collected in the Koran. The prophet's flight, or *hegira,* from Mecca under the threat of a murder plot in the year 622 is now considered the beginning of the Muslim era, the date from which the calendar is calculated. Muhammad spent the rest of his life in Medina, but captured Mecca in a bloodless battle in 630, to complete his conquest of Arabia. Each of the 1.1 billion Muslims in the world is required to pray five times a day while facing Mecca, regarded as the holiest city of Islam. No non-Muslims are per-

mitted to enter the city, and every one of the faithful who is financially able is required to make the annual *hajj,* or pilgrimage, to Mecca at least once.

7. **namby-pamby** (nam'bē pam'bē) The term "namby-pamby," used to describe anything *weakly sentimental, pretentious, or affected,* comes from Henry Carey's parody of Ambrose Philips's sentimental children's poems. Carey titled his parody "Namby Pamby," taking the "namby" from the diminutive of "Ambrose" and using the first letter of his surname, "P," for the alliteration. Following a bitter quarrel with Philips, Alexander Pope seized upon Carey's parody in the second edition of his *Dunciad* in 1733. Through the popularity of Pope's poem, the term "namby-pamby" passed into general usage.

8. **mountebank** (moun'tə bangk') During the Middle Ages, Italians conducted their banking in the streets, setting up business on convenient benches. In fact, the Italian word "banca" has given us our word "bank." People with less honest intentions realized that it would be relatively easy to cheat the people who assembled around these benches. To attract a crowd, these con men often worked with jugglers, clowns, rope dancers, or singers. Since they always worked around a bench, they were known as "montimbancos." Although the word was Anglicized to "mountebank," it still refers to *a huckster or charlatan who sells quack medicines from a platform in a public place, appealing to his audience by using tricks, storytelling, and so forth.*

9. **Svengali** (sven gä'lē) In one of his most memorable film roles, the great matinee idol John Barrymore steals the show as the evil hypnotist Svengali, a mad genius whose intense, piercing gaze is irresistible to the innocent artist's model Trilby, the heroine of the novel published in 1894 by George Du Maurier. Under his tutelage, Trilby is transformed into a great singer. Barrymore appears as a ghoulish, bearded creature dressed in disheveled clothing like a sort of dissolute monk. The 1931 film, of course, was called *Svengali,* not (like the original novel) *Trilby.* His is the image we summon up when we think of a "Svengali," *a person who completely dominates another, usually with evil or selfish motives.*

10. **mugwump** (mug'wump') This word entered the English language in a most curious fashion. In the mid-1600s, the clergyman John Eliot, known as the Apostle to the Indians, translated the Bible into the Algonquian language. When he came to the thirty-sixth chapter of Genesis, he had no word for "duke," so he used "mugquomp," an Algonquian term for *chief* or *great man.* Historians of the language theorize that the term might

already have been in circulation at that time, but they know for certain that by 1884 it was in fairly general use. In the presidential election that year, a group of Republicans threw their support to Grover Cleveland rather than to the party's nominee, James G. Blaine. The newspapers scorned the renegade Republicans as "mugwumps," those who thought themselves too good to vote for Blaine. The scorned Republicans got the last word when they adopted the same term to describe themselves, saying they were independent men proud to call themselves "mugwumps," or *great men.* Today we use the term "mugwump" to describe *a person who takes an independent position* or *one who is neutral on a controversial issue.*

Quiz 19: True/False

In the space provided, write T if the definition of the numbered word is true or F if it is false.

		T or F
1. **toady**	sycophant	_____
2. **miscreant**	sociable person	_____
3. **mugwump**	political ally	_____
4. **namby-pamby**	cereal	_____
5. **gregarious**	affable	_____
6. **Svengali**	politician	_____
7. **mountebank**	impostor	_____
8. **meerschaum**	mixup	_____
9. **mecca**	shrine	_____
10. **sinecure**	sincere	_____

Quiz 20: Matching

Match each of the following numbered words with its closest synonym. Write your answer in the space provided.

1. **mountebank**	a. easy job	_____
2. **gregarious**	b. knave	_____
3. **mecca**	c. charlatan	_____
4. **toady**	d. master	_____
5. **miscreant**	e. sociable	_____
6. **mugwump**	f. independent	_____
7. **namby-pamby**	g. sycophant	_____
8. **sinecure**	h. pipe	_____
9. **Svengali**	i. place of pilgrimage	_____
10. **meerschaum**	j. sentimental	_____

Lesson 11

Here are ten new words to enhance your word power. When you have finished reading the history of each word, complete the quizzes.

1. **oscillate** (os′ə lāt′) In ancient Rome, the grape growers hung little images with the face of Bacchus, the god of wine, on their vines. Since the Latin word for face is "os," a little face would be called an "oscillum." Because the images swung in the wind, some students of language concluded that the Latin verb "oscillare" came from a description of this motion. Most scholars have declined to make this connection, saying only that our present word "oscillate," *to swing to and fro,* is derived from Latin "oscillare," *to swing,* which in turn comes from "oscillum," *a swing.*

2. **nabob** (nā′bob) The Mogul emperors, who ruled India from the sixteenth until the middle of the nineteenth century, delegated authority to men who acted as governors of various parts of India. To the native Indians, such a ruler was known as a "nawwab," *deputy.* The word was changed by the Europeans into "nabob." The nabobs were supposed to tithe money to the central government, but some of the nabobs withheld the money, and thereby became enormously wealthy. From their fortunes came the European custom of using the word "nabob" to refer to a person, especially a European, who had attained great wealth in India or another country of the East. The usage spread to England, and today we use the term to describe *any very wealthy or powerful person.*

3. **pander** (pan′dər) "Pander," *to act as a go-between in amorous intrigues* or *to act as a pimp* or *procurer* or *to cater basely,* comes from the medieval story of Troilus and Cressida. In his retelling, Chaucer describes how the love-stricken Troilus calls upon his friend Pandarus, kin to Cressida, to aid him in his quest for her love. Much of Chaucer's tale is devoted to the different means used by Pandarus to help Troilus win his love. Shakespeare later recycled the same legend. As the story gained in popularity the name "Pandarus" was changed in English to "pandare" and then to "pander." The noun now has the negative connotation of *pimp* or *procurer for illicit sexual intercourse.*

4. **pedagogue** (ped′ə gog′, -gôg′) Wealthy Greek families kept a special slave to supervise their sons. The slave's responsibilities included accompanying the boys as they traveled to and from

school and walked in the public streets. To describe a slave's chores, the Greeks coined the term "paidagogos," *a leader of boys.* Occasionally, when the slave was an educated man captured in warfare and sold into slavery, the slave also tutored his charges. From the Greek word we derived the English "pedagogue," *teacher* or *educator.*

5. **quack** (kwak) Noticing how the raucous shouts of the charlatans selling useless concoctions sounded like the strident quacks of ducks, the sixteenth-century Dutch called these charlatans "quacksalvers"—literally, *ducks quacking over their salves.* The term quickly spread through Europe. The English shortened it to "quack," and used it to describe *any fraudulent or ignorant pretender to medical skills,* the meaning we retain today.

6. **nepotism** (nep'ə tiz'əm) This word for *patronage bestowed or favoritism shown on the basis of family relationships,* as in business or politics, can be traced to the popes of the fifteenth and sixteenth centuries. To increase their power, these men surrounded themselves with people they knew would be loyal—members of their own family. Among the most popular candidates were the popes' own illegitimate sons, called "nephews," from the Latin "nepos," *a descendant,* as a mark of respect. Eventually the term "nepotism" came to mean favoritism to all family members, not just nephews.

7. **pompadour** (pom'pə dôr', -dŏor') Sheltered by a wealthy family and educated as though she were their own daughter, at twenty the exquisite Jeanne Antoinette Poisson Le Normant d'Étioles married her protector's nephew and began her reign over the world of Parisian fashion. Soon after, King Louis XV took her as his mistress, established her at the court of Versailles, and gave her the estate of Pompadour. The Marquise de Pompadour created a large and high-swept hairstyle memorialized by her name. The upswept style is still known by her name whether it is used to describe a man's or women's hairdo.

8. **nostrum** (nos'trəm) The word "nostrum," *a patent or quack medicine,* became current around the time of the Great Plague in the mid-seventeenth century. Doctors were helpless to combat the disease, so charlatans and quacks flooded the market with their own "secret"—and useless—concoctions. To make their medicines seem more effective, they labeled them with the Latin word "nostrum." The term came to be used as a general word for any quack medicine. Ironically, "nostrum" means *our own,* as in "nostrum remedium," *our own remedy;* thus it makes no claims at all for the remedy's effectiveness.

9. **narcissism** (när′sə siz′əm) The word "narcissism," *inordinate fascination with oneself,* comes from the Greek myth of Narcissus. According to one version of the legend, an exceptionally handsome young man fell in love with his own image reflected in a pool. When he tried to embrace his image, he drowned. According to another version, Narcissus fell in love with his identical twin sister. After her death, he sat and stared at his own reflection in the pool until he died from grief.

10. **nepenthe** (ni pen′thē) According to Greek legend, when Paris kidnapped Helen and took her to Troy, he wanted her to forget her previous life. In Homer's version of the tale, Paris gave Helen a drug thought to cause loss of memory. The drug was called "nepenthes." The word has come down to us with its meaning intact: *anything inducing a pleasurable sensation of forgetfulness.*

Quiz 21: True/False

In the space provided, write T if the definition of the numbered word is true or F if it is false.

		T or F
1. **nepenthe**	remembrance	_____
2. **nepotism**	impartiality	_____
3. **pander**	procurer	_____
4. **pompadour**	crewcut	_____
5. **oscillate**	swing	_____
6. **pedagogue**	teacher	_____
7. **narcissism**	self-love	_____
8. **nabob**	pauper	_____
9. **nostrum**	patent medicine	_____
10. **quack**	expert	_____

Quiz 22: Defining Words

Define each of the following words.

1. pompadour _____

2. nepenthe _____

3. oscillate _____

4. nostrum _____

5. quack _____

6. nabob _____

7. pander _____

8. nepotism _____

9. pedagogue _____

10. narcissism _____

Suggested Answers   1. upswept hairstyle 2. something inducing forgetfulness 3. to swing back and forth 4. patent or useless remedy 5. medical charlatan 6. wealthy, powerful person 7. pimp or procurer 8. patronage given to family members 9. teacher 10. excessive self-love

Lesson 12

Each of these ten words beginning with the letter "p" has a particularly captivating tale behind it. Read the stories, then complete the two quizzes at the end of the lesson.

1. **palaver** (pə lav′ər, -lä′vər) The word "palaver" derives ultimately from the Greek word "parabola," *comparison,* literally *a placing beside.* From this came English "parable," *a story that makes comparisons.* In Latin the word came to mean *speech, talk, word.* Later, Portuguese traders carried the term to Africa in the form "palavra" and used it to refer to the long talks with native chiefs required by local custom. English traders picked up the word in the eighteenth century, spelling it as we do today. The word retains its last meaning, *a long parley, especially one with people indigenous to a region* or *profuse, idle talk.*

2. **pharisaic** (far′ə sā′ik) The Pharisees were one of the two great Jewish sects of the Old Testament; their opponents were known as Sadducees. The Pharisees placed great emphasis on the strict observance of religious law, rites, and ceremonies. By the time of Jesus, many of the common people had become alienated from the Pharisees, who, according to the Gospels, "preach but do not practice." The word "pharisaic" reflects this New Testament view of the Pharisees and now means *practicing external ceremonies without regard to the spirit; hypocritical.*

3. **pariah** (pə rī′ə) The term "pariah," *an outcast,* comes from the name of one of the lowest castes in India. Composed of agricultural laborers and household servants, it is not the lowest caste, but its members are still considered untouchable by the Brahmans. The British used the term "pariah" for anyone of low social standing. The term "pariah" now is used for *any outcast among his or her own people.*

4. **pecuniary** (pi kyoo′nē er′ē) The Romans measured a man's worth

by the number of animals he kept on his farm. They adapted the Latin word for a farm animal, "pecu," to refer to individual wealth. But as people acquired new ways of measuring wealth, such as money and land, the Roman word evolved into "pecunia," which referred most specifically to money. From this came the adjective "pecuniary," *pertaining to or consisting of money.*

5. **phantasmagoria** (fan taz′mə gôr′ē ə) In the early years of the nineteenth century, an inventor named Philipstal created a wondrous device for producing optical illusions. By projecting colored slides onto a thin silk screen, Philipstal made his spectral images appear to move. Today, of course, we take such motion-picture illusions for granted, but in the age of the magic lantern, such visions were marvelous indeed. Philipstal named his invention "phantasmagoria," which we now apply to *a shifting series of phantasms or deceptive appearances, as in a dream.*

6. **pooh-bah** (pōō′bä′) *The Mikado* (1885) is probably the most popular light opera written by the collaborative team of Gilbert and Sullivan. Ostensibly the story of the thwarted love of Nanki-Poo for the beauteous Yum-Yum, set at the imperial court of Japan, it is actually an incisive satire on the society of the Victorian era. The absurd character of the overbearing high official known as Pooh-Bah has given us this generic term meaning *a person who holds several positions at once* or—more pungently—*any pompous, self-important person.*

7. **precipitate** (pri sip′i tāt′) The word "precipitate" is based on the Latin root "caput," meaning *head.* In fact, the word was first used to apply to those who had been executed or killed themselves by being hurled or jumping headlong from a "precipice" or high place. Later, the word came to mean *to rush headlong.* From this has come today's meaning, *to hasten the occurrence of; to bring about prematurely.*

8. **precocious** (pri kō′shəs) To the Romans, the Latin word "praecox," the source of English "precocious," was a culinary term meaning *precooked.* In time, however, its meaning was extended to *acting prematurely.* It is this later meaning of "precocious" that we use today, *unusually advanced in development, especially mental development.*

9. **pretext** (prē′tekst) "Pretext" comes from the Latin word "praetexta," meaning *an ornament,* such as the purple markings on a toga denoting rank. In addition to its literal sense, however, the word carried the connotation of something to cloak one's true

identity. We have retained only the word's figurative meaning, *something that is put forward to conceal a true purpose or object, an ostensible reason.*

10. **procrustean** (prō krus'tē ən) According to one version of the Greek myth, Procrustes was a bandit who made his living way-laying unsuspecting travelers. He tied everyone who fell into his grasp to an iron bed. If they were longer than the bed, he cut short their legs to make their bodies fit; if they were shorter, he stretched their bodies until they fit tightly. Hence, "pro-crustean" means *tending to produce conformity through violent or arbitrary means.*

Quiz 23: True/False

In the space provided, write T if the definition of the numbered word is true or F if it is false.

			T or F
1.	procrustean	marine life	_____
2.	pecuniary	picayune	_____
3.	precipitate	play	_____
4.	pretext	falsification	_____
5.	pariah	outcast	_____
6.	pooh-bah	denunciation	_____
7.	palaver	serving tray	_____
8.	precocious	advanced	_____
9.	pharisaic	hypocritical	_____
10.	phantasmagoria	illusions	_____

Quiz 24: Matching

Match each of the following numbered words with its closest syn-onym. Write your answer in the space provided.

1.	pooh-bah	a. excuse	_____
2.	palaver	b. producing conformity by violent means	_____
3.	pecuniary	c. pompous fool	_____
4.	phantasmagoria	d. fantasy	_____
5.	pretext	e. expedite	_____
6.	precocious	f. idle chatter	_____
7.	precipitate	g. advanced	_____
8.	pariah	h. outcast	_____
9.	procrustean	i. hypocritical	_____
10.	pharisaic	j. monetary	_____

Lesson 13

Here is a *potpourri* or *ollo* or *gallimaufry* (all meaning "mixed bag") of ten more fascinating words. Read through the interesting stories behind them. Then work through the two quizzes to see how many of the words you can use correctly.

1. **proletariat** (prō′li tär′ē ət) "Proletariat" derives from the Latin "proletarius," *a Roman freeman who lacked property and money.* The word came from "proles," *offspring, children.* Although the freemen had the vote, many wealthy Romans despised them, saying they were useful only to have children. They called them "proletarii," *producers of children.* Karl Marx picked up the word in the mid-nineteenth century as a label for the lower-class working people of his age. "Proletariat" retains the same meaning today: *members of the working class, especially those who do not possess capital and must sell their labor to survive.*

2. **Arcadian** (är kā′dē ən) The residents of landlocked Arcadia, in ancient Greece, did not venture to other lands. As a result, they maintained traditional ways and lived what others imagined to be a simpler life. Ancient classical poets made "Arcadia" a symbol for a land of pastoral happiness. In the sixteenth century, English poet Sir Philip Sidney imagined a bucolic land he called "Arcadia." The word has retained this meaning, and today we consider residents of an "Arcadian" place to be *rustic, simple, and innocent.*

3. **rake** (rāk) "Rake," meaning *a dissolute person, especially a man,* was originally "rakehell." In the sixteenth century, this colorful term was used to describe a person so dissipated that he would "rake hell" to find his pleasures. "Rakehell" is now considered a somewhat archaic term to describe such roués; "rake" is the more common word.

4. **pygmy** (pig′mē) The ancient Greeks were entranced by stories of a tribe of dwarfs in the Upper Nile who were so small that they could be swallowed by cranes. To describe these tiny people, the Greeks used the word "pygmaios," which also referred to the distance on a person's arm from the elbow to the knuckles. The word became English "pygmy," *a tiny person or thing; a person or thing of small importance.*

5. **sardonic** (sär don′ik) The ancient Greeks described a plant on the island of Sardinia whose flesh, if eaten, caused the victim's face to become grotesquely convulsed, as if in scornful laughter. The Greek name for Sardinia was "Sardos"; therefore, "sardonios" came to refer to any mocking laughter. The English word

eventually became "sardonic," *characterized by bitter irony or scornful derision.*

6. **tartar** (tär′tər) The fierce Genghis Khan and his successors led an army of bloodthirsty warriors, including the Ta-ta Mongols, in a series of conquests throughout Asia and into Europe. Their name, "Tartar" or "Tatar," became closely associated with brutal massacres. Today the word "tartar" refers to *a savage, ill-tempered, or intractable person.*

7. **argosy** (är′gə sē) In the Middle Ages, cities on the Mediterranean coast maintained large fleets to ship goods around the known world. Ragusa was a Sicilian city well known for its large ships, called "ragusea." In English, the initial two letters became switched, creating "argusea." From there it was a short step to "argosy," *a large merchant ship, especially one with a rich cargo.* Because of Ragusa's wealth, the word "argosy" also came to mean *an opulent supply or collection.*

8. **Balkanize** (bôl′kə nīz′) After centuries of war, in 1912 the Balkan nations united to conquer the Turks and divide the spoils among themselves. The following year, however, the Balkan nations quarreled over how to divide their booty and began to fight among themselves. From this experience comes the verb "Balkanize," *to divide a country or territory into small, quarrelsome, ineffectual states.* The term has taken on new pungency since the breakup of the former Yugoslavia in the 1990s.

9. **Rabelaisian** (rab′ə lā′zē ən, -zhən) A classic old *New Yorker* cartoon shows two laughing men in Renaissance dress, one of whom is saying, "Ho ho ho! Monsieur Rabelais, there is just no word to describe that earthy humor of yours!" The joke is that there *is* one and only one such word, and that word is "Rabelaisian." The masterpiece of François Rabelais, *Gargantua and Pantagruel,* contains serious discussions of education, politics, and philosophy, but it is most remarkable for its broad, ribald, often scatalogical humor—a humor unique in world literature for its daring and immodest hilarity that has given birth to the word "Rabelaisian," meaning *coarsely humorous.*

10. **hegira** (hi jī′rə, hej′ər ə) Around the year 600, the prophet Muhammad began to preach the new faith of Islam. To escape persecution, he was forced to flee his home in Mecca. Eventually, his followers increased, and by his death in 632, he controlled Arabia. Within a century, the empire of Islam had spread throughout western Asia and northern Africa. The turning point, Muhammad's flight from Mecca, came to be called

the "Hegira," after the Arabic word for *flight* or *emigration*. The "Hegira" is the starting point on the Muslim calendar, and we now apply the word to *any flight or journey to a desirable or congenial place.*

Quiz 25: True/False

In the space provided, write T if the definition of the numbered word is true or F if it is false.

			T or F
1.	rake	roué	_____
2.	proletariat	wealthy persons	_____
3.	hegira	flight	_____
4.	Rabelaisian	modest	_____
5.	tartar	disciple	_____
6.	arcadian	rustic	_____
7.	sardonic	derisive	_____
8.	pygmy	monkey	_____
9.	argosy	rich supply	_____
10.	Balkanize	vulcanize	_____

Quiz 26: Matching

Select the best definition for each numbered word. Write your answer in the space provided.

1.	rake	a.	bucolic	_____
2.	pygmy	b.	merchant ship	_____
3.	Rabelaisian	c.	midget	_____
4.	arcadian	d.	break up into antagonistic units	_____
5.	argosy	e.	the working class	_____
6.	hegira	f.	scornful; mocking	_____
7.	Balkanize	g.	ribald	_____
8.	proletariat	h.	bad-tempered person	_____
9.	sardonic	i.	journey or flight	_____
10.	tartar	j.	roué	_____

Lesson 14

The following ten words have peculiar backgrounds that might make them hard to decipher without a little help from a word historian. First review the stories behind them. Then complete the two quizzes to help you add them to your vocabulary.

1. **ballyhoo** (bal′ē hoo′) The word "ballyhoo" is of uncertain origin. Some, however, have connected it with the Irish town of Bally-hooy, known for the rowdy and often uncontrolled quarrels of its inhabitants. Today "ballyhoo" is an Americanism with a specific meaning: *a clamorous attempt to win customers or advance a cause; blatant advertising or publicity.*

2. **tawdry** (tô′drē) In the seventh century, an Englishwoman named Etheldreda fled her husband to establish an abbey. When the Venerable Bede recounted her story in the early eighth century, he claimed that her death had been caused by a tumor in her throat, which she believed was a punishment for her early vanity of wearing jewelry about her neck. Her abbey eventually became the Cathedral of Ely; her name, Audrey. In her honor, the cathedral town held an annual fair where "trifling objects" were hawked. One theory as to the development of the word "tawdry" relates to the hawkers' cry, "Saint Audrey's lace!" This became "Sin t'Audrey lace" and then "tawdry lace." By association with these cheap trinkets, the word "tawdry" has come to mean *gaudy, showy,* or *cheap.*

3. **phoenix** (fē′niks) According to legend, the phoenix was a fabulous Arabian bird that ignited itself on a pyre of flames after its allotted life span of 500 years and then arose from its ashes to live through another cycle. Thus, the symbol of the phoenix has often been used to designate the cycle of death and resurrection. We use the word to describe *a person or thing that has been restored after suffering calamity or apparent annihilation.*

4. **wiseacre** (wīz′ā′kər) Although the word "acre" in "wiseacre" makes it appear that the term refers to a unit of measurement, "wiseacre" is actually used contemptuously to mean a *wise guy* or a *smart aleck.* The term comes from the Dutch "wijssegger," which means *soothsayer.* Since soooothsayers were considered learned, it was logical to call them "wise," which is what "wijs" means. The word "acre" is a mispronunciation of the Dutch "segger," *sayer.* There is a famous story in which the word was used in its present sense. In reponse to the bragging of a wealthy landowner, the English playwright Ben Jonson is said to have replied, "What care we for your dirt and clods? Where you have an acre of land, I have ten acres of wit." The chastened landowner is reported to have muttered: "He's Mr. Wiseacre."

5. **carpetbagger** (kär′pit bag′ər) After the Civil War, many unscrupulous Northern adventurers flocked to the South to become profiteers and to seize political power during the chaotic Reconstruction period. The epithet "carpetbagger" referred to

the unstable future symbolized by the flimsy carpetbags in which they carried their possessions. We still use this vivid term to describe *any person, especially a politician, who takes up residence in a new place for opportunistic reasons.*

6. **silhouette** (sil′oo et′) At the urging of his mistress, Madame de Pompadour, the French king Louis XV appointed Etienne de Silhouette as his finance minister. His mission was to enact strict economy measures to rescue the government from near-bankruptcy. At the same time, there was a revival of the practice of tracing profiles created by shadows. Since they replaced more costly paintings, these outlines came to be derided as "à la Silhouette"—another of his money-saving measures. Although Silhouette lasted in office less than a year, he achieved a sort of immortality when his name became permanently associated with *a two-dimensional representation of the outline of an object, as a person's profile, generally filled in with black.*

7. **philistine** (fil′ə stēn′,-stīn′) The Philistines were a non-Semitic people who settled in ancient Palestine after their migration from the Aegean area in the twelfth century B.C.E. As rivals of the Israelites for many centuries, they have long suffered from an undeserved bad reputation: There is no real historical proof to indicate that they were as rough and uncivilized as the modern word "philistine" suggests. The word is used to refer to *a person who is lacking in or smugly indifferent to culture and aesthetic refinement; one who is contentedly commonplace in ideas and tastes.*

8. **caprice** (kə prēs′) "Caprice," *a sudden, unpredictable change of mind, a whim,* doesn't remind us of hedgehogs, yet these animals probably played a role in this word's past. "Caprice" comes ultimately from the Italian word "capriccio," which originally meant *fright, horror.* The word is thought to be a compound of "capo," *head,* and "riccio," *hedgehog,* because when people are very frightened, their hair stands on end, like a hedgehog's spines.

9. **treacle** (trē′kəl) Originally, "treacle" was an ointment used by the ancient Romans and Greeks against the bite of wild animals. But in the eighteenth and nineteenth centuries, competing quack medicine hawkers added sweetening to make their bitter potions more palatable. After a while, the sweetening agent itself, usually molasses, came to be called "treacle." We retain this meaning and have extended it to refer figuratively to *contrived or unrestrained sentimentality* as well.

10. **billingsgate** (bil′ingz gāt′) In the 1500s, Belin's gate, a walled town

within London, was primarily a fish market. The name was soon distorted to "billingsgate," and since many fishwives and seamen were known for their salty tongues, the word "billingsgate" came to mean *coarse or vulgar abusive language.*

Quiz 27: True/False

In the space provided, write T if the definition of the numbered word is true or F if it is false.

			T or F
1.	wiseacre	large ranch	_____
2.	caprice	capable	_____
3.	philistine	lover	_____
4.	carpetbagger	skinflint	_____
5.	ballyhoo	dance	_____
6.	tawdry	gaudy	_____
7.	billingsgate	profane language	_____
8.	phoenix	reborn person	_____
9.	treacle	sugar	_____
10.	silhouette	outline	_____

Quiz 28: Matching

Match each of the following numbered words with its closest synonym. Write your answer in the space provided.

1.	phoenix	a. whim	_____
2.	ballyhoo	b. cheap	_____
3.	treacle	c. verbal abuse	_____
4.	tawdry	d. comeback kid	_____
5.	carpetbagger	e. outline	_____
6.	wiseacre	f. clamor	_____
7.	silhouette	g. smarty-pants	_____
8.	caprice	h. mawkish sentimentality	_____
9.	philistine	i. boor	_____
10.	billingsgate	j. opportunist	_____

Lesson 15

The stories behind these ten words provide intriguing reading and can add muscle to your vocabulary. After you study the words, complete the two quizzes to see how many of them you can use correctly.

1. **apartheid** (ə pärt′hāt, -hīt) "Apartheid," the term for *a policy of racial segregation and discrimination against non-whites,* entered English from Afrikaans, the language of South Africa's Dutch settlers, the Boers. They created the word from the Dutch word for "apart" and the suffix "-heid," related to our suffix "-hood." Thus, the word literally means *apartness* or *separateness.* It was first used in 1947, in a South African newspaper. Apartheid is no longer practiced in South Africa, but the term has passed into general use to describe *extreme racism.*

2. **quixotic** (kwik sot′ik) The word "quixotic," meaning *extravagantly chivalrous or romantic,* is based on the character of Don Quixote, the chivalrous knight in Cervantes' 1605 masterpiece *Don Quixote de la Mancha.* The impractical, visionary knight was ludicrously blind to the false nature of his dreams.

3. **bromide** (brō′mīd) "Bromides" are chemicals, several of which can be used as sedatives. In 1906, the American humorist Gelett Burgess first used the word to mean *a boring person,* one who is likely to serve the same purpose as a sedative. The term was then extended to mean *a platitude,* the kind of remark one could expect from a tiresome person.

4. **profane** (prə fān′, prō-) Only fully initiated men were allowed to participate in Greek and Roman religious rites; those not admitted were called "profane," from "pro," *outside,* and "fanum," *temple.* When the word came into English, it was applied to persons or things not part of Christianity. Probably in reference to the contempt of nonbelievers, "profane" now means *characterized by irreverence for God or sacred things.*

5. **rialto** (rē al′tō) In the late sixteenth century, the Venetians erected a bridge across the Grand Canal. Since the bridge spanned deep waters, it was called the "Rialto," *deep stream.* The bridge led to the creation of a busy shopping area in the center of the city. From this shopping center we derive our present meaning of "rialto," *an exchange or mart.* The word is also used to refer to a theater district, especially Broadway, in New York City.

6. **thespian** (thes′pē ən) A Greek poet named Thespis, who flourished circa 534 B.C., enlarged the traditional celebrations at the festival of Dionysus by writing verses to be chanted alternately by individuals and the chorus. This opportunity to be a solo performer was a first. From the poet's name we derive the word "thespian," *an actor or actress.*

7. **siren** (sī′rən) The Sirens of Greek legend were three sea nymphs with the head of a woman and the body of a bird who inhab-

ited an island surrounded by rocky shoals and lured passing mariners to their death with their enchanting songs. Jason and the Argonauts were saved from them by the lyre-playing of Orpheus, which was even sweeter than the Sirens' song. Odysseus, who could not resist the temptation of listening to them, instructed his shipmates to tie him to the mast and plug up their own ears to avoid a shipwreck. Today a "siren" is *a seductively beautiful or charming woman, especially one who beguiles men; an enchantress.*

8. **chagrin** (shə grin′) The word "chagrin," meaning *a feeling of vexation due to disappointment,* does not derive from "shagreen," *a piece of hard, abrasive leather used to polish metal,* even though both words are spelled identically in French. French scholars connect "chagrin," *vexation, grief,* with an Old French verb, "chagreiner," *to turn melancholy or gloomy,* which evolved in part from a Germanic word related to English "grim."

9. **shibboleth** (shib′ə lith, -leth′) In the twelfth chapter of Judges, Jephthah and his men gained a victory over the warriors of Ephraim. After the battle, Jephthah gave his guards the password "shibboleth" to distinguish friends from foes; he picked the word because the Ephraimites could not pronounce the "sh" sound. His choice was shrewd, and many of his enemies were captured and killed. Thus, "shibboleth" has come to mean *a peculiarity of pronunciation, usage, or behavior that distinguishes a particular class or set of persons.* It also can mean *slogan; catchword.*

10. **vie** (vī) The word "vie," *to strive in competition or rivalry with another, to contend for superiority,* was originally a shortened version of "envien," a sixteenth-century gaming term meaning *to raise the stake.* The contraction, "vie," came to mean *to contend, compete.*

Quiz 29: True/False

In the space provided, write T if the definition of the numbered word is true or F if it is false.

		T or F
1. **chagrin**	chafe	_____
2. **vie**	accede	_____
3. **profane**	irreverent	_____
4. **siren**	seductress	_____
5. **quixotic**	ill-tempered	_____
6. **rialto**	marketplace	_____
7. **apartheid**	foreigner	_____

8. **shibboleth**   platitude   _____
9. **thespian**   actor   _____
10. **bromide**   explosive   _____

Quiz 30: Definitions

Select the best definition for each numbered word. Write your answer in the space provided.

_____   1. bromide
                 a. cliché   b. effervescence   c. angst
_____   2. vie
                 a. treat   b. contend   c. despise
_____   3. quixotic
                 a. alien   b. romantic   c. fictional
_____   4. siren
                 a. frump   b. noisemaker   c. enchantress
_____   5. shibboleth
                 a. peculiarity   b. forbidden   c. murdered
_____   6. profane
                 a. pious   b. irreverent   c. exploding
_____   7. thespian
                 a. actress   b. speech impairment   c. playwright
_____   8. apartheid
                 a. discrimination   b. unity   c. hopelessness
_____   9. rialto
                 a. shipyard   b. reality   c. exchange
_____   10. chagrin
                 a. stiff   b. vexation   c. smirk

Lesson 16

The following ten words are derived from earlier terms that can provide a window on the past, as well as suggesting the ways in which the genius of the English language borrows and adapts words for its own purposes. Study the words, then work through the two quizzes that follow.

1. **Promethean** (prə mē′thē ən) According to Greek myth, as punishment for stealing fire from the gods and giving it to mortal humans, Prometheus was bound to the side of a mountain, where he was attacked daily by a fierce bird that feasted upon his liver. At night his wounds healed; the next day he was attacked anew. Because of his extraordinary boldness in stealing

the divine fire, the word "Promethean" has come to mean *creative, boldly original.*

2. **sarcophagus** (sär kof′ə gəs) Although the majority of ancient Greeks favored burial or cremation, some obtained limestone coffins that could dissolve a body in little over a month. The coffin was called a "sarcophagus," from the Greek "sarx," *flesh,* and "phagos," *eating.* Today we use the term to refer to *a stone coffin, especially one bearing sculpture, an inscription, etc., often displayed as a monument.*

3. **quorum** (kwôr′əm) The word "quorum" was first used as part of a Latin phrase meaning *to select people for official court business.* Ultimately, it came to mean *the number of members of a group or organization required to be present to transact business; legally, usually a majority.*

4. **antimacassar** (an′ti mə kas′ər) In the 1800s, macassar oil was imported from Indonesia to England as a popular remedy for baldness. Based on its reputation, men began to apply it liberally to their scalps, but the oil stained the backs of sofas and chairs where they rested their oily heads. Therefore, homemakers began to place pieces of fabric over sofa and chair backs, since these scraps could be washed more easily than stained upholstery. These fabric pieces came to be called "antimacassars"—*against macassar oil.* These *little doilies* are now regarded as highly collectible relics of the Victorian era because of their elaborate designs and fine handiwork—now a lost art.

5. **lackey** (lak′ē) After their invasion of Spain in 711, the Moors conquered nearly the entire country and established a glittering civilization. But it was not to last. By 1100, Christians had already wrested half of Spain from the Moors. Two hundred years later, the Moors retained only a small toehold; and a hundred years after that, they were driven out of Europe entirely. As the Moors suffered repeated defeats, their captured soldiers became servants to their Spanish conquerors. They were called "alacayo." The initial "a" was later dropped, and the word was rendered in English as "lackey," *a servile follower.*

6. **Sisyphean** (sis′ə f ē′ən) In Greek mythology, Sisyphus was the founder and king of Corinth who was condemned to Tartarus for his disrespect to Zeus. There he performed the eternal task of rolling a heavy stone to the top of a steep hill, where it inevitably slipped away from him and rolled back down again. His punishment has given us the term "Sisyphean," meaning *futile* or *hopeless,* especially in relation to an impossible task. In a 1942 essay, the existentialist

writer Albert Camus (1913–60) popularized the myth as a metaphor for modern life.

7. **paladin** (pal'ə din) The original paladins were Charlemagne's twelve knights. According to legend, the famous paladin Roland was caught in an ambush and fought valiantly with his small band of followers to the last man. Because of his actions, "paladin" has come down to us as *any champion of noble causes.*

8. **hobnob** (hob'nob') Those who "hobnob" with their buddies *associate on very friendly terms* or *drink together.* The word comes from the Anglo-Saxon "haebbe" and "naebbe," *to have* and *to have not.* In the 1700s, "hobnob" meant *to toast friends and host alternate rounds of drinks.* Each person thus had the pleasure of treating, creating a sense of familiarity. Today this usage survives, even if those hobnobbing are teetotalers.

9. **helot** (hel'ət, hē'lət) Around the eighth century B.C., the Spartans conquered and enslaved the people of the southern half of the Peloponnesus. They called these slaves "helots," perhaps from the Greek word meaning *to enslave.* Today "helot" still means *serf or slave; bondsman.* Fans of the 1941 movie *Meet John Doe* may recall that this is the favorite epithet of Gary Cooper's hobo sidekick, played by Walter Brennan, which he applies to anyone who threatens his freewheeling lifestyle.

10. **kowtow** (kow'tou') The Chinese people, who were largely isolated from the West until Portuguese traders established a post outside Canton, regarded their emperor as a representation of God on earth. Those approaching the emperor had to fall to the ground and strike their heads against the floor as a sign of humility. This was called a "kowtow," from the Chinese word that meant *knock-head.* As a verb, the English word follows the original meaning, *to touch the forehead to the ground while kneeling, as an act of worship;* but from this meaning we have derived a figurative use as well: *to act in an obsequious manner, show servile deference.*

Quiz 31: Defining Words

Define each of the following words.

1. Sisyphean _____

2. Promethean _____

3. helot _____

4. sarcophagus _____

5. kowtow _____

6. lackey _____

7. antimacassar _____

8. hobnob _____

9. quorum _____

10. paladin _____

Suggested Answers 1. impossible; hopeless 2. creative, boldly original 3. serf, slave 4. coffin 5. deference 6. a servile follower 7. doily 8. associate on friendly terms; drink together 9. majority 10. champion

Quiz 32: True/False

In the space provided, write T if the definition of the numbered word is true or F if it is false.

			T or F
1.	**lackey**	servant	_____
2.	**quorum**	majority	_____
3.	**Sisyphean**	futile	_____
4.	**hobnob**	twisted logic	_____
5.	**promethean**	creative	_____
6.	**sarcophagus**	cremation	_____
7.	**helot**	hell-on-wheels	_____
8.	**antimacassar**	against travel	_____
9.	**kowtow**	bow low	_____
10.	**paladin**	villain	_____

Lesson 17

The quirky stories behind the following ten words can help you understand and remember them better. Read through the histories and complete the two quizzes to add to your mastery of language.

1. **quahog** (kwô′hôg, -hog) Despite the "hog" at the end of the word, a "quahog" has nothing to do with a pig. Rather, it is a clam; the word comes from the Algonquian (Narragansett) word "poquauhock." It is one of many terms the European settlers adopted from the Native Americans to describe the local wildlife. Other such borrowings include *raccoon, opossum, moose, skunk, woodchuck, squash, maize, tomato, chocolate,* and *cocoa.*

2. **protean** (prō′tē ən) According to Greek legend, Proteus was a sea god who possessed the power to change his shape at will. He

also had the ability to foretell the future, but those wishing to avail themselves of his power first had to steal up on him at noon when he checked his herds of sea calves, catch him, and bind him securely. Thus bound, Proteus would change shape furiously, but the petitioner who could keep him restrained until he returned to his original shape would receive the answer to his question—if he still remembered what he wanted to know. From Proteus, then, we get the word "protean," *readily assuming different forms or characters; variable.*

3. **noisome** (noi'səm) Although the words appear to have the same root, "noisome" bears no relation to "noise." "Noisome" means *offensive* or *disgusting,* as an odor, and comes from the Middle English word "noy," meaning *harm.* The root is related, however, to the word "annoy," *to molest or bother.*

4. **chimerical** (ki mer'i kəl, -mēr'-) The Chimera was originally a fire-breathing monster of classical myth that was represented as having a lion's head, a goat's body, and a serpent's tail. According to Greek myth, it was slain by the gallant warrior Bellerophon, who attacked it astride the winged horse Pegasus. Later the word meant *any horrible or grotesque imaginary creature;* then, *a fancy or dream.* Today we use "chimerical" to mean *unreal or imaginary; wildly fanciful or unrealistic.*

5. **simony** (sī'mə nē, sim'ə-) Simon the sorcerer offered to pay the Apostle Peter to teach him the wondrous cures he had seen Peter perform, not understanding that his feats were miracles rather than magic tricks. From Simon's name comes the term "simony," *the sin of buying or selling ecclesiastical preferments.*

6. **rigmarole** (rig'mə rōl') In fourteenth-century England, a register of names was called a "rageman." Later it became a "ragman," then "ragman roll." As it changed, the term evolved to refer to a series of unconnected statements. By the 1700s, the word had become "rigmarole," with its present meaning, *an elaborate or complicated procedure.*

7. **bolshevik** (bōl'shə vik) At a rally of Communist leaders in 1903, Lenin garnered a majority of the votes. He cleverly dubbed his supporters "Bolsheviks," meaning *the majority.* His move was effective propaganda. Even though his supporters actually comprised only a minority, the name stuck and came to be associated with *a member of the Russian Communist party.* The word is also used in a derogatory sense to denote *an extreme political radical; a revolutionary.*

8. **jingoism** (jing'gō iz'əm) This word, meaning *belligerent patriotism and the advocacy of an aggressive foreign policy,* has a rather

obscure source. It was extrapolated from the phrase "by jingo" in a political song written by George Ward Hunt supporting the entrance of England and the use of British forces in the Russo-Turkish War of 1877–78 on the side of the Turks. Fortunately, cooler heads prevailed, but the term has been current ever since to describe such hotheaded, opportunistic aggression.

9. **Tweedledum and Tweedledee** (twēd'l dum' ən twēd'l dē'), The chubby schoolboy characters of Tweedledum and Tweedledee famous for their recitation in Lewis Carroll's *Through the Looking Glass* of "The Walrus and the Carpenter" actually have an earlier historical counterpart. This humorous coinage, devised in imitation of the sounds of their musical compositions, was apparently first applied to Italian composer Giovanni Bononcini (1670–1747) and his German-born rival Georg Friedrich Handel (1685–1759). Whichever reference you prefer, the term "Tweedledum and Tweedledee" still means *two persons nominally different but practically the same; a nearly identical pair.*

10. **sylph** (silf) A German alchemist of the 1700s coined the term "Sylphis" to describe the spirits of the air. He envisioned them as looking like humans but able to move more swiftly and gracefully. Over the years, the word evolved to mean *a slender, graceful girl or woman.*

Quiz 33: True/False

In the space provided, write T if the definition of the numbered word is true or F if it is false.

		T or F
1. **jingoism**	happiness	_____
2. **chimerical**	unreal	_____
3. **simony**	slickness	_____
4. **bolshevik**	sheik	_____
5. **protean**	changeable	_____
6. **noisome**	clamorous	_____
7. **sylph**	svelte female	_____
8. **quahog**	bivalve	_____
9. **rigmarole**	simplification	_____
10. **Tweedledum and Tweedledee**	identical couple	_____

Quiz 34: Matching

Match each of the numbered words with its closest synonym from the list of lettered words in the second column. Write your answer in the space provided.

1. **sylph**	a. indistinguishable pair	_____
2. **quahog**	b. bellicose patriotism	_____
3. **Tweedledum and**		
Tweedledee	c. ecclesiastical favors	_____
4. **bolshevik**	d. slender girl	_____
5. **chimerical**	e. Communist	_____
6. **jingoism**	f. involved process	_____
7. **noisome**	g. variable	_____
8. **protean**	h. clam	_____
9. **rigmarole**	i. foul	_____
10. **simony**	j. fanciful	_____

Lesson 18

Now read the histories of these ten unique words. Fix them in your memory by completing the two quizzes that follow and devising some new sentences of your own. The words can make your speech and writing more colorful, interesting, and effective.

1. **solomonic** (sol′ə mon′ik) Solomon, the tenth-century B.C.E. Hebrew king who was the son and successor of David, was renowned for his wisdom. Probably most famous was his decision in the case of the two women who claimed to be the mother of the same infant. When Solomon announced his decision to resolve the bitter dispute by severing the child in two and awarding one half to each of the disputants, one woman enthusiastically agreed to comply with his judgment while the other offered to give up the child rather than seeing it murdered before her eyes. Solomon handed over the child to the second woman, whom he deemed to be its true mother. Thus, we say that a "solomonic" decision or person is one that is *wise or reasonable in character, sagacious.*

2. **sybarite** (sib′ə rīt′) The ancient Greek colony of Sybaris in southern Italy was known for its luxurious life style. The residents were so famous for their opulent ways that the word "sybarite" came to be used for *any person devoted to luxury and pleasure.*

3. **rostrum** (ros′trəm) Today a "rostrum" is *any platform, stage, or the like for public speaking.* The word comes from the victory in 338 B.C. of the Romans over the pirates of Antium (Anzio), off the Italian coast. The victorious consul took back to Rome the prows of the six ships he had captured. These were attached to the lecterns used by Roman speakers. They came to be called "rostra," or *beaks.* We use the singular, "rostrum."

4. **draconian** (drā kō′nē ən, drə-) Draco (fl. 621 B.C.E.) was a Greek politician who is most famous for his codification of Athenian customary law. Though little of his code is extant, later commentators on his work indicated that the death penalty was prescribed for the most trivial offenses. Therefore, his name has come down to us to refer to punishment or rule that is *unusually cruel or severe.*

5. **spoonerism** (spoo′nə riz′əm) The English clergyman W. A. Spooner (1844–1930) was notorious for his habit of transposing the initial letters or other sounds of words, as in "a blushing crow" for "a crushing blow." Since the good reverend was not unique in his affliction, we use the word "spoonerism" to describe these *unintentional transpositions of sounds.*

6. **Pyrrhic victory** (pir′ik) Pyrrhus (c. 318–272 B.C.E.) was a Greek warrior-king whose incessant warfare against the Romans as well as fellow Greeks ultimately brought ruin on his own kingdom. Though he defeated the Romans at Aesculum in 279, his losses were so heavy that he was later said by the Greek historian and biographer Plutarch to have declared, "One more such victory and I am undone." Thus a "Pyrrhic victory" is *a victory or attainment achieved at too great a cost to be worthwhile.*

7. **pundit** (pun′dit) Today we use the word "pundit" to mean *an expert or authority;* but in the nineteenth century, the word was usually applied to a learned person in India. It comes from the Hindi word "pandit," meaning *learned man,* a Brahman with profound knowledge of Sanskrit, Hindu law, and so forth.

8. **yahoo** (yä′hoo) This word for a *coarse, uncouth person* was coined by Jonathan Swift in his 1726 novel *Gulliver's Travels.* In Swift's satire, the Yahoos were a race of humanoid brutes ruled by the Houyhnhnms, civilized horses.

9. **stoic** (stō′ik) The Stoics were philosophers of ancient Greece who believed in self-restraint. Their name comes from Greek *stoa,* "porch," where they habitually walked. Hence the word "stoic," which describes a person who is *impassive, calm, and austere.*

10. **wormwood** (wûrm′wood′) "Wormwood" is the active narcotic ingredient of absinthe, a bitter green liqueur now banned in most Western countries. Originally, however, the herb was used as a folk remedy for worms in the body. Because of the herb's bitter qualities, we also use it figuratively to mean *something bitter, grievous, or extremely unpleasant.*

Quiz 35: True/False

In the space provided, write T if the definition of the numbered word is true or F if it is false.

			T or F
1.	spoonerism	Midwesterner	_____
2.	yahoo	oaf	_____
3.	wormwood	bitterness	_____
4.	solomonic	love-struck	_____
5.	pundit	bad kick	_____
6.	draconian	harsh	_____
7.	sybarite	slender	_____
8.	stoic	austere	_____
9.	Pyrrhic victory	enslavement	_____
10.	rostrum	register	_____

Quiz 36: Matching

Select the best definition for each numbered word. Write your answer in the space provided.

1. rostrum	a. wise		
2. yahoo	b. something bitter		_____
3. solomonic	c. cruel		_____
4. spoonerism	d. victory at too great a cost		_____
5. wormwood	e. impassive		_____
6. sybarite	f. stage or platform		_____
7. draconian	g. authority		_____
8. pundit	h. lover of luxury		_____
9. Pyrric victory	i. transposition of sounds in words		_____
10. stoic	j. boor		_____

Lesson 19

Here are ten more words with intriguing pasts. Read through the histories, then complete the quizzes that follow. Spend a few minutes devising sentences for each of the words to help you make them part of your regular speech and writing.

1. **termagant** (tûr′mə gənt) The word "termagant," meaning *a violent, turbulent, or brawling woman,* comes from a mythical deity that many Europeans of the Middle Ages believed was worshiped by the Muslims. It often appeared in morality plays as

a violent, overbearing personage in long robes. In modern usage, "termagant" is applied only to women.

2. **blarney** (blär'nē) According to Irish legend, anyone who kisses a magical stone set twenty feet beneath the ground of a castle near the village of Blarney, in Ireland, will henceforth possess the gift of eloquence. One story claims the Blarney stone got its powers from the eloquence of the seventeenth-century Irish patriot Cormac McCarthy, whose soft speech won favorable terms from Elizabeth I after an Irish uprising. From this stone-kissing custom, "blarney" has come to mean *flattering or wheedling talk; cajolery.*

3. **charlatan** (shär'lə tn) During the Renaissance, the village of Cerreto, in Umbria, Italy, was noted for its medical quacks, who became known as "cerretanos," after the town's name. The combination of "cerretano" with "ciartatore," an imitative word meaning *chatterer,* created the Italian term "cialatano." When the word was transplanted to the shores of England, it remained nearly intact as "charlatan," *a person who pretends to special knowledge or skill; fraud.*

4. **eunuch** (yōo'nək) A "eunuch" is *a castrated man,* especially formerly, one employed by Oriental rulers as a harem attendant. The word is based on the Greek "eunouchos," from "eune," *bed,* and "echein," *to keep,* since a eunuch is perfectly suited for guarding a woman's bed. The word is used figuratively to refer to *a weak, powerless person.*

5. **tartuffe** (tär tōof', -tōof') The French actor and playwright Molière (1622–73) is famed for his farces and comedies of manners, which ridicule human foibles and excesses in the person of a main character that epitomizes such vices as hypocrisy, misanthropy, affected intellectualism, and social snobbery. The title character of *Le Tartuffe,* first performed in 1664, is the source for this word meaning *a hypocritical pretender to piety; a religious hypocrite.*

6. **shrew** (shrōo) In Old English, the word "shrew" described *a small, fierce rodent.* The word was later applied to *a person with a violent temper and tenacious personality* similar to the rodent's. Although "shrew" has retained this meaning, it is usually applied only to a woman.

7. **kudos** (kōo'dōz, kyōo'-) Although "kudos" has come down to us from the Greek intact in both form and meaning—*praise, glory*—in the process it has come to be regarded as a plural word, although it is singular. As a result, another new word has been formed, "kudo." Although purists still prefer "kudos

is" to "kudos are," only time will tell if the transformation to kudo/kudos becomes permanent.

8. **bohemian** (bō hē′mē ən) In the early fifteenth century, a band of vagabond peasants took up residence in Paris. Knowing that they had come from somewhere in central Europe, the French dubbed the gypsies "Bohemians," in the belief that they were natives of Bohemia. Working from the stereotyped view of gypsies as free spirits, the French then applied the term "bohemian" to *a person, typically one with artistic or intellectual aspirations, who lives an unconventional life.*

9. **rhubarb** (rōō′bärb) In conventional usage, the word refers to *a long-stalked plant, used in tart conserves and pie fillings;* it is also a slang term for *quarrel* or *squabble.* The ancient Greeks gave the plant its name. Since it grew in an area outside of Greece, they called it "rha barbaron." "Rha" was the name of the plant and "barbaron" meant *foreign.*

10. **lacuna** (lə kyōō′nə) "Lacuna," *a gap or missing part; hiatus,* comes from the identical Latin word, "lacuna," meaning *a hollow.* It first entered English to refer to a missing part in a manuscript. It is also the root of "lagoon."

Quiz 37: True/False

In the space provided, write T if the definition of the numbered word is true or F if it is false.

			T or F
1. **kudos**	compliment		_____
2. **blarney**	cajolery		_____
3. **shrew**	cleverness		_____
4. **tartuffe**	pious hypocrite		_____
5. **lacuna**	hiatus		_____
6. **termagant**	intermediate		_____
7. **bohemian**	businesslike		_____
8. **charlatan**	quack		_____
9. **rhubarb**	sweet		_____
10. **eunuch**	castrated man		_____

Quiz 38: Definitions

Select the best definition for each numbered word. Write your answer in the space provided.

_____   1. kudos
a. enclave   b. martial arts   c. acclaim   d. humiliation

_____ 2. eunuch
a. hero   b. warrior   c. castle   d. castrated man

_____ 3. bohemian
a. free spirit   b. butcher   c. foreigner   d. master chef

_____ 4. shrew
a. virago   b. sly   c. bibliophile   d. hearty

_____ 5. lacuna
a. hot tub   b. gap   c. lake   d. cool water

_____ 6. termagant
a. lease   b. eternal   c. possessive   d. brawling woman

_____ 7. charlatan
a. expert   b. aristocrat   c. doctor   d. fraud

_____ 8. rhubarb
a. root   b. ridicule   c. squabble   d. arrow

_____ 9. blarney
a. mountain climbing   b. sweet talk   c. sightseeing
d. luncheon meats

_____ 10. tartuffe
a. religious hypocrite   b. renegade   c. saint
d. ruthless fighter

Lesson 20

Familiarizing yourself with the history of these ten words can help you retain their meanings and make them part of your stock of words. Go through the following word histories and complete the quizzes that follow. Then review the histories to help you remember the words.

1. **solecism** (sol′ə siz′əm, sō′lə-) To the ancient Greeks, the people of the colony of Soloi spoke inexcusably poor Greek. The Greeks were perhaps most offended by the Solois' errors in grammar and usage. They called such barbarous speech "soloikismos," *the language of Soloi.* Through Latin, the word became "solecism," *a substandard or ungrammatical usage, a breach of good manners or etiquette.*

2. **requiem** (rek′wē əm) A "requiem" is *a mass celebrated for the repose of the souls of the dead.* It comes from the opening line of the Roman Catholic mass for the dead. "Requiem aeternam dona ers, Domine," meaning *Give them eternal rest, Lord.* It can refer more loosely to *any memorial for the dead,* or *a tribute,* as in the title of the film *Requiem for a Heavyweight,* about a washed-up prizefighter.

3. **tariff** (tar'if) "Tariff," *an official schedule of duties or customs imposed by a government on imports and exports,* comes from the Arabic term for *inventory,* "ta῾rif." Perhaps because this story is so unexciting, a false etymology claims that the word instead comes from the name of a Moorish town near the straits of Gibraltar formerly used as a base for daring pirate raids. Colorful, but not true. The word is also used more loosely to mean *cost* or *price of admission.*

4. **blitzkrieg** (blits'krēg') The German word "Blitzkrieg," literally *a lightning war,* describes the overwhelming Nazi attacks on Poland in 1940. In two weeks, Germany pounded Poland into submission; in six weeks, it crushed the French army. Although ultimately the Germans met defeat, their method of attack has found a place in our language, and "blitzkrieg" has come to denote *an overwhelming, all-out attack.*

5. **spartan** (spär'tn) Sparta was the rival city-state of ancient Greece that ultimately destroyed the high civilization of Athens in the petty squabbles of the Peloponnesian War (431–404 B.C.E.). Though both empires were equally ruthless, the Spartans were renowned for their superior military discipline, which began in early childhood. A famous story tells of the proud stoicism of a boy who allowed a fox smuggled into school under his clothing to slowly disembowel him rather than cry out and admit his transgression. So extreme was their emphasis on the virtues of self-denial and toughness that the word "spartan" came to be synonymous with *a person who is sternly disciplined and rigorously simple, frugal, or austere.*

6. **pecksniffian** (pek snif'ē ən) The often lovable, sometimes villainous, but always memorable eccentrics that populate the literary universe of Charles Dickens made him one of the most popular and enduring English novelists of the nineteenth century. Indeed we often speak of peculiar characters with notable quirks as being "Dickensian." Everyone knows that a "scrooge" is a miser, thanks to the numerous versions of *A Christmas Carol* that are performed every year at Christmas time. Far fewer people are familiar with Seth Pecksniff, a minor character in *Martin Chuzzlewit* (1843), one of Dickens' lesser-known works. But he so thoroughly embodies the trait of *hypocritically affecting benevolence or high moral principles* that we can find no better word to describe such pious frauds than "pecksniffian."

7. **bacchanalia** (bak'ə nā'lē ə, -nāl'yə) In Greek times, a Bacchanalia was originally a religious festival in honor of Bacchus, the god of wine and protector of the vineyards. Bacchus was also a god of vegetation and fertility, and his religious ceremonies

ultimately degenerated into occasions for drunkenness, lewd behavior, and other excesses. Therefore, the word "bacchanalia" (or "bacchanal") has come to mean *drunken revelry; orgy.*

8. **kibitzer** (kib'it sər) A "kibitzer" is *a spectator, especially at a card game, who gives unwanted advice to a player; a meddler.* This word came from Yiddish, which derived it from the German verb "kiebitzen," *to be a busybody, give unwanted advice to card players.* The verb, in turn, came from "Kiebitz," the German word for a lapwing, an inquisitive little bird given to shrill cries.

9. **lampoon** (lam pōōn') "Lampoon," *a sharp, often virulent satire* comes from the French word "lampon," which is thought to come from "lampons," *let's drink,* a common ending to seventeenth-century French satirical drinking songs. We also use the word as a verb meaning *to mock or ridicule.*

10. **scapegoat** (skāp'gōt') The term "scapegoat," *a person made to bear the blame for others or to suffer in their place,* comes from the sixteenth chapter of Leviticus, which describes how the high priest Aaron was directed to select two goats. One goat was to be a burnt offering to the Lord; the other, an "escape goat" for atonement, was presented alive to the Lord and sent away into the wilderness to carry away the sins of the people. The word "scape" was a shortening of "escape."

Quiz 39: True/False

In the space provided, write T if the definition of the numbered word is true or F if it is false.

		T or F
1. **kibitzer**	busybody	_____
2. **bacchanalia**	tea party	_____
3. **blitzkrieg**	negotiations	_____
4. **solecism**	bad grammar	_____
5. **tariff**	price of admission	_____
6. **pecksniffian**	villainous	_____
7. **requiem**	revival	_____
8. **lampoon**	enlighten	_____
9. **scapegoat**	substitute victim	_____
10. **spartan**	austere	_____

Quiz 40: Matching

Match each of the following numbered words with its closest synonym. Write your answer in the space provided.

1. **tariff**
2. **lampoon**
3. **kibitzer**
4. **scapegoat**
5. **bacchanalia**
6. **requiem**
7. **solecism**
8. **blitzkrieg**
9. **pecksniffian**
10. **spartan**

a. feigning kindness
b. mock
c. funeral mass
d. drunken orgy
e. customs duties
f. disciplined person
g. busybody
h. grammatical error
i. victim
j. all-out attack

_____
_____
_____
_____
_____
_____
_____
_____
_____
_____

Answers to Quizzes in Chapter 7

Answers to Quiz 1

1. f 2. d 3. b 4. g 5. e 6. h 7. i 8. c 9. j 10. a

Answers to Quiz 2

1. T 2. F 3. F 4. F 5. T 6. F 7. T 8. T 9. F 10. F

Answers to Quiz 3

1. F 2. T 3. F 4. T 5. F 6. F 7. F 8. F 9. T 10. T

Answers to Quiz 4

1. c 2. f 3. i 4. g 5. b 6. h 7. d 8. a 9. j 10. e

Answers to Quiz 5

1. c 2. b 3. a 4. c 5. c 6. b 7. a 8. c 9. a 10. b

Answers to Quiz 6

1. d 2. c 3. i 4. a 5. g 6. j 7. b 8. e 9. f 10. h

Answers to Quiz 7

1. T 2. F 3. F 4. T 5. F 6. T 7. T 8. T 9. F 10. F

Answers to Quiz 9

1. c 2. a 3. d 4. d 5. c 6. a 7. b 8. b 9. a 10. b

Answers to Quiz 10

1. T 2. T 3. T 4. T 5. T 6. T 7. F 8. F 9. F 10. T

Answers to Quiz 11

1. b 2. f 3. a 4. j 5. i 6. d 7. g 8. c 9. h 10. e

Answers to Quiz 13
1. T 2. F 3. F 4. F 5. F 6. F 7. F 8. T 9. T 10. T

Answers to Quiz 14
1. e 2. j 3. h 4. a 5. i 6. b 7. d 8. f 9. c 10. g

Answers to Quiz 15
1. d 2. e 3. f 4. j 5. h 6. i 7. c 8. a 9. b 10. g

Answers to Quiz 16
1. T 2. F 3. F 4. T 5. T 6. F 7. F 8. F 9. T 10. F

Answers to Quiz 17
1. meander 2. maudlin 3. martinet 4. lilliputian 5. Pollyanna 6. garret 7. Olympian 8. gossamer 9. gazette 10. gorgon

Answers to Quiz 18
1. a 2. b 3. c 4. d 5. d 6. b 7. c 8. a 9. a 10. c

Answers to Quiz 19
1. T 2. F 3. F 4. F 5. T 6. F 7. T 8. F 9. T 10. F

Answers to Quiz 20
1. c 2. e 3. i 4. g 5. b 6. f 7. j 8. a 9. d 10. h

Answers to Quiz 21
1. F 2. F 3. T 4. F 5. T 6. T 7. T 8. F 9. T 10. F

Answers to Quiz 23
1. F 2. F 3. F 4. T 5. T 6. F 7. F 8. T 9. T 10. T

Answers to Quiz 24
1. c 2. f 3. j 4. d 5. a 6. g 7. e 8. h 9. b 10. i

Answers to Quiz 25
1. T 2. F 3. T 4. F 5. F 6. T 7. T 8. F 9. T 10. F

Answers to Quiz 26
1. j 2. c 3. g 4. a 5. b 6. i 7. d 8. e 9. f 10. h

Answers to Quiz 27
1. F 2. F 3. F 4. F 5. F 6. T 7. T 8. T 9. F 10. T

Answers to Quiz 28

1. d 2. f 3. h 4. b 5. j 6. g 7. e 8. a 9. i 10. c

Answers to Quiz 29

1. F 2. F 3. T 4. T 5. F 6. T 7. F 8. F 9. T 10. F

Answers to Quiz 30

1. a 2. b 3. b 4. c 5. a 6. b 7. a 8. a 9. c 10. b

Answers to Quiz 32

1. T 2. T 3. T 4. F 5. T 6. F 7. F 8. F 9. T 10. F

Answers to Quiz 33

1. F 2. T 3. F 4. F 5. T 6. F 7. T 8. T 9. F 10. T

Answers to Quiz 34

1. d 2. h 3. a 4. e 5. j 6. b 7. i 8. g 9. f 10. c

Answers to Quiz 35

1. F 2. T 3. T 4. F 5. F 6. T 7. F 8. T 9. F 10. F

Answers to Quiz 36

1. f 2. j 3. a 4. i 5. b 6. h 7. c 8. g 9. d 10. e

Answers to Quiz 37

1. T 2. T 3. F 4. T 5. T 6. F 7. F 8. T 9. F 10. T

Answers to Quiz 38

1. c 2. d 3. a 4. a 5. b 6. d 7. d 8. c 9. b 10. a

Answers to Quiz 39

1. T 2. F 3. F 4. T 5. T 6. F 7. F 8. F 9. T 10. T

Answers to Quiz 40

1. e 2. b 3. g 4. i 5. d 6. c 7. h 8. j 9. a 10. f

8

Words Borrowed from Other Languages

The roots of English are Anglo-Saxon, but there have been so many other influences over the centuries that we can hardly recognize ourselves as speaking a Germanic language. Nevertheless, though only around one-fifth of our vocabulary stems from those Germanic roots, these basic words comprise the vast majority of the ones we use to communicate with each other every day. It is estimated that around three-fifths of our vocabulary derives from French, Latin, and Greek; the remaining one-fifth has been borrowed from languages all around the globe.

The Norman Conquest of England in 1066 brought about the first sea change in English, as the language of the French conquerors became grafted onto the trunk of the Anglo-Saxon idiom. In general, French was the language of the court, the clergy, and the aristocracy; not surprisingly, the everyday speech of the common people continued to rely on the plainer words of Anglo-Saxon origin, known as Old English. The rapid melding of the two cultures over several succeeding centuries produced the hybrid Middle English. Modern English—the language we speak today—is said to have developed sometime after 1450, during the Renaissance era. Thus, *The Canterbury Tales* of Geoffrey Chaucer (1340?–1400) were written in Middle English and are quite difficult reading for students, whereas the plays of William Shakespeare (1564–1616) are relatively accessible to the average reader. The revival of classical learning during the Renaissance also led to the importation of an enormous number of Greek and Latin terms.

A second sea change is associated with the establishment of the

English colonies in North America. American and British English began to diverge in the seventeenth century, and Americans have been far more prone than the British to innovate in their vocabulary. Among the more significant influences that have contributed to the growth of American English are Native American languages, Dutch, German, Spanish, and Yiddish, but every ethnic group that has assimilated into the American population has contributed something of its culture and byways to our ever-evolving language. (For an entertaining and comprehensive overview, see H. L. Mencken, *The American Language.*)

English is a flexible, multivalent language that has adapted itself quite beautifully to the changing needs of its speakers. It continues to enrich itself by coining new words as well as borrowing or adapting tried-and-true foreign terms that are often not quite translatable. This selection of "imported" words should help to illustrate that process while improving your ability to express your own thoughts and feelings.

French

We've borrowed so many words from the French that someone once half-seriously claimed that English is little more than French badly pronounced. Some of these words have kept their original spelling, while others have become so Anglicized you may not recognize them as originally French. Nearly half of our French borrowings came into English before the fifteenth century; thereafter, the adaptations tended to be of a more literary nature. Indeed French has always been regarded as the language of the educated and elite classes. However, a little bit of French goes a long way; its overuse can make the speaker or writer seem affected and pretentious. But French terms can lend both elegance and precision to your self-expression, as well as a certain charm, or what the French call *je ne sais quoi* (literally, "I don't know what")—an indefinable stylish quality that enhances your presentation of yourself.

Lesson 1

1. **avant-garde** (ə vänt′gärd′, ə vant′-, av′änt-, ä′vänt-) the advance group in any field, especially in the visual, literary, or musical arts, whose works are unorthodox and experimental.

2. **bon vivant** (bon'vē vänt', bôn'vē väɴ') a person who lives luxuriously and enjoys good food and drink.
3. **cause célèbre** (kôz'sə leb', -leb'rə) any controversy that attracts great public attention.
4. **coup d'état** (kōō' dā tä') a sudden and decisive action in politics, especially one effecting a change of government, illegally or by force.
5. **cul-de-sac** (kul'də sak') a street, lane, etc., closed at one end; blind alley.
6. **demimonde** (dem' ē mond') a group that has lost status or lacks respectability.
7. **envoy** (en'voi, än'-) a diplomatic agent; an accredited messenger or representative.
8. **esprit de corps** (e sprē' də kôr') a sense of union and of common interests and responsibilities, as developed among a group of persons associated together.
9. **idée fixe** (ē'dā fēks') a fixed idea; obsession.
10. **joie de vivre** (zhwä'də vēv', vē'vrə) a delight in being alive.
11. **laissez-faire** (les'ā fâr') the theory that government should intervene as little as possible in economic affairs.
12. **milieu** (mil yōō', mēl-) an environment; medium.
13. **rapport** (ra pôr', rə-) a harmonious or sympathetic relationship or connection.
14. **rendezvous** (rän'də vōō', -dā-) an agreement between two or more people to meet at a certain time and place.
15. **repartee** (rep'ər tē', -tā', -är-) witty conversation; a quick reply.

Quiz 1: Matching

Match each of the following numbered words with its closest synonym. Write your answer in the space provided.

1. **rendezvous**	a. team spirit	_____
2. **rapport**	b. experimental artists	_____
3. **cul-de-sac**	c. hands-off policy	_____
4. **bon vivant**	d. love of life	_____
5. **idée fixe**	e. meeting	_____
6. **joie de vivre**	f. environment	_____
7. **repartee**	g. diplomatic agent	_____
8. **milieu**	h. harmony	_____
9. **avant-garde**	i. controversy	_____
10. **coup d'état**	j. government overthrow	_____
11. **demimonde**	k. dead end	_____
12. **esprit de corps**	l. disreputable group	_____

13. envoy   m. big spender   _____
14. cause célèbre   n. clever banter   _____
15. laissez-faire   o. obsession   _____

Quiz 2: True/False

In the space provided, write T if the definition of the numbered word is true or F if it is false.

		T or F
1. laissez-faire	a policy of leaving alone	_____
2. esprit de corps	harmony and union	_____
3. milieu	setting	_____
4. rendezvous	meeting	_____
5. idée fixe	obsession	_____
6. repartee	departure	_____
7. envoy	letter	_____
8. rapport	announcement	_____
9. joie de vivre	good vintage	_____
10. coup d'état	headache	_____
11. cause célèbre	controversy	_____
12. cul-de-sac	dead end	_____
13. bon vivant	high liver	_____
14. demimonde	underworld	_____
15. avant-garde	front-runners	_____

Lesson 2

1. **agent provocateur** (ā′jənt prə vok′ə tûr′, tŏor′) outside agitator.
2. **chic** (shēk) attractive and fashionable in style; stylish.
3. **connoisseur** (kon′ə sûr′, -sŏor′) a person who is especially competent to pass critical judgments in art or in matters of taste.
4. **decolletage** (dā′kol täzh′) the neckline of a dress cut low in the front or back and often across the shoulders.
5. **éminence grise** (ā mē näns grēz′) a person who exercises power unofficially and surreptitiously.
6. **en masse** (än mas′) as a group.
7. **mêlée** (mā′lā, mā lā′) a confused, general hand-to-hand fight.
8. **pièce de résistance** (pyes də Rā zē stäNs′) showpiece; principal object or event.
9. **poseur** (pôzûr′) a person who attempts to impress others by assuming or affecting a manner, degree of elegance, etc.
10. **protégé** (prō′tə zhā′, prō′tə zhā′) a person under the patronage or care of someone influential who can further his or her career.

11. **raconteur** (rak´on tûr´, -to͞or´) a person who is skilled in relating anecdotes.
12. **riposte** (ri pōst´) a quick, sharp retort; retaliation.
13. **saboteur** (sab´ə tûr´) a person who deliberately destroys property, obstructs services, or undermines a cause.
14. **tour de force** (to͞or´də fôrs´) an exceptional achievement using the full skill, ingenuity, and resources of a person, country, or group.
15. **vis-à-vis** (vē´zə vē´) face to face; opposite; in relation to.

Quiz 3: Defining Words

Define each of the following words.

1. pièce de résistance _____

2. riposte _____

3. éminence grise _____

4. vis-à-vis _____

5. décolletage _____

6. en masse _____

7. tour de force _____

8. chic _____

9. protégé _____

10. connoisseur _____

11. raconteur _____

12. mêlée _____

13. saboteur _____

14. poseur _____

15. agent provocateur _____

Suggested Answers 1. showpiece 2. retort 3. an unofficial power 4. in relation to everybody 5. a low-cut neckline or backless dress 6. as a group 7. an exceptional achievement using the full skill, ingenuity, and resources of a person, country or group 8. attractive and fashionable in style 9. a person under the patronage or care of someone influential who can further his or her career 10. a person who is especially competent to pass critical judgments in art, especially one of the fine arts, or in matters of taste 11. a person who is skilled in relating anecdotes 12. a confused, general hand-to-hand fight 13. a person who destroys property, obstructs services, or subverts a cause 14. a person who attempts to impress others by assuming or affecting a manner, degree of elegance, etc. 15. outside agitator

Quiz 4: Synonyms

Each of the following phrases contains an italicized word. Select the best synonym for each word from the choices provided.

1. a daring *décolletage*
   a. low-cut neckline   b. dance   c. acrobatics   d. behavior
2. a *chic* hat
   a. French   b. imported   c. expensive   d. stylish
3. a daring *agent provocateur*
   a. actor   b. secret agent   c. talent scout   d. striptease artist
4. sitting *vis-à vis* an opponent
   a. next to   b. astride   c. facing   d. below
5. the entertaining *raconteur*
   a. comedian   b. storyteller   c. singer   d. poet
6. an amazing *tour de force*
   a. voyage   b. war victory   c. humiliation   d. achievement
7. to act *en masse*
   a. all together   b. religiously   c. stupidly   d. separately
8. a transparent *poseur*
   a. model   b. prank   c. fraud   d. gag
9. a captured *saboteur*
   a. spy   b. weapon   c. turncoat   d. revolutionary
10. my *protégé*
    a. mentor   b. tutor   c. proponent   d. dependent
11. a mighty *éminence grise*
    a. old man   b. battleship   c. soldier   d. secret power
12. a violent *mêlée*
    a. free-for-all   b. storm   c. criminal   d. sea
13. a noted *connoisseur*
    a. expert   b. politician   c. hostess   d. professor
14. a magnificent *pièce de résistance*
    a. argument   b. rebellion   c. centerpiece   d. fortress
15. a disarming *riposte*
    a. letter   b. artwork   c. weapon   d. swift reply

Lesson 3

arriviste (ar′ē vēst′) a person who has recently acquired wealth or status; upstart.

au courant (ō′ kōō räN′) up-to-date; fully aware; cognizant.

au fait (ō fe′) well-versed; expert; experienced.

beau monde (bō′ mond′, -môNd′) the fashionable world; high society.

bête noir (bāt′ nwär′) pet peeve; annoyance.

bonhomie (bon′ə mē′, bō′nə-) good nature; geniality.
bon mot (bôN mō′) clever turn of phrase; witticism.
cachet (ka shā′) superior status; prestige; a distinguishing feature.
canaille (kə nī′, -nāl′) the common people; rabble.
carte blanche (kärt′ blänch′, bläNsh′) full authority or access; unconditional authority.
causerie (kō′zə rē′) informal conversation; chat.
comme il faut (kô mēl f ō′) as it should be; proper; appropriate.
contretemps (kon′trə täN′) mishap; inconvenience.
coterie (kō′tə rē) a group of close associates; exclusive group or clique.
coup de grâce (kōō′ də gräs′) final blow; a finishing or decisive stroke.

Quiz 5: True/False

In the space provided, write T if the definition of the numbered word or phrase is true or F if it is false.

			T or F
1.	coterie	close associates	_____
2.	bête noir	annoyance	_____
3.	au courant	out of sync	_____
4.	contretemps	tempo	_____
5.	coup de grâce	final stroke	_____
6.	arriviste	newly rich person	_____
7.	comme il faut	proper	_____
8.	beau monde	high society	_____
9.	bon mot	good taste	_____
10.	causerie	chat	_____
11.	cachet	notebook	_____
12.	bonhomie	old friend	_____
13.	canaille	rabble	_____
14.	au fait	accomplished	_____
15.	carte blanche	unconditional authority	_____

Quiz 6: Synonyms

Each of the following sentences contains an italicized word or phrase. From the selection provided, pick the closest definition.

1. She aspired to be a member of the *beau monde.*
   a. athletic team   b. acting profession   c. underworld
   d. fashionable society
2. His *bon mot* brought a smile to everyone's lips.
   a. witticism   b. social blunder   c. somersault   d. fine cooking
3. She considered herself superior to the *canaille.*
   a. neighbors   b. common people   c. snobs   d. artistocrats

4. Reading the newspaper will keep you *au courant.*
   a. nervous   b. busy   c. ignorant   d. in the know
5. Her boss gave her *carte blanche* to negotiate the contract.
   a. a piece of paper   b. confidence   c. full authority   d. a high salary
6. His *bonhomie* won him many friends.
   a. good nature   b. stylishness   c. wealth   d. humility
7. His opponent administered the *coup de grâce* with enthusiasm.
   a. first strike   b. gracious bow   c. illegal hit   d. death blow
8. No one takes that *arriviste* seriously.
   a. tourist   b. clown   c. upstart   d. amateur
9. She is *au fait* in the ways of the world.
   a. awkward   b. experienced   c. old-fashioned   d. ignorant
10. His elegant wardrobe gave him a certain *cachet.*
    a. prestige   b. arrogance   c. contempt   d. debt
11. Slangy speech was his *bête noir.*
    a. specialty   b. worst fault   c. pet peeve   d. source of amusement
12. It was difficult to gain admission to their *coterie.*
    a. clique   b. nightclub   c. confidence   d. estate
13. They were engaged in a private *causerie.*
    a. love affair   b. argument   c. conversation   d. political movement
14. The unfortunate *contretemps* created a great deal of confusion.
    a. bad timing   b. mishap   c. counterstrike   d. rebuttal
15. She was hired to ensure that everything would be done *comme il faut.*
    a. as it should be   b. rapidly   c. on time   d. at great expense

Lesson 4

déclassé (dā′kla sā′, -klä-) reduced to or having low status.

denouement (dā′nōō mäN′) resolution or outcome, especially of a story.

de rigueur (də ri gûr′, -rē) strictly according to the rules; required.

dernier cri (dern′yā krē′) the last word; the ultimate; latest fashion.

detritus (di trī′təs) debris; rubbish.

de trop (də trō′) too much or too many; unwanted; in the way.

divertissement (di vûr′tis mənt; *Fr.* dē veR tēs -mäN′) a diversion or entertainment.

doyen (doi en′; *Fr.* dwA yaN′) the senior member of a group or profession; a leader or ultimate authority in a field.

echelon (esh′ə lon′) a level of authority, rank, or command.

éclat (ā klä′) flair, dash; brilliance; showy or elaborate display; acclaim or acclamation.

élan (ā län′, ā läN′) vivacity; verve.

enfant terrible (*Fr.* äN fäN te Rē′blə) irresponsible person; unconventional or shocking person; incorrigible child.

engagé (*Fr.* äN gA zhä′) politically committed; involved in a cause.
ennui (än wē′) boredom; a sense of weariness and discontent.
en passant (än′ pa säN′, äN′) in passing; by the way.

Quiz 7: Matching

Match each of the following numbered words and phrases with their closest synonyms. Write your answer in the space provided.

1.	dernier cri	a.	acclamation	_____
2.	enfant terrible	b.	by the way	_____
3.	divertissement	c.	too many	_____
4.	déclassé	d.	by the rules	_____
5.	éclat	e.	the ultimate	_____
6.	de rigueur	f.	vivacity	_____
7.	echelon	g.	boredom	_____
8.	ennui	h.	incorrigible person	_____
9.	de trop	i.	involved in a cause	_____
10.	engagé	j.	amusement	_____
11.	denouement	k.	having low status	_____
12.	doyen	l.	level of authority	_____
13.	élan	m.	debris	_____
14.	detritus	n.	outcome	_____
15.	en passant	o.	senior member	_____

Quiz 8: Synonyms

Each of the following sentences contains an italicized word or phrase. Choose the best synonym from the selection provided.

1. She rose to the highest *echelon* of her profession.
   a. rank   b. demands   c. challenge   d. temptation
2. The affair ultimately had a satisfactory *denouement*.
   a. division   b. prosecution   c. resolution   d. marriage
3. Their presence was regarded as *de trop* by the event's organizers.
   a. desirable   b. essential   c. awkward   d. unwanted
4. I mentioned it to her *en passant*.
   a. secretly   b. in the hallway   c. in passing   d. in a low voice
5. Her new book is the *dernier cri.*
   a. latest thing   b. laughingstock   c. mistaken notion   d. critical success
6. He is the *doyen* of art criticism.
   a. opponent   b. student   c. amateur   d. leading authority
7. His performance was marked by great *éclat.*
   a. brilliance   b. awkwardness   c. noisiness   d. mediocrity

8. Formal dress is *de rigueur* for this event.
    a. too much   b. optional   c. required   d. inappropriate
9. Even the thought of visiting them fills me with *ennui.*
    a. elation   b. weariness   c. fear   d. excitement
10. Playing cards provided a *divertissement* for their guests.
    a. hardship   b. expense   c. entertainment   d. boring pastime
11. The *engagé* students mounted a protest in support of the striking workers.
    a. married   b. busy   c. politically committed   d. immature
12. Somebody has to deal with the *detritus* after the party.
    a. rubbish   b. stragglers   c. bills   d. complaints
13. That *enfant terrible* tries our patience at times.
    a. political activist   b. irresponsible person   c. bore
    d. Neanderthal
14. Loud, pushy people are so *déclassé.*
    a. annoying   b. inconsiderate   c. low-status   d. exhilarating
15. The *élan* she brings to her work is infectious.
    a. high spirits   b. bad temper   c. meticulousness   d. boredom

Lesson 5

fait accompli (*Fr.* fe tA kôN plē′) accomplished act; done deal.
fracas (frā′kəs, frak′əs) noisy disturbance; disorderly fight.
gaffe (gaf) blunder; faux pas.
gaucherie (gō′shə rē′) awkwardness; vulgarity.
Grand Guignol (*Fr.* gRäN gē nyôl′) a drama emphasizing horror or sensationalism.
habitué (hə bich′o͞o ā′) a frequent visitor to a place; regular client; devotee.
hauteur (hō tûr′, ō tûr′) snobbishness; aloofness; superior air; haughtiness; arrogance.
ingénue (an′zhə no͞o′, aN ′-) a naive or innocent young woman.
lèse majesty (lēz′ maj′ə stē) an attack on a ruler or established authority; an affront to dignity.
maladroit (mal′ə droit′) lacking in adroitness; awkward.
mélange (mā läNzh′, -länj′) mixture; medley.
métier (mā′tyā, mā tyā′) vocation or calling; forte.
motif (mō tēf′) a recurring theme; a repeated element of design.
mot juste (*Fr.* mō zhYst′) precise word; pithy phrase.
mystique (mi stēk′) an aura of mystery; a framework of beliefs lending enhanced value or meaning to a person or thing.

Quiz 9: True/False

In the space provided, write T if the definition of the numbered word is true or F if it is false.

T or F

1. **métier**	rhythm	_____
2. **Grand Guignol**	sensationalistic drama	_____
3. **fracas**	breakage	_____
4. **habitué**	devotee	_____
5. **gaffe**	long pole	_____
6. **mot juste**	pithy phrase	_____
7. **ingénue**	naive girl	_____
8. **fait accompli**	accomplished act	_____
9. **gaucherie**	awkwardness	_____
10. **mystique**	secret plot	_____
11. **maladroit**	clumsy	_____
12. **mélange**	medley	_____
13. **motif**	intention	_____
14. **hauteur**	arrogance	_____
15. **lèse-majesty**	affront to dignity	_____

Quiz 10: Synonyms

Each of the following sentences contains an italicized word or phrase. Choose the best definition from the selection provided.

1. Her *hauteur* made her unpopular.
   a. height   b. low status   c. awkwardness   d. haughtiness
2. He had a certain gift for the *mot juste.*
   a. bargain   b. most clues   c. precise word   d. right answer
3. Garbo's *mystique* lingered long after her retirement from the movies.
   a. mysterious aura   b. popularity   c. income   d. illness
4. Their *fracas* broke up the party.
   a. complaints   b. embarrassment   c. noisy fight   d. boring speeches
5. The artist was a *habitué* of the small café.
   a. critic   b. regular   c. debtor   d. employee
6. His *gaucherie* embarrassed everyone in the room.
   a. shabby clothing   b. lies   c. snobbishness   d. vulgarity
7. The publication was an act of *lèse-majesty.*
   a. groveling   b. courage   c. noninterference in policy   d. attack on authority
8. Her performance as an aging movie queen turned psychotic was pure *Grand Guignol.*
   a. comedy   b. sensational horror   c. ham acting   d. sentimentality
9. His *maladroit* behavior marked him as an ill-bred person.
   a. evil   b. inconsiderate   c. awkward   d. snobbish

10. The wallpaper had a floral *motif.*
    a. repeated design   b. centerpiece   c. border   d. hint
11. The alliance was by then a *fait accompli.*
    a. failure   b. fated   c. old news   d. done deal
12. His *gaffe* cost him his job.
    a. laughter   b. error   c. insubordination   d. arrogance
13. She chose her *métier* after years of indecision.
    a. spouse   b. vocation   c. favorite poem   d. major subject
14. The *ingénue* was dressed in a demure fashion.
    a. unworldly girl   b. infant   c. sophisticate   d. engineer
15. His art was a *mélange* of different elements.
    a. satire   b. mixture   c. denial   d. derivation

Lesson 6

nom de guerre (nom′ də gâr′) an assumed name; pseudonym; stage name; alias.

nouveau riche (nōō′vō rēsh′) a newly rich person, especially one who is ostentatious or uncultivated.

parvenu (pär′və nōō′, -nyōō′) newcomer; upstart.

penchant (pen′chənt) a strong inclination, taste, or liking for something.

pied-à-terre (pē ā′də târ′) a part-time or temporary residence.

précis (prā sē′, prā′sē) a short, concise summary.

rapprochement (rap′rōsh mäN′) an establishment or renewal of friendly relations.

recherché (rə shâr′shā) esoteric or obscure; select or rare; mannered or affected.

risqué (ri skā′) racy, indelicate, or suggestive.

sang-froid (*Fr.* säN frwA′) self-possession; composure; calmness or equanimity.

savoir-faire (sav′wär fâr′) know-how; tact; social polish.

soigné (swän yā′) well-groomed; carefully or elegantly done.

succès d'estime (*Fr.* sYk se des tēm′) critical success; success achieved by merit rather than popularity.

tête-à-tête (tāt′ə tāt′, tet′ə tet′) intimate, private conversation.

volte-face (volt fäs′, vōlt-) reversal; turnabout; about-face.

Quiz 11: Matching

Match each of the following numbered words or phrases with its closest synonym. Write your answer in the space provided.

1. **rapprochement**   a. private conversation   _____
2. **sang-froid**   b. about-face   _____
3. **nom de guerre**   c. elegantly done   _____
4. **penchant**   d. indelicate   _____

5. savoir-faire	e. renewal of relations	_____
6. volte-face	f. self-possession	_____
7. recherché	g. temporary residence	_____
8. nouveau riche	h. affected	_____
9. pied-à-terre	i. critical success	_____
10. tête-à-tête	j. assumed name	_____
11. risqué	k. inclination	_____
12. succès d'estime	l. know-how	_____
13. précis	m. concise summary	_____
14. parvenu	n. newly rich person	_____
15. soigné	o. upstart	_____

Quiz 12: Synonyms

Each of the following sentences contains an italicized word or phrase. From the selection provided, choose the best definition.

1. The assignment was to write a *précis* of the essay.
   a. criticism   b. summary   c. outline   d. fictionalization
2. *Lady Chatterley's Lover* is *risqué*.
   a. risky   b. scholarly   c. racy   d. sentimental
3. A *soigné* escort is every woman's best accessory.
   a. well-groomed   b. wealthy   c. polite   d. helpful
4. The foreign film was a *succès d'estime* but it lost money at the box office.
   a. critical favorite   b. diatribe   c. successful remake
   d. tearjerker
5. The divorced couple reached a *rapprochement*.
   a. impasse   b. disagreement   c. state of friendly relations
   d. boiling point
6. We maintain a *pied-à-terre* in the city.
   a. part-time residence   b. small garden   c. business office   d. old friend
7. The text is too *recherché* to appeal to a wide audience.
   a. pornographic   b. well-researched   c. obscure   d. expensive
8. She maintained her *sang-froid* in the face of criticism.
   a. composure   b. options   c. combativeness   d. ability to speak well
9. When he was confronted with the evidence, he did a *volte-face*.
   a. special plea   b. impersonation   c. admission of guilt
   d. reversal
10. The *nouveau riche* businessman tried to buy social acceptance.
    a. newly rich   b. impoverished   c. avant-garde   d. haughty

11. He is more well known by his *nom de guerre*.
    a. war exploits   b. bad reputation   c. alias   d. birth name
12. He asked her to join him at the café for a *tête-à-tête*.
    a. light meal   b. intimate chat   c. debate   d. love affair
13. His *savoir-faire* helped him to smooth over a difficult situation.
    a. manservant   b. physical attractiveness   c. impersonation
    d. social tact
14. She's only a *parvenu* in that field.
    a. newcomer   b. part-time worker   c. dabbler   d. outsider
15. His home reflects a *penchant* for Oriental art.
    a. expertise   b. distaste   c. misunderstanding   d. strong liking

Greek

To the Ancient Greeks, philosophy (from *philos* "loving" and *sophia* "skill, wisdom") encompassed logic, science, ethics, politics, psychology, and even poetics. Like their art and architecture, Greek thought is concerned with order and harmony; it has provided the rational foundations of Western civilization. Indeed, the concept of democracy is Greek (from *demos* "people, population" and *kratos* "rule, strength, might"). Under the great statesman Pericles (c. 495–429 B.C.E.), the people of Athens instituted the first constitution, an assembly of 500 senators, and a system of trial by jury. In addition, Greek festivals in honor of the wine and fertility god Dionysus gave birth to the theater of Aeschylus, Sophocles, and Euripides. The very words "theater," "drama," "comedy," and "tragedy" are all gifts of the Greeks.

Though we have already seen the influence of Ancient Greek on the English language in some earlier chapters, there are still a number of terms that are so pungent and precise that they survive in our vocabulary to this day. In many cases, Greek terms embody abstract concepts that are otherwise hard to describe in English. Studying these lists will give you some insight into the Greek mind and perhaps help you to understand the roots of European culture, while also greatly enhancing your ability to express your own ideas.

Lesson 7

acedia (ə sē′dē ə) listlessness, sloth; indifference; apathy.
alpha and omega (al′fə and ō mā′gə, ō mē′gə) the beginning and the end; the basic or essential elements.

anathema (ə nath′ə mə) detested or loathed thing or person; curse.
anomie (an′ə mē′) a sense of dislocation; alienation; despair.
catharsis (kə thär′sis) a purging of emotion or release of emotional tensions.
charisma (kə riz′mə) personal magnetism; the capacity to lead or inspire others.
despot (des′pət, -pot) absolute ruler; tyrant or oppressor.
diatribe (dī′ə trīb′) a bitter denunciation; abusive criticism.
enigma (ə nig′mə) puzzle, riddle; a person or thing of a confusing and contradictory nature.
ephemera (i fem′ər ə) short-lived or transitory things.
epiphany (i pif′ə nē) revelation; sudden, intuitive insight into reality.
epitome (i pit′ə mē) embodiment; a person or thing that is typical of a whole class.

Quiz 13: True/False

In the space provided, write T if the definition of the numbered word is true or F if it is false.

		T or F
1. **enigma**	distinctive feature	_____
2. **catharsis**	release of tension	_____
3. **alpha and omega**	married couple	_____
4. **despot**	absolute ruler	_____
5. **ephemera**	short poem	_____
6. **anathema**	curse	_____
7. **diatribe**	sharp criticism	_____
8. **epitome**	large book	_____
9. **acedia**	apathy	_____
10. **charisma**	attractive aura	_____
11. **anomie**	despair	_____
12. **epiphany**	sudden insight	_____

Quiz 14: Synonyms

Each of the following sentences contains an italicized word or phrase. Select the best synonym from the choices provided.

1. After the fall of the republic, the empire was ruled by a succession of *despots.*
   a. madmen   b. drunkards   c. tyrants   d. illiterates
2. Rock and roll was *anathema* to the classical musician.
   a. revolutionary   b. loathsome   c. inspiring   d. noisy
3. The candidate's *charisma* ensured his election to national office.
   a. personal magnetism   b. credit   c. following
   d. cheerfulness

4. All of Samuel Beckett's characters are afflicted with *anomie.*
   a. hunger   b. halitosis   c. alienation   d. poverty
5. She wastes all her time with *ephemera.*
   a. jewels   b. insignificant things   c. false friends   d. magic
6. Her changeable moods made her something of an *enigma* to her friends.
   a. puzzle   b. annoyance   c. delight   d. bore
7. Food and wine are the *alpha and omega* of the gourmet's existence.
   a. pitfalls   b. end-all and be-all   c. expenses   d. amusements
8. A severe attack of *acedia* kept him from meeting his deadline.
   a. indigestion   b. anxiety   c. insects   d. listlessness
9. The solution to the math problem came to him in an *epiphany.*
   a. envelope   b. sudden revelation   c. graveyard   d. pithy saying
10. The dramatic events of the play caused a general *catharsis* among the members of the audience.
    a. riot   b. exodus   c. emotional purging   d. noisy complaint
11. Jackie was the *epitome* of style and elegance.
    a. embodiment   b. sworn enemy   c. proponent   d. antithesis
12. He had few friends left after his outspoken *diatribe.*
    a. commendation   b. filibuster   c. gibberish   d. denunciation

Lesson 8

ethos (ē'thos, ē'thōs) the fundamental character or spirit of a culture; distinguishing character or disposition of a group.

euphoria (yŏŏ fôr'ē ə) elation; strong feeling of happiness, confidence, or well-being.

exegesis (ek'si jē'sis) a critical explanation or interpretation, especially of a text.

halcyon (hal'sē ən) happy, joyful, or carefree; prosperous; calm, peaceful, or tranquil.

hedonist (hēd'n ist) a person who is devoted to self-gratification as a way of life; pleasure-seeker.

hoi polloi (hoi' pə loi') the common people; the masses.

hubris (hyŏŏ'bris, hōō'-) excessive pride or self-confidence; arrogance.

iota (ī ō'tə) a very small quantity; jot; whit.

metamorphosis (met'ə môr'fə sis) transformation; profound or complete change.

miasma (mī az'mə) noxious fumes; poisonous effluvia; a dangerous, foreboding, or deathlike influence or atmosphere.

myriad (mir'ē əd) of an indefinitely great number; innumerable.

omphalos (om'fə ləs) navel; central point.

Quiz 15: Matching

Match each of the following numbered words or phrases with its closest synonym. Write your answer in the space provided.

1. **myriad**	a. interpretation	_____
2. **omphalos**	b. elation	_____
3. **exegesis**	c. prosperous	_____
4. **hubris**	d. the masses	_____
5. **miasma**	e. cultural spirit	_____
6. **euphoria**	f. whit	_____
7. **hoi polloi**	g. uncountable	_____
8. **ethos**	h. navel	_____
9. **halcyon**	i. transformation	_____
10. **iota**	j. arrogance	_____
11. **metamorphosis**	k. poisonous atmosphere	_____
12. **hedonist**	l. pleasure-seeker	_____

Quiz 16: Synonyms

For each of the italicized words or phrases in the following sentences, select the best synonym from the choices provided.

1. He expressed his contempt for the *hoi polloi.*
   a. tasteless food   b. cheap gifts   c. common people   d. baseless accusations
2. His newfound love filled him with *euphoria.*
   a. fear   b. happiness   c. arrogance   d. suspicion
3. The ancient people built their temple at the *omphalos* of the kingdom.
   a. center   b. end   c. highest point   d. beginning
4. She longed for the *halcyon* days of her youth.
   a. carefree   b. bohemian   c. expatriate   d. studious
5. When they donned their costumes, the *metamorphosis* was complete.
   a. deception   b. party   c. examination   d. transformation
6. She was trapped in the *miasma* of her own sins.
   a. dangerous atmosphere   b. outcome   c. awkwardness   d. pride
7. The anthropologist studied the *ethos* of the tribe.
   a. anatomy   b. underlying beliefs   c. love life   d. military practices
8. Don Juan was a *hedonist.*
   a. pleasure-seeker   b. Spaniard   c. courtier   d. ruffian
9. Leonardo da Vinci had *myriad* talents.
   a. artistic   b. limited   c. innumerable   d. diplomatic

10. The scholar spent many years refining his *exegesis.*
    a. library   b. prose style   c. rejection   d. interpretation
11. Not one *iota* of your argument is acceptable to me.
    a. little bit   b. idea   c. excuse   d. interpretation
12. Tragic heroes are destroyed by their own *hubris.*
    a. armies   b. language   c. pride   d. followers

Lesson 9

panacea (pan′ə sē′ə) cure-all; a solution for all difficulties.
pantheon (pan′thē on′) the realm of the heroes or idols of any group; illustrious leaders.
paradigm (par′ə dīm′) an example serving as a model; pattern.
pathos (pā′thos, -thōs) pity; compassion; suffering.
pedagogue (ped′ə gog′, -gôg′) a teacher; a person who is pedantic, dogmatic, and formal.
plethora (pleth′ər ə) overabundance; excess; a great number.
protagonist (prō tag′ə nist) an actor who plays the main role; the chief proponent or leader of a movement or cause.
psyche (sī′kē) the human soul, spirit, or mind.
stasis (stā′sis) equilibrium or inactivity; stagnation.
stigma (stig′mə) a stain or reproach on one's reputation; a mark or defect of a disease.
trauma (trou′mə, trô′-) wound or shock; a wrenching or distressing experience.
troglodyte (trog′lə dīt′) cave dweller or Neanderthal; brutal or degraded person; reactionary.

Quiz 17: True/False

In the space provided, write T if the definition of the word is true or F if it is false.

			T or F
1.	**pedagogue**	teacher	_____
2.	**troglodyte**	reactionary	_____
3.	**panacea**	poison	_____
4.	**plethora**	plea	_____
5.	**stigma**	stain	_____
6.	**trauma**	wound	_____
7.	**paradigm**	nonsense	_____
8.	**psyche**	spirit	_____
9.	**stasis**	equilibrium	_____
10.	**pantheon**	wild animal	_____
11.	**pathos**	pity	_____
12.	**protagonist**	enemy	_____

Quiz 18: Synonyms

Each of the following sentences contains an italicized word. From the selection provided, find the best synonym for that word.

1. Her dilemma evoked great *pathos* in the onlookers.
   a. contempt   b. amusement   c. compassion   d. contributions
2. He could never escape the *stigma* associated with his criminal conviction.
   a. misery   b. puzzle   c. victim   d. bad reputation
3. That professor has a reputation as a *pedagogue*.
   a. tyrant   b. sex fiend   c. athlete   d. pedant
4. The *trauma* of her childhood led her to seek therapy.
   a. distress   b. grandparents   c. poverty   d. dreams
5. The resilience of the human *psyche* is an amazing thing.
   a. body   b. spirit   c. love life   d. family
6. She was elevated into the *pantheon*.
   a. stratosphere   b. attic   c. realm of heroes   d. executive ranks
7. Booze and drugs reduced him to the status of a *troglodyte*.
   a. brute   b. outcast   c. bankrupt   d. academic dropout
8. *Stasis* is the enemy of progress in society.
   a. moral turpitude   b. criminality   c. national pride
   d. stagnation
9. She is the *paradigm* of what a woman should be.
   a. opposite   b. model   c. teacher   d. failure
10. There is always a *plethora* of junk mail on my desk.
    a. excess   b. pleasing amount   c. variety   d. lack
11. Che is remembered as the *protagonist* of the revolution.
    a. destroyer   b. loser   c. dead hero   d. proponent
12. She thought her divorce from her first husband would work as a *panacea*.
    a. cure for all problems   b. inspiration   c. example   d. source of wealth

Latin

The Ancient Romans were great borrowers; they are more distinguished for their military exploits and legal traditions than their cultural values or artistic accomplishments. The Roman Empire was acquired by dint of a superior fighting force and rigorous military discipline, but it was maintained by Roman law. Thus, we should not be surprised that so many Latin legal terms have been carried over into English.

While the empire stretched as far north as Scotland, as an occupying force the Romans did not integrate with the native population to make a notable impression on the language during the centuries-long Roman presence in ancient Britain, even though remains of their civil engineering feats—roads, forts, aqueducts, baths, and walls—still survive in England today. Indeed, the Latin influence on the English language comes primarily through the Romance languages, particularly French and to a lesser degree Italian, as well as through the borrowings associated with the renewed interest in classical sources during the Renaissance.

Not all of the following terms are strictly legal, but they suggest the precision and practicality of the Latin mind and will also help you to clarify your speech and writing.

Lesson 10

ad hoc (ad hok′, hōk′) for a specific or particular purpose.
antebellum (an′tē bel′əm) prewar.
caveat (kav′ē ät′) a warning or caution; admonition.
decorum (di kôr′əm) dignity; proper behavior, manners, or appearance.
de facto (dē fak′tō, dā) in fact; in reality; actually existing.
de profundis (dā prō fo͞on′dis) out of the depths of sorrow or despair.
dementia (di men′shə) madness; insanity; severely impaired mental function.
desideratum (di sid′ə rā′təm, -rä′-) something wanted or needed.
dolor (dō′lər) sorrow; grief.
ex cathedra (eks′ kə thē′drə) from the seat of authority; by virtue of one's office.
exemplar (ig zem′plər, -plär) model or pattern; example or instance; original or archetype.
exigent (ek′si jənt) urgent; pressing.

Quiz 19: Matching

Match each of the following numbered words or phrases with its closest synonym. Write your answer in the space provided.

1. **desideratum**	a. grief	_____
2. **exigent**	b. madness	_____
3. **caveat**	c. prewar	_____
4. **dementia**	d. from the depths	_____
5. **decorum**	e. in fact	_____
6. **antebellum**	f. urgent	_____
7. **exemplar**	g. with special purpose	_____

  8. **dolor**
  9. **ad hoc**
10. **ex cathedra**
11. **de facto**
12. **de profundis**

h. caution   _____
i. necessary thing   _____
j. archetype   _____
k. dignity   _____
l. official   _____

Quiz 20: Synonyms

Each of the following sentences contains an italicized word or phrase. Choose the best synonym from the selection provided.

  1. Nothing could assuage his *dolor.*
     a. courage   b. sadness   c. anger   d. impatience
  2. The *antebellum* plantation fell into disrepair.
     a. Southern   b. magnificent   c. enemy   d. prewar
  3. She ignored his *caveat.*
     a. tie   b. small dog   c. warning   d. example
  4. Their leader made an *ex cathedra* pronouncement.
     a. authoritative   b. religious   c. profane   d. revolutionary
  5. They formed an *ad hoc* committee to address the problem.
     a. warlike   b. finance   c. permanent   d. limited-purpose
  6. An *exigent* matter requires immediate action.
     a. dangerous   b. pressing   c. confusing   d. scandalous
  7. Her *decorum* at the ball convinced everyone that Eliza was a lady.
     a. proper behavior   b. fancy dress   c. conversation   d. arrogance
  8. The prince was given to fits of *dementia.*
     a. laughter   b. laziness   c. insanity   d. indecision
  9. Having a comfortable home was her main *desideratum.*
     a. expense   b. wish   c. failure   d. occupation
10. The leader served as an *exemplar* for the rest of the group.
     a. model   b. tyrant   c. encouragement   d. warning
11. The tortured soul gave a cry *de profundis.*
     a. of exultation   b. suddenly   c. out of the depths   d. of relief
12. The *de facto* government operated without a constitution.
     a. lawful   b. efficient   c. unfair   d. actually existing

Lesson 11

ex nihilo (eks nī′hi lō′, nē′-) out of nothing.
ex post facto (eks′ pōst′ fak′tō) after the fact; subsequently; retroactively.
factotum (fak tō′təm) assistant or aide; deputy.
imprimatur (im′pri mä′tər) sanction; approval.
in toto (in tō′tō) in all; completely, entirely; wholly.
literati (lit′ə rä′tē) intellectuals or scholars; highly educated persons.
mea culpa (mā′ə kul′pə) my fault; an admission of guilt.

modus operandi (mō'dəs op'ə ran'dē, -dī) way of operating; method of working.

non compos mentis (non' kom'pəs men'tis) of unsound mind; mentally incompetent.

nonsequitur (non sek'wi tər) something that does not follow from the preceding series; illogical conclusion.

odium (ō'dē əm) intense hatred or dislike; reproach or discredit.

pro forma (prō fôr'mə) done perfunctorily; done as a formality.

Quiz 21: True/False

In the space provided, write T if the definition of the numbered word or phrase is true or F if it is false.

			T or F
1.	in toto	completely	_____
2.	ex post facto	after the fact	_____
3.	nonsequitur	logical series	_____
4.	ex nihilo	from the top	_____
5.	modus operandi	dishonest tactics	_____
6.	pro forma	as a formality	_____
7.	imprimatur	blessing	_____
8.	mea culpa	mean person	_____
9.	odium	bad debt	_____
10.	literati	educated persons	_____
11.	factotum	fact sheet	_____
12.	non compos mentis	mentally incompetent	_____

Quiz 22: Synonyms

Each of the following sentences contains an italicized word or phrase. From the choices provided, choose the best definition.

1. The plan has the *imprimatur* of the highest authority.
   a. contempt   b. approval   b. semblance   c. arrogance
2. He inspired intense *odium* in everyone who knew him.
   a. admiration   b. excitement   c. hatred   d. curiosity
3. The defendant was acquitted on grounds of *non compos mentis.*
   a. innocence   b. extenuating circumstances   c. youth   d. insanity
4. He built an empire *ex nihilo.*
   a. out of nothing   b. illegally   c. rapidly   d. extravagantly
5. All the *literati* were in attendance at the ceremony.
   a. litterbugs   b. students   c. movie stars   d. intellectuals
6. His speech was filled with *nonsequiturs.*
   a. nonsense words   b. faulty logic   c. sound arguments
   d. condemnations

7. She offered a *pro forma* apology for her lapse in manners.
   a. lengthy   b. informal   c. perfect   d. perfunctory
8. All the details were handled by her *factotum.*
   a. father   b. accountant   c. deputy   d. factory
9. The posse was composed of twelve members *in toto.*
   a. in all   b. in disguise   c. as a rule   d. on foot
10. Her *modus operandi* is slow but efficient.
    a. means of conveyance   b. argument   c. way of working
    d. dressmaker
11. An *ex post facto* law is unfair.
    a. strict   b. arbitrary   c. foreign   d. retroactive
12. All his *mea culpas* did not soften her anger.
    a. confessions of guilt   b. gifts   c. poor excuses   d. entreaties

Lesson 12

prolix (prō liks′, prō′liks) wordy; talkative; tediously long.
quidnunc (kwid′nungk′) busybody; a person eager to know the latest gossip.
quid pro quo (kwid′ prō kwō′) equal exchange; substitute; something given or taken in return for something else.
rara avis (râr′ə ā′vis) a rare person or thing; anything unusual; rarity.
sanctum sanctorum (sangk′təm sangk tôr′əm) sacred place; the holiest of places.
sine qua non (sin′ā kwä nōn′) an indispensable condition; prerequisite.
status quo (stā′təs kwō, stat′əs) conditions as they are now; the existing state.
sub rosa (sub rō′zə) confidentially; secretly; privately; undercover.
sui generis (sōō′ē jen′ər is) of its own kind; unique; one of a kind; unparalleled.
terra incognita (ter′ə in kog′ni tə) unknown territory; an unexplored region; uncharted ground.
viva voce (vī′və vō′sē) aloud, orally; by word of mouth.
vox populi (voks′ pop′yə lī′) popular opinion; the voice of the people.

Quiz 23: Matching

Match each of the following numbered words or phrases with its closest definition. Write your answer in the space provided.

1. **sui generis**	a. unusual thing	_____
2. **rara avis**	b. substitute	_____
3. **quidnunc**	c. unparalleled	_____
4. **terra incognita**	d. existing state	_____
5. **sine qua non**	e. privately	_____
6. **prolix**	f. uncharted ground	

7. **sub rosa**   g. by word of mouth   _____
8. **viva voce**   h. wordy   _____
9. **status quo**   i. voice of the people   _____
10. **vox populi**   j. gossip   _____
11. **sanctum sanctorum**   k. necessary condition   _____
12. **quid pro quo**   l. holy place   _____

Quiz 24: Synonyms

Each of the following sentences contains an italicized word or phrase. Choose the best definition from the selection of synonyms provided.

1. The students took their exams *viva voce.*
   a. secretly   b. orally   c. outdoors   d. with lively enthusiasm
2. He retreated to the *sanctum sanctorum* of his den.
   a. sacred place   b. chaotic mess   c. workshop   d. worldly comforts
3. A true friend is a *rara avis.*
   a. temporary thing   b. necessity   c. rarity   d. phantasm
4. The revolutionary is never satisfied with the *status quo.*
   a. corrupt government   b. common people   c. agenda   d. things as they are
5. Outer space remains *terra incognita.*
   a. unknown territory   b. terrifying   c. fascinating   d. an object of study
6. If you offer them a *quid pro quo,* it will settle the dispute once and for all.
   a. apology   b. ultimatum   c. small bonus   d. equal exchange
7. The *vox populi* called for his acquittal.
   a. popular opinion   b. rabble   c. senate   d. loudmouths
8. The conspirators met *sub rosa.*
   a. in the garden   b. secretly   c. as a group   d. in the open air
9. None of the students wanted to attend his *prolix* lectures.
   a. scholarly   b. informal   c. frequent   d. tediously long
10. Her *sui generis* prose style attracted the attention of the critics.
    a. unique   b. flamboyant   c. formal   d. simple
11. None of the neighbors welcomed the presence of that *quidnunc.*
    a. unruly child   b. glutton   c. meddlesome person   d. liar
12. Mutual trust is the *sine qua non* of a lasting relationship.
    a. secret ingredient   b. embodiment   c. outcome   d. prerequisite

Italian

After French, Italian has had the greatest influence on English of all the modern European languages, but most of our borrowings have long been Anglicized beyond recognition. Though most Italian-Americans emigrated around the beginning of the twentieth century, the language probably had its greatest impact in the Renaissance, when Italian culture was at its height. It was so pervasive in England that several sixteenth-century writers complained about its corrupting influence on the language.

Many of the words that survive intact in the English vocabulary are musical, artistic, and architectural terms that reflect the Italian emphasis on refinement and good living. In addition, many French-appearing terms are barely disguised versions of the original Italian *(caricature, burlesque, carnival, buffoon, façade)*. Other Italian importations are evidence of the love of intrigue shared by the descendants of Niccolò Machiavelli (1469–1527), the political philosopher whose surname has given us the highly descriptive term *Machiavellian* ("characterized by unscrupulous cunning, deception, or expediency").

Lesson 13

al fresco (al fres'kō) out-of-doors; in the open air.
bravura (brə vyŏor'ə, -vŏor'ə) a florid, brilliant style; a display of daring.
dolce far niente (dōl'chä fär nyen'tä) sweet inactivity.
focaccia (fō kä'chə) a round, flat Italian bread, sprinkled with oil and herbs before baking.
imbroglio (im brōl'yō) a confused state of affairs; a complicated or difficult situation; bitter misunderstanding.
inamorata (in am'ə rä'tə, in'am-) a female sweetheart or lover.
incognito (in'kog nē'tō) with one's identity hidden or unknown; in disguise.
la dolce vita (lä dōl'chä vē'tä) the good life.
manifesto (man'ə fes'tō) a public declaration of intentions, opinions, or objectives, as issued by an organization.
panache (pə nash', -näsh') a grand or flamboyant manner; flair; verve; stylishness.
punctilio (pungk til'ē ō') strict or exact observance of formalities; fine point or detail of conduct or procedure.
vendetta (ven det'ə) a prolonged or bitter feud or rivalry; the pursuit of vengeance.

Quiz 25: True/False

In the space provided, write T if the definition of the numbered word or phrase is true or F if it is false.

			T or F
1.	**vendetta**	saleswoman	_____
2.	**incognito**	hidden identity	_____
3.	**la dolce vita**	easy living	_____
4.	**bravura**	acclamation	_____
5.	**punctilio**	proper procedure	_____
6.	**focaccia**	thin pancake	_____
7.	**dolce far niente**	leisure time	_____
8.	**panache**	flamboyant manner	_____
9.	**imbroglio**	embroidery	_____
10.	**al fresco**	in the open air	_____
11.	**inamorata**	unloving	_____
12.	**manifesto**	open apology	_____

Quiz 26: Synonyms

Each of the following sentences contains an italicized word or phrase. Select the best synonym from the choices provided.

1. Cut the *focaccia* into eight pieces.
   a. pie   b. cake   c. bread   d. pizza
2. He wrote poetry for his *inamorata.*
   a. patron   b. teacher   c. self-satisfaction   d. sweetheart
3. The family liked to dine *al fresco.*
   a. outdoors   b. at restaurants   c. in formal dress   d. late at night
4. The revolutionaries issued a *manifesto.*
   a. barrage of gunfire   b. apology   c. map   d. statement of purpose
5. The soprano's *bravura* performance brought down the house.
   a. off-key   b. brilliant   c. unexpected   d. improvised
6. The royal family was traveling *incognito.*
   a. at night   b. at great expense   c. in disguise   d. forcibly
7. The ambassador performed his duties with *punctilio.*
   a. speed   b. arrogance   c. timeliness   d. strict formality
8. They looked forward to living *la dolce vita* after their retirement.
   a. the good life   b. inexpensively   c. quietly   d. in seclusion
9. Their longstanding *vendetta* led to ruin for both parties.
   a. debts   b. feud   c. business deal   d. love affair
10. Coco always dressed with *panache.*
    a. carelessness   b. great speed   c. stylishness   d. bad taste

11. His scandalous behavior created an *imbroglio* for his government.
   a. difficult situation   b. diversion   c. opportunity   d. expense
12. The playboy lived a life of *dolce far niente*.
   a. erotic pleasure   b. ambition   c. artistic pursuits   d. sweet inactivity

Lesson 14

chiaroscuro (kē är′ə skyŏŏr′ō, -skŏŏr′ō) the distribution of light and dark areas, as in a picture.
cognoscenti (kon′yə shen′tē, kog′nə-) those in the know; intellectuals; well-informed persons.
crescendo (kri shen′dō, -sen′dō) a steady increase in force or loudness; a climactic point or peak.
dilettante (dil′i tänt′, dil′i tän′tā) dabbler; amateur; devotee.
diva (dē′və) an exalted female singer; any goddess-like woman.
impresario (im′prə sär′ ē ō′) a person who organizes public entertainments; an entrepreneur, promoter, or director.
pentimento (pen′tə men′tō) the reappearance of an earlier stage, as in a painting.
prima donna (prē′mə don′ə) the principal singer in an opera company; any vain, temperamental person who expects privileged treatment.
sotto voce (sot′ō vō′chē) in a soft, low voice, so as not to be overheard.
staccato (stə kä′tō) abruptly disconnected; disjointed; herky-jerky.
tempo (tem′pō) rate of speed; rhythm or pattern.
virtuoso (vûr′chŏŏ ō′sō) highly skilled performer; a person who has special knowledge or skill in a field; highly cultivated person.

Quiz 27: Matching

Match each of the following numbered words or phrases with its closest synonym. Write your answer in the space provided.

1. **diva**	a. in a low voice	_____
2. **virtuoso**	b. amateur	_____
3. **pentimento**	c. goddess	_____
4. **crescendo**	d. rate of speed	_____
5. **chiaroscuro**	e. skilled performer	_____
6. **sotto voce**	f. emergence of an earlier stage	_____
7. **cognoscenti**	g. temperamental person	_____
8. **impresario**	h. climactic point	_____
9. **tempo**	i. pattern of light and shadow	_____
10. **staccato**	j. intellectuals	_____

11. **dilettante**   k. entrepreneur   _____
12. **prima donna**   l. disjointed   _____

Quiz 28: Synonyms

Each of the following sentences contains an italicized word or phrase. Select the best synonym from the choices provided.

1. She is a *virtuoso* in her field.
   a. skilled person   b. moral person   c. failure   d. celebrity
2. Diaghilev was the most famous *impresario* of his age.
   a. emperor   b. performer   c. artistic promoter   d. statesman
3. The *prima donna* always got her way.
   a. consort   b. president's wife   c. temperamental woman   d. saint
4. Lillian Hellman's memoir of her youth was aptly entitled *Pentimento.*
   a. regrets   b. sentiments   c. reemergence of an earlier stage   d. souvenirs
5. The parade proceeded at a *staccato* pace.
   a. smooth   b. rapid   c. staggering   d. stop-and-go
6. Rock and roll has as many *divas* as the world of opera.
   a. goddesses   b. hangouts   c. devotees   d. flops
7. A *dilettante* has passion but no real talent.
   a. watercolorist   b. lawyer   c. accompanist   d. dabbler
8. The *cognoscenti* are flocking to this new play.
   a. ignoramuses   b. well-informed people   c. rich people   d. tourists
9. The conspirators conversed *sotto voce.*
   a. loudly   b. seductively   c. in a low voice   d. under the stairs
10. The candlelight bathed the room in *chiaroscuro.*
    a. romance   b. brilliance   c. sweet smells   d. areas of light and shadow
11. His anger reached a *crescendo.*
    a. peak   b. credibility   c. turning point   d. decrease
12. He never quite adjusted to the *tempo* of city life.
    a. cruelty   b. sophistication   c. anonymity   d. rhythms

Spanish

Spanish has had a less pervasive influence on the English language than some other European sources, but we have borrowed a substantial number of useful words from the Spanish culture of the Southwest. A number of unique American terms are actually mispronunciations of the original Spanish words: *vamoose, mus-*

tang, calaboose, lariat, buckaroo, and *hoosegow* are all coinages that evoke the bygone world of the American cowboy.

But as more Latin-Americans emigrate to the United States, bringing their culture and customs with them, we may see the introduction of some new Spanish terms. Learning some of these words borrowed from the Spanish will widen your cultural horizons and add spice and piquancy to your vocabulary.

Lesson 15

aficionado (ə fish'yə nä'dō) fan; enthusiast; ardent devotee.
bonanza (bə nan'zə) stroke of luck; sudden source of wealth; spectacular windfall.
bravado (brə vä'dō) swaggering display of courage.
desperado (des'pə rä'dō) a bold, reckless criminal; outlaw.
duenna (dōō en'ə, dyōō-) chaperone; an older woman who serves as an escort for young ladies.
embargo (em bär'gō) a government order restricting commerce; any restraint or prohibition.
fiesta (fē es'tə) a festival or feast; any joyous or merry celebration.
incommunicado (in'kə myōō'ni kä'dō) in solitary confinement; without any means of communicating with others.
lagniappe (lan yap', lan'yap) bonus; gratuity or tip.
machismo (mä chēz'mō) an exaggerated sense of masculinity; boastful or swaggering virility.
peccadillo (pek'ə dil'ō) a minor offense; venial sin.
siesta (sē es'tə) a midafternoon rest; nap.

Quiz 29: Matching

Match each of the following numbered words with its closest synonym. Write your answer in the space provided.

1. **machismo**	a. official restraint	_____
2. **bravado**	b. chaperone	_____
3. **desperado**	c. gratuity	_____
4. **aficionado**	d. exaggerated masculinity	_____
5. **lagniappe**	e. venial sin	_____
6. **duenna**	f. celebration	_____
7. **peccadillo**	g. midafternoon rest	_____
8. **bonanza**	h. enthusiast	_____
9. **siesta**	i. stroke of luck	_____
10. **embargo**	j. pretense of courage	_____
11. **incommunicado**	k. in seclusion	_____
12. **fiesta**	l. bold criminal	_____

Quiz 30: Synonyms

Each of the following sentences contains an italicized word. From the choices provided, select the closest definition.

1. She never went anywhere without her *duenna.*
   a. best friend   b. chaperone   c. handbag   d. identification card
2. They kept the prisoner *incommunicado.*
   a. under guard   b. in a public place   c. in solitary   d. in disguise
3. There is an *embargo* on new shipments.
   a. tax   b. watchman   c. prohibition   d. quota
4. She was given a small *lagniappe* for her services.
   a. punishment   b. bonus   c. checklist   d. salary
5. She is a sports *aficionado.*
   a. fan   b. competitor   c. commentator   d. hater
6. He forgave her for her *peccadillo.*
   a. serious violation   b. bad taste   c. minor sin   d. breach of trust
7. A little *siesta* will make you feel refreshed.
   a. bath   b. nap   c. snack   d. encouragement
8. The posse captured the *desperado.*
   a. outlaw   b. public imagination   c. wild horse   d. runaway child
9. The villagers held an annual *fiesta.*
   a. potluck supper   b. bonfire   c. election   d. festival
10. The unexpected inheritance proved to be a genuine *bonanza.*
    a. disappointment   b. windfall   c. fraud   d. burden
11. An exaggerated sense of *machismo* turned him into a bully.
    a. virility   b. justice   c. fear   d. vengeance
12. His *bravado* masked the genuine terror he felt on the battlefield.
    a. bravery   b. laughter   c. swaggering manner   d. self-mockery

Lesson 16

bodega (bō dä′gə) small grocery store; wineshop.

campesino (kam′pə sē′nō) a farmer or peasant.

caudillo (kou dē′lyō, -dē′yō) a head of state, especially a military dictator.

compañero (kom′pən yâr′ō) companion; partner; bosom buddy.

embarcadero (em bär′kə dâr′ō) a pier, wharf, or jetty.

garrote (gə rot′, -rōt′) to strangle or throttle.

guerrilla (gə ril′ə) a member of a small, independent band of soldiers that harass the enemy by surprise raids, sabotage, etc.

junta (ho͞on′tə, jun′tə) a small group ruling a country, especially after a revolutionary seizure of power.

peon (pē′ən, pē′on) a farm worker or unskilled laborer; a person of low social status who does menial work; drudge.

presidio (pri sid′ē ō′) fort or garrison; military post.
ramada (rə mä′də) an open shelter with a thatched roof.
vigilante (vij′ə lan′tē) an unauthorized volunteer who takes the law into his
or her own hands; a self-appointed avenger of injustice.

Quiz 31: True/False

In the space provided, write T if the definition of the numbered
word is true or F if it is false.

		T or F
1. **compañero**	companion	_____
2. **junta**	joint rulers	_____
3. **vigilante**	watchman	_____
4. **bodega**	lottery	_____
5. **peon**	drudge	_____
6. **guerrilla**	reactionary	_____
7. **campesino**	peasant	_____
8. **presidio**	judge	_____
9. **garrote**	strangle	_____
10. **ramada**	lean-to	_____
11. **embarcadero**	pier	_____
12. **caudillo**	head of state	_____

Quiz 32: Synonyms

Each of the following sentences contains an italicized word. From
the choices provided, select the best definition.

1. The enemy attacked the *presidio.*
   a. president   b. occupying forces   c. military post   d. seaport
2. The rule of the *junta* was harsh.
   a. king   b. enemy   c. conservatives   d. ruling coalition
3. I relied on the support of my *compañero.*
   a. spouse   b. partner   c. political party   d. employer
4. *Vigilante* law was tolerated in the Old West.
   a. immediate vengeance   b. inefficient   c. unpopular   d. harsh
5. Menial tasks were done by the *peons.*
   a. immigrants   b. unskilled laborers   c. victims of prejudice
   d. young people
6. The *guerrillas* hid in the mountainous areas of the country.
   a. shepherds   b. great apes   c. escaped criminals   d.
   revolutionary soldiers
7. We strolled along the *embarcadero.*
   a. wharf   b. highway   c. mountain ridge   d. shopping district

8. Everyone dreaded the *caudillo.*
   a. hot weather   b. revolutionaries   c. military dictator
   d. monster
9. The *ramada* offered very little protection.
   a. band of soldiers   b. military fort   c. thatched lean-to   d. naval forces
10. The owners of the *bodega* were well-respected in the community.
    a. ranch   b. small grocery   c. restaurant   d. pier
11. They enlisted the aid of the *campesinos.*
    a. small farmers   b. clergy   c. cowboys   d. outdoor campers
12. He *garroted* his victim.
    a. throttled   b. mocked   c. stabbed   d. threatened

German

English is a Germanic language, but it diverged from the language that is the ancestor of Modern German about 1,500 years ago. Most English words that come from German are relatively recent borrowings. German borrowings are especially common in intellectual fields, including science, philosophy, and psychology.

Note that all nouns in German are capitalized; in English they sometimes have a capital and sometimes don't, depending on whether they are felt to be German words used in English or fully naturalized borrowings. In the following lists, we have given everything in lowercase.

Lesson 17

angst (ängkst) a feeling of dread, anxiety, or anguish.

ersatz (er′zäts, -säts) fake; synthetic; artificial.

festschrift (fest′shrift′) a volume of scholarly articles contributed by many authors to commemorate a senior scholar or teacher.

gemütlichkeit (*Ger.* gə mүt′likн kīt′) comfortable friendliness; cordiality; congeniality.

gestalt (gə shtält′) a form having properties that cannot be derived by the summation of its component parts.

götterdämmerung (got′ər dam′ə ro͝ong′) total destruction or downfall, as in a great final battle.

kitsch (kich) something of tawdry design, appearance, or content created to appeal to people having popular or undiscriminating taste.

lebensraum (lā′bəns roum′) additional space needed to function.

realpolitik (rä äl′pō′ lē tēk′) political realism; specifically, a policy based on power rather than ideals.

schadenfreude (shäd′n froi′də) pleasure felt at another's misfortune.
weltanschauung (vel′tän shou′ŏŏng) world-view; a comprehensive conception of the universe and humanity's relation to it.
weltschmerz (velt′shmerts′) sorrow that one feels is one's necessary portion
in life; sentimental pessimism.

Quiz 33: True/False

In the space provided, write T if the definition of the numbered
word is true or F if it is false.

			T or F
1.	**gestalt**	guesswork	_____
2.	**schadenfreude**	despair	_____
3.	**götterdämmerung**	apocalypse	_____
4.	**weltanschauung**	overview	_____
5.	**angst**	anxiety	_____
6.	**realpolitik**	political idealism	_____
7.	**festschrift**	forbidden act	_____
8.	**kitsch**	bad taste	_____
9.	**weltschmerz**	sorrow	_____
10.	**ersatz**	phony	_____
11.	**lebensraum**	abandonment	_____
12.	**gemütlichkeit**	friendliness	_____

Quiz 34: Synonyms

Each of the following sentences contains an italicized word. Select
the closest synonym from the choices provided.

1. The *festschrift* was timed to coincide with the professor's
   retirement.
   a. festival   b. conference   c. debate   d. commemorative volume
2. Her sympathy for her rival was *ersatz*.
   a. genuine   b. fake   c. powerful   d. well known
3. The Romantic poet was afflicted with *weltschmerz*.
   a. sentimental pessimism   b. negative criticism   c. an artificial
   style   d. a desire to travel
4. The country inn was known for its *gemütlichkeit*.
   a. fine cooking   b. remoteness   c. homey atmosphere   d. bad
   taste
5. The prophet predicted *götterdämmerung*.
   a. victory   b. total devastation   c. drought   d. prosperity
6. The prospect of meeting her at last filled him with *angst*.
   a. dread   b. anticipation   c. elation   d. lust

7. Her whole house is decorated in *kitsch.*
   a. country style   b. tawdry objects   c. elegant taste   d. bright colors
8. The dictator's excuse for the invasion was a need for *lebensraum.*
   a. slave labor   b. power   c. food   d. more space
9. The president's closest adviser was an advocate of *realpolitik.*
   a. political realism   b. liberalism   c. war games   d. peace
10. She felt a twinge of *schadenfreude* at his bad luck.
    a. guilt   b. sympathy   c. anguish   d. pleasure in another's misfortune
11. His novels reflect a pessimistic *weltanschauung.*
    a. world-view   b. political realism   c. sorrow   d. bias
12. She finally grasped the *gestalt* of the matter through an intuitive insight.
    a. hopelessness   b. falsity   c. whole sense   d. peculiarity

Lesson 18

doppelgänger (dop'əl gang'ər) phantom double; a ghostly counterpart of a living person; alter ego; dead ringer.

echt (ekht) real; authentic; genuine.

kaput (kä pōōt', -pŏŏt') finished, ruined; broken.

leitmotif (līt'mō tēf') a recurring theme; a motif in a dramatic work that is associated with a particular person, idea, or situation.

lumpenproletariat (lum'pən prō'li târ'ē ət) a crude and uneducated underclass comprising unskilled laborers, vagrants, and criminals.

poltergeist (pōl'tər gīst') a ghost that makes loud knocking or rapping noises.

sturm and drang (shtŏŏrm' ōont dräng') turmoil; tumult; upheaval; extreme emotionalism.

übermensch (ōō'bər mensh') superman; an ideal superior being.

verboten (fər bōt'n, vər-) forbidden; prohibited.

wanderlust (won'dər lust') a strong desire to travel.

wunderkind (vŏŏn'dər kind', wun'-) prodigy; gifted child; a person who succeeds at an early age.

zeitgeist (tsīt'gīst', zīt'-) the spirit of the time; the general trend of thought and feeling that is characteristic of the era.

Quiz 35: Matching

Match each of the following numbered words or phrases with its closest definition. Write your answer in the space provided.

1. **verboten**   a. turmoil   _____
2. **echt**   b. gifted child   _____

3. **kaput**   c. riffraff   _____
4. **wunderkind**   d. superior being   _____
5. **lumpenproletariat**   e. spirit of the age   _____
6. **wanderlust**   f. recurrent theme   _____
7. **doppelgänger**   g. prohibited   _____
8. **leitmotif**   h. ruined   _____
9. **sturm und drang**   i. desire to travel   _____
10. **poltergeist**   j. genuine   _____
11. **zeitgeist**   k. phantom double   _____
12. **übermensch**   l. noisy ghost   _____

Quiz 36: Synonyms

Each of the following sentences contains an italicized word or phrase. Choose the closest synonym from the selection provided.

1. After graduation, she was seized with *wanderlust.*
   a. sexual desire   b. intense boredom   c. a desire to travel
   d. joyfulness
2. My TV set is *kaput.*
   a. broken   b. first-rate   c. secondhand   d. repaired
3. Mozart was a world-renowned *wunderkind.*
   a. wonderful friend   b. prodigy   c. late bloomer   d. unique
   person
4. Adolescence is a period of *sturm und drang.*
   a. rapid growth   b. great freedom   c. emotional upheaval
   d. romantic affairs
5. Smoking is *verboten.*
   a. forbidden   b. unhealthful   c. permitted   d. very bad
6. The *übermensch* is not subject to the same laws as ordinary people.
   a. aristocrat   b. ghost   c. criminal   d. superman
7. She was an *echt* genius.
   a. self-described   b. authentic   c. arrogant   d. child
8. The support of the *lumpenproletariat* brought the fascists to power.
   a. unions   b. artistocrats   c. liberals   d. rabble
9. If it wasn't you, it must have been your *doppelgänger.*
   a. accomplice   b. factotum   c. distant relative   d. phantom
   double
10. The townspeople were prejudiced against the *gastarbeiters.*
    a. migrant workers   b. local artisans   c. bohemians   d. young
    people
11. All great artists are tuned in to the *zeitgeist.*
    a. sense of sorrow   b. godhead   c. spirit of the age   d. romantic
    feelings

12. The loss of innocence is a *leitmotif* of the novel.
   a. motive   b. recurring theme   c. flawed conception   d. false lead

Yiddish

Yiddish, the language spoken by the Jews of Eastern Europe, derives from the German of the Middle Ages, with the addition of many Hebrew and Aramaic words, but it has absorbed many other words and expressions from the native cultures of the countries where the Jews have settled. Since Hebrew is the traditional means of expression of learned Jews, Yiddish tends to be a folksy, colorful language that expresses the day-to-day concerns of the common people. After World War I, when many Jews were forced by political upheavals to emigrate, the United States became a center of Yiddish literary activity. The integration of this population into the American mainstream occurred so rapidly that many people who employ Yiddish terms do not even recognize their source.

Yiddish is earthy, blunt, emotional, and direct. Therefore, in many contexts it serves an expressive purpose that no English word can quite approximate. Be careful, however, since Yiddish is rarely appropriate in a formal context.

You will probably be familiar with many of the words in this selection of Yiddish expressions, and if you muse long enough over those you don't know, you will probably discover that many of them are precisely the words you've been looking for to describe the little frustrations of everyday life.

Lesson 19

chutzpah (κнoot′spə, hoot′-) gall; nerve; brashness.
golem (gō′ləm) robot; lifelike creature.
gonif (gon′əf) a thief, swindler, crook, or rascal.
haimish (hā′mish) homey; cozy.
klutz (kluts) clumsy or awkward person.
kvell (kvel) be delighted; take pleasure.
kvetch (kvech) complain, whine, nag; crotchety person.
macher (mä′κнər) wheeler-dealer; big shot.
maven (mā′vən) expert; connoisseur.
megillah (mə gil′ə) tediously long story; rigmarole; complicated matter.
mensch (mensh) admirable person; decent human being.
meshuga (mə shoog′ə) crazy; mad; nutty.
nebbish (neb′ish) nobody; loser; hapless person.

nosh (nosh) snack; nibble.
nudge (nŏŏj) nag; annoy or pester; a pest or annoying person.

Quiz 37: Matching

Match each of the following numbered words with its closest synonym. Write your answer in the space provided.

1. maven	a. nibble	_____
2. klutz	b. be pleased	_____
3. mensch	c. pester	_____
4. kvell	d. nutty	_____
5. nosh	e. robot	_____
6. chutzpah	f. admirable person	_____
7. kvetch	g. expert	_____
8. macher	h. thief	_____
9. meshuga	i. big shot	_____
10. golem	j. clumsy person	_____
11. nebbish	k. loser	_____
12. haimish	l. brashness	_____
13. gonif	m. rigmarole	_____
14. nudge	n. homey	_____
15. megillah	o. complain	_____

Quiz 38: Synonyms

Each of the following sentences contains an italicized word. From the selection provided, choose the closest definition.

1. He's a big *macher* out in Hollywood.
   a. moocher   b. engineer   c. troublemaker   d. wheeler-dealer
2. She *kvelled* over the news about her son.
   a. wept   b. complained   c. took pleasure   d. fainted
3. His apartment is very *haimish*.
   a. cozy   b. cluttered   c. expensive   d. uncomfortable
4. He got the job through sheer *chutzpah*.
   a. hard work   b. nerve   c. good humor   d. pull
5. She liked to have a little *nosh* in the midafternoon.
   a. nap   b. drink   c. snack   d. chat
6. Give me the facts, not a whole *megillah*.
   a. document   b. testimony   c. excuse   d. lengthy explanation
7. Walter Mitty was a *nebbish* who lived in his daydreams.
   a. nobody   b. liar   c. psychotic   d. visionary
8. Her dance instructor told her she was a *klutz*.
   a. beginner   b. graceful person   c. clumsy person   d. failure

9. I should never have trusted that *gonif.*
   a. gossip   b. swindler   c. incompetent   d. amateur
10. He's like an unthinking *golem.*
    a. boxer   b. scientist   c. servant   d. robot
11. Everyone who attended the funeral service said he was a *mensch.*
    a. decent person   b. crook   c. wheeler-dealer   d. connoisseur
12. Her continual *kvetching* gets on my nerves.
    a. pushiness   b. gossiping   c. whining   d. bragging
13. Pay no attention to his *meshuga* ideas.
    a. crazy   b. old-fashioned   c. immature   d. ambitious
14. The opera *maven* had a vast collection of old records.
    a. performer   b. impresario   c. connoisseur   d. amateur
15. His mother *nudged* him to get married.
    a. helped   b. forbade   c. discouraged   d. needled

Lesson 20

schlemiel (shlə mēl′) unlucky person; misfit; failure; awkward person.
schlep (shlep) drag or lug around; trudge; a slow, awkward person; a tedious journey.
schlock (shlok) shoddy merchandise; junk.
schmaltz (shmälts) mawkishness; sentimentality; mush.
schmatte (shmä′tə) rag; article of cheap clothing.
schmooze (shmo͞oz) chitchat; gab; gossip.
schmutz (shmo͞ots) dirt; garbage.
schnook (shno͝ok) pathetic person; sucker, easy mark; lovable fool.
schnorrer (shnôr′ər) sponger; parasite.
shtick (shtik) comic routine; special interest or talent.
tchotchkes (choch′kəz) knickknacks; baubles or trinkets.
tsuris (tso͞or′is, tsûr′-) worries; woes; afflictions.
tzimmes (tsim′əs) fuss, to-do; uproar, disturbance.
yenta (yen′tə) busybody; gossip; nosy old woman.
zaftig (zäf′tik, -tig) juicy; plump; voluptuous; curvy.

Quiz 39: True/False

In the space provided, write T if the definition of the numbered word is true or F if it is false.

			T or F
1. **tsuris**	uproar		_____
2. **schmatte**	rag		_____
3. **schmutz**	garbage		_____
4. **yenta**	busybody		_____

5. schlock	crazy person	_____
6. tchotchkes	bric-a-brac	_____
7. schlemiel	big shot	_____
8. tzimmes	to-do	_____
9. schlep	awkward person	_____
10. zaftig	magic	_____
11. schmaltz	snack	_____
12. schnorrer	tedious person	_____
13. schmooze	chitchat	_____
14. shtick	sadness	_____
15. schnook	easy mark	_____

Quiz 40: Synonyms

Each of the following sentences contains an italicized word. Choose the nearest definition from the selection provided.

1. She says her kids give her nothing but *tsuris*.
   a. joy   b. troubles   c. knickknacks   d. junk
2. She wiped the *schmutz* off her face.
   a. smile   b. sorrow   c. dirt   d. makeup
3. The women in the paintings of Rubens are *zaftig*.
   a. plump   b. skinny   c. magnificent   d. cheap-looking
4. They like to *schmooze* after work.
   a. nap   b. stroll   c. snack   d. gab
5. All the merchandise at that store is *schlock*.
   a. discount   b. junk   c. first-rate   d. expensive
6. She came to the door in her *schmatte*.
   a. bad temper   b. designer dress   c. cheap dress
   d. underwear
7. They had a collection of *tchotchkes* from their trips abroad.
   a. knickknacks   b. memories   c. fine art   d. tedious stories
8. That new movie is pure *schmaltz*.
   a. comedy   b. junk   c. genius   d. mush
9. Don't ever invite that *schnorrer* to my house again.
   a. noisy person   b. gossip   c. sponger   d. bore
10. She *schlepped* all over town.
    a. celebrated   b. trudged   c. shopped   d. gossiped
11. Chaplin's signal character was a *schnook*.
    a. lovable fool   b. parasite   c. big shot   d. clumsy person
12. Her closest confidante turned out to be a *yenta*.
    a. fool   b. parasite   c. gossip   d. liar
13. The *schlemiel* frittered away his inheritance.
    a. playboy   b. wheeler-dealer   c. idealist   d. unlucky person

14. Doing impersonations of celebrities is his *shtick*.
    a. special talent   b. worst fault   c. tedious habit   d. aspiration
15. They made a *tzimmes* out of nothing.
    a. fuss   b. snack   c. fortune   d. pack of lies

Japanese

Though the first European contact with Japan was made by Portuguese sailors in the sixteenth century, it was not until the middle of the nineteenth century that the United States forced the opening of trade with the West. As this small island nation has developed into a great economic power in the last generation, we have become more familiar with its traditions. Many of our more recent borrowings from the Japanese are business terms; others are artistic or religious. The growing popularity of the martial arts has given us still other new words and concepts.

The following selection of Japanese words is designed to introduce you to this increasingly important culture and perhaps even give you some insight into the Japanese mind.

Lesson 21

futon (fo͞o'ton) a thick, quiltlike mattress placed on the floor for sleeping and folded up for seating or storage.

geisha (gā'shə, gē'-) a young woman trained as a gracious companion for men; hostess.

haiku (hī'ko͞o) a short, pithy verse in three lines of five, seven, and five syllables.

kabuki (kə bo͞o'kē) a popular entertainment characterized by stylized acting, elaborate costumes, and exaggerated makeup.

karaoke (kar'ē ō'kē) an act of singing along to a music video, especially one that has had the original vocals electronically eliminated.

koan (kō'än) a nonsensical proposition or paradoxical question presented to a student of Zen as an object of meditation; unsolvable riddle.

noh (nō) classical lyric drama characterized by chants, the wearing of wooden masks, and highly stylized movements drawn from religious rites.

origami (ôr'i gä'mē) the art of folding paper into representational forms.

roshi (rō'shē) a Zen master; a teacher in a monastery.

satori (sə tôr'ē) enlightenment; ultimate insight into the nature of reality.

Shinto (shin'tō) the traditional Japanese system of nature and ancestor worship.

shoji (shō'jē) a room divider or sliding screen made of translucent paper.

tanka (täng'kə) traditional verse form having five-line stanzas with alternate lines of five and seven syllables.

tatami (tə tä′mē) a woven straw mat used as a floor covering.
tsunami (tsōō nä′mē) a huge sea wave produced by an undersea earthquake or volcanic eruption.
Zen (zen) a sect of Buddhism that emphasizes enlightenment through meditation.

Quiz 41: Matching

Match each of the following numbered words with its closest synonym. Write your answer in the space provided.

1. **tatami**	a. riddle	_____
2. **karaoke**	b. classical drama	_____
3. **geisha**	c. enlightenment	_____
4. **noh**	d. ancestor worship	_____
5. **shoji**	e. short poem	_____
6. **Zen**	f. paper folding	_____
7. **kabuki**	g. singalong	_____
8. **origami**	h. paper screen	_____
9. **tsunami**	i. straw mat	_____
10. **futon**	j. popular entertainment	_____
11. **satori**	k. Buddhist school	_____
12. **haiku**	l. long poem	_____
13. **koan**	m. tidal wave	_____
14. **Shinto**	n. mattress	_____
15. **tanka**	o. female companion	_____
16. **roshi**	p. Buddhist priest	_____

Quiz 42: Synonyms

Each of the following sentences contains an italicized word. From the selection provided, choose the best definition.

1. After work, the businessmen enjoy *karaoke* bars.
   a. underworld   b. singalong   c. health food   d. sex
2. The small island community was threatened by a *tsunami*.
   a. war lord   b. tornado   c. epidemic   d. tidal wave
3. She was trained to be a *geisha*.
   a. hostess   b. ballerina   c. businessperson   d. teacher
4. *Origami* requires great skill and dexterity.
   a. traditional drama   b. painting   c. calligraphy   d. paper folding
5. She meditated on the *koan* her teacher set before her.
   a. straw mat   b. poem   c. sofa   d. riddle

6. *Noh* is a very ancient art that requires many years of training.
   a. classical drama   b. paper folding   c. scroll painting
   d. meditation
7. *Kabuki* is an entertainment enjoyed by all social classes.
   a. the art of self-defense   b. singing   c. telling riddles
   d. popular drama
8. He sat cross-legged on the *tatami*.
   a. mattress   b. straw mat   c. low table   d. sofa
9. She was admitted through the *shoji*.
   a. solution to a riddle   b. poetry competition   c. sliding screen
   d. school
10. He achieved *satori* after many years of study.
    a. enlightenment   b. an acting role   c. a poetry prize   d. honor
11. Put the *futon* on the floor.
    a. mattress   b. straw mat   c. rice paper   d. sandals
12. He was the acknowledged master of the *tanka*.
    a. classical drama   b. art of paper folding   c. traditional poem
    d. Zen student
13. *Shinto* is the ancient religion of Japan.
    a. Confucianism   b. ancestor worship   c. meditation
    d. monotheism
14. They competed to see who could produce the best *haiku*.
    a. woodblock   b. lyric drama   c. scroll painting   d. short, pithy
    verse
15. His *Zen* teacher slapped him hard across the face to provoke him.
    a. martial arts   b. Buddhism   c. poetry   d. acting
16. She bowed before the *roshi*.
    a. emperor   b. Zen master   c. business executive   d. poet

Lesson 22

aikido (ī kē′dō) a form of self-defense using wrist, joint, and elbow grips to immobilize or throw one's opponent.

bushido (boo′shē dō′) the code of honor of the samurai, stressing loyalty and obedience.

dojo (dō′jō) a school or practice hall where martial arts are taught.

hara-kiri (här′ə kēr′ē, har′ə-) ritual suicide by disembowelment; any self-destructive act.

judo (joo′dō) a martial art based on jujitsu that bans dangerous blows or throws, stressing the athletic or sport element.

jujitsu (joo jit′soo) a method of self-defense that uses the strength and weight of one's opponent to disable him or her.

kamikaze (kä′mi kä′zē) person on a suicide mission; a wild or reckless act.
karate (kə rä′tē) self-defense using fast, hard blows with the hands, elbows, knees, or feet.
keiretsu (kā ret′sōo) a loose coalition of business groups.
ninja (nin′jə) a mercenary trained in martial arts and stealth.
samurai (sam′ōo rī′) a noble warrior; warrior class.
shogun (shō′gən, -gun) a military commander; war lord.
sumo (sōo′mō) a form of wrestling aimed at forcing one's opponent out of the ring or causing him to touch the ground with any body part other than the soles of the feet.
tycoon (tī kōon′) a businessperson of great wealth or power; magnate.
yakuza (yä′kōo zä′) a member of a crime syndicate; racketeer; gangster.
zaibatsu (zī bät′ sōo) a great industrial or financial conglomerate.

Quiz 43: True/False

In the space provided, write T if the definition of the numbered word is true or F if it is false.

			T or F
1.	**sumo**	wrestling	_____
2.	**kamikaze**	reckless act	_____
3.	**jujitsu**	chewy candies	_____
4.	**dojo**	priest	_____
5.	**aikido**	artwork	_____
6.	**zaibatsu**	poetry competition	_____
7.	**yakuza**	racketeer	_____
8.	**bushido**	code of ethics	_____
9.	**judo**	martial sport	_____
10.	**keiretsu**	business coalition	_____
11.	**shogun**	war lord	_____
12.	**hara-kiri**	ritual suicide	_____
13.	**tycoon**	whirlwind	_____
14.	**samurai**	warrior	_____
15.	**karate**	fit for consumption	_____
16.	**ninja**	soldier for hire	_____

Quiz 44: Synonyms

Each of the following sentences contains an italicized word. Choose the best definition from the selection provided.

1. She was honored to be accepted by the *dojo*.
   a. financial conglomerate   b. Zen master   c. school of martial arts   d. acting company

2. The *ninja* offered his services for hire.
   a. noble warrior   b. suicidal pilot   c. martial artist
   d. mercenary soldier
3. An act of *hara-kiri* will redeem his honor.
   a. ceremonial suicide   b. self-defense   c. war
   d. meditation
4. She practiced her *aikido* moves.
   a. calligraphy   b. business   c. self-defense   d. paper folding
5. Practitioners of *judo* never intentionally hurt each other.
   a. big business   b. meditation   c. poetry   d. a martial art that
   bans dangerous blows
6. He adhered strictly to the principles of the *bushido*.
   a. self-defense   b. crime syndicate   c. code of honor   d. suicide
   mission
7. The *zaibatsu* wielded enormous economic power.
   a. war lord   b. crime syndicate   c. priest   d. financial
   conglomerate
8. They agreed to join the *keiretsu*.
   a. coalition of business groups   b. crime syndicate   c. school of
   martial arts   d. suicide mission
9. The *yakuza* swore a bloody vengeance.
   a. person on a suicide mission   b. crime syndicate   c. business
   magnate   d. military commander
10. Women who practice *jujitsu* may have an advantage over their
    male attackers.
    a. self-defense that focuses on an opponent's size   b. wrestling
    c. meditation   d. unfair business practices
11. The *kamikaze* acts out of a sense of honor and duty.
    a. mercenary   b. person on a suicide mission   c. guerrilla
    d. female companion
12. The *tycoon* expected absolute loyalty from his underlings.
    a. war lord   b. gangster   c. business magnate
    d. Zen teacher
13. The *samurai* are a hereditary class in Japan.
    a. gangsters   b. noble warriors   c. Zen masters   d. classical
    actors
14. The *shogun* was the real power behind the emperor.
    a. military commander   b. business coalition   c. crime syndicate
    d. female companion
15. *Sumo* requires superior height and weight.
    a. kick boxing   b. Japanese-style wrestling   c. success in business
    d. arm wrestling

16. *Karate* requires speed, concentration, and the intimidation of one's opponent.
    a. wrestling   b. self-defense based on fast, hard blows   c. chess
    d. success in business

Answers to Quizzes in Chapter 8

Answers to Quiz 1

1. e 2. h 3. k 4. m 5. o 6. d 7. n 8. f 9. b 10. j 11. 1 12. a 13. g 14. i 15. c

Answers to Quiz 2

1. T 2. T 3. T 4. T 5. T 6. F 7. F 8. F 9. F 10. F 11. T 12. T 13. T 14. T 15. T

Answers to Quiz 4

1. a 2. d 3. b 4. c 5. b 6. d 7. a 8. c 9. a 10. d 11. d 12. a 13. a 14. c 15. d

Answers to Quiz 5

1. T 2. T 3. F 4. F 5. T 6. T 7. T 8. T 9. F 10. T 11. F 12. F 13. T 14. T 15. T

Answers to Quiz 6

1. d 2. a 3. b 4. d 5. c 6. a 7. d 8. c 9. b 10. a 11. c 12. a 13. c 14. b 15. a

Answers to Quiz 7

1. e 2. h 3. j 4. k 5. a 6. d 7. 1 8. g 9. c 10. i 11. n 12. o 13. f 14. m 15. b

Answers to Quiz 8

1. a 2. c 3. d 4. c 5. a 6. d 7. a 8. c 9. b 10. c 11. c 12. a 13. b 14. c 15. a

Answers to Quiz 9

1. F 2. T 3. F 4. T 5. F 6. T 7. T 8. T 9. T 10. F 11. T 12. T 13. F 14. T 15. T

Answers to Quiz 10

1. d 2. c 3. a 4. c 5. b 6. d 7. d 8. b 9. c 10. a 11. d 12. b 13. b 14. a 15. b

Answers to Quiz 11

1. e 2. f 3. j 4. k 5. 1 6. b 7. h 8. n 9. g 10. a 11. d 12. i 13. m 14. o 15. c

Answers to Quiz 12

1. b 2. c 3. a 4. a 5. c 6. a 7. c 8. a 9. d 10. a 11. c 12. b 13. d 14. a 15. d

Answers to Quiz 13

1. F 2. T 3. F 4. T 5. F 6. T 7. T 8. F 9. T 10. T 11. T 12. T

Answers to Quiz 14

1. c 2. b 3. a 4. c 5. b 6. a 7. b 8. d 9. b 10. c 11. a 12. d

Answers to Quiz 15

1. g 2. h 3. a 4. j 5. k 6. b 7. d 8. e 9. c 10. f 11. i 12. d

Answers to Quiz 16

1. c 2. b 3. a 4. a 5. d 6. a 7. b 8. a 9. c 10. d 11. a 12. c

Answers to Quiz 17

1. T 2. T 3. F 4. F 5. T 6. T 7. F 8. T 9. T 10. F 11. T 12. F

Answers to Quiz 18

1. c 2. d 3. d 4. a 5. b 6. c 7. a 8. d 9. b 10. a 11. d 12. a

Answers to Quiz 19

1. i 2. f 3. h 4. b 5. k 6. c 7. j 8. a 9. g 10. 1 11. e 12. d

Answers to Quiz 20

1. b 2. d 3. c 4. a 5. d 6. b 7. a 8. c 9. b 10. a 11. c 12. d

Answers to Quiz 21

1. T 2. T 3. F 4. F 5. F 6. T 7. T 8. F 9. F 10. T 11. F 12. T

Answers to Quiz 22

1. b 2. e 3. d 4. a 5. d 6. b 7. d 8. c 9. a 10. c 11. d 12. a

Answers to Quiz 23

1. c 2. a 3. j 4. f 5. k 6. h 7. e 8. g 9. d 10. i 11. 1 12. b

Answers to Quiz 24

1. b 2. a 3. c 4. d 5. a 6. d 7. a 8. b 9. d 10. a 11. c 12. d

Answers to Quiz 25

1. F 2. T 3. T 4. F 5. T 6. F 7. T 8. T 9. F 10. T 11. F 12. F

Answers to Quiz 26

1. c 2. d 3. a 4. d 5. b 6. c 7. d 8. a 9. b 10. c 11. a 12. d

Answers to Quiz 27
1. c 2. e 3. f 4. h 5. i 6. a 7. j 8. k 9. d 10. l 11. b 12. g

Answers to Quiz 28
1. a 2. c 3. c 4. c 5. d 6. a 7. d 8. b 9. c 10. d 11. a 12. d

Answers to Quiz 29
1. d 2. j 3. l 4. h 5. c 6. b 7. e 8. i 9. g 10. a 11. k 12. f

Answers to Quiz 30
1. b 2. c 3. c 4. b 5. a 6. c 7. b 8. a 9. d 10. b 11. a 12. e

Answers to Quiz 31
1. T 2. T 3. F 4. F 5. T 6. F 7. T 8. F 9. T 10. T 11. T 12. T

Answers to Quiz 32
1. c 2. d 3. b 4. a 5. b 6. d 7. a 8. c 9. c 10. b 11. a 12. a

Answers to Quiz 33
1. F 2. F 3. T 4. T 5. T 6. F 7. F 8. T 9. T 10. T 11. F 12. T

Answers to Quiz 34
1. d 2. b 3. a 4. c 5. b 6. a 7. b 8. d 9. a 10. d 11. a 12. c

Answers to Quiz 35
1. g 2. j 3. h 4. b 5. c 6. i 7. k 8. f 9. a 10. l 11. e 12. d

Answers to Quiz 36
1. e 2. a 3. b 4. c 5. a 6. d 7. b 8. d 9. d 10. a 11. c 12. b

Answers to Quiz 37
1. g 2. j 3. f 4. b 5. a 6. l 7. o 8. i 9. d 10. e 11. k 12. n 13. h 14. c 15. m

Answers to Quiz 38
1. d 2. c 3. a 4. b 5. c 6. d 7. a 8. c 9. b 10. d 11. a 12. c 13. a 14. c 15. d

Answers to Quiz 39
1. F 2. T 3. T 4. T 5. F 6. T 7. F 8. T 9. T 10. F 11. F 12. F 13. T 14. F 15. T

Answers to Quiz 40
1. b 2. c 3. a 4. d 5. b 6. c 7. a 8. d 9. c 10. b 11. a 12. c 13. d 14. a 15. a

Answers to Quiz 41

1. i 2. g 3. o 4. b 5. h 6. k 7. j 8. f 9. m 10. n 11. c 12. e 13. a 14. d 15. l
16. p

Answers to Quiz 42

1. b 2. d 3. a 4. d 5. d 6. a 7. d 8. b 9. c 10. a 11. a 12. c 13. b 14. d 15. b
16. b

Answers to Quiz 43

1. T 2. T 3. F 4. F 5. F 6. F 7. T 8. T 9. T 10. T 11. T 12. T 13. F 14. T
15. F 16. T

Answers to Quiz 44

1. c 2. d 3. a 4. c 5. d 6. c 7. d 8. a 9. b 10. a 11. b 12. c 13. b 14. a 15. b
16. b

9

Specialized Vocabularies

Even after you have acquired a more powerful general vocabulary, you may still encounter terms that are unfamiliar to you because they are part of the special vocabulary of a discipline you have not studied. Many of these fields are central to modern life. Computer literacy, for example, is fast becoming a necessity for people in virtually all trades and professions, and everyone is bound to have some dealings with the legal profession at some time.

Here is a brief selection of current and basic terminology drawn from seven important spheres of American life—business, science, computers, law, fashion, and sports. These terms will provide an introduction and orientation to the current status of each of these professions.

A. Business

The vocabulary of business has grown at an astonishing rate. The executive, the student, the investor, the job seeker, the consumer are all affected by the world of business, and all of them need to be familiar with its specialized terminology. Even an experienced business professional may need to learn terminology that is outside his or her particular field. The novice or layperson can benefit by learning the technical vocabulary, the jargon peculiar to business, even though many of these terms have already passed into the general vocabulary. For example, *bottom line* refers to the last line of a financial statement but also means "the crucial factor" or "the outcome."

The common thread that runs through the world of business is the making, marketing, and management of a product or service. The catchall term "business" encompasses fields as diverse as personal finance, economics, insurance, manufacturing, retailing, marketing, and much more. Here is a selection of new or useful terms.

Specialized/Technical Terms

bear   a person who believes that stock prices will decline.

bull   a person who believes that stock prices will rise.

proxy   a written authorization for one person to act for another, as at a meeting of stockholders.

securities   stocks and bonds.

contrarian   a person who rejects the majority opinion, especially an investor who buys when others are selling, and vice versa.

drive time   the rush hour, when commuters listen to car radios: perceived as a time for generating advertising revenue.

emerging market   a market in a less developed country whose economy is just beginning to grow.

mutual fund   an investment company that invests its pooled funds in a diversified list of securities.

golden parachute   an employment agreement guaranteeing an executive substantial compensation in the event of dismissal.

small-cap   referring to a stock with a market capitalization of under $500 million, and considered to have more growth potential.

large-cap   referring to a stock with a market capitalization of $1 billion or more.

superstore   a very large store that stocks a great variety of merchandise.

hedge fund   an investment company that uses high-risk speculative methods to obtain large profits.

flexdollars   money given by an employer that an employee can apply to any of various benefits.

outsourcing   the purchase of goods or contracting of services from an outside company.

short selling   borrowing shares from a broker and selling them, then buying back the same shares at a lower price.

capital gains   income from the sale of assets, such as bonds or real estate.

Informal or Slang

bean counter   a person who makes judgments based primarily on numerical calculations.

dead-cat bounce   a temporary recovery in stock prices after a steep decline, often resulting from the purchase of securities that have been sold short.

road warrior   a person who travels extensively on business.

comp time   compensatory time off from work, granted to an employee in lieu of overtime pay.

Acronyms

COBRA   Consolidated Omnibus Budget Reconciliation Act: a federal law guaranteeing the right to continue participation in an employee health plan after coverage has been terminated due to layoff, divorce, etc.

SKU   stockkeeping unit: a retailer-defined coding system used to distinguish individual items within a retailer's accounting and warehousing systems.
REIT   real estate investment trust: a mutual fund that invests in real estate and must distribute at least 90% of its income as dividends.

Abbreviations

IPO   initial public offering: a company's first stock offering to the public.
NAV   net asset value: the price of a share in a mutual fund, equal to the total value of the fund's securities divided by the number of shares outstanding.
UGMA   Uniform Gifts to Minors Act: a law that provides a means to transfer securities or money to a minor without establishing a formal trust, the assets being managed by a custodian.
APR   annual percentage rate: the annual rate of interest, or the total interest to be paid in a year divided by the balance due.

Usage Issues

Journalese, bureaucratese, computerese, and legalese all afflict the uninitiated. As with other specialized industries, occupations, and academic disciplines, the language of business has been criticized and ridiculed for its overuse of jargon. The following is a discussion of usage issues that relate to the business field. Other, more general usage issues are discussed in Chapter 4.

impact   The figurative use of this verb, in the sense "to have an influence or effect (on)," has been criticized in recent years. However, this use is fully standard and fairly well established in the language. There are many examples in business and financial contexts: *to impact sales; to impact profits; to impact on the bottom line.*
proactive   This adjective means "serving to prepare for, intervene in, or control an expected occurrence or situation." It has been criticized for overuse and stigmatized as jargon: *proactive measures against corruption; a proactive approach to fighting crime.*
price point   This noun means "the price for which something is sold on the retail market." Some usage experts point out that it is redundant, since the word "price" has almost the same meaning. However, the term "price point" emphasizes the price of something in contrast to competitive prices for the same item: *The price point of this paperback is too high for the student market.*
incentivize   This verb means "to give incentives to": *The government should incentivize the private sector to create jobs.* Many verbs ending in -*ize* have been disapproved of in recent years, particularly "finalize" and "prioritize." Although fully standard, such words are most often criticized when they become vogue terms, heard and seen everywhere. They are especially used in the contexts of advertising, commerce, and government—forces claimed to have a corrupting influence on the language.

B. Science

Vocabulary in the world of science has undergone a virtual explosion during the past few decades. This growth of new terms is the result not only of the accelerated progress of scientific discovery but also a number of crucial changes in emerging scientific theory. Nowhere is this more apparent than in the fields of physics, astronomy, and cosmology.

Some new theories have raised fundamental, often controversial questions, including a renewed debate over the origin of the universe. Whatever your perspective may be on these issues, it is important to familiarize yourself with the language that expresses them.

Here are some basic terms, as well as some of the newer ones you may encounter in discussions of current issues in the world of science.

antigravity a hypothesized force that behaves in ways opposite to gravity and repels matter.

antimatter matter composed only of antiparticles, which have attributes that are the reverse of those of matter. The basic difference between matter and antimatter is in the electric charge (negative vs. positive); for each particle of matter, there is a particle of antimatter.

antiparticle a particle whose properties, as mass, spin, or electric charge, have the same magnitude as, but the opposite algebraic sign of, a specific elementary particle. Where one is positive, the other is negative.

astronomy the science that deals with the universe beyond the earth's atmosphere, including the other planets in Earth's solar system, the stars, galaxies other than our own, and various other phenomena, such as quarks and black holes.

atom the basic component of an element, consisting of a nucleus containing combinations of neutrons and protons and one or more electrons bound to the nucleus by electrical attraction.

atomic weight the average weight of an atom of an element.

baryon a proton, neutron, or any elementary particle that decays into a set of particles that includes a proton.

Big Bang theory a theory that holds that our universe had its origins in an explosive cataclysm. Before that, the entire substance of the universe existed in a dense, compact kind of "cosmic soup"; since then, it has been expanding.

black hole a massive object in space, formed by the collapse of a star at the end of its life, whose gravitational field is so intense that no electromagnetic radiation can escape, not even light.

cosmology the branch of astronomy that deals with the general structure and evolution of the universe.

coulomb the basic unit of quantity of electricity, equal to the quantity of electric charge transferred in one second across a conductor.

cyclotron an accelerator in which particles are propelled in spiral paths by the use of a constant magnetic field. It is used to initiate nuclear transformations.

dark matter a hypothetical form of matter, probably making up over ninety percent of the mass of the universe, that is invisible to electromagnetic radiation and therefore undetectable. It is thought to account for the gravitational forces that are observable in the universe.

electric charge one of the basic properties of the elementary particles of matter giving rise to all electric and magnetic forces and interactions. The two kinds of charge are given negative and positive algebraic signs.

element one of a class of substances that cannot be separated into simpler substances by chemical means.

galaxy a large system of stars, such as our own Milky Way, held together by mutual gravitation and isolated from similar systems by vast regions of space.

gluon an unobserved massless particle that is believed to transmit the strong force between quarks, binding them together into baryons and mesons.

gravity the force of attraction by which terrestrial bodies tend to fall toward the center of the earth. It is also the similar attractive effect, considered as extending throughout space, of matter on other matter, including light.

MACHOs Massive Astrophysical Compact Halo Objects; brown dwarfs (small, cold stars), planets, or other objects hypothesized as constituting part of the dark matter in the halo of the Milky Way.

mass the quantity of matter in a body as determined from its weight or measured by its motion.

matter the substance or substances of which any physical object consists or is composed. Matter is made up of atoms; it has mass and can be measured.

meson any strongly interacting, unstable subatomic particle, other than a baryon, made up of two quarks.

Milky Way the spiral galaxy containing our solar system. With the naked eye it is observed as a faint luminous band stretching across the heavens, composed of at least 100 billion stars, including the sun, most of which are too distant to be seen individually.

neutrino any of three uncharged elementary particles or antiparticles having virtually no mass.

neutron an elementary particle having no electric charge, and having mass slightly greater than that of a proton.

neutron star an extremely dense, compact star composed primarily of neutrons, especially the collapsed core of a supernova.

nova a star that suddenly becomes thousands of times brighter and then gradually fades to its original intensity.

nuclear fission the splitting of the nucleus of an atom into nuclei of lighter atoms, accompanied by the release of great amounts of energy.

nuclear fusion a thermonuclear reaction in which nuclei of light atoms are fused, joining to form nuclei of heavier atoms, and releasing large amounts of energy.

nucleus the positively charged mass within an atom, composed of neutrons and protons, and possessing most of the mass but occupying only a small fraction of the volume of the atom.

particle 1. one of the extremely small constituents of matter, as an atom or nucleus. **2.** an elementary particle, quark, or gluon.

periodic table a table illustrating the periodic system, in which the chemical elements, formerly arranged in the order of their atomic weights and now according to their atomic numbers, are shown in related groups.

physics the science that deals with matter, energy, motion, and force.

planet 1. any of the nine large heavenly bodies revolving about the sun and shining by reflected light. In the order of their proximity to the sun, they are: Mercury, Venus, Earth, Mars, Jupiter, Saturn, Uranus, Neptune, and Pluto. **2.** a similar body revolving about a star other than the sun.

proton a positively charged elementary particle that is a fundamental constituent of all atomic nuclei. It is the lightest and most stable baryon, having an electric charge equal in magnitude to that of the electron.

pulsar one of several hundred known celestial objects, generally believed to be rapidly rotating neutron stars, that emit pulses of radiation, especially radio waves, with a high degree of regularity.

quark any of the hypothetical particles that, together with their antiparticles, are believed to constitute all the elementary particles classed as baryons and mesons; they are distinguished by their flavors, designated as up (u), down (d), strange (s), charm (c), bottom or beauty (b), and top or truth (t), and their colors, red, green, and blue.

radio astronomy the branch of astronomy that uses extraterrestrial radiation in radio wavelengths for the study of the universe, rather than using visible light.

SETI Search for Extraterrestrial Intelligence; any of several research projects designed to explore the universe for signs of patterned signals that would indicate the presence of intelligent life in outer space.

solar system the sun together with all the planets and other bodies that revolve around it.

space-time the four-dimensional continuum, a combination of space and time, having three spatial coordinates and one temporal coordinate, in which all physical quantities may be located. The implication is that space and time are one thing, not separate.

spin the intrinsic angular momentum characterizing each kind of elementary particle, which exists even when the particle is at rest.

steady-state theory a theory in which the universe is assumed to have average properties that are constant in space and time so that new matter must be continuously and spontaneously created to maintain average densities as the universe expands. This theory is now largely discredited in its original form. See Big Bang theory.

supernova the explosion of a star, possibly caused by gravitational collapse, during which the star's luminosity increases by as much as twenty magnitudes and most of the star's mass is blown away at very high velocity, sometimes leaving behind an extremely dense core.

Theory of Everything a theory, sought by scientists, that would show that the weak, strong, and gravitational forces of the universe are components of a single force. This theory would unify all the forces of nature.

universe the totality of known or supposed objects and phenomena throughout space; the cosmos; macrocosm. Originally thought to include only the solar system, then expanded to admit our Milky Way galaxy, the concept of the universe now encompasses everything known or not yet known in space.

C. Computers

Since the 1980s, a new kind of literacy, computer literacy, has come to be prized as an aid to advancement in school and at work. Computer literacy is normally defined as familiarity with computers and how they work. But the term means more than that. Computer literacy is not just the ability to sit at a computer and use it to perform a few practical tasks, such as word processing or calculating interest payments with a spreadsheet program; it requires an understanding of the basic vocabulary of computer hardware and software. Without this vocabulary, it is difficult to make sensible decisions about choosing and working with computer software and hardware.

Remember, computer literacy does not compete with literacy in the more usual sense. It merely enables you to be comfortable with computer technology, which provides you with an additional tool for accomplishing productive and creative tasks.

Here are a few of the essential terms and concepts you may need from the world of personal computers.

alpha test an early test of new or updated computer software conducted by the developers of the program prior to beta testing by potential users.

American Standard Code for Information Interchange See ASCII.

applet a small application program that can be called up for use while working in another application. A typical example would be an on-screen calculator that you can use while working in a word processor.

application a specific kind of task, as database management or word processing, that can be done using an application program.

application program a computer program created for use in accomplishing a specific kind of task, as word processing or desktop publishing.

ASCII American Standard Code for Information Interchange: a standardized code in which characters are represented for computer storage and transmission by the numbers 0 through 127. See also UNICODE.

backup a copy or duplicate version, especially of a data file or program, retained for use in the event that the original becomes unusable or unavailable.

bay an open compartment in the console housing a computer's CPU in which a disk drive, tape drive, etc., may be installed. Also called **drive bay.**

beta test a test of new or updated computer software or hardware conducted at select user sites just prior to release of the product. Experienced beta testers try to push a new program to its limits, to see what kinds of behavior will make it break. This helps the programmers to eliminate bugs.

boot to start (a computer) by loading the operating system.

bug a defect, error, or imperfection, as in computer software.

byte a group of adjacent bits, usually eight, processed by a computer as a unit.

cache (pronounced like cash, not catch) a piece of computer hardware or a section of RAM dedicated to selectively storing and speeding access to frequently used program commands or data.

central processing unit See CPU.

CD-ROM a compact disc on which a large amount of digitized read-only data can be stored.

chat to engage in dialogue by exchanging electronic messages, usually in real time.

click to depress and release a mouse button rapidly, as to select an icon. Some functions in a program require a single click, some a double click.

compression reduction of the size of computer data by efficient storage. Compressed data can be stored in fewer bits than uncompressed data, and therefore takes up less space. This is useful not only for saving space on a hard disk, for example, but also for communicating data through a modem more rapidly.

copy protection a method of preventing users of a computer program from making unauthorized copies, usually through hidden instructions contained in the program code.

CPU Central Processing Unit: the key component of a computer. It houses the essential electronic circuitry that allows the computer to interpret and execute program instructions.

crash (of a computer) to suffer a major failure because of a malfunction of hardware or software. A crash is usually not the user's fault.

cursor a movable, sometimes blinking, symbol used to indicate where data (as text, commands, etc.) may be input on a computer screen.

cyber- a combining form representing "computer" *(cybertalk; cyberart).*

cyberspace the realm of electronic communication, as exemplified by the Internet.

database a collection of ordered, related data in electronic form that can be accessed and manipulated by specialized computer software. Commonly, database information is organized by RECORDS, which are in turn divided into FIELDS.

desktop publishing the design and production of publications by means of specialized software enabling a personal computer to generate typeset-quality text and graphics. The kinds of publications that can be produced by means of desktop publishing now range from something as small as a business card to large books.

directory See FOLDER.

drive bay a compartment in the console that houses a computer's CPU in which a storage device, like a disk drive or tape drive, may be installed. Internal bays hold mass storage devices, like hard disks, while external, or open, bays house devices that give the user access to removable disks, tape, compact discs, etc.

documentation instructional materials for computer software or hardware. Some of these materials still come in print, in books or brochures, but increasingly, documentation is available primarily on line, as through a program's Help files.

dot pitch a measure of the distance between each pixel on a computer screen. A lower number indicates a sharper image.

download to transfer (software or data) from a computer or network to a smaller computer or a peripheral device.

export to save (documents, data, etc.) in a format usable by another application program.

fax modem a modem that can fax electronic data, as documents or pictures, directly from a computer. Many fax modems can also receive faxes, in electronic form, which can then be printed out.

field a unit of information, as a person's name, that combines with related fields, as an official title, an address, or a company name, to form one complete record in a computerized database.

file a collection of related computer data or program records stored by name, as on a disk.

flame *Slang.* (esp. on a computer network) **1.** an act or instance of angry criticism or disparagement. **2.** to behave in an offensive manner; rant. **3.** to insult or criticize angrily.

floppy disk a thin, portable, flexible plastic disk coated with magnetic material, for storing computer data and programs. Currently, the 3 1/2–inch disk, housed in a square rigid envelope, is the common size used with personal computers.

folder a place on a disk for holding multiple files. Using folders, disks can be organized in a hierarchical structure, with folders contained within other folders. The designation folder is used in environments with a graphical user interface. The equivalent term in operating systems like DOS and Unix, known as command-line systems, and in early versions of Windows, was directory.

font a set of characters that have a given shape or design. The characters in a scalable font can be enlarged or reduced. A given font is a combination of the typeface, size, pitch, weight, and spacing.

freeware computer software distributed without charge. Compare SHAREWARE.

FTP File Transfer Protocol: a software protocol for exchanging information between computers over a network. Files are commonly downloaded from the Internet using FTP.

gigabyte a measure of data storage capacity equal to a little over one billion (10^9) BYTES, or 1,024 MEGABYTES. Hard disk drives with a capacity of several gigabytes are no longer uncommon.

graphical user interface a software interface designed to standardize and simplify the use of computer programs, as by using a mouse to manipulate text and images on a display screen featuring icons, windows, and menus. Also called **GUI.**

hard copy computer output printed on paper; printout.

hard disk a rigid disk coated with magnetic material. Hard disks are used for storing programs and relatively large amounts of data. Such storage is permanent, in that a disk's contents remain on the disk when the computer is shut off and can be accessed again when the computer is turned on.

hardware all the physical devices included in a computer system, as the CPU, keyboard, monitor, internal and external disk drives, and separate peripherals, like a printer or scanner.

HTML HyperText Markup Language: a set of standards, a variety of SGML, used to tag the elements of a hypertext document: the standard for documents on the World Wide Web.

hypertext data, as electronic text, graphics, or sound, linked to one another in paths determined by the creator of the material. Hypertext is usually stored with the links overtly marked, so that a computer user can move nonsequentially through a link from one object or document to another.

icon a small graphic image on a computer screen representing a disk drive, a file, or a software command, as a picture of a wastebasket to which a file one wishes to delete can be dragged with a mouse, or a picture of a printer that can be pointed at and clicked on to print a file.

inkjet printer a computer printer that prints text or graphics by spraying jets of ink onto paper to form a high-quality image approaching that of a laser printer.

install to put in place or connect for service or use: to install software on a computer; to install a scanner in one's computer system.

interface computer hardware or software designed to communicate information between hardware devices, between software programs, between devices and programs, or between a computer and a user.

Internet a large computer network linking smaller computer networks worldwide.

laptop a portable personal computer that is small, light, and thin enough to rest on the lap while in use. The screen is usually on the inside of the hinged top cover, becoming visible when when one opens the computer. Most laptops can be operated either through an electrical connection or batteries.

laser printer a high-speed, high-resolution computer printer that uses a laser to form dot-matrix patterns and an electrostatic process to print a page at a time.

macro a single instruction, for use in a computer program, that represents a sequence of instructions or keystrokes.

megabyte a measure of data storage capacity equal to approximately one million bytes.

memory the capacity of a computer to store information, especially internally in RAM, while electrical power is on. Do not confuse memory with storage.

menu a list, displayed on a computer screen, from which one can choose options or commands.

modem an electronic device that allows the transmission of data to or from a computer via telephone or other communication lines.

monitor a component part of a computer system that includes a display screen for viewing computer data.

multimedia the combined use of several media, such as sound, text, graphics, animation, and video, in computer applications. Multimedia is featured, for example, in games and in reference works on CD-ROMs.

newsgroup a discussion group maintained on a computer network, usually focused on a specific topic.

notebook a small, lightweight laptop computer.

OCR Optical Character Recognition: the reading of printed or typed text by electronic means, as by using a scanner and OCR software. In this process, the text is converted to digital data, which can then be manipulated and edited on the computer by using an application program, such as a word processor, spreadsheet, or database.

peripheral an external hardware device connected to a computer's CPU. Examples are printers, keyboards, and scanners.

printout computer output produced by a printer; hard copy.

RAM Random Access Memory: volatile computer memory that can store information while the electrical power is on. The information disappears when the computer is shut off. The amount of RAM a computer has is determined by the number and capacity of the RAM chips in the computer.

record a group of related FIELDS treated as a unit in a DATABASE.

SGML Standard Generalized Markup Language: a set of standards enabling a user to create an appropriate scheme for tagging the elements of an electronic document.

resolution the degree of sharpness of a computer-generated image, as on a display screen or printout. Resolution is measured by the number of pixels across and down on a screen and by the number of dots per linear inch on hard copy.

shareware computer software distributed without initial charge but for which the user is encouraged to pay a nominal registration fee after trying the program out. Such fees cover support for continued use and often entitle the user to inexpensive updates.

software programs for directing the operation of a computer or for processing electronic data. Software is, roughly, divided into utility programs and application programs.

spreadsheet a large electronic ledger sheet that can be used for financial planning. Electronic spreadsheets provide "what if" calculations, enabling the user to change estimated figures and see immediately what effect that change will have on the rest of the calculations in the spreadsheet.

storage the capacity of a device, such as a hard disk or a CD-ROM, to hold programs or data permanently. In the case of hard disks, one can remove such programs or data deliberately. Do not confuse storage with memory.

surge protector a device to protect computer circuitry from electrical spikes and surges by diverting the excess voltage through an alternate pathway.

typeface a design for a set of characters, especially numbers and letters, devised to provide the group of symbols with a unified look. Some popular typefaces often found on computer systems include Courier, Times Roman, and Helvetica, but the number of available typefaces has reached the thousands.

Unicode a standard for coding alphanumeric characters using sixteen bits for each character. Unlike ASCII, which uses eight-bit characters, Unicode can represent 65,000 unique characters. This allows a user of software that is Unicode-compatible to access the characters of most European and Asian languages.

URL Uniform Resource Locater: a protocol for specifying addresses on the Internet.

utility program a system program used to simplify standard computer operations, as sorting, copying, or deleting files.

virtual temporarily simulated by software. You can have *virtual memory* on a hard disk or *virtual storage* in RAM. *Virtual reality* simulates a real-world environment.

Web site a connected group of pages on the World Wide Web regarded as a single entity, usually maintained by one person or organization and devoted to one single topic or several closely related topics.

word processing the automated production and storage of documents using computers, electronic printers, and text-editing software.

World Wide Web a system of extensively linked hypertext documents; a branch of the Internet.

WYSIWYG What You See Is What You Get: of, pertaining to, or being a screen display that shows text as it will appear when printed, as by using display-screen versions of the printer's typefaces.

D. Politics

For as long as America has existed as a country, its people have been obsessed with politics. The speeches of politicians are learned in history classes, our important documents are still debated in the newspapers every day, and political campaigns are constantly claiming the interest of the public.

The words used to discuss politics have likewise generated great interest. Sometimes politicians speak so as to evade issues, other times they create memorable words or expressions to memorialize their efforts. Below are some of the many words you will encounter while following that great American spectator sport of Government.

Beltway, the the Washington, D.C., area; the U.S. government (used with *inside* or *outside*).
bloviate to speak pompously.
bork to systematically attack (a candidate or the like), especially in the media.

curve the forefront of any issue: *ahead of the curve; behind the curve.*

dirty tricks unethical or illegal activities directed against a political opponent.
dove a person who advocates peace or a conciliatory military position.

full-court press an all-out effort.

-gate (used to indicate political scandals, especially ones resulting from a cover-up): *Watergate; Irangate.*
goo-goo an idealistic supporter of political reform.
gridlock a complete stoppage of normal activity: *legislative gridlock.*

hawk a person who advocates war or a belligerent military position.
Hill, the the United States Congress; Capitol Hill.
hot-button arousing passionate emotions: *hot-button issues.*

policy wonk a person obsessively devoted to the most intricate details of policy.
pork political appropriations or appointments made solely for political reasons.
pork barrel a government bill, policy, or appropriation that supplies funds for local improvements, designed to ingratiate legislators with their constituents.

smoking gun indisputable evidence or proof, as of a crime or misdeed.
sound bite a brief, striking remark taken from a speech for use in a news story.
spin a particular viewpoint or bias, as on a news issue; *(as a verb)* to put a spin on: *The press secretary spun the debate to make it look like his candidate won.*

spin doctor an expert in spinning.

Teflon impervious to blame or criticism: *the Teflon president.*

wedge issue an issue that divides an otherwise united group or political party.

E. Law

Rarely has a profession captivated the public imagination more thoroughly than law. With its theatrical courtrooms, intense conflicts, powerful personalities, and intriguing mysteries surrounding the issues of guilt and innocence, the law often occupies center stage in both fiction and reality. New celebrities—actors in both fictional and real courtroom dramas—are often created overnight, and the law seems to permeate our lives.

Whether your goal is to enrich your understanding of these events and stories or to deal with the mundane, practical legal matters in your personal and professional life, exposure to legal terminology is a necessity. Much of the vocabulary encountered in legal contexts is common enough to require little interpretation. No one has any trouble with *court, judge, defense attorney,* and similar terms, but some legal language is unfamiliar or just plain difficult. What follows is a representative sample of terms from the language of the law.

abet to encourage, instigate, or support some criminal activity. Used almost exclusively in the phrase *aid and abet.*

abscond to leave a jurisdiction in order to avoid arrest, service of a summons, or other imposition of justice.

abuse mistreatment of someone, such as physical abuse, psychological abuse, or sexual abuse. Abusive actions subject to legal intervention include (but are not limited to) child abuse and spousal abuse.

accessory a person who assists a criminal in committing a crime without being present when the crime is committed. An accessory is considered as culpable as someone who actually commits the crime.

adjourn to suspend or postpone a legal proceeding, either temporarily or indefinitely.

adjudication the hearing and disposition of a case in a proper court or agency. Adjudication includes a decision, as by a judge or jury, and, when appropriate, sentencing.

affidavit a formal written statement swearing to the truth of the facts stated and signed before a notary public. Dishonesty in an affidavit is either FALSE SWEARING or PERJURY.

amicus curiae, *pl.* **amici curiae** (literally, "friend of the court") someone who, although not a party to the litigation, volunteers or is invited by the court to submit views on the issues in the case.

arraignment the proceeding in which a criminal defendant is brought before the court, formally advised of charges, and required to enter a plea.

attachment the seizing or freezing of property by court order, either to resolve a dispute over ownership or to make the property available to satisfy a judgment against the owner.

certiorari a writ issuing from a superior court calling up the record of a proceeding in an inferior court for review. Also called **writ of certiorari.**

charge **1.** a judge's instruction to the jury on a particular point of law. **2.** a formal allegation that a person has violated a criminal law. **3.** to make or deliver a charge.

conflict of interest the circumstance of a public officeholder, business executive, or the like, whose personal interests might benefit from his or her official actions or influence, especially when those personal interests conflict with one's duty.

contract an agreement between two or more parties for one to do or not do something specified in exchange for something done or promised by the other(s).

counterclaim a claim made to offset another claim, especially one made by the defendant against the plaintiff in a legal action.

cross examination an examination, usually by a lawyer, of a witness for the opposing side, especially for the purpose of discrediting the witness's testimony.

due process fair administration of the law in accordance with established procedures and with due regard for the fundamental rights and liberties of people in a free society.

escheat the reverting of property to the state when there are no persons that can be found who are legally qualified to inherit or to claim.

exclusionary rule a rule that forbids the introduction of illegally obtained evidence in a criminal trial.

extradition the surrender of a suspect by one state, nation, or authority to another.

false swearing the crime of making a false statement, as under oath (for example, in a civil case), knowing that the statement is not true. *False swearing* is not considered as serious a crime as PERJURY.

garnishment the attachment of money or property so they can be used to satisfy a debt.

grand jury a group of citizens assembled to hear evidence presented by a prosecutor against a particular person for a particular crime. A *grand jury* is convened in order to determine whether or not there is sufficient evidence to issue an indictment. The standards for indictment are considerably less than those for conviction at trial.

gravamen the fundamental part of an accusation; the essence of a complaint or charge.

hearsay evidence testimony based on what a witness has heard from another person rather than on direct personal knowledge or experience.

hostile witness a witness called by one side in a case who is known to be friendly to the other side or who turns out to be evasive in answering questions.

impeachment the institution of formal misconduct charges against a government official as a basis for removal from office.

in flagrante delicto in the very act of committing the offense: *They were caught in flagrante delicto.*

judicial district a geographic division established for the purpose of organizing a court system.

jurisdiction the geographic area throughout which the authority of a court, legislative body, law enforcement agency, or other governmental unit extends.

kangaroo court a mock court convened to reach a predetermined verdict of guilty, such as one set up by vigilantes.

litigant a party to a lawsuit.

litigation the process of making something the subject of a lawsuit; contesting an issue in a judicial proceeding.

litigator a lawyer who specializes in litigation.

malfeasance the performance by a public official of an act that is legally unjustified, harmful, or contrary to law.

mandamus a writ from a superior court to an inferior court or to an officer, corporation, etc., commanding that a specified thing be done; usually issued only in rare cases, to remedy an injustice.

monopoly the intentional acquisition or retention of exclusive control of a commodity or service in a particular market, especially so as to exclude competition and make possible the manipulation of prices.

nolo contendere (in a criminal case) a defendant's pleading that does not admit guilt but subjects him or her to punishment as though a guilty plea had been entered. Unlike a guilty plea, however, a plea of *nolo contendere* cannot be used as proof of guilt in a subsequent civil proceeding.

perjury the willful giving of false testimony under oath or affirmation, in a judicial or administrative proceeding, upon a point material to a legal inquiry. Compare FALSE SWEARING.

plaintiff the person who starts a lawsuit by serving or filing a complaint.

plea a criminal defendant's formal response to charges. The defendant may plead *guilty, not guilty,* or *nolo contendere.*

prima facie (of a case, evidence, or proof) sufficient to support a contending party's claim and to warrant a verdict in favor of that party regarding that issue.

pro bono (of legal services) performed without fee, for the sake of the public good.

replevin an action for the recovery of tangible personal property wrongfully taken or detained by another.

special prosecutor an outside person appointed to investigate and, if warranted, prosecute a case in which the prosecutor who would normally handle the case has a conflict of interest.

statute of limitations a statute defining the period of time after an event within which legal action arising from that event may be taken.

subornation of perjury the crime of inducing another person to commit perjury.

surrogate court (in some states) a court having jurisdiction over the probate of wills, the administration of estates, etc.

venue the county or judicial district where the courts have jurisdiction to consider a case.

voir dire an examination of a proposed witness or juror to determine if there are possible sources of bias that would militate against his or her objectivity in serving on a jury; an oath administered to a prospective witness or juror by which he or she is sworn to speak the truth so that the examiner can ascertain his or her competence.

writ a court order by which a court commands a certain official or body to carry out a certain action.

F. Fashion

Dressing stylishly is an important means of self-expression for many people, and the fashion industry is one of the biggest businesses in America, with its own customs, its own newspapers, and its own language. Here is a selection of recent words referring to clothing and fashion, along with definitions of some enduring classics.

asymmetrical-cut referring to necklines or hemlines that are not symmetrical.

atelier a workshop or studio of a high-fashion designer.

backpack a pack or knapsack carried on one's back to keep the hands free; first popularized by campers and students, later made in leather and adopted by fashionable women in lieu of a handbag.

ballerina flats low-heeled women's shoes modeled on the soft exercise slippers worn by dancers.

bandage dress a dress of spandex that totally conforms to the wearer's body; originated by Hervé Leger.

bell-bottoms trousers with wide, flaring legs, modeled on sailor's pants.

bespoke (of menswear) referring to hand-tailored suits, custom-fitted shirts, bench-made shoes, etc.

bias-cut referring to fabric cut on the bias to drape gracefully on the body.

Birkenstocks ™ open leather sandals.

blouson a full-cut shirt or jacket tied at the waist for a balloon effect.

boat shoes rubber-soled mocassins worn to provide a firm grip on a boat's deck.

bodysuit a short, one-piece garment for women with a snap closure at the crotch, designed to eliminate bunching at the waist and create a smooth line under a skirt or pants; adapted from a dancer's leotard.

bomber jacket a short jacket with a fitted or elasticized waist, often made of leather and lined with fleece; originally worn by fliers.

bustier a women's tight-fitting, sleeveless, strapless top worn as a blouse and usually exposing decolletage; modeled on the corset.

button-down (of a collar) having buttonholes at the ends with which it can be buttoned to the front of the garment.

caftan a full, long robe with loose sleeves, worn for lounging; based on similar Middle Eastern garments.

camisole a women's waist-length top with skinny shoulder straps, usually worn under a sheer bodice.

cargo pants loose-cut trousers with a number of deep pockets on the legs to accommodate extra baggage; originally a military style.

casual day a day (usually Friday) on which office workers are permitted to dress in sportswear. Also **dress-down day.**

catsuit a one-piece garment for women with long sleeves and leggings, often made of a polyester fabric to cling tightly to the shape of the wearer.

Chanel bag a women's handbag of quilted leather suspended from the shoulder on a gold chain.

Chanel suit a women's suit usually with a cropped jacket having a round neck, several buttons, and often braid trim, worn with a skirt.

chesterfield a single- or double-breasted overcoat with a velvet collar, often made of herringbone wool.

cornrows narrow braids of hair plaited tightly against the scalp.

cowboy boots chunky-heeled boots with a pointed toe and highly decorative stitching and embossing.

cowlneck sweater a sweater with a neckline made of softly draped fabric.

crop top a casual pullover sport shirt cut short to expose the midriff.

cross-trainers athletic shoes designed to be used for more than one sport.

dreadlocks a hairstyle of many long, ropelike braids.

driving shoes soft, semi-flexible leather or suede loafers with a rubber sole designed to grip the pedals of a car.

duffel coat a hooded overcoat of sturdy wool, usually fastened with toggle buttons.

espadrilles flat shoes with a cloth upper, a rope sole, and sometimes lacing around the ankles.

fashionista an influential person in the fashion world; a devotee of fashion.

fashion police a jocular imaginary force invoked as criticism of a person who is badly or unstylishly dressed.

fashion victim a person whose attempts to follow the dictates of fashion have backfired ludicrously; one whose obsession with fashion is excessive.

faux fur artificial fleece dyed and styled to resemble animal fur.

fisherman's sweater an elaborately designed, solid-color, hand-knit and cable-stitched sweater of heavy wool; originally made by the wives of sailors in the Aran Islands of Ireland.

French cuffs generous foldover shirt cuffs that require cufflinks or studs.

fun fur a fur jacket or coat dyed and cut in an outré style to be worn as sportswear.

gangsta a style derived from the inner-city ghetto emphasizing baggy clothing, designer sportswear, cutting-edge athletic shoes, and sometimes gold jewelry. Also **hip-hop.**

Gore-Tex ™ a breathable, water-repellent fabric laminate originally used for outdoor sportswear, often produced in bright colors.

Gothic look a style marked by bizarre or outré makeup (for men as well as women), dress, and hairstyle in a Romantic vein reminiscent of classic horror films. Also **Goth.**

grunge a style marked by dirty, unkempt, often torn, secondhand clothing.

hair extensions false hair woven into a person's natural hair to give the illusion of greater length and fullness.

haute couture high fashion; the most fashionable, exclusive, and expensive designer clothing, made to measure of luxurious fabrics after extensive fittings.

Hawaiian shirt a loose-fitting, button-front, short-sleeved cotton shirt with a turnover collar, made in bright colors and loud patterns with a tropical theme, such as palm trees or parrots.

high tops sneakers with fabric extending to the ankles.

jellies transparent polyurethane shoes with a cross-strap and very low heels.

Kelly bag a squarish or slightly trapezoidal women's handbag first made by Hermès for Princess Grace of Monaco.

kente a colorful striped fabric of Ghanaian origin often worn as a symbol of African-American pride.

khakis loose-fitting trousers made of a stout beige fabric, worn as casual sportswear.

leggings tight-fitting elasticized pants for women; modeled on dancer's tights.

little black dress a basic, unadorned black dress popularized by Coco Chanel in the early twentieth century for its flexibility and utility as a wardrobe mainstay, especially as a cocktail dress.

maxi coat a full-length overcoat extending to the ankles.

microfiber an extremely fine polyester fiber used in clothing.

motorcycle jacket a short leather jacket resembling a bomber jacket, but usually embellished with zippers, buckles, studs, etc.

palazzo pants women's wide-legged trousers cut to resemble a long skirt.

pantsuit a softened version for women of the classic menswear suit, having a jacket with lapels and tailored trousers.

pareo a length of fabric tied at the side to drape over the hips, usually worn over a matching bathing suit. Also **sarong.**

parka a hooded, straight-cut jacket made of materials that provide warmth against very cold temperatures; often a down- or polyester-filled nylon shell, sometimes quilted for extra warmth.

pea jacket a heavy, double-breasted, short wool jacket; originally worn by seamen. Also **peacoat.**

pedal pushers casual slacks reaching to mid-calf. Also **capri pants; clam diggers.**

platforms shoes with a thick insert of leather, cork, plastic, or other sturdy material between the upper and the sole.

polo coat a tailored overcoat of camel's hair or a similar fabric, single- or double-breasted and often belted or half-belted.

polo shirt a cotton pullover sport shirt with a round neck or turnover collar, usually with short sleeves.

power suit a tailored women's suit with jacket and skirt designed in imitation of a man's business suit and usually including shoulder pads; popular among businesswomen of the 1980s.

racer back a tank top with the back cut out to expose the shoulder blades; modeled on similar designs in bathing suits designed to cut friction in speed-swimming contests.

ready-to-wear ready-made clothing. Also **prêt-à-porter; off-the-peg; off-the-rack.**

Rugby shirt a full-cut, usually broad-striped cotton pullover with a contrasting white turnover collar and three-button placket; modeled on shirts worn by English Rugby or soccer players.

Saville Row an area of London specializing in elegant and classic hand-tailored menswear.

sheath a close-fitting, simple, unbelted dress with a straight drape, usually sleeveless with a plain neckline.

shell a short, sleeveless, usually round-necked blouse for women, often worn under a jacket.

ski pants snug-fitting pants of a stretch fabric, usually having straps for the feet to keep them from bunching at the boot line.

skort a women's garment for the lower body that resembles a skirt but has separate openings for the legs.

slides backless women's shoes of varying heights. Also **mules.**

slingbacks open-backed women's shoes with a strap to secure the heel.

slip dress a loose-fitting unadorned dress with skinny straps, modeled on women's undergarments of the earlier twentieth century.

spandex a polyurethane fabric with elastic properties.

stilettos very high, narrow heels that taper to a point, used on women's shoes. Also **spike heels.**

supermodel a prominent fashion model who commands the highest fees and can usually be recognized by first name only.

sweater set a short-sleeved, round-necked sweater for women accompanied by a matching cardigan. Also **twin set.**

tank top a low-cut, sleeveless pullover with shoulder straps, often made of a lightweight knit.

thigh-cut referring to bathing suits cut high on the thigh to expose the hip.

thigh-highs stockings that come to mid-thigh, often worn under a short skirt so that the stocking tops are visible.

thong a skimpy garment for the lower body that exposes the buttocks, usually having a strip of fabric passing between the legs attached to a waistband.

vintage referring to clothing purchased at resale shops that evokes the style of an earlier era in fashion.

weave false hair woven into the natural hair.

wedgies women's shoes with a heel formed by a roughly triangular or wedgelike piece that extends from the front or middle to the back of the sole.

wrap dress a patterned polyester or cotton knit dress that ties on the side to drape naturally over the wearer's body; originated by Diane Von Furstenburg in the 1970s and revived in the 1990s.

G. Sports

The American devotion to sports is almost religious in its fervor. The main team sports—baseball, football, basketball, and to a lesser degree hockey—remain incredibly popular; but other sports, such as figure skating, mountain biking, snowboarding, in-line skating, and beach volleyball are gaining more and more attention. Every sport has its own complicated rules and language; there are entire books devoted to sports terminology. Here is a short list of some recent sports-related words and expressions.

beach volleyball competitive volleyball played outdoors on sand.

bungee jumping jumping from a high surface to which one is attached by elasticized cords, so that the body bounces back before hitting the ground.

extreme sports sports that are viewed as being very dangerous, such as bungee-jumping or sky surfing.

full-court press a defensive strategy in basketball in which the defensive team pressures the offensive team the entire length of the court.

Hacky Sack™ a small leather beanbag juggled with the feet as a game.

Hail Mary a long football pass thrown in desperation, with a low chance of being caught.

high five a gesture of greeting or congratulation where one person slaps the open palm of another as it is held at head level.

in-line skate a roller skate having typically four hard-rubber wheels in a line resembling the blade of an ice skate.

in-your-face (in basketball) confrontational; provocative.

Jet Ski™ a small jet-propelled boat ridden like a motorcycle.

Rollerblade™ a brand of in-line skates.

sky surfing jumping from a plane with a parachute while wearing a board resembling a snowboard, so that one can "skate" on the air currents.

snowboard a board for gliding on the snow, resembling a wide ski, that one rides in an upright, standing position resembling the motion of surfing.

triathlon an athletic contest consisting of swimming, running, and cycling.

trash-talking (in basketball) the use of aggressive, boastful, or insulting language.

Zamboni™ a machine for smoothing the ice at a rink.

10

Slang, Jargon, and Dialect

Lesson 1. Slang

Many people think that the word *slang* refers to any sort of language that is nonstandard, but this is not the case. Slang is a special part of the language, not just ungrammatical or "dirty" or "funny-sounding" speech.

It is hard to define *slang* precisely, but a working definition might be that it is a highly informal, nontechnical vocabulary composed chiefly of novel-sounding synonyms for standard expressions, and that it packs some kind of rhetorical "punch." A slang word must *sound* slangy; it must have that special effect that a standard word doesn't have. Slang is typically more metaphorical, playful, elliptical, vivid, and ephemeral than ordinary language.

Slang can arise in any group; there is medical slang just as there is sexual slang. But because of the subversive nature of slang, it is more likely to come from "outsider" social groups. Almost any unfamiliar word invented by teenagers or drug users is likely to be considered slang, but only the most obviously slangy lawyers' terms would be called slang. Some of the subcultures that generate a great deal of slang are adolescents, ethnic minorities (especially African-Americans, who have contributed greatly to slang in the United States), sports groups (including fans and players), criminals, drug users, and the military. Among the concepts that generate many slang synonyms are sex, alcohol or drug use, body parts, violence, and terms (often disparaging) for other people.

Slang expressions develop the same way other vocabulary does.

Most slang comes from standard English words that have taken on new meanings. For example, *dog* has many slang senses, including "a sausage; hot dog"; "a slow or worthless horse"; "a person's foot"; "an inferior or defective manufactured product"; and "an ugly person."

While slang that has become established in the language tends to stay around for longer than many people think, it is also true that slang can become outdated very quickly. A word like *groovy,* meaning "very pleasing; attractive; wonderful; exciting" is still familiar, but it is a stereotyped word of the late 1960s, and no one would use it seriously any more. *Twenty-three skiddoo,* used as an exclamation of excitement; *the cat's meow,* referring to anything wonderful; *hepster,* to describe a person who is fashionable; and *jalopy,* for a broken-down car, are all slang words that were once common but have now become obsolescent.

Slang often invigorates a language, giving it freshness and energy, but it is important to be aware of what is appropriate. In formal situations, slang should be avoided. You can use slang occasionally to flavor your speech or writing, but be careful to choose words that suit your audience and your purpose.

Here are fifteen relatively recent slang words and expressions that are in popular use. How many of them are familiar to you?

attitude a hostile or belligerent disposition. "Calm down, and stop giving me all that *attitude."*

the bomb wonderful; exciting; great. "That new record is *the bomb!"*

chill [out] to relax; calm down. "It's no big deal, man. You should *chill out."*
chump change a relatively small or insignificant amount of money. "I worked all weekend for *chump change."*

dis to show disrespect for; affront. "She *dissed* me by making fun of my outfit."
dope wonderful; exciting; great. "He's wearing some *dope kicks."*

hang to relax; loiter. "I'm just gonna go *hang* with my friends."
homey a close friend. "You're my *homey.* I'll always help you out."
hoochie a young woman who dresses provocatively. "Check out that *hoochie* over there."

in-your-face confrontational; provocative; defiant. "He gave me this *in-your-face* glare and walked right out of class."

kicks shoes; sneakers.

my bad my fault; I'm sorry. "Whoops, *my bad.*"

not! (used after a statement to contradict it). "I can't wait to go back to school. *Not!*"

scrunchie an elastic band used by girls to tie up their hair. "She was wearing this ugly purple *scrunchie* in her hair."

yada-yada-yada (used as an interjection to mean) and so on; and so forth; et cetera. "They told me I needed to improve my attitude, get better grades, *yada-yada-yada.*"

Quiz 1: Write In

Each of the following sentences contains an italicized slang word or expression that is perfectly appropriate in the context of informal conversation. For each sentence, replace the slang word with a word or phrase that would be better suited to more formal usage and notice the effect of the change. Write your answer in the space provided.

_____ 1. He really *bugs* me when he does that.
_____ 2. Watch out! There's a *Five-O* around the corner!
_____ 3. That chore was a real *pain in the neck.*
_____ 4. Johnny was hit on the *bean* with the softball.
_____ 5. I had a lot of *moola* riding on that bet.
_____ 6. I *blew* it all at the races.
_____ 7. That franchise deal was a *ripoff.*
_____ 8. If you keep on drinking like that, you're going to get *wasted.*
_____ 9. I wish he'd quit his *bellyaching.*
_____ 10. When she's in one of those moods, she's a real *sourpuss.*
_____ 11. He *zapped* the figures marching across the screen and defeated his opponent.
_____ 12. What's your *beef?*
_____ 13. I told him to *bug off.*
_____ 14. If he doesn't start studying soon, he's going to *flunk* this course.
_____ 15. Mike is *hooked on* video games.

Suggested Answers   1. annoys, bothers 2. police officer 3. nuisance, bother 4. head 5. money 6. spent, wasted 7. fraud, swindle 8. drunk 9. complaining, grumbling 10. complainer, grumbler, grouch 11. hit, destroyed, demolished 12. complaint 13. leave, depart 14. fail 15. addicted to, obsessed with

Lesson 2. Jargon and Argot

"Get him in here stat," the doctor ordered. *Stat,* a word adopted by the medical establishment from Latin "statim," is medical argot for "immediately" and is used when doctors and their assistants want to communicate quickly and efficiently. Both "jargon" and "argot" refer to the vocabulary that is peculiar to a specific group of people and that has been devised for intergroup communication or identification. Its use is also a means of restricting access by the uninitiated and creating a sense of exclusivity among group members. Though the words "jargon" and "argot" are interchangeable, "jargon" has derogatory connotations and one of its common meanings is *gibberish, nonsense.* For that reason we shall use the designation "argot" for specialized terminology.

While some argot does pass into general circulation, most of it remains incomprehensible to the layperson. Argot should be used only within the field to which it belongs; otherwise, it will probably fail to communicate your meaning. Here are some examples of argot drawn from different fields.

Legal Argot

on all fours	a legal precedent exactly on the mark
blacklining	marking up a legal document for changes
nit	a small point
conformed copy	a legal document with a printed rather than a signed name
counterparts	identical copies signed by different parties

Publishing Argot

dummy	a mocked-up copy to be checked, as for pagination
proof	a trial impression of composed type taken to correct errors and make alterations
gutter	the white space formed by the inner margins of two facing pages of a book
slush pile	unsolicited manuscripts

Printing Argot

bleed	illustration or printing that extends beyond the edges of the page

roll size   paper width
live art   the actual art being used
blanket   the rubber sheet in a printing press that transfers the
                image from the plate to the paper

Theater Argot

angel   a theatrical backer
spot   a spotlight
apron   the part of a stage in front of the curtain
ice   free tickets

Aeronautics Argot

jig   a device in which an airplane part can be held while it is being
            worked on
BAFO   best and final offer
RFQ   request for quote
CDRL   contract data requirements list

Quiz 2: Matching

Below are some examples of baseball argot. See how closely you can match each word or phrase with its meaning. Write your answer in the space provided.

_____   1. fungo   a. a high fly ball that's easy to catch

_____   2. around the horn   b. batter hits the ball down so it will
                                     bounce high

_____   3. hit for the cycle   c. a baseball tossed in the air and
                                     struck as it comes down

_____   4. can of corn   d. a home run with three runners on
                                     base

_____   5. grand slam   e. to get a single, double, triple, and
                                     home run in one game

_____   6. Baltimore chop   f. a double play started by the third
                                     baseman

Lesson 3. Dialect and Briticisms

A dialect is a version of language spoken in a particular geographic region or by a specific group of people. Dialects frequently contain words, pronunciations, and grammatical structures that are not accepted as standard English. For example, in the British Yorkshire dialect, "something" would be rendered as "summat." For more on dialects, refer to Chapter 1.

Although the Americans and the British have little difficulty communicating with each other, each country nevertheless retains a vocabulary of its own. Words used specifically by the British are known as Briticisms. Here are some of the more common ones.

Briticism	Americanism
pub	bar
redundant	laid off (from a job)
mackintosh	raincoat
torch	flashlight
bloke	guy
sweet-shop	candy store
flat	apartment
chemist	druggist
telly	TV
petrol	gasoline
lift	elevator
ladder	run (in a stocking)
settee	sofa
underground, tube	subway
bonnet	hood (of a car)
nappie	diaper
serviette	napkin
lorry	truck
nick	jail
cooker	stove

Quiz 3: Matching

Match each Briticism with its American counterpart. Write your answer in the space provided.

1. **lift**	a. napkin		_____
2. **underground**	b. sofa		_____
3. **telly**	c. hood (of a car)		_____
4. **flat**	d. truck		_____
5. **cooker**	e. guy		_____
6. **redundant**	f. elevator		_____
7. **settee**	g. druggist		_____
8. **petrol**	h. TV		_____
9. **bloke**	i. flashlight		_____
10. **torch**	j. run (in a stocking)		_____

11. **lorry**	k. subway	_____
12. **chemist**	l. apartment	_____
13. **nick**	m. jail	_____
14. **mackintosh**	n. gasoline	_____
15. **serviette**	o. raincoat	_____
16. **pub**	p. stove	_____
17. **sweet-shop**	q. bar	_____
18. **ladder**	r. laid off	_____
19. **bonnet**	s. candy store	_____
20. **nappie**	t. diaper	_____

Answers to Quizzes in Chapter 10

Answers to Quiz 2

1. c 2. f 3. e 4. a 5. d 6. b

Answers to Quiz 3

1. f 2. k 3. h 4. l 5. p 6. r 7. b 8. n 9. e 10. i 11. d 12. g 13. m 14. o 15. a
16. q 17. s 18. j 19. c 20. t

11

Shortened Forms in English

Though some language experts regard the modern predilection for abbreviations and shortened forms as a kind of barbarism, it is a trend that reflects the pressures of modern life, as we attempt to compress long utterances into more compact expressive forms. Abbreviations are also a natural outgrowth of the underlying preference of English speakers for monosyllabic forms.

Here is an overview of shortened forms in English, along with some notes on their formation and use.

An *abbreviation* is a shortened or contracted form created from the initial or first few letters, or any group of letters, of a word or series of words. The series of words in the full form can be a title, name, or set phrase. Examples: *E* (for East); *Dr.* (for Doctor); *lb.* (for Latin "libra," pound); *etc.* (for et cetera).

An *initialism* is a shortened form created from the initial letters of a series of words, with each letter pronounced separately. Examples: *FDR* (for Franklin Delano Roosevelt); *CIA* (for Central Intelligence Agency).

An *acronym* is a pronounceable word created from the initial or first few letters of a series of words. Sometimes a vowel is inserted in the acronym to aid pronunciation. Very often the full or expanded form of an acronym is not widely known; few people know what the letters in *laser* stand for. The acronym may be a word that already exists in the language, such as *CARE* and *SHAPE*. Examples: *NASA* (for National Aeronautics and Space Administration); *scuba* (for self-contained underwater breathing apparatus).

A *hybrid* is a shortened form that cannot be neatly classified as an abbreviation, initialism, or acronym. One type of hybrid can be pronounced as the word it spells or as a series of letters, as *AWOL*. Another type of hybrid is an initialism that is pronounced as a word, as *SCSI* (skuz′ē). There are also shortened forms composed of a short form and a word, as *D-day* and *CAT scan*. Sometimes a shortened form can be considered both an abbreviation and a word, as *math* (for mathematics) and *prof* (for professor).

A *symbol* is a letter, figure, or other conventional mark, or a combination of letters, used to designate an object, quality, process, etc. Symbols are used in specialized fields, as physics and music. Examples: *Au* (for gold, the chemical element); *X* (for ten, the Roman numeral).

The Formation and Use of Short Forms

Short forms are commonly encountered in newspapers, magazines, advertising, and daily conversation. In addition to the forms in general, everyday use, each specialized field has its own set of technical short forms.

Abbreviations, acronyms, and symbols are created for several reasons. They are easy to pronounce or remember, and they save time in speaking and writing. Many are catchy, such as *GUI* (Graphical User Interface) and *WYSIWYG* (What You See Is What You Get), or useful in advertising slogans and newspaper headlines. Some serve as euphemisms, such as *B.O.* for body odor.

A full form may have several different short forms in common use. Not all are equally correct, acceptable, or widespread. For example, *acct.* is more common than *acc.* as an abbreviation for "account."

Many short forms are informal or slang, as *P.D.Q.* (for pretty damn quick) and *OK*. Others are formal or fully standard in the language. In fact, some short forms are used instead of their corresponding full forms. We commonly speak of *VCRs, TVs,* and *HMOs,* but rarely of *videocassette recorders, televisions,* and *health maintenance organizations.*

Although short forms are acceptable and widely used, some are not immediately recognizable. They may be derived from foreign words or phrases, such as *no.* from Latin "numero." Some short forms stand for more than one full form and are therefore ambiguous. These forms should be defined the first time they are mentioned, and the short form can be used thereafter. Example: *The Central Intelligence Agency (CIA) was established in 1947. The CIA is a federal agency that conducts intelligence activities outside the United States.*

For abbreviations and initialisms, the trend is to leave out the periods, especially in scientific and technical notation and in capitalized forms, such as *F* (for Fahrenheit) and *RNA*. However, some short forms always take periods to avoid confusion, as *B.A.* (for Bachelor of Arts), *art.* (for article), *D.C.* (District of Columbia), and *no.* (for number).

The great majority of abbreviations are written with capital letters regardless of whether the constituent words are usually capitalized, as *LCD* (for liquid-crystal display). Acronyms are usually capitalized, as *NATO,* but common ones often appear in lowercase, as *radar.* Short forms standing for proper nouns or important words in names or titles are usually capitalized, as *UFT* (for United Federation of Teachers) and *Span.* (for Spanish). Short forms standing for common nouns, adjectives, or adverbs are usually lowercased, as *spec.* (for special). Units of weight and measure, such as *kg* and *hr,* are written in lowercase. Symbols for chemical elements have only the first letter capitalized, as *Fe* (for iron).

The plural of a short form is often the same as the singular; in fact, there is a trend toward abolishing all pluralized forms. Short forms may be pluralized by adding "s" or "es," as *lbs.* (pounds), *nos.* (numbers), *HMOs* (health maintenance organizations), and *PCs* (personal computers). Sometimes apostrophes are used in plural forms, as *pj's.* There is a small group of abbreviations that form the plural by doubling a consonant, as *mss* (manuscripts), *ll* (lines), and *pp.* (pages).

Short forms can function as more than one part of speech. For example, *OK* is used as a noun, interjection, verb, adjective, and adverb. In these cases, the form is inflected in a predictable manner: *OK'ed* (or *OK'd*), *OK'ing.*

12

Guide to Sensitivity in Language

This chapter is intended as a general guide to language that can, intentionally or not, cause offense or perpetuate discriminatory values and practices by emphasizing the differences between people or implying that one group is superior to another. Its purpose is to make you aware of the possible consequences of the words you choose. Before looking at the words themselves, it is important to note that offensive or insensitive speech is not limited to a specific group of words. Anyone can be hurtful and insulting by using any type of vocabulary, if that is the intent. While in most cases it is easy to avoid blatantly offensive slurs and comments, more subtle bias that is an inherent part of our language or that is the habit of a lifetime is much harder to change.

Certain words are labeled in the dictionary as *vulgar, offensive,* or *disparaging.* Words in these categories, which include those referring to sexual or excretory functions and racial, ethnic, or social groups, are usually inappropriate and should be treated with caution. While there are some circumstances where these words are accepted, there are many others where their use can be hurtful and upsetting. For example, consider such words as *Nazi* or *nigger.*

Other factors complicate the question. A group may disagree within itself as to what is acceptable and what is not. Many seemingly inoffensive terms develop negative connotations over time and become dated or go out of style as awareness changes. A "within the group" rule often applies, which allows a member of a group to use terms freely that would be considered offensive if used by a nonmember of the group.

What is considered acceptable shifts constantly as people become more aware of language and its power. The rapid changes of the last few decades have left many people puzzled and afraid of unintentionally insulting someone. At the same time, these changes have angered others, who decry what they see as extremes of "political correctness" in rules and locutions that alter language to the point of obscuring, even destroying, its meaning. The abandonment of traditional usages has also upset many people. But while it is true that some of the more extreme attempts to avoid offending language have resulted in ludicrous obfuscation (is *animal companion* necessary as a replacement for *pet?*), it is also true that heightened sensitivity in language is a statement of respect, indicates a precision of thought, and is a positive move toward rectifying the unequal social status between one group and another.

Suggestions for avoiding language that reinforces stereotypes or excludes certain groups of people are given in the following pages. In each case, the suggested terms are given on the right. While these suggestions can reflect trends, they cannot dictate or predict the preferences of each individual.

Lesson 1. Sexism

Sexism is the most difficult bias to avoid, in part because of the convention of using *man* or *men* and *he* or *his* to refer to people of either sex. Other, more disrespectful conventions include giving descriptions of women in terms of age and appearance while describing men in terms of accomplishment, and neglecting to use parallel terms to refer to men and women. Some suggestions for avoiding sexism in language are given below.

1. Replacing *man* or *men,* or words or expressions containing either, when they are clearly intended to refer to a person of either sex or to include members of both sexes.

Instead of	Consider using
man	human being, human, person, individual
mankind, man (collectively)	human beings, humans, humankind, humanity, people, human race, human species, society, men and women
man-made	synthetic, artificial
workingman	worker, wage earner
man in the street	average person, ordinary person

2. Using gender-neutral terms wherever possible to designate occupations, positions, roles, etc., rather than terms that specify sex. A full list of nonsexist job designations can be found in the *Dictionary of Occupational Titles* published by the U.S. Department of Labor.

   a. Avoiding terms ending in -*man* or other gender-specific forms. One approach is to use words ending in -*person.* Some of these terms, like *salesperson* and *spokesperson,* have achieved wide acceptance; others, like *councilperson* and *weatherperson,* still sound awkward to many people. When discussing an individual whose sex is known, gender-specific terms such as *anchorwoman, businessman, saleswoman,* and *salesman* can be used, although in this situation, too, many people still prefer the neutral terms.

Instead of	Consider using
anchorman	anchor
bellman, bellboy	bellhop
businessman	businessperson *or more specifically* business executive, manager, business owner, retailer, etc.
cameraman	camera operator, cinematographer
chairman	chair, chairperson
cleaning lady, cleaning woman	housecleaner, office cleaner, housekeeper
clergyman	member of the clergy, cleric *or more specifically* minister, rabbi, priest, pastor, etc.
congressman	representative, member of Congress, legislator
fireman	firefighter
forefather	ancestor
housewife	homemaker
insurance man	insurance agent
layman	layperson, nonspecialist, nonprofessional
mailman, postman	mail carrier, letter carrier
policeman	police officer, law enforcement officer
salesman	salesperson, sales representative
spokesman	spokesperson, representative
stewardess, steward	flight attendant
weatherman	weather reporter, weathercaster, meteorologist
workman	worker

b. Avoiding "feminine" suffixes such as *-ess, -ette, -trix,* and *-enne.* Words with these suffixes are often regarded as implying a triviality or inferiority on the part of the person or role involved, as well as making unnecessary reference to the person's sex.

Instead of	Consider using
authoress	author
aviatrix	aviator
poetess	poet
proprietress	proprietor
sculptress	sculptor
suffragette	suffragist
usherette	usher

A few such terms, like *actress, heiress,* and *hostess,* remain in active use, though many women prefer the terms *actor, heir,* and *host.* Several substitutions for both *waitress* and *waiter*—*waitperson, waitron,* and *server*—are gaining ground, but none has yet replaced the traditional designations. Legal terms like *executrix* and *testatrix* are still used, but with diminishing frequency.

c. Eliminating as modifiers the words *lady, female, girl, male,* and the like for terms that otherwise have no gender designation, as in *lady doctor, female lawyer, girl athlete,* or *male secretary,* unless they serve to clarify meaning. Such expressions tend to patronize the individual involved by suggesting that the norm for the role is the gender *not* specified, and that for someone of the gender specified to be found in that role is somehow remarkable or peculiar. When it is necessary to point out the female aspect of a person in a given role or occupation, using *female* or *woman* as a modifier is preferable to *lady: My grandmother was the first woman doctor to practice in this town.*

3. Referring to members of both sexes by parallel terms, names, or titles.

Instead of	Consider using
men and ladies	men and women, ladies and gentlemen
10 men and 13 females	10 men and 13 women
Betty Schmidt, an attractive 49-year-old physician, and her husband, Alan Schmidt, a noted editor	Betty Schmidt, a physician, and her husband, Alan Schmidt, an editor

Mr. David Kim and Mrs. Betty Harrow	Mr. David Kim and Ms. Betty Harrow (unless *Mrs.* is her known preference)
man and wife	husband and wife
Dear Sir:	Dear Sir/Madam:
	Dear Madam or Sir:
	To whom it may concern:
Mrs. Smith and President Jones	Governor Smith and President Jones

4. Avoiding the third person singular masculine pronoun when referring to an individual who could be of either sex, as in *When a reporter covers a controversial story, he has a responsibility to present both sides of the issue.* Rephrasing the sentence in any of the following ways will circumvent this situation:

a. Structuring the sentence in the plural and using the third person plural pronouns *they/their/theirs/them: When reporters cover controversial stories, they have a responsibility. . . .* (Some people approve the use of a plural pronoun to refer to an indefinite like *everyone* or *anyone,* as in *Everyone packed their own lunch,* but many people do not, at least in formal writing.)

b. Using either first or second person pronouns—*I/me/my/mine, we/us/our/ours, you/your/yours*—that do not specify sex. *As a reporter covering a controversial story, I have a responsibility. . . .* or *As reporters covering controversial stories, we have a responsibility . . .* or *When you are a reporter covering a controversial story, you have a responsibility . . .*

c. Using the third person *one: As a reporter covering a controversial story, one has a responsibility. . . .* (Although common in British usage, *one* can seem stilted or excessively formal to Americans. This pronoun is most effective when used sparingly.)

d. Using both the masculine and feminine singular pronouns: *When a reporter covers a controversial story, he or she* (or *she or he*) *has a responsibility. . . .* (This approach is the one most likely to produce awkwardness. But if the pronouns are not repeated too often, it may sometimes be the most satisfactory solution.) The abbreviated forms *he/she, his/her, him/her* (and the reverse forms, with the feminine pronoun first) are also available, though they are not widely used in formal writing. The blend *s/he* is also used by some people.

e. Using the passive voice: *When controversial stories are covered, there is a responsibility to present both sides of the issue* (or *both sides of the issue should be presented*).

f. Rephrasing the sentence to avoid any pronoun: *When covering a controversial story, a reporter has a responsibility. . . .*

    g. Using nouns, like *person, individual,* or a synonym appropriate to the context, instead of pronouns: *Reporters often cover controversial stories. In such cases the journalist has a responsibility. . . .*

    h. Using a relative clause: *A reporter who covers a controversial story has a responsibility. . . .*

Different solutions will work better in different contexts.

5. Avoiding language that disparages, stereotypes, or patronizes either sex.

    a. Avoiding referring to an adult female as a *girl;* to women collectively as *the distaff side* or *the fair sex;* to a wife as *the little woman,* to a female college student as a *coed;* to an unmarried woman as a *bachelor girl, spinster,* or *old maid.*

    b. Being aware that such generalized phrases as *lawyers/doctors/ farmers and their wives* or *a teacher and her students* or *a secretary and her boss* can be taken to exclude an entire sex from even the possibility of occupying a role. It is possible to choose words or forms that specify neither sex or acknowledge both sexes, as in *lawyers and their spouses* (or *families* or *companions*), *a teacher and his or her students* (or *a teacher and students* or *teachers and their students*); *a secretary and his or her boss* (or *a secretary and boss*).

    c. Avoiding terms like *womanly, manly, feminine,* or *masculine* in referring to traits stereotypically associated with one sex or the other. English abounds in adjectives that describe such qualities as strength or weakness, nurturing or determination or sensitivity, without intrinsic reference to maleness or femaleness.

Lesson 2. Race, Ethnicity, and National Origin

Some words and phrases that refer to racial and ethnic groups are clearly offensive and are labeled as such in a dictionary. Other words (e.g., *Indian, Oriental, colored*) are outdated or inaccurate. *Hispanic* is generally accepted as a broad term for Spanish-speaking people of the Western Hemisphere, but more specific terms *(Latino, Mexican American, Cuban American)* are also acceptable and in some cases preferred. *Mixed race* or *multiracial* are acceptable terms for people who identify with more than one race.

Instead of	*Consider using*
Negro, colored, Afro-American	black, African-American (generally preferred to *Afro-American*)

Oriental, Asiatic	Asian, or more specific designations such as Pacific Islander, Chinese American, Korean
Indian	*Indian* properly refers to people who live in or come from India. *American Indian, Native American,* or more specific designations (Lakota, Chinook, Hopi), are usually preferred when referring to the native peoples of the Western Hemisphere. *Red man* and *Red Indian* are considered offensive.
Eskimo	Inuit, Alaska natives,
native (n.)	native peoples, early inhabitants, aboriginal peoples (but not *aborigines*)
(of countries) underdeveloped, less developed, primitive, poor	developing, Third World (although this continues in common use, the disappearance of the Second World has left its context in question)

Lesson 3. Age

The concept of aging is changing in our society as people are living longer and more active lives. Be aware of word choices that reinforce stereotypes *(decrepit, senile)* and avoid mentioning age unless it is relevant to the subject at hand. As with other groups, preferred terms for referring to older people are changing, and individual preferences may vary.

Instead of	*Consider using*
elderly, aged, old, geriatric, the elderly, the aged	older person, senior citizen, older people, senior citizens, seniors

Lesson 4. Sexual Orientation

The term *homosexual* to describe a man or a woman is increasingly replaced by the terms *gay* for men and *lesbian* for women. Among homosexuals, certain terms (such as *queer* and *dyke*) that are usually considered offensive have been gaining currency in recent years, particularly among radicals and in the academic community. However, it is still prudent to avoid these terms in standard contexts. The term *life partner* is frequently used when referring to one member of a committed gay relationship as well as to members of heterosexual relationships. *Sexual orientation* has replaced *sexual preference,* which implies choice. In some contexts, *same-sex* is appropriate: *same-sex marriage, same-sex parents.*

Lesson 5. Avoiding Depersonalization of Persons with Disabilities or Illnesses

Terminology that emphasizes the person rather than the disability is generally preferred when referring to a person with a physical or mental impairment or disability. *Handicap* is used to refer to the environmental barrier that affects the person. (Stairs handicap a person who uses a wheelchair.) While words such as *crazy, demented,* and *insane* are used in facetious or informal contexts, these terms are no longer in technical use and are not used to describe people with clinical diagnoses of mental illness. The euphemisms *challenged, differently abled,* and *special* are preferred by some people, but are often ridiculed and are best avoided.

Instead of	*Consider using*
Mongoloid	person with Down syndrome
wheelchair-bound	a person who uses a wheelchair
AIDS sufferer, person afflicted with AIDS, AIDS victim	person with AIDS, P.W.A., HIV+ (someone who tests positive for HIV but does not yet show symptoms of AIDS)
polio victim	has/had polio
the handicapped, the disabled, cripple	persons with disabilities, person with a disability *or* person who uses crutches *or* other more specific description
deaf-mute, deaf and dumb	deaf person

Lesson 6. Avoiding Patronizing or Demeaning Expressions

Some expressions can offend, regardless of the speaker's intention. References to age, sex, religion, race, and the like should only be included if they are relevant.

Instead of	Consider using
girls (when referring to adult women), the fair sex	women
sweetie, dear, dearie, honey	(usually not appropriate with strangers or in public situations)
old maid, spinster, bachelorette	single woman, woman, divorced woman (but only if one would specify "divorced man" in the same context)
the little woman, old lady, ball and chain	wife
boy (when referring to or addressing an adult man)	man, sir

Lesson 7. Avoiding Language that Excludes or Unnecessarily Emphasizes Differences

These expressions can also be offensive, regardless of intention. References to age, sex, religion, race, and the like should only be included if they are relevant.

Instead of	Consider using
lawyers and their wives	lawyers and their spouses
a secretary and her boss	a secretary and boss, a secretary and his or her boss
a good female surgeon	a good surgeon
the male nurse	the nurse
Arab man denies assault charge	Man denies assault charge
the articulate black student	the articulate student
Marie Curie was a great woman scientist	Marie Curie was a great scientist. (unless the intent is to compare her only with other women in the sciences)
Christian name	given name, personal name, first name
Mr. Johnson, the black representative, met with the president today to discuss civil rights legislation.	Mr. Johnson, a member of the Congressional Black Caucus, met with the president today to discuss civil rights legislation.

13

Word Power for Nonnative Speakers

A full mastery of English is hard enough even for native-born speakers. The most comprehensive dictionaries of modern English list over half a million words, including specialized terms, trade jargon, and slang—words that are not strictly necessary for the vast majority of us. However, the vocabulary of the average adult includes only around 30,000–60,000 words. Furthermore, it has been estimated that the works of Shakespeare are based on only around 20,000 words, while the King James Bible uses fewer than 6,000. Thus, the core vocabulary needed to communicate effectively in English is actually surprisingly small. Nevertheless, it is difficult to convey complex concepts and ideas without a fairly extensive vocabulary.

Here are a few specific suggestions to guide the nonnative speaker in the quest for a more sophisticated command of English. Refer also to Chapters 3 and 4 for some helpful tips on usage and a list of words that are often confused even by native English speakers.

General and Specialized Vocabulary

Nonnative learners of English must begin by mastering the basic vocabulary. The use of learner's dictionaries and flashcards have proven to be effective tools for the study of vocabulary. However, knowing the meaning(s) of a word is not enough. A learner must know the limitations on the use of a particular term, so as not to make an error in word choice. Certain words, such as the adverb *just* and the verb *mean,* are used more frequently in conversational speech than in writing. Other words are only used in formal contexts, as in business letters, official documents, or public speeches.

Familiarity with the most frequently used words will enable the learner to understand the spoken language and to read newspapers and magazines. More difficult words can be acquired gradually over the course of time. However, the workplace presents an additional hurdle for the learner of English. Each field of activity, whether it be computers, banking, or law, has its own specialized terminology. Specialized dictionaries and glossaries can be of help, but the advanced learner will have to absorb this technical vocabulary in much the same way as the native speaker.

Synonyms

The study of synonym groups is a useful method of vocabulary-building. A particular sense or meaning can be expressed by several different words. In order to select the most suitable word, the learner must be able to distinguish among the different shades of meaning. Most standard and learner's dictionaries have "synonym studies," and there are many thesauruses, dictionaries of synonyms, and other word finders. See page 381 for a list of helpful resources.

Idioms

An idiom or verb phrase must be learned as a whole because its meaning is not evident from the meanings of its individual words. Most standard dictionaries list idioms and verb phrases at the main-entry word. For example, *crack up* would appear at the entry for *crack,* and *off the cuff* would appear at the entry for *cuff.*

New Words

New words in English represent a variety of subject areas, both general and specialized. A study of these new words will give the learner a great deal of information about cultural and social trends, values, and customs. Not only does English add new vocabulary, but existing words change, broaden, or narrow their meanings over time. For example, the word *input,* meaning "something that is put in, or the process of putting in" has gained the new sense "data to be entered into a computer for processing."

For a list of recent additions to the English vocabulary, see Chapter 14, "Power Vocabulary for the Year 2000."

Irregular Verbs

An *irregular verb* is one that does not conform to a standard pattern. In English, regular verbs form their past tense by adding an *-ed* ending. Other verbs are irregular. The only way to learn these verbs is by memorizing them; fortunately, there aren't very many. The following list contains most of the irregular verbs you are likely to encounter.

Root Form	Past Tense	Past Participle
arise	arose	arisen
awake	awoke, awaked	awoke, awaked, awoken
be	was	been
bear	bore	borne
beat	beat	beaten, beat
become	became	become
begin	began	begun
bend	bent	bent
bereave	bereaved, bereft	bereaved, bereft
beseech	besought, beseeched	besought, beseeched
bet	bet, betted	bet, betted
bid	bade, bid	bidden, bid
bind	bound	bound
bite	bit	bitten
bleed	bled	bled
blow	blew	blown
break	broke	broken
breed	bred	bred
bring	brought	brought
broadcast	broadcast, broadcasted	broadcast, broadcasted
build	built	built
burn	burned, burnt	burned, burnt
burst	burst	burst
buy	bought	bought
cast	cast	cast
catch	caught	caught

Root Form	Past Tense	Past Participle
choose	chose	chosen
cling	clung	clung
clothe	clothed, clad	clothed, clad
come	came	came
cost	cost	cost
creep	crept	crept
cut	cut	cut
deal	dealt	dealt
dig	dug	dug
dive	dived, dove	dived
do	did	done
draw	drew	drawn
dream	dream, dreamt	dreamed, dreamt
drink	drank	drunk
drive	drove	driven
dwell	dwelt, dwelled	dwelt, dwelled
eat	ate	eaten
fall	fell	fallen
feed	fed	fed
feel	felt	felt
fight	fought	fought
find	found	found
flee	fled	fled
fling	flung	flung
fly	flew	flown
forget	forgot	forgotten
forgive	forgave	forgiven
forsake	forsook	forsaken
freeze	froze	frozen
get	got	gotten
give	gave	given
go	went	gone
grind	ground	ground
grow	grew	grown
hang	hung, hanged	hung, hanged
have	had	had
hear	heard	heard
hide	hid	hidden, hid
hit	hit	hit
hold	held	held
hurt	hurt	hurt
keep	kept	kept

Root Form	Past Tense	Past Participle
kneel	knelt, kneeled	knelt, kneeled
know	knew	known
lay	laid	laid
lead	led	led
leap	leaped, leapt	leaped, leapt
leave	left	left
lend	lent	lent
let	let	let
lie	lay	lain
light	lighted, lit	lighted, lit
lose	lost	lost
make	made	made
mean	meant	meant
meet	met	met
mistake	mistook	mistaken
misunderstand	misunderstood	misunderstood
outdo	outdid	outdone
overcome	overcame	overcome
overdo	overdid	overdone
overhear	overheard	overheard
overrun	overran	overrun
oversee	oversaw	overseen
oversleep	overslept	overslept
overtake	overtook	overtaken
overthrow	overthrew	overthrown
partake	partook	partaken
pay	paid	paid
prove	proved	proved, proven
put	put	put
read	read	read
relay	relayed	relayed
rend	rent	rent
rid	rid, ridded	rid, ridded
ride	rode	ridden
ring	rang	rung
rise	rose	risen
run	ran	run
say	said	said
see	saw	seen
seek	sought	sought
sell	sold	sold
send	sent	sent

Root Form	Past Tense	Past Participle
set	set	set
sew	sewed	sewn, sewed
shake	shook	shaken
shave	shaved	shaved, shaven
shed	shed	shed
shine	shone	shone
shoot	shot	shot
show	showed	shown, showed
shrink	shrank, shrunk	shrunk, shrunken
shut	shut	shut
sing	sang	sung
sink	sank, sunk	sunk, sunken
sit	sat	sat
slay	slew	slain
sleep	slept	slept
slide	slid	slid
sling	slung	slung
slink	slunk	slunk
slit	slit	slit
smell	smelled, smelt	smelt
smite	smote	smitten, smit, smote
sow	sowed	sown, sowed
speak	spoke	spoken
speed	sped, speeded	sped, speeded
spend	spent	spent
spill	spilled, split	spilled, split
spin	spun	spun
spit	spit, spat	spit, spat
split	split	split
spoil	spoiled, spoilt	spoiled, spoilt
spread	spread	spread
spring	sprang, sprung	sprung
stand	stood	stood
steal	stole	stolen
stick	stuck	stuck
sting	stung	stung
stink	stank, stunk	stunk
stride	strode	stridden
strike	struck	struck, stricken
string	strung	strung
strive	strove, strived	striven, strived
swear	swore	sworn

Root Form	Past Tense	Past Participle
sweep	swept	swept
swell	swelled	swollen, swelled
swim	swam	swum
swing	swung	swung
take	took	taken
teach	taught	taught
tear	tore	torn
tell	told	told
think	thought	thought
thrive	thrived, throve	thrived, thriven
throw	threw	thrown
thrust	thrust	thrust
tread	trod	trodden, trod
undergo	underwent	undergone
understand	understood	understood
undertake	undertook	undertaken
undo	undid	undone
unwind	unwound	unwound
uphold	upheld	upheld
upset	upset	upset
wake	waked, woke	waked, woken
wear	wore	worn
weave	wove, weaved	woven, wove
wed	wedded, wed	wedded, wed
wet	wet, wetted	wet, wetted
win	won	won
wind	wound	wound
withdraw	withdrew	withdrawn
withhold	withheld	withheld
withstand	withstood	withstood
wring	wrung	wrung
write	wrote	written

Nouns with Irregular or Alternate Plurals

Most nouns in English form plurals by adding an -s or -es to the end of a word. However, there are many exceptions to this rule. Some nouns have unchanged plurals, while others, borrowed from foreign languages, form their plurals the way the other language does. Any good dictionary will show unusual plurals, but the following list includes most of the ones you'll need to know.

Singular	Plural	Alternate Plural
addendum	addenda	
adieu	adieus	adieux
alga	algae	
alto	altos	
alumna	alumnae	
alumnus	alumni	
analysis	analyses	
antelope	antelopes	antelope
antenna	antennas	antennae
apex	apexes	apices
appendix	appendixes	appendices
aquarium	aquariums	aquaria
archipelago	archipelagos	archipelagoes
attorney general	attorneys general	attorney generals
automaton	automatons	automata
axis	axes	
bacillus	bacilli	
bacterium	bacteria	
banjo	banjoes	banjos
basis	bases	
brother-in-law	brothers-in-law	
buffalo	buffalos	buffaloes
bureau	bureaus	bureaux
cactus	cacti	cactuses
calf	calves	
cargo	cargoes	cargos
cello	cellos	
chamois	chamois	chamoix
chassis	chassis	
cherub	cherubs	cherubim
child	children	
codex	codices	
commando	commandos	commandoes
concerto	concertos	concerti
contralto	contraltos	
corpus	corpora	corpuses
court-martial	courts-martial	court-martials
crisis	crises	
criterion	criteria	
datum	data	
deer	deer	
diagnosis	diagnoses	

Singular	Plural	Alternate Plural
dwarf	dwarfs	dwarves
dynamo	dynamos	
elf	elves	
embryo	embryos	
epoch	epochs	
father-in-law	fathers-in-law	
faux pas	faux pas	
fish	fish	fishes
flounder	flounder	flounders
focus	focuses	foci
foot	feet	
formula	formulas	formulae
fungus	fungi	funguses
ganglion	ganglia	ganglions
genesis	geneses	
genus	genera	genuses
goose	geese	
half	halves	
halo	halos	haloes
herring	herrings	herring
hippopotamus	hippopotamuses	hippopotami
hoof	hoofs	hooves
hypothesis	hypotheses	
index	indexes	indices
isthmus	isthmuses	isthmi
kibbutz	kibbutzim	
kilo	kilos	
knife	knives	
lady-in-waiting	ladies-in-waiting	
larva	larvae	
leaf	leaves	
libretto	librettos	libretti
life	lives	
loaf	loaves	
locus	loci	
louse	lice	
man	men	
manservant	manservants	
matrix	matrices	matrixes
medium	mediums	media
memorandum	memorandums	memoranda
monarch	monarchs	

Singular	Plural	Alternate Plural
money	monies	
moose	moose	
moratorium	moratoria	moratoriums
mosquito	mosquitoes	mosquitos
mother-in-law	mothers-in-law	
motto	mottoes	mottos
mouse	mice	
nebula	nebulae	nebulas
nemesis	nemeses	
nucleus	nuclei	nucleuses
oasis	oases	
octopus	octopuses	octopi
offspring	offspring	
ovum	ova	
ox	oxen	
parenthesis	parentheses	
passerby	passersby	
patois	patois	
phenomenon	phenomena	phenomenons
photo	photos	
piano	pianos	
piccolo	piccolos	
plateau	plateaus	plateaux
portmanteau	portmanteaus	portmanteaux
potato	potatoes	
quarto	quartos	
quiz	quizzes	
radius	radii	radiuses
reindeer	reindeer	reindeers
scarf	scarfs	scarves
self	selves	
seraph	seraphs	seraphim
series	series	
sheaf	sheaves	
sheep	sheep	
shelf	shelves	
silo	silos	
sister-in-law	sisters-in-law	
solo	solos	
soprano	sopranos	
stand-by	stand-bys	
stimulus	stimuli	

Singular	Plural	Alternate Plural
stratum	strata	stratums
stylus	styli	styluses
Swiss	Swiss	
syllabus	syllabuses	syllabi
symposium	symposiums	symposia
synopsis	synopses	
tableau	tableaux	tableaus
tango	tangos	
tempo	tempos	tempi
terminus	termini	terminuses
thesis	theses	
thief	thieves	
tobacco	tobaccos	tobaccoes
tomato	tomatoes	
tooth	teeth	
tornado	tornadoes	tornados
trousseau	trousseaux	trousseaus
trout	trout	trouts
ultimatum	ultimatums	ultimata
vertebra	vertebrae	vertebras
virtuoso	virtuosos	virtuosi
volcano	volcanoes	volcanos
vortex	vortexes	vortices
wharf	wharves	wharfs
wife	wives	
wolf	wolves	
woman	women	
zero	zeros	zeroes

14

Power Vocabulary for the Year 2000

The vocabulary of English, especially American English, is growing at a remarkable rate. Among all the varieties of English around the world, including British English, it is American English that changes the fastest, adding more new words each year. New terms have entered the language mostly as a result of recent inventions or knowledge in the fields of science and technology. Social and cultural trends and fashions have also contributed to the great expansion of the English vocabulary. These new terms represent a variety of subject categories, both general and specialized.

Many new terms are borrowed from other languages, such as *pita* (from modern Greek) and *karaoke* (from Japanese). Other terms are formed by combining or blending two or more existing words, such as *camcorder* (from *camera* and *recorder*) and *alternative medicine*. The creation of abbreviations is another common method of word formation in English. The abbreviation *ATM* is certainly more convenient to use than the full phrase "automated-teller machine"; the shortened form *AIDS* is easier to pronounce and remember than the full form "acquired immune deficiency syndrome." New words are commonly derived from existing words by the addition of a prefix or suffix: *superstore* (prefix *super-*) and *cyberspace* (prefix *cyber-*). The coinage of new words that are not based on existing words is quite uncommon. Nevertheless, individuals have invented terms that are both clever and descriptive. A large number of coinages are names of people or places.

Not only does the language add new vocabulary, but existing words change, broaden, or narrow their meanings over time. The new sense of *rocket scientist* (highly intelligent person) extends the original meaning (specialist in rocket design).

New terms are popularized and given life in our newspapers, magazines, books, and electronic documents, not to mention radio and television shows, motion pictures, and plays. Some new terms last only for the moment, as a passing fad, and are forgotten soon after their introduction. Other new terms are controversial because of their slang status, or because they are perceived to be offensive. It is not possible to foretell the future of a particular word. As for the future of English, the language is certain to continue its expansion in the course of the 21st century.

It is a difficult enough task to master the extensive vocabulary of English, but a command of the language is not complete unless you are familiar with the terms that have entered English in recent years. A careful study of the following selection of words will reveal a great deal about our changing world.

abs   the muscles of the stomach; abdominal muscles.

alternative medicine   health care and treatments, including traditional Chinese medicine and folk medicine, that try to avoid the use of surgery and drugs.

answering machine   an electronic device that answers telephone calls with a recorded message and records the callers' messages on a tape.

aromatherapy   **1.** the use of pleasant fragrances to affect or change a person's mood or behavior. **2.** treatment of the skin by the application of fragrant oils from flowers or herbs.

aspartame   an artificially made white powder that is much sweeter than sucrose and is used as a low-calorie sugar substitute.

assisted suicide   suicide in which a physician helps the person to commit suicide, as by supplying a poison.

audio book   a recording on cassette in which a book is read aloud, usually by the author or a professional actor.

body piercing   the piercing of a part of the body, such as the navel or the nose, in order to insert a metal ring or other ornament.

boom box   a large, powerful radio or combination radio and cassette player that can be carried around.

brewpub   a bar or small restaurant serving beer that is brewed at a microbrewery located in the same building.

bulimia   a disturbance in eating habits marked by repeated instances of overeating followed by intentional vomiting or fasting.

carjacking   the crime of stealing a vehicle from its driver by using force or threats.

challenged   (a polite word used to avoid offending someone) disabled or handicapped: *Several children in the school are physically or mentally challenged.*

chronic fatigue syndrome   a disease in which the person is always tired and has flu-like symptoms.

codependent   of or relating to a relationship in which one person is addicted to alcohol or drugs and tries to manipulate or control the other person.

control freak   a person having a strong need to control or manipulate situations, events, and other people.

copay   a fixed sum, or a percentage of the customary fee, required by an health-insurance company to be paid by a patient to a health-care provider.

cyberspace   the worldwide system of linked computer networks, thought of as being a limitless environment for exchange of information and electronic communication.

defining moment   a point at which the basic nature or character of a person, group, etc., is revealed or identified.

digerati   people who are skilled with or knowledgeable about computers.

dweeb   a person who is considered to be unfashionable, socially awkward, or unpopular.

factoid   **1.** something that is untrue or unproven but is presented as fact and believed to be true because of constant repetition. **2.** an insignificant or unimportant fact.

fajitas   a Mexican dish consisting of thin strips of grilled beef or chicken with sliced peppers and onions, usually wrapped in tortillas.

focus group   a representative group of people brought together and questioned about their opinions on political issues, new products, etc.

food court   a space, usually in a shopping mall, with a variety of fast-food stalls and a common eating area.

foodie   a person who is very interested in food, esp. a gourmet.

401(k)   a savings plan that allows employees to contribute part of their income to an account whose funds are invested and usually withdrawn after retirement.

frequent flier   an airline passenger participating in a program that provides bonuses based on distance traveled.

GED   an abbreviation of: general equivalency diploma, a diploma that can be earned by people who have left high school before graduating.

geek   a person who is considered to be different from others, esp. a teenager who is socially awkward or spends too much time studying.

high-definition television   a television system that produces a sharper image and greater picture detail. *Abbr.:* HDTV

home office   a room or space in one's home that is equipped and used as an office.

homeschooling   the practice of teaching one's own children at home instead of sending them to school.

HOV lane   a highway or street lane reserved for high-occupancy vehicles with two or more passengers, usually marked with diamond shapes on the road.

hypertext   text, pictures, or other data stored in a computer and linked so that a user can move from an item in one electronic document to a related item in another document.

infomercial   a television commercial similar in length and format to a regular program, disguising the fact that it is an advertisement.

information superhighway   the worldwide network of computers, providing access to electronic databases, e-mail, video materials, and a variety of other services.

in-line skate   a roller skate with four hard-rubber wheels in a straight line.

in-your-face   marked by or being bold and aggressive; provocative.

latte   hot espresso served mixed with hot milk.

level playing field   a state of equality; an equal opportunity.

managed care   comprehensive health care provided by a health maintenance organization or similar system.

microbrewery   a small brewery usually producing unique or high quality beer.

microfiber   a very fine lightweight polyester fiber, used especially for clothing.

micromanage   to manage or control with great or too much attention to minor details.

minivan   a small passenger van, usually seating six or more people.

morphing   a technique in which one image is gradually and smoothly changed into another by means of a computer, as in a motion picture or video.

mountain bike   a bicycle designed for use on unpaved or hilly roads, having a sturdy frame and wider tires than a standard bicycle.

MRI   an abbreviation of: magnetic resonance imaging, a technique that produces images of tissues and organs of the body by means of a strong magnetic field and low-energy radio waves.

nail-biter   a situation that is marked by anxiety or tension.

no-brainer   anything requiring little thought or effort; something easy or simple to understand or do.

outsourcing   the business practice of purchasing supplies, parts, or finished products from another company, or of using outside workers in the manufacturing process.

paparazzo   a freelance photographer, especially one who takes candid photographs of celebrities for publication in magazines and newspapers.

personal trainer   a person who works with a individual client to plan or carry out an exercise or fitness program.

primary care   medical care by a physician who is the patient's first contact with the healthcare system and who may recommend a specialist if necessary.

repetitive strain injury   any of a group of medical conditions caused by the stress of repeated movements, marked by pain, numbness, or tingling in the hand or arm.

rightsize   to adjust to an appropriate size: *We will have to fire about 50 workers in order to rightsize our staff.*

road kill   the body of an animal killed on a road by a motor vehicle.

rocket science   **1.** the science of rocket design and flight; rocketry. **2.** something requiring great intelligence, especially mathematical ability.

rocket scientist   **1.** a specialist in rocket design. **2.** a highly intelligent person, especially one with mathematical ability.

secondhand smoke   tobacco smoke that is involuntarily inhaled when one is near or in the same room as a smoker.

shock jock   a radio disc jockey who features offensive or controversial material.

snail mail   standard postal service, as contrasted with electronic mail.

snowboard   a board that resembles a wide ski, used for gliding on snow while in a standing position.

sport-utility vehicle   a sturdy passenger vehicle with a trucklike frame, designed for occasional use on hilly or unpaved roads.

telecommuting   the act or practice of working at home using a computer terminal that is electronically linked to one's office.

theme park   an amusement park whose attractions and rides are based on various themes, such as fairy tales or the American West.

trophy wife   the young, often second, wife of a rich middle-aged man.

V-chip   a computer chip or other electronic device that blocks television reception of programs with violent or sexual content.

virtual reality   the computer simulation of a realistic, three-dimensional environment, allowing the user to become an active participant through the use of special gloves, headphones, and goggles.

voice mail   a computerized system that answers telephone calls and records phone messages for later playback, used esp. in offices.

Quizzes

To help you keep up with many of the new words and meanings that are now part of modern American English, we have put together the following vocabulary quizzes. These quizzes are arranged according to general subjects. How word-savvy are you? How many of these new terms are you familiar with?

Based on what you may have heard in everyday talk, match each of the numbered words with the closest synonym or definition. Write your answer in the space provided.

Quiz 1. General Vocabulary

1. **agita**	a. low-wage job	_____
2. **kenbei**	b. wonderful	_____
3. **frequent flier**	c. anxiety	_____
4. **doula**	d. excited	_____
5. **McJob**	e. suburban area	_____
6. **hissy**	f. fast route	_____
7. **superhighway**	g. midwife	_____
8. **phat**	h. temper tantrum	_____
9. **stoked**	i. anti-American sentiment	_____
10. **edge city**	j. regular airline passenger	_____

Quiz 2. Science, Medicine, and Technology

1. **anyon**
2. **necropsy**

3. **extrachromosomal**
4. **antirejection**
5. **clone**

a. genetic replica
b. DNA acting
   independently
c. autopsy
d. elementary particle
e. preventing refusal of
   transplants

Quiz 3. Computers and Cyberspace

1. **cyber-**
2. **newbie**

3. **snail mail**
4. **dongle**

5. **application**

a. uninitiated Internet user
b. device preventing
   unauthorized use
c. computer program
d. physical delivery of
   information
e. pertaining to the
   Internet

Quiz 4. Business, Economics, and Law

1. **bork**
2. **euro**
3. **quant**
4. **stockist**

5. **maquiladora**

a. European monetary unit
b. U.S. factory in Mexico
c. attack through media
d. place stocking
   merchandise
e. numbers expert

Quiz 5. Sensitivity and Religion

1. **ableism**

2. **don't ask, don't tell**
3. **challenged**

4. **ageism**

5. **superchurch**

a. policy of tolerance but
   not approval
b. handicapped
c. large congregation with
   facilities
d. discrimination against
   older people
e. discrimination against
   the disabled

Quiz 6. Music, Art, and the Media

1. **mosh**
2. **rave**

a. raucous dance
b. rap music

3. hip-hop   c. bold radio personality   _____
4. metafiction   d. fiction that analyzes
            another work of fiction   _____
5. shock jock   e. rowdy dance party   _____

Quiz 7. Fashion and Food

1. brewski   a. espresso with milk   _____
2. basmati   b. Ghanaian cloth   _____
3. latte   c. Indian rice   _____
4. kente   d. glamorous
            spokesperson   _____
5. spokesmodel   e. beer   _____

Quiz 8. Sports and Games

1. undercard   a. supporting event to a
            feature event   _____
2. Zamboni™   b. high lob in tennis   _____
3. cruciverbalist   c. long pass of
            desperation   _____
4. moonball   d. designer of crossword
            puzzles   _____
5. Hail Mary   e. ice-smoothening vehicle   _____

Answers to Quizzes in Chapter 13

Answers to Quiz 1

1. c 2. i 3. j 4. g 5. a 6. h 7. f 8. b 9. d 10. e

Answers to Quiz 2

1. d 2. c 3. b 4. b 5. a

Answers to Quiz 3

1. e 2. a 3. d 4. b 5. c

Answers to Quiz 4

1. c 2. a 3. e 4. d 5. b

Answers to Quiz 5

1. e 2. a 3. b 4. d 5. c

Answers to Quiz 6

1. a 2. e 3. b 4. d 5. c

Answers to Quiz 7

1. e 2. c 3. a 4. b 5. d

Answers to Quiz 8

1. a 2. e 3. d 4. b 5. c

15

Vocabulary-Building Puzzles

It's no surprise that people who love to solve word puzzles have superior vocabularies. Here are a number of different puzzles designed to add to *your* word power. There are three different types of puzzles to tease your brain and augment your vocabulary. Have fun!

Puzzle 1. Super Six

Most of the words in this puzzle have six letters; two of them have five. Your job is to fit each word listed below in its proper place in the puzzle. To help you get started, we've filled in one word, "mantra."

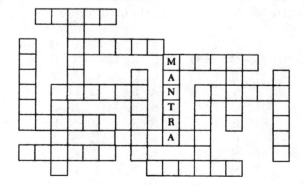

Word List

1. **cabal** (kə bal´) a small group of conspirators, especially one plotting against a government.

2. **fecund** (fē′kund, fek′und) prolific, fertile, or fruitful.
3. **bisque** (bisk) a heavy cream soup of puréed shellfish or vegetables; ice cream made with powdered macaroons or nuts.
4. **drivel** (driv′əl) nonsense.
5. **bungle** (bung′gəl) to do clumsily or awkwardly; botch.
6. **wimple** (wim′pəl) a woman's headcloth drawn in folds under the chin, formerly worn out of doors, and still in use by nuns.
7. **morose** (mə rōs′) gloomy; depressed.
8. **balsam** (bôl′səm) a fragrant resin exuded from certain trees.
9. **demean** (di mēn′) to lower in dignity or standing; debase.
10. **petard** (pi tärd′) an engine of war or an explosive device formerly used to blow in a door or gate, form a breach in a wall, etc.
11. **mantra** (man′trə, män′-) a word or formula to be recited or sung.
12. **feisty** (fī′stē) animated, energetic, spirited, or plucky.
13. **welter** (wel′tər) to roll, toss, or heave, as waves; to wallow or become deeply involved.
14. **supine** (sō͞o pīn′) lying on the back.
15. **beadle** (bēd′l) in British universities, an official who supervises and leads processions, macebearer; a parish officer who keeps order during services, waits on the clergy, etc.
16. **duress** (dō͞o res′, dyō͞o-) coercion, force, or constraint.
17. **sinew** (sin′yō͞o) a tendon; a source of strength.

Puzzle 2. Word Find 1

There are seventeen words hidden in this word-find puzzle. To complete the puzzle, locate and circle all the words. The words may be written forward, backward, up, or down.

```
C  A  T  A  F  A  L  Q  U  E  D
R  D  N  U  C  I  B  U  R  T  E
U  E  P  O  I  L  L  A  C  A  T
C  S  C  A  R  A  B  G  D  G  A
I  O  Z  O  B  E  R  M  I  E  C
B  E  L  B  U  A  B  I  C  N  I
L  E  Z  A  R  A  S  R  U  B  T
E  F  O  N  T  A  N  E  L  A  S
B  S  A  T  U  R  N  A  L  I  A
M  S  I  P  O  R  P  A  L  A  M
```

Word List:

1. **malapropism** (mal′ə prop iz′əm) the act or habit of misusing words ridiculously.

2. **rubicund** (r$\overline{oo}$'bi kund') red or reddish.
3. **saturnalia** (sat'ər nā'lē ə) unrestrained revelry; orgy.
4. **catafalque** (kat'ə fôk', -fôlk', -falk') a raised structure on which the body of a deceased person lies in state.
5. **quagmire** (kwag'mī°r', kwog'-) an area of miry or boggy ground.
6. **lucid** (l$\overline{oo}$'sid) crystal-clear.
7. **bauble** (bô'bəl) a cheap piece of ornamentation; gewgaw.
8. **masticated** (mas'ti kā'tid) chewed.
9. **calliope** (kə lī'ə pē') a musical instrument consisting of a set of harsh-sounding steam whistles that are activated by a keyboard.
10. **rebozo** (ri bō'sō, -zō) a long woven scarf, worn over the head and shoulders, especially by Mexican women.
11. **rubric** (r$\overline{oo}$'brik) a title, heading, direction, or the like, in a book, written or printed in red or otherwise distinguished from the rest of the text.
12. **fontanel** (fon'tn el') one of the spaces, covered by a membrane, between the bones of the fetal or young skull.
13. **raze** (rāz) to wreck or demolish.
14. **scarab** (skar'əb) a beetle regarded as sacred by the ancient Egyptians, a representation or image of a beetle, much used by the ancient Egyptians.
15. **abnegate** (ab'ni gāt') to surrender or renounce (rights, conveniences, etc.); deny oneself.
16. **bursar** (bûr'sər, -sär) a treasurer or business officer, especially of a college or university.
17. **crucible** (kr$\overline{oo}$'sə bəl) a vessel of metal or refractory material employed for heating substances to a high temperature.

Puzzle 3. Acrostic 1

First unscramble each of the seven vocabulary words so that it matches its definition. Then use the words to fill in the appropriate spaces on the correspondingly numbered lines. When you have completed the entire puzzle, another vocabulary word will read vertically in the first spaces.

1. PONILANER having no equal
2. YOGLUE a speech or writing in praise of a person
3. MERRYPUT nonsense
4. REESIO an evening party or social gathering
5. HUNRIC a mischievous child
6. SIKKO an open pavilion
7. TEARRA errors in writing or printing

1. __ __ __ __ __ __ __ __ __
2. __ __ __ __ __ __
3. __ __ __ __ __ __ __ __
4. __ __ __ __ __ __
5. __ __ __ __ __ __
6. __ __ __ __ __
7. __ __ __ __ __ __

Word List:

soiree	errata	nonpareil
eulogy	trumpery	kiosk
urchin		

Puzzle 4. Word Find 2

There are eighteen words hidden in this word-find puzzle. To complete the puzzle, locate and circle all the words. The words may be written forward, backward, up, or down. Good luck!

```
N O N S E Q U I T U R
E B G A D F L Y B O E
T A U T O L O G Y E M
T L D U E U R O D N O
L U A R P U R L O I N
E S M N A C L O Y T S
S T S I J S U X E N T
O R O N E C N O N O R
M A N E M L O D B T A
E D S O D E N R U O T
P E J O R A T I V E E
```

Word List:

1. **nonce** (nons) the present; the immediate occasion or purpose.
2. **damson** (dam′zən, -sən) a small dark-blue or purple plum.
3. **nexus** (nek′səs) a means of connecting; tie; link.
4. **jape** (jāp) to jest; joke; jibe.
5. **tontine** (ton′tēn, ton tēn′) an annuity scheme in which subscribers share a common fund with the benefit of survivorship, the survivors' shares being increased as the subscribers die, until the whole goes to the last survivor.

6. **balustrade** (bal′ə strād′, -sträd′) a railing.
7. **doxology** (dok sol′ə jē) a hymn or form of words containing an ascription of praise to God.
8. **non sequitur** (non sek′wi tər, -to͝or′) an inference or conclusion that does not follow from the premises.
9. **purloin** (pər loin′, pûr′loin) to take dishonestly; steal.
10. **dolmen** (dōl′men, -mən, dol′-) a structure, usually regarded as a tomb, consisting of two or more large, upright stones set with a space between and capped by a horizontal stone.
11. **doyen** (doi en′, doi′ən) the senior member, as in age or rank, of a group.
12. **remonstrate** (ri mon′strāt) to protest.
13. **nettlesome** (net′l səm) annoying or disturbing.
14. **tautology** (tô tol′ə jē) needless repetition of an idea in different words, as in "widow woman."
15. **rue** (ro͞o) to deplore; mourn; regret.
16. **gadfly** (gad′flī′) a person who repeatedly and persistently annoys or stirs up others with provocative criticism.
17. **pejorative** (pə jôr′ə tiv, -jor′-) having a disparaging, derogatory, or belittling effect or force.
18. **saturnine** (sat′ər nīn′) having or showing a sluggish, gloomy temperament.

Puzzle 5. Acrostic 2

First unscramble each of the seven vocabulary words so that it matches its definition. Then use the words to fill in the appropriate spaces on the correspondingly numbered lines. When you have completed the entire puzzle, another vocabulary word will read vertically in the first spaces.

1. RACEUSA a break, usually in the middle of a verse
2. ORAMIRE a large wardrobe
3. BAMNELT moving lightly over a surface
4. SOURIOUX doting upon or submissive to one's wife
5. CANDIMENT a beggar
6. MYPONE a person, real or imaginary, from whom something, as a tribe, nation, or place, takes its name
7. FITFIN a light lunch (British usage)

1. __ __ __ __ __ __ __
2. __ __ __ __ __ __ __
3. __ __ __ __ __ __ __

4. __ __ __ __ __ __ __ __

5. __ __ __ __ __ __ __ __ __

6. __ __ __ __ __ __

7. __ __ __ __ __ __

Word List:

tiffin   lambent   mendicant
eponym   caesura   armoire
uxorious

Puzzle 6. Word Find 3

There are fourteen words hidden in this word-find puzzle. To complete the puzzle, locate and circle all the words. The words may be written forward, backward, up, or down. Good luck!

```
D N U B R E M M U C
U N A M S D U B M O
L C O B E Z A G A M
C O A L E S C E H P
I I M Y R I A D O O
M F E Y N E E R U T
E T I O L O G Y T E
R O U S T A B O U T
```

Word List:

1. **gazebo** (gə zā′bō, -zē′-) a structure, as a summerhouse or pavilion, built on a site affording a pleasant view.
2. **roustabout** (roust′ə bout′) a wharf laborer or deck hand; a circus laborer.
3. **compote** (kom′pōt) fruit stewed or cooked in syrup.
4. **coif** (kwäf, koif) a hairstyle.
5. **cummerbund** (kum′ər bund′) a wide sash worn as a waistband, especially one with horizontal pleats worn beneath a dinner jacket.
6. **seer** (sēr) a prophet; mystic.
7. **ombudsman** (om′bədz mən′, -man′, -bŏŏdz-, ôm′-) a commissioner appointed by a legislature to hear and investigate complaints by private citizens against government officials and agencies.
8. **mahout** (mə hout′) the keeper or driver of an elephant.

9. **tureen** (tŏo rēn', tyŏo-) a large, deep covered dish for serving soup or stew.
10. **coalesce** (kō'ə les') to blend; join.
11. **fey** (fā) fairylike; whimsical or strange; supernatural, enchanted; in unnaturally high spirits.
12. **etiology** (ē'tē ol'ə jē) the study of the causes of diseases.
13. **dulcimer** (dul'sə mər) a trapezoidal zither with metal strings that are struck with light hammers.
14. **myriad** (mir'ē əd) many; innumerable.

Puzzle 7. The "P" Patch

Each of the words in this puzzle begins with the letter "p." Your job is to fit each of the words listed below in its proper place in the puzzle. To help you get started, we've filled in one word, "pimpernel."

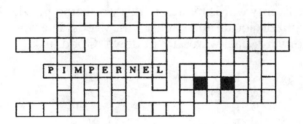

Word List:

1. **patois** (pat'wä, pā'twä, pa twä') a rural or provincial form of speech, especially of French.
2. **parse** (pärs, pärz) to describe (a word or series of words) grammatically, telling the parts of speech, inflectional forms, etc.
3. **poteen** (pə tēn', -chēn') illicitly distilled whiskey.
4. **pimpernel** (pim'pər nel', -nl) a plant of the primrose family, having scarlet, purplish, or white flowers that close at the approach of bad weather.
5. **piebald** (pī'bôld') having patches of black and white or of other colors.
6. **paean** (pē'ən) any song of praise, joy, or thanksgiving.
7. **prosody** (pros'ə dē) the science or study of poetic meters and versification.
8. **pica** (pī' kə) a type size measuring twelve points; a morbid craving for substances not fit to eat, such as clay or chalk.
9. **pout** (pout) to sulk; look sullen.

10. **pastiche** (pa stēsh′, pä-) a literary, musical, or artistic piece consisting wholly or chiefly of motifs or techniques borrowed from one or more sources.
11. **pariah** (pə rī′ə) an outcast.
12. **piddle** (pid′l) to waste time; dawdle.
13. **placebo** (plə sē′bō) a substance having no pharmacological effect but given to a patient or subject of an experiment who supposes it to be a medicine.
14. **paucity** (pô′si tē) scarcity; meagerness or scantiness.
15. **peon** (pē′ən, -on) an unskilled laborer; drudge; person of low social status.
16. **pupa** (pyoō′pə) an insect in the nonfeeding, usually immobile, transformation stage between the larva and the imago.
17. **pinto** (pin′tō, pēn′-) piebald; mottled; spotted; a pinto horse.

Puzzle 8. Word Find 4

There are twenty words hidden in this word-find puzzle. To complete the puzzle, locate and circle all the words. The words may be written forward, backward, up, or down. Good luck!

```
T  S  I  T  A  M  S  I  M  U  N  B
C  A  C  H  E  P  O  T  U  O  L  F
A  P  F  E  R  A  L  R  S  E  E  R
L  X  R  A  M  S  A  I  M  R  N  E
L  U  D  D  I  T  E  A  O  T  G  N
O  A  Z  Y  A  I  K  G  I  U  I  E
U  F  A  D  O  C  H  E  R  O  O  T
S  S  C  A  T  H  A  R  S  I  S  I
C  A  S  E  M  E  N  T  Y  O  L  C
```

Word List:

1. **triage** (trē äzh′) the process of sorting victims, as of a battle or disaster, to determine priority of medical treatment.
2. **cachepot** (kash′pot′, -pō′) an ornamental container for holding or concealing a flowerpot.
3. **frenetic** (frə net′ik) highly excited.
4. **callous** (kal′əs) unfeeling.
5. **miasma** (mī az′mə, mē-) noxious exhalations from putrescent matter.
6. **outré** (oō trā′) beyond the bounds of what is usual or considered proper.

7. **cheroot** (shə roo͞t′) a cigar having open, untapered ends.
8. **feral** (fēr′əl, fer′-) wild; primitive.
9. **flout** (flout) to treat with disdain, scorn, or contempt; scoff at.
10. **catharsis** (kə thär′sis) purging of the emotions, especially through a work of art.
11. **Luddite** (lud′īt) a member of any of various bands of English workers (1811–16) who destroyed industrial machinery in the belief that its use diminished employment; any opponent of new technologies.
12. **faux pas** (fō pä′) a social gaffe; error.
13. **soigné** (swän yā′) carefully or elegantly done; well-groomed.
14. **seer** (sēr) a prophet; mystic.
15. **numismatist** (noo͞ miz′mə tist, -mis′-, nyoo͞-) a person who collects coins.
16. **pastiche** (pa stēsh′, pä-) a literary, musical, or artistic piece consisting wholly or chiefly of motifs or techniques borrowed from one or more sources.
17. **heady** (hed′ē) intoxicating; exciting.
18. **coda** (kō′də) a passage concluding a musical composition.
19. **cloy** (kloi) to weary by excess, as of food, sweetness, or pleasure; surfeit or sate.
20. **casement** (kās′mənt) a window sash opening on hinges.

Puzzle 9. Acrostic 3

First unscramble each of the seven vocabulary words so that it matches its definition. Then use the words to fill in the appropriate spaces on the correspondingly numbered lines. When you have completed the entire puzzle, another vocabulary word will read vertically in the first spaces.

1. ZIMZUNE a crier who calls Muslims to prayer
2. NEXUPGE to erase
3. DAILYRAP the art of cutting and polishing gems; highly exact and refined in style.
4. PARTIFIE a small alcoholic drink taken before dinner
5. COCARMENNY black magic; conjuration
6. TIGMEL a small tool, a cocktail
7. WESHEC to shun, avoid

1. __ __ __ __ __ __ __

2. __ __ __ __ __ __ __

3. __ __ __ __ __ __ __ __

4. __ __ __ __ __ __ __ __

5. __ __ __ __ __ __ __ __ __ __

6. __ __ __ __ __ __

7. __ __ __ __ __ __

Word List:

eschew   necromancy   lapidary
gimlet   muezzin   apéritif
expunge

Puzzle 10. Word Find 5

There are thirteen words hidden in this word-find puzzle. To complete the puzzle, locate and circle all the words. The words may be written forward, backward, up, or down. Good luck!

```
S L U M G U L L I O N S M
C I T C E L C E N B O R I
A N E D E M A N A V R I N
B A H E G E M O N Y O X A
R E C A N T E D E R M I R
O A A E P I P H A N Y L E
U P C E T A U N E T X E T
S A N C T I M O N I O U S
```

Word List:

1. **slumgullion** (slum gul′yən, slum′gul′-) a stew of meat, potatoes, and vegetables.
2. **oxymoron** (ok′si môr′on) a figure of speech in which a locution produces an effect by seeming self-contradictory, as in "cruel kindness" or "to make haste slowly."
3. **paean** (pē′ən) any song of praise, joy, or thanksgiving.
4. **minarets** (min′ə rets′, min′ə rets′) slender towers or turrets that are attached to a mosque and from which a muezzin calls the people to prayer.
5. **sanctimonious** (sangk′tə mō′nē əs) insincere; hypocritical.
6. **hegemony** (hi jem′ə nē, hej′ə mō′nē) leadership or predominant influence.
7. **inane** (i nān′) pointless; silly.
8. **extenuate** (ik sten′yoo āt′) to make or try to make seem less serious, especially by offering excuses.
9. **nirvana** (nir vä′nə, -van′ə, nər-) in Buddhism, freedom from the

endless cycle of personal reincarnations, with their consequent suffering, as a result of the extinction of individual passion, hatred, and delusion.

10. **recanted** (ri kan′tid) retracted; denied.
11. **edema** (i dē′mə) abnormal accumulation of fluids in body tissues, causing swelling.
12. **epiphany** (i pif′ə nē) an appearance or manifestation, especially of a deity.
13. **eclectic** (i klek′tik) selecting; choosing from various sources.

Puzzle 11. Spectacular Seven

Each of the words in this puzzle has seven letters. Your job is to fit each of the words listed below in its proper place in the puzzle. To help you get started, we've filled in one word, "heinous," which means *reprehensible* or *evil*.

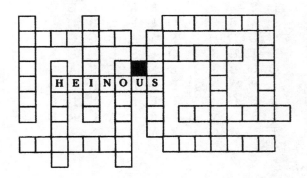

Word List:

1. **acolyte** (ak′ə līt′) an altar boy.
2. **pismire** (pis′mī³ r′, piz′-) an ant.
3. **shoguns** (shō′gənz, -gunz) the chief Japanese military commanders from the eighth to twelfth centuries, or the hereditary officials who governed Japan, with the emperor as nominal ruler, until 1868.
4. **panacea** (pan′ə sē′ə) a remedy for all ills; cure-all.
5. **pooh-bah** (poo͞′bä′) a person who holds several positions, especially ones that give him importance; a pompous person.
6. **hirsute** (hûr′soo͞t, hûr soo͞t′) hairy.
7. **foibles** (foi′bəlz) minor weaknesses or failings of character.
8. **debacle** (də bä′kəl, -bak′əl, dā-) a general breakup or dispersion; sudden collapse.

9. **carping** (kär′ping) fault-finding; critical.
10. **cuckold** (kuk′əld) the husband of an unfaithful wife.
11. **distaff** (dis′taf) a staff with a cleft end for holding wool, flax, etc., from which the thread is drawn in spinning by hand; the female sex; woman's work.
12. **palfrey** (pôl′frē) a riding horse, as distinguished from a war horse; a saddle horse particularly suitable for a woman.
13. **winsome** (win′səm) cute; charming.

Puzzle 12. Word Find 6

There are nineteen words hidden in this word-find puzzle. To complete the puzzle, locate and circle all the words. The words may be written forward, backward, up, or down. Good luck!

```
P R E L A P S A R I A N
E E M E T I E R V U E O
I M B R O G L I O B H I
G O D H A R M A O G C T
N T E S P O U S E H U A
O I B T I B M A G E A R
I P A N D E M I C R G O
R E C A F F E F A K I R
R S A V O I R F A I R E
T N A C I R Y G E N A P
```

Word List:

1. **peroration** (per′ə rā′shən) the concluding part of a speech or discourse.
2. **oeuvre** (ûrv, ûrv′rə) the works of a writer, painter, or the like, taken as a whole.
3. **prelapsarian** (prē′lap sâr′ē ən) pertaining to conditions existing before the fall of humankind.
4. **mummery** (mum′ə rē) an empty or ostentatious performance.
5. **gherkin** (gûr′kin) a pickle.
6. **fakir** (fə kēr′, fā′kər) a Muslim or Hindu religious ascetic or mendicant monk commonly considered a wonder worker.
7. **métier** (mā′tyā, mā tyā′) an occupation.
8. **peignoir** (pān wär′, pen-, pān′wär, pen′-) a woman's dressing gown.
9. **pandemic** (pan dem′ik) (of a disease) prevalent throughout an entire country or continent or the whole world.

10. **savoir faire** (sav′wär fâr′) a knowledge of just what to do in any situation; tact.
11. **gauche** (gōsh) uncouth; awkward.
12. **imbroglio** (im brōl′yō) a confused state of affairs.
13. **panegyric** (pan′i jir′ik, -jī′rik) an oration, discourse, or writing in praise of a person or thing.
14. **dharma** (där′mə, dûr′-) in Buddhism, the essential quality or nature, as of the cosmos or one's own character.
15. **efface** (i fās′) to wipe out; cancel or obliterate; make (oneself) inconspicuous.
16. **espouse** (i spouz′, i spous′) to advocate or support; marry.
17. **epitome** (i pit′ə mē) a person or thing that is typical of or possesses to a high degree the features of a whole class; embodiment.
18. **gambit** (gam′bit) in chess, an opening in which a player seeks by sacrificing a pawn or piece to obtain some advantage; any maneuver by which one seeks to gain an advantage.
19. **cant** (kant) deceit, insincerity or hypocrisy; the private language of a group, class, or profession; singsong or whining speech.

Answers to Puzzles

Answers to Puzzle 1

Answers to Puzzle 2

Answers to Puzzle 3

nonpareil	having no equal
eulogy	a speech or writing in praise of a person
trumpery	nonsense
soirée	an evening party or social gathering
urchin	a mischievous child
kiosk	an open pavilion
errata	errors in writing or printing

(netsuke (net′skē, -skā) in Japanese art, a small carved figure, originally used as a button-like fixture on a man's sash)

Answers to Puzzle 4

Answers to Puzzle 5

caesura	a break, usually in the middle of a verse
armoire	a large wardrobe
lambent	moving lightly over a surface
uxorious	doting upon or submissive to one's wife
mendicant	a beggar
eponym	a person, real or imaginary, from whom something as a tribe, nation, or place takes its name
tiffin	a light lunch (British usage)

Answers to Puzzle 7

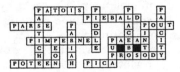

Answers to Puzzle 9

muezzin	a crier who calls Muslims to prayer
expunge	to erase
lapidary	the art of cutting and polishing gems, highly exact and refined in style
apéritif	a small alcoholic drink taken before dinner
necromancy	black magic; conjuration
gimlet	a small tool, a cocktail
eschew	to shun, avoid

(mélange (mā lāNzh′, -lānj′) a mixture or medley)

Answers to Puzzle 11

Answers to Puzzle 6

Answers to Puzzle 8

Answers to Puzzle 10

Answers to Puzzle 12

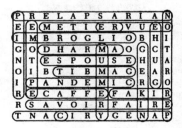

Glossaries

A. Important Prefixes to Know

a-¹, *prefix.* from Old English, used **1.** before some nouns to make them into adverbs showing "place where": *a- + shore → ashore = on (or into) the shore.* **2.** before some verbs to make them into words showing a state or process: *a- + sleep → asleep (= sleeping); a- + blaze → ablaze (= blazing).*

a-², *prefix.* a variant spelling of **an-**. It comes from Latin and is used before some adjectives to mean "not"; *a- + moral → amoral (= without morals); a- + tonal → atonal (= without tone).*

ab-, *prefix.* from Latin, used before some words and roots to mean "off, away": *abnormal (= away from what is normal).* Compare A-².

ad-, *prefix.* from Latin, meaning "toward" and indicating direction or tendency: *ad- + join → adjoin* (= join toward, attack).

ambi-, *prefix.* from Latin, meaning "both" and "around." These meanings are found in such words as: *ambiguous, ambivalence, ambiance.*

amphi- *prefix.* from Greek, meaning "both; on two sides." This meaning is found in such words as: *amphibian, amphibious, amphitheater.*

an-, *prefix.* from Greek, used before roots or stems beginning with a vowel or *h,* meaning "not; without; lacking": *anaerobic (= without oxygen); anonymous (= without name).* Compare A-².

ante-, *prefix.* from Latin, used before roots, meaning **1.** "happening before": *antebellum (= before the war).* **2.** "located in front of": *anteroom (= room located in front of another).*

anti-, *prefix.* from Greek, used before nouns and adjectives, meaning **1.** against, opposed to: *anti-Semitic, antislavery.* **2.** preventing, counteracting, or working against: *anticoagulant, antifreeze.* **3.** destroying or disabling: *antiaircraft, antipersonnel.* **4.** identical to in form or function, but lacking in some important ways: *anticlimax, antihero, antiparticle.* **5.** an antagonist or rival of: *Antichrist, antipope.* **6.** situated opposite: *Anti-Lebanon.* Also, *before a vowel,* **ant-.**

apo-, *prefix.* from Greek, meaning "away, off, apart": *apo- + strophe → apostrophe* (= a turn away, digression).

aqua-, *prefix.* from Latin, meaning "water." This meaning is found in such words as: *aquaculture, aqualung, aquarium, aquatic, aqueduct, aqueous, aquifer.*

auto-, *prefix.* from Greek, meaning "self." This meaning is found in such words as: *autocrat, autograph, autonomous, autonomy, autopsy.* Also, *esp. before a vowel,* **aut-.**

baro-, *prefix.* from Greek, meaning "weight." This meaning is found in such words as: *barograph, barometer, baroreceptor.*

be-, *prefix.* from Old English, used **1.** to make verbs meaning "to make, become, treat as": *be- + cloud → becloud (= make like a cloud, hard to see); be- + friend → befriend (= treat someone as a friend).* **2.** before adjectives and verbs ending in *-ed* to mean "covered all over; completely; all around": *be- + decked → bedecked (= decked or covered all over); be- + jeweled → bejeweled (= covered with jewels).*

bi-, *prefix.* from Latin, meaning "twice, two." This meaning is found in such words as: *biennial, bisect, bicentennial, bigamy, biped, binoculars, bilateral, bipartisan, biweekly.* —**Usage.** In some words, especially words referring to time periods, the prefix *bi-* has two meanings: "twice a + ~" and "every two + ~-s". Thus, *biannual* means both "twice a year" and "every two years." Be careful; check many of these words.

bio-, *prefix.* from Greek, meaning "life." This meaning is found in such words as: *biodegradable, biology, biosphere.*

centi-, *prefix.* from Latin, used before roots to mean "hundredth" or "hundred": *centiliter (= one hundredth of a liter); centipede (= (creature having) one hundred feet).*

chiro-, *prefix.* from Greek, meaning "hand." This meaning is found in such words as: *chirography, chiropodist, chiropractor, chiromancy.*

circum-, *prefix.* from Latin, meaning "round, around." This meaning is found in such words as *circuit, circuitous, circumcise, circumference, circumnavigate, circumstance, circumvent, circumlocution, circus.*

co-, *prefix.* from Latin, meaning **1.** "joint, jointly, together." This meaning is found in such words as: *cochair, costar, coworker.* **2.** "auxiliary, helping." This meaning is found in such words as: *copilot.*

col-¹, var. of COM- before *l: collateral.*

col-², var. of COLO- before a vowel: *colectomy.*

com-, *prefix.* from Latin, meaning "with, together with." This meaning is found in such words as: *combine, compare, commingle.* For variants before other sounds, see CO-, COL-¹, CON-, COR-.

con-, *prefix.* a variant spelling of COM-. It comes from Latin, meaning "together, with." This meaning is found in such words as: *convene, condone, connection.*

contra-, *prefix.* from Latin, meaning "against, opposite, opposing." This meaning is found in such words as: *contraband, contraception, contradict, contrary.*

cor-, *prefix.* another form of COM- that is used before roots beginning with *r: correlate.*

counter-, *prefix.* from Middle English, meaning "against, counter to, opposed to." This meaning is found in such words as: *counterattack, counteroffer, counterclockwise.*

de-, *prefix.* from Latin, used to form verbs and some adjectives meaning **1.** motion or being carried down from, away, or off: *deplane (= move down or off an airplane); descend (= move or go down);* **2.** reversing or undoing the effects of an action: *deflate (= reverse the flow of air out of something); dehumanize (= reverse the positive, humanizing effects of something);* **3.** taking out or removal of a thing: *decaffeinate (= take out the caffeine from something); declaw (= re-*

move the claws of an animal); **4.** finishing or completeness of an action: *defunct (= completely non-functioning); despoil (= completely spoil).*

deci-, *prefix.* from Latin, meaning "ten." This meaning now appears in the names of units of measurement that are one tenth the size of the unit named by the second element of the compound: *decibel (= one tenth of a bel); deciliter (= one-tenth of a liter).* See the root -DEC-.

dem-, *prefix.* from Greek, meaning "people." This meaning is found in such words as: *demagogue, democracy, demography.*

demi-, *prefix.* from French, meaning "half." This meaning is found in such words as: *demigod, demitasse.*

demo-, *prefix.* like DEM-, from Greek, meaning "people, population." This meaning is found in such words as: *democracy, demography.*

di-, *prefix.* from Greek, meaning "two, double." This meaning is found in such words as: *diptych, dioxide.*

dia-, *prefix.* from Greek, meaning "through, across, from point to point; completely." These meanings are found in such words as: *diachronic, diagnosis, dialogue, dialysis, diameter, diaphanous, diarrhea, diathermy.*

dis-, *prefix.* from Latin, meaning "apart." It now has the following meanings: **1.** opposite of: *disagreement (= opposite of agreement).* **2.** not: *disapprove: (= not to approve); dishonest (= not honest); disobey (= not obey).* **3.** reverse; remove: *disconnect (= to remove the connection of); discontinue (= to stop continuing); dissolve (= remove the solidness of; make liquid).*

dys-, *prefix.* from Greek, meaning "ill, bad." This meaning is found in such words as: *dysentery, dyslexia, dyspepsia.*

electro-, *prefix.* from New Latin, meaning "electric" or "electricity": *electro- + magnetic → electromagnetic.*

em-, *prefix.* a form of EN- used before roots beginning with *b, p,* and sometimes *m: embalm.* Compare IM-[1].

en-, *prefix.* ultimately from Latin, used before adjectives or nouns to form verbs meaning **1.** to cause (a person or thing) to be in (the place, condition, or state mentioned); to keep in or place in: *en- + rich → enrich (= to cause to be rich); en- + tomb → entomb (= to cause to be in a tomb);* **2.** to restrict on all sides, completely: *en- + circle → encircle (= to restrict on all sides within a circle).*

epi-, *prefix.* from Greek, meaning "on, upon, at" (*epicenter*), "outer, exterior" (*epidermis*), "accompanying, additional" (*epiphenomenon*).

eu-, *prefix.* from Greek, meaning "good, well"; it now sometimes means "true, genuine." This meaning is found in such words as: *eugenics, eulogize, eulogy, euphemism, euphoria, euthanasia.*

Euro-, *prefix.* contraction of "Europe," used with roots and means "Europe," "Western Europe," or "the European Community": *Euro- + -centric → Eurocentric (= centered on Europe); Euro- + -crat → Eurocrat (= bureaucrat in the European Community).* Also, *esp. before a vowel,* **Eur-.**

ex-, *prefix.* from Latin, meaning **1.** "out, out of, away, forth." It is found in such words as: *exclude, exhale, exit, export, extract.* **2.** "former; formerly having been": *ex-member (= former member).*

exo-, *prefix.* from Greek, meaning "outside, outer, external": *exocentric.* Also, *before a vowel,* **ex-.**

extra-, *prefix.* from Latin, meaning "outside of; beyond": *extra- + galactic → extragalactic (= outside the galaxy); extra- + sensory → extrasensory (= beyond the senses).*

fore-, *prefix.* from Old English, used before nouns, meaning **1.** before (in space, time, condition, etc.): *fore- + -cast → forecast (= prediction before weather comes); fore- + taste → foretaste (= a taste before the event takes place); fore- + warn → forewarn (= to warn ahead of time).* **2.** front: *fore- + head → forehead (= front of the head).* **3.** preceding: *fore- + father → forefather (= father that came before).* **4.** superior: *fore- + man → foreman (= superior to the other workers).*

hemo- (or **hema-**), *prefix.* from Greek, meaning "blood." This meaning is found in such words as: *hemoglobin, hemophilia, hemorrhage, hemorrhoid.* Also, *esp. before a vowel,* **hem-.**

hyper-, *prefix.* from Greek, used **1.** before nouns and adjectives meaning "excessive; overly; too much; unusual": *hyper- + critical → hypercritical (= overly critical); hyper- + inflation → hyperinflation (= inflation that is unusual or too high).* Compare SUPER-. **2.** in computer words to refer to anything not rigidly connected in a step-by-step manner: *hyper- + text → hypertext (= text or information that the user can gain access to in the order he or she chooses).*

hypo-, *prefix.* from Greek, used before roots, meaning "under, below": *hypo- + dermic → hypodermic (= under the skin); hypo- + thermia → hypothermia (= heat or temperature below what it should be).* Also, *esp. before a vowel,* **hyp-.**

il-[1], *prefix.* another form of IN-[2] that is used before roots beginning with *l;* it means "not": *il- + legible → illegible (= that cannot be easily read).*

il-[2], *prefix.* another form of IN-[1] that is used before roots beginning with *l;* it means "in, into": *il- + -luminate (= light) → illuminate (= shine on or into).*

im-[1], *prefix.* another form of IN-[2] that is used before roots beginning with *p, b,* and *m;* it means "not": *im- + possible → impossible (= that is not possible).*

im-[2], *prefix.* another form of IN-[1] that is used before roots beginning with *p, b,* and *m;* it means "in, into": *im- + -migrate → immigrate (= travel in or into).*

in-[1], *prefix.* from Old English, used before verbs and nouns and means "in; into; on": *in- + come → income (= money coming in); in- + corporate (= body) → incorporate (= make into one body); in- + land → inland (= in the land).*

in-[2], *prefix.* from Latin, used before adjectives, meaning "not": *in- + accurate → inaccurate (= not accurate); in- + capable → incapable (= not capable); in- + direct → indirect (= not direct).* For variants before other sounds, see IM-, IL-, IR-.

inter-, *prefix.* from Latin, meaning "between, among": *intercity (= between cities); interdepartmental (= between or among departments).*

intra-, *prefix.* from Latin, meaning "within": *intraspecies (= within species).* Compare INTRO-, INTER-.

intro-, *prefix.* from Latin, meaning "inside, within": *intro- + -duce (= lead) → in-*

troduce (= bring inside or within to meet someone); intro- + -version (= a turning) → *introversion (= a turning inside or within).* Compare INTRA-.

ir-¹, *prefix.* another form of IN-¹ that is used before roots beginning with *r: ir- + radiate* → *irradiate.*

ir-², *prefix.* another form of IN-² that is used before roots beginning with *r: ir- + reducible* → *irreducible.*

iso-, *prefix.* from Greek, meaning "equal." This meaning is found in such scientific and chemical words as: *isochromatic.*

kilo-, *prefix.* from Greek, used before quantities, meaning "thousand": *kilo- + liter* → *kiloliter (= one thousand liters); kilo- + watt* → *kilowatt (= one thousand watts).*

mal-, *prefix.* from Latin, meaning "bad; wrongful; ill." This meaning is found in such words as: *maladroit, malcontent, malfunction.*

maxi-, *prefix.* contraction of the word *maximum,* meaning "very large or long in comparison with others of its kind." This meaning is found in such words as: *maxiskirt.*

mega-, *prefix.* from Greek, meaning **1.** extremely large, huge: *megalith (= extremely large stone or rock); meagstructure (= a huge structure).* **2.** one million of the units of (the base root or word): *megahertz (= one million hertz); megaton (= one million tons).* **3.** very large quantities or amounts: *megabucks (= a great deal of money); megadose (= a large dose of medicine)* **4.** things that are extraordinary examples of their kind: *megahit (= a smash movie or stage hit); megatrend (= important, very popular trend).*

meta-, *prefix.* from Greek, meaning "after, along with, beyond, among, behind." These meanings are found in such words as: *metabolism, metamorphosis, metaphor, metaphysics.*

micro-, *prefix.* from Latin, meaning **1.** small or very small in comparison with others of its kind: *micro- + organism* → *microorganism (= very small living creature).* **2.** restricted in scope: *micro- + habitat* → *microhabitat; micro- + economics* → *microeconomics.* **3.** containing or dealing with texts that require enlargement to be read: *micro- + film* → *microfilm.* **4.** one millionth: *micro- + gram* → *microgram.* Also, *esp. before a vowel,* **micr-.**

mid-, *prefix.* from Old English, meaning "being at or near the middle point of": *midday; mid-Victorian; mid-twentieth century.*

milli-, *prefix.* from Latin, meaning **1.** one thousand: *milli- + -pede (= foot)* → *millipede (= a small creature with very many legs).* **2.** (in the metric system) equal to 1/1000 of the unit mentioned: *milli- + meter* → *millimeter (= 1/1000 of a meter).*

mini-, *prefix.* contraction of the word *minimum,* meaning **1.** of a small or reduced size in comparison with others of its kind: *mini- + car* → *minicar; mini- + gun* → *minigun.* **2.** limited in scope, intensity, or duration: *mini- + boom (= economic upturn)* → *miniboom (= short-lived economic boom); mini- + course* → *minicourse (= short course of study).* **3.** (of clothing) short; not reaching the knee: *mini- + dress* → *minidress; mini- + skirt* → *miniskirt.* See -MIN-, -MICRO-.

mis-, *prefix.* from Old English, used before nouns, verbs, and adjectives meaning **1.** mistaken; wrong; wrongly; incorrectly: *mis- + trial → mistrial (= a trial conducted improperly); mis- + print → misprint (= something incorrectly printed); misfire: (= fail to fire properly).* **2.** the opposite of: *mis- + trust → mistrust (= the opposite of trust).*

mono-, *prefix.* from Greek, meaning "one, single, lone." This meaning is found in such words as: *monarch, monastery, monochrome, monocle, monogamy, monogram, monograph, monolingual, monolith, monologue, mononucleosis, monopoly, monopterous, monorail, monosyllable, monotonous.*

multi-, *prefix.* from Latin, meaning "many, much, multiple, many times, more than one, composed of many like parts, in many respects": *multi- + colored → multicolored (= having many colors); multi- + vitamin → multivitamin (= composed of many vitamins).*

neo-, *prefix.* from Greek, meaning "new." It has come to mean "new, recent, revived, changed": *neo- + colonialism → neocolonialism (= colonialism that has been revived); neo- + -lithic → neolithic (= of a recent Stone Age).* Also, *esp. before a vowel,* **ne-.**

neuro-, *prefix.* from Greek, meaning "nerve, nerves." Its meaning now includes "nervous system," and this meaning is found in such words as: *neurology, neurosurgery.*

non-, *prefix.* from Latin, usually meaning "not," used **1.** before adjectives and adverbs and means a simple negative or absence of something: *non- + violent → nonviolent.* **2.** before a noun of action and means the failure of such action: *non- + payment → nonpayment (= failure to pay).* **3.** before a noun to suggest that the thing mentioned is not true, real, or worthy of the name, as in *nonbook, noncandidate, non-event.*

ob-, *prefix.* from Latin, used before roots, meaning "toward," "to," "on," "over," "against": *ob- + -jec- → object.*

octa-, *prefix.* from Greek, meaning "eight": *octa- + -gon → octagon (= eight-sided figure).*

omni-, *prefix.* from Latin, meaning "all": *omni- + directional → omnidirectional (= in all directions).*

ortho-, *prefix.* from Greek, meaning "straight, upright, right, correct": *ortho- + graph → orthography (= correct writing); ortho- + dontics → orthodontics (= dentistry dealing with straightening teeth); ortho- + pedic → orthopedic (= correction of improper bone structure from childhood).*

out-, *prefix.* from Old English, used **1.** before verbs, meaning "going beyond, surpassing, or outdoing (the action of the verb)": *out- + bid → outbid; out- + do → outdo; out- + last → outlast.* **2.** before nouns to form certain compounds meaning "outside; out": *out- + cast → outcast; out- + come → outcome; out- + side → outside.*

over-, *prefix.* from Old English, meaning **1.** the same as the adverb or adjective OVER, as in: *overboard; overcoat; overhang; overlord; overthrow.* **2.** "over the limit; to excess; too much; too": *overact (= to act too much); overcrowd (= to crowd too many people or things into); overaggressive (= too aggressive); over-*

full; overweight. **3.** "outer," as when referring to an outer covering: *overskirt (= a skirt worn over something, such as a gown).*

pan-, *prefix.* from Greek, meaning "all." This meaning is found in such words as: *panorama; pantheism.* It is also used esp. in terms that imply or suggest the union of all branches of a group: *Pan-American; Pan- + hellenic (Greek) → Panhellenic (= all Greeks united in one group); Pan-Slavism (= all the people of Slavic background united).*

para-¹, *prefix.* from Greek, meaning 1. "at or to one side of, beside, side by side." This meaning is found in such words as: *parabola; paragraph.* 2. "beyond, past, by": *paradox.* 3. "abnormal, defective": *paranoia.* 4. (before names of jobs or occupations) "ancilliary, subsidiary, assisting." This meaning is found in such words as: *paralegal; paraprofessional.* Also, *esp. before a vowel,* **par-.**

para-², *prefix.* taken from PARACHUTE, and is used to form compounds that refer to persons or things that use parachutes or that are landed by parachute: *paratrooper.*

penta-, *prefix.* from Greek, meaning "five": *penta- + -gon → pentagon (= five-sided figure).*

per-, *prefix.* from Latin, used before roots, meaning "through, thoroughly, completely, very": *per- + -vert → pervert (= a person completely turned away from the normal); per- + -fect → perfect (= thoroughly or completely done).*

peri-, *prefix.* from Greek, used before roots, meaning **1.** "about, around": *peri- + meter → perimeter (= distance around an area); peri- + -scope → periscope (= instrument for looking around oneself).* **2.** "enclosing, surrounding": *peri- + cardium → pericardium (= a sac surrounding the heart).* **3.** "near": *peri- + he-lion → perihelion (= point of an orbit nearest to the sun).*

petro-¹, *prefix.* from Greek, meaning "rock, stone": *petro- + -ology → petrology (= the study of rocks or stone).*

petro-², *prefix.* taken from PETROLEUM and used to form compounds: *petro- + chemistry → petrochemistry; petro- + power → petropower (= power derived from petroleum).*

photo-, *prefix.* from Greek, meaning "light": *photo- + biology → photobiology; photo- + -on → photon (= elementary "particle" of light).* Also means "photographic" or "photograph": *photo- + copy → photocopy.*

poly-, *prefix.* from Greek, meaning "much, many": *polyandry (= the custom of having many husbands); polyglot (= speaking many languages).*

post-, *prefix.* from Latin, meaning "after (in time), following (some event)"; "behind, at the rear or end of": *post- + industrial → postindustrial (= after the industrial age); post- + war → postwar (= after the war).*

pre-, *prefix.* from Latin, **1.** meaning "before, in front of," "prior to, in advance of," "being more than, surpassing": *pre- + -dict → predict (= say in advance of something); pre- + eminent → preeminent (= surpassing or being more than eminent); pre- + face → preface (= something written in front of a book, etc.)* **2.** used before verbs to form new verbs that refer to an activity taking place before or instead of the usual occurrence of the same activity: *pre- + board → preboard (= to board an airplane before the other passengers); pre- + cook → precook (= cook before regular cooking).* **3.** used in forming adjectives that refer to a period of time before the event, period, person, etc., mentioned in the root: *pre-* + *school* → *preschool* (*= before the age of starting school*); *pre-* + *war* → *prewar* (*= before the war started*).

pro-¹, *prefix.* from Latin, **1.** meaning "forward, forward movement or location; advancement": *proceed; progress; prominent; promote; propose.* **2.** used before roots and words, meaning "bringing into existence": *procreate; produce.* **3.** used before roots and words, meaning "in place of": *pronoun.* **4.** used to form adjectives, meaning "favoring the group, interests, course of action, etc., named by the noun; calling for the interests named by the noun": *pro-* + *choice* → *pro-choice* (*= in favor of allowing a choice to be made regarding abortions*); *pro-* + *war* → *prowar* (*= in favor of fighting a war*).

pro-², *prefix.* from Greek, meaning **1.** "before, beforehand, in front of": *prognosis; prophylactic; prothesis; proboscis.* **2.** "primitive or early form": *prodrug; prosimian.*

proto-, *prefix.* from Greek, meaning "first, foremost, earliest form of": *proto-* + *lithic* → *protolithic; protoplasm.* Also, *esp. before a vowel,* **prot-**.

pseudo-, *prefix.* from Greek, meaning **1.** "false; pretended; unreal": *pseudo-* + *intellectual* → *pseudointellectual* (*= a person pretending to be an intellectual*). **2.** "closely or deceptively resembling": *pseudo-* + *carp* → *pseudocarp* (*= a fish closely resembling a carp*); *pseudo-* + *-pod-* → *pseudopod* (*= a part of an animal that closely resembles a foot*). Also, *esp. before a vowel,* **pseud-**.

psycho-, *prefix.* from Greek, meaning "soul; mind." This meaning is found in such words as: *parapsychology, psychedelic, psychiatry, psychic, psychological, psychology, psychopath, psychosis, psychotic.*

pyro-, *prefix.* from Greek, meaning "fire, heat, high temperature": *pyromaniac, pyrotechnics.*

quasi-, *prefix.* from Latin, meaning "as if, as though." It is used before adjectives and nouns and means "having some of the features but not all; resembling; almost the same as": *quasi-scientific, quasiparticle, quasi-stellar.*

radio-, *prefix.* ultimately from Latin *radius,* meaning "beam, ray." It is used before roots and nouns and means "radiant energy": *radiometer.* It is also used to mean "radio waves": *radiolocation; radiotelephone.* Other meanings are: **1.** the giving off of rays as a result of the breakup of atomic nuclei: *radioactivity; radiocarbon.* **2.** x-rays: *radiograph; radiotherapy.*

re-, *prefix.* from Latin, used **1.** before roots and sometimes words to form verbs and nouns meaning or referring to action in a backward direction: *re-* + *-cede-* → *recede* (*= fall back*); *re-* + *-vert-* → *revert* (*= turn back*). **2.** to form verbs or nouns showing action in answer to or intended to undo or reverse a situation: *rebel; remove; respond; restore; revoke.* **3.** to form verbs or nouns showing action that is done over, often with the meaning that the outcome of the original action was in some way not enough or not long lasting, or that the performance of the new action brings back an earlier state of affairs: *recapture; reoccur; repossess; resole* (*= put another sole on a shoe*); *retype.*

retro-, *prefix.* from Latin, meaning "back, backward": *retro-* + *-gress* → *retrogress* (*= proceed backward*); *retro-* + *rocket* → *retrorocket.*

self-, *prefix.* from Old English, used **1.** before nouns to refer to something that one does by oneself or to oneself: *self-control (= control of oneself); self-government; self-help; self-portrait.* **2.** before adjectives and nouns to refer to an action that is done without assistance: *self-adhesive; a self-loading gun; self-study.*

semi-, *prefix.* from Latin, meaning **1.** "half": *semiannual; semicircle.* **2.** "partially; partly; somewhat": *semiautomatic; semidetached; semiformal.* **3.** "happening or occurring twice in (a certain length of time)": *semiannual.*

sex-, *prefix.* from Latin, meaning "six": *sexpartite (= having six parts or divisions).*

socio-, *prefix.* from Latin, used before roots and sometimes words, meaning "social; sociological; society": *socio- + economic → socioeconomic; socio- + -metry → sociometry (= social statistics).*

step-, *prefix.* from Old English, used before words to name a member of a family related by the remarriage of a parent and not by blood: *When my father married his second wife, she already had a son who became my stepbrother.*

sub-, *prefix.* from Latin, meaning **1.** "under, below, beneath": *subsoil; subway.* **2.** "just outside of, near": *subalpine; subtropical.* **3.** "less than, not quite": *subhuman; subteen.* **4.** "secondary, at a lower point in a hierarchy": *subcommittee; subplot.* Sometimes this prefix is spelled as **su-, suc-, suf-, sug-, sum-, sup-, sur-, sus-.**

super-, *prefix.* from Latin, meaning **1.** "above, beyond; above or over (another); situated or located over": *superimpose, superstructure, superficial.* **2.** "an individual, thing, or property that surpasses customary or normal amounts or levels, as being larger, more powerful, or having something to a great degree or to too great a degree": *superconductivity, superman, supercomputer, superhighway, superhuman, supercritical, supercool.*

supra-, *prefix.* from Latin, meaning "above, over; beyond the limits of": *supraorbital; supranational.* Compare SUPER-.

sur-, *prefix.* from French, meaning "over, above, in addition": *surcharge; surname; surrender.*

sym-, *prefix.* another form of the prefix SYN-. It appears before roots beginning with *b, p, m: symbol; symphony; symmetry.*

syn-, *prefix.* from Greek, meaning "with; together." This meaning is found in such words as: *synchronous, idiosyncrasy, photosynthesis, synagogue, synchronize, synonym, synthesis.* See SYM-.

tele-, *prefix.* **1.** from Greek, meaning "far." It is used before roots and sometimes words and means "reaching over a distance, carried out between two remote points, performed or operating through electronic transmissions": *telegraph; telekinesis; teletypewriter.* **2.** *tele-* is also used to mean "television:" *telegenic; telethon.* Also, *esp. before a vowel,* **tel-.**

trans-, *prefix.* from Latin, used **1.** before verb roots that refer to movement or carrying from one place to another; it means "across; through": *transfer; transmit; transplant.* **2.** to mean "complete change": *transform; transmute.* **3.** before roots to form adjectives that mean "crossing, going beyond, on the other side of (the place or thing named)": *transnational; trans-Siberian.*

tri-, *prefix.* from Latin, meaning "three": *triatomic; trilateral.*

ultra-, *prefix.* from Latin, meaning **1.** "located beyond, on the far side of": *ultraviolet.* **2.** "carrying to the furthest degree possible, on the fringe of": *ultraleft; ultramodern.* **3.** "extremely": *ultralight.* **4.** "going beyond normal or customary bounds or limits": *ultramicroscope; ultrasound; ultrastructure.*

un-[1]**,** *prefix.* from Old English, used very freely to form adjectives and the adverbs and nouns formed from these adjectives. It means "not," and it brings negative or opposite force: *unfair, unfairly, unfairness; unfelt; unseen; unfitting; unformed; unheard-of; unrest; unemployment.*

un-[2]**,** *prefix.* from Old English, used **1.** before verbs, meaning "a reversal of some action or state, or a removal, a taking away, or a release": *unbend; uncork; unfasten.* **2.** before some verbs to intensify the meaning: *unloose (= let loose with force).*

under-, *prefix.* from Old English, meaning **1.** "a place or situation below or beneath": *underbrush; undertow.* **2.** "lower in grade, rank or dignity": *undersheriff; understudy.* **3.** before adjectives to mean "of lesser degree, extent, or amount": *undersized.* **4.** "not showing enough; too little": *underfed.*

vice-, *prefix.* from Latin, meaning "in place of, instead of." It is used before roots and sometimes words and means "deputy"; it is used esp. in the titles of officials who serve in the absence of the official named by the base word: *viceroy (→ vice- + roy, "king"); vice-chancellor; vice-chairman.*

B. Important Suffixes to Know

-ability, *suffix.* ultimately from Latin, a combination of -ABLE and -ITY, used to form nouns from adjectives that end in *-able: capable (adjective) → capability (noun); reliable (adjective) → reliability (noun).*

-able, *suffix.* ultimately from Latin, added to verbs to form adjectives meaning "capable of, fit for, tending to": *teach + -able → teachable (= capable of being taught); photograph + -able → photographable = (fit for photographing).* Compare -IBLE.

-aceous, *suffix.* from Latin, meaning "having the nature of, made of." This meaning is found in such words as *herbaceous, cretaceous.*

-acious, *suffix.* from Latin, used after some roots to form adjectives meaning "tending to; abounding in": *tenacious (from ten- "hold on" + -acious) = tending to hold on; loquacious (from loq(u)- "talk" + -acious) = tending to talk.* Compare -OUS.

-acity, *suffix.* from Middle English, used after some roots to form nouns with the meaning "tendency toward; abundance in": *tenacity (from- ten- "hold on" + -acity) = tendency toward holding on.*

-age, *suffix.* ultimately from Latin, used to form noncount mass or abstract nouns **1.** from other nouns, with meanings such as "collection" (*coinage = a collection or group of coins*) and "quantity or measure" (*footage = quantity of feet in measurement*). **2.** from verbs, with meanings such as "process" (*coverage = the act or process of covering*), "the outcome of, the fact of" or "the physical effect or remains of" (*spoilage = the result of spoiling; wreckage = the remains of wrecking*), and "amount charged" (*towage = charge for towing; postage = amount charged for posting, that is, sending through the mail*).

-aholic, *suffix.* (originally taken from the word ALCOHOLIC) used to form new words with the general meaning "a person who is addicted to or strongly desires" the activity being shown by the initial part of the word. Thus, a *charge-aholic* is someone who uses a charge card a lot; a *foodaholic* is someone who always wants food. Compare -HOLIC.

-al¹, *suffix.* from Latin, added to nouns to form adjectives meaning "relating to, of the kind of, having the form or character of": *autumn + -al → autumnal (= relating to the season autumn); nature + -al → natural (= having the character of nature).*

-al², *suffix.* from Latin, added to verbs to form nouns meaning "the act of": *deny + -al → denial (= the act of denying); refuse + -al → refusal (= the act of refusing).*

-ally, *suffix.* form from **-al¹** + **-ly**, used to form adverbs from certain adjectives ending in -IC: *terrific (adj.) + -ally → terrifically (adverb).*

-an, *suffix.* from Latin, meaning "of, pertaining to, having qualities of," **1.** added to names of places or people to form adjectives and nouns meaning **a.** being connected with a place: *Chicago + -an → Chicagoan;* **b.** having membership in a group of: *Episcopal + -(i)an → Episcopalian;* **2.** used to form adjectives meaning "of or like (someone); supporter or believer of": *Christ + -(i)an → Christian; Freud + -(i)an → Freudian (= supporter of or believer in the theories of Sigmund Freud).* **3.** used to form nouns from words ending in -ic or -y meaning "one who works with": *electric + -(i)an → electrician; comedy + -an → comedian.*

-ance, *suffix.* ultimately from Latin, used **1.** after some adjectives ending in -ANT to form nouns meaning "quality or state of": *brilliant + -ance → brilliance.* **2.** *after some verb roots to form nouns: appear + -ance → appearance; resemble + -ance → resemblance.* See -ANT, -ENCE.

-ant, *suffix.* from Latin, used **1.** after some verbs to form adjectives meaning "doing or performing (the action of the verb)": *please + -ant → pleasant (= doing the pleasing).* **2.** after some verbs to form nouns meaning "one who does or performs (the action of the verb, often a formal action)": *serve + -ant → servant (= one who serves); apply (+ ic) + -ant → applicant (= one who formally applies, as for a job).* **3.** after some verbs to form nouns meaning: "substance that does or performs (the action of the verb)": *cool (verb = "to make cool") + -ant → coolant (= substance to keep engines cool).* See -ENT.

-ar, *suffix.* from Latin, used **1.** after some nouns (many of which have an *l* before the end) to form adjectives: *circle + -ar → circular; single + -ar → singular.* **2.** after some verbs to form nouns meaning "one who does or performs an act of": *beg + -ar → beggar; lie + -ar → liar.*

-ard, *suffix.* from French, used after some verbs and nouns to form nouns that refer to persons who regularly do an activity, or who are characterized in a certain way, as indicated by the stem: *dullard (= one who is dull); drunkard (= one who is drunk).*

-arian, *suffix.* from Latin, used **1.** after some nouns and adjectives that end in

-ARY to form personal nouns: *library* + *-arian* → *librarian; seminary* + *-arian* → *seminarian; veterinary* + *-arian* → *veterinarian.* **2.** after some roots to form nouns meaning "a person who supports, calls for, or practices the principles of (the root noun)": *authority* + *-arian* → *authoritarian (= one who believes in central authority); totality* + *-arian* → *totalitarian (= one who believes in total governmental rule).*

-art, *suffix.* variant form of -ARD, found in such words as: *braggart.*

-ary, *suffix.* from Latin, used **1.** after some nouns to form adjectives meaning: "relating to, connected with": *element* + *-ary* → *elementary; honor* + *-ary* → *honorary.* **2.** after some roots to form personal nouns, or nouns that refer to objects that hold or contain things: *secretary; -libr- (= root meaning "book")* + *-ary* → *library (= place for holding books); glossary (= place containing specialized words and their meanings).* **3.** after some nouns to form adjectives meaning "contributing to; for the purpose of": *inflation* + *-ary* → *inflationary (= contributing to inflation); compliment* + *-ary* → *complimentary (= for the purpose of complimenting).*

-ate, *suffix.* **1.** from Latin, used to form adjectives meaning "showing; full of": *passion* + *-ate* → *passionate (= showing passion); consider* + *-ate* → *considerate (= showing the action of considering); literate.* **2.** used to form verbs meaning "cause to become (like); act as": *regular* + *-ate* → *regulate (= make regular, act by rule); active* + *-ate* → *activate (= cause to become active); hyphenate; calibrate.* **3.** used to form nouns meaning **a.** a group of people: *elector* + *-ate* → *electorate (= group who elect).* **b.** an area ruled by: *caliph (a kind of ruler)* + *-ate* → *caliphate (= area ruled by a caliph); protector* + *-ate* → *protectorate (= area ruled by a protecting nation).* **c.** the office, institution, or function of: *consul* + *-ate* → *consulate; magistrate; potentate.*

-ation, *suffix.* from Latin, used after some verbs or adjectives (some of which end in -ATE) to form nouns meaning "state or process of": *starve* + *-ation* → *starvation (= condition of starving); separate* + *-ation* → *separation (= state of being separate).*

-ative, *suffix.* from Latin, used after some verbs (some of which end in -ATE) and nouns to form adjectives: *regulate* + *-ative* → *regulative (= with the power to regulate); norm (= rule)* + *-ative* → *normative (= having rules).*

-ator, *suffix.* from Latin, used after verbs ending in -ATE to form nouns meaning "person or thing that does or performs (the action of the verb)": *agitate* + *-ator* → *agitator (= person who agitates; machine that agitates); vibrate* + *-ator* → *vibrator (= thing that vibrates); narrator, generator, mediator, incubator.*

-based, *suffix.* from the word *base,* used **1.** after nouns to form adjectives. **2.** after nouns of place to form adjectives meaning "operating or working from": *ground* + *-based* → *ground-based (= operating from the ground); New York* + *-based* → *New York-based (= working from New York).* **3.** after nouns to form adjectives meaning "making use of": *computer* + *based* → *computer-based (= making use of computers; "as in "computer-based instruction"); logic* + *-based* → *logic-based (= making use of logic).*

-burger, *suffix.* (originally taken from the word *hamburger*) used after roots and some words to form nouns that mean "the food added to, or substituted for, a basic hamburger": *cheese + -burger → cheeseburger (= a hamburger with cheese added on top); fish + -burger → fishburger (= fish substituted for the meat of a hamburger).*

-cracy, *suffix.* ultimately from Greek, meaning "power; rule; government," used after roots to form nouns meaning "rule; government": *auto- + -cracy → autocracy (-government by one ruler); theo- ("God") + -cracy → theocracy (-a country governed by the rule of God or a god).* Compare -CRAT.

-crat, *suffix.* ultimately from Greek, meaning "ruler; person having power," used after roots to form nouns meaning "ruler; member of a ruling body": *auto- + -crat → autocrat (= a ruler governing alone).* Compare -CRACY.

-cy, *suffix.* from French and Latin, used **1.** to form nouns from adjectives that have stems that end in *-t, -te, -tic,* and esp. *-nt* **a.** to form abstract nouns: *democrat + -cy → democracy; accurate + -cy → accuracy; expedient + -cy → expediency; lunatic + -cy → lunacy.* **b.** to form action nouns: *vacant + -cy → vacancy; occupant + -cy → occupancy.* **2.** *to form nouns meaning "rank or office of": captain + -cy → captaincy (= rank or office of a captain); magistra(te) + -cy → magistracy (= office of a magistrate).*

-dom, *suffix.* from Old English, used after some nouns and adjectives to form nouns meaning **1.** domain or area ruled: *king + -dom → kingdom (= area a king rules).* **2.** collection of persons: *official + -dom → officialdom (= a collection of officials).* **3.** rank: *earl + -dom → earldom (= the rank or position of an earl).* **4.** general condition: *free + -dom → freedom (= general condition of being free).*

-ed, *suffix.* from Old English, **1.** added to words with the following rules of form: **a.** For most regular verbs that end in a consonant, *-ed* is added directly afterwards: *cross + -ed → crossed.* When the verb ends in *-y,* the *-y* changes to *-i* and *-ed* is added: *ready + -ed → readied.* If the root ends in *-e,* an *e* is dropped: *save + -ed → saved.* **b.** The pronunciation of the suffix *-ed* depends on the *sound* that appears before it. After the sounds *p, k, f, th, s, sh,* and *ch* the suffix is pronounced *(t): cross + -ed → crossed (krôst);* after the sounds *t, d* it is pronounced *(id): edit + -ed → edited (ed'i tid);* after all other sounds it is pronounced *(d): budge + -ed → budged (bujd).* **2.** carries a number of different meanings. It is used **a.** to form the past tense and past participle of regular verbs: *He crossed the river. He had crossed the river when we got there.* **b.** to form an adjective indicating a condition or quality due to action of the verb: *inflated balloons (= balloons that have been inflated).* **c.** after nouns to form adjectives meaning "possessing, having, or characterized by (whatever the noun base is)": *beard + -ed → bearded (= possessing or having a beard).*

-ee, *suffix.* from French, used **1.** after verbs that take an object to form nouns meaning "the person who is the object of the action of the verb": *address + -ee → addressee (= the person whom someone else addresses).* **2.** after verbs that do not take an object to form nouns meaning "the one doing or performing the act of the verb": *escape + -ee → escapee (= one performing the act* *of escaping).* **3.** after other words to form nouns meaning "the one who is or does": *absent + -ee → absentee (= one who is absent).*

-eer, *suffix.* from French, used to form nouns meaning "the person who produces, handles, or is associated with" the base word: *engine + -eer → engineer (= person handling an engine).*

-en, *suffix.* from Old English, used **1. a.** after some adjectives to form verbs meaning "to be or make": *hard + -en → harden (= to be or make hard).* **b.** after some nouns to form verbs meaning "to add to, cause to be, or have": *length + -en → lengthen (= to add length to; make long).* **2.** after some nouns that are materials or sources of something to form adjectives that describe the source or material: *gold + -en → golden (= like gold).*

-ence, *suffix.* from Latin, used **1.** after some adjectives ending in -ENT to form nouns meaning "quality or state of": *abstin(ent) + -ence → abstinence.* **2.** after some verb roots to form nouns: *depend + -ence → dependence.* See -ANCE, -ENT.

-ent, *suffix.* from Latin, used **1.** after some verbs to form adjectives meaning "doing or performing (the action of the verb)": *differ + -ent → different.* **2.** after some verbs to form nouns meaning "one who does or performs (the action)": *stud(y) + -ent → student (= one who studies).* See -ANT, -ENCE.

-er¹, *suffix.* from Old English, used **1.** after verbs to form nouns meaning "a person, animal or thing that performs the action of the verb" or "the person, animal or thing used in performing the action of the verb": *bake + -er → baker (= a person who bakes); teach + -er → teacher (= a person who teaches); fertilize + -er → fertilizer (= a thing that is used to fertilize)* **2.** after nouns to form new nouns that refer to the occupation, work, or labor of the root noun: *hat + -er → hatter (= one whose work is making hats); roof + -er → roofer (= one whose occupation is repairing roofs).* **3.** after nouns to form new nouns that refer to the place of origin, or the dwelling place, of the root noun: *Iceland + -er → Icelander (= person who originally comes from Iceland); southern + -er → southerner (= a person who originally comes from, or lives in, the south).* Compare -IER, -OR.

-er², *suffix.* from Middle English, regularly used to form the comparative form of short adjectives and adverbs: *hard + -er → harder; small + -er → smaller; fast + -er → faster.*

-ery (or **-ry**), *suffix.* from French, used **1.** to form nouns that refer to **a.** things in a collection: *green + -ery → greenery (= green plants as a group); machine + -ery → machinery (= a group or collection of machines)* **b.** people in a collection: *Jew + -ry → Jewry (= Jews as a group); peasant + -ry → peasantry (= peasants as a group)* **c.** an occupation, activity, or condition: *dentist + -ry → dentistry (= occupation of a dentist); rival + -ry → rivalry (= condition of being a rival); rob + -ery → robbery (= activity of robbing or being robbed).* **2.** to form nouns that refer to a place where the activity of the root is done: *bake + -ery → bakery (= place where baking is done); wine + -ery → winery (= place where wine is made).*

-ese, *suffix.* ultimately from Latin, used **1.** after nouns that refer to place names: **a.** to form adjectives to describe things made in or relating to the place: *Japan + -ese → Japanese (= of or relating to Japan or its people); Vienna + -ese →*

Viennese (= of or relating to Vienna or its people) **b.** to form nouns with the meanings "the people living in (the place)" or "the language of (the place)": *Vietnam + -ese → Vietnamese (= the people living in/the language spoken in Vietnam)*. **2.** to form nouns that describe in an insulting or humorous way the language characteristic of or typical of the base word: *Brooklyn + -ese → Brooklynese (= the language characteristic of Brooklyn); journal + -ese → journalese (= the language typical of journalists)*.

-esque, *suffix.* from French, used after nouns and proper names to form adjectives meaning "resembling," "in the style or manner of," "suggesting the work of" the person or thing denoted by the base word: *Kafka + -esque → Kafkaesque (= in the style or manner of Franz Kafka); Lincoln + -esque → Lincolnesque (= in the style of Abraham Lincoln); picture + -esque → picturesque (= resembling or suggesting a picture)*.

-ess, *suffix.* from French, used to form a feminine noun: *count + -ess → countess; god + -ess → goddess; lion + -ess → lioness.* —**Usage.** *The use of words ending in -ESS has declined sharply in the latter half of the 20th century, but some are still current: actress (but some women prefer actor); adventuress; enchantress; governess (only in its child-care sense); heiress (largely in journalistic writing); hostess (but women who conduct radio and television programs are hosts); seamstress; seductress; temptress; and waitress.*

-est, *suffix.* from Old English, regularly used to form the superlative form of short adjectives and adverbs: *fast + -est → fastest; soon + -est → soonest; warm + -est → warmest.*

-ette, *suffix.* from French, used **1.** after nouns to form nouns that refer to a smaller version of the original noun or root: *kitchen + -ette → kitchenette (= small kitchen); novel + -ette → novelette (= smaller novel)*. **2.** after nouns to form nouns that refer specifically to a female: *major + -ette → majorette (= female leader of a band, or baton twirler); usher + -ette → usherette (= female usher in a movie theater)*. **3.** after nouns to form nouns that refer to a name that is an imitation product of the root: *leather + -ette → leatherette (= imitation leather product)*. —**Usage.** *English nouns in which -ETTE signifies a feminine role or identity have been thought of as implying inferiority or unimportance and are now generally avoided. Only (drum) majorette is still widely used, usually indicating a young woman who twirls a baton with a marching band.*

-ferous, *suffix.* from the root *-fer* + the suffix *-ous.* This suffix is found in such words as: *coniferous, pestiferous.*

-fest, *suffix.* from German, added to nouns to form nouns meaning "an assembly of people engaged in a common activity" named by the first element of the compound: *gab + -fest → gabfest (= group of people gabbing or talking a lot); song + -fest → songfest (= assembly of people singing together)*.

-fold, *suffix.* from Old English, used after words that refer to a number or quantity to form adjectives meaning "having the number of kinds or parts" or "multiplied the number of times": *four + -fold → fourfold (= multiplied four times); many + -fold → manyfold (= having many parts or kinds)*.

-footed, *suffix.* from the word *foot,* added to nouns to form adjectives meaning "having (the kind of, number of, etc.) a foot or feet indicated": *a four-footed animal (= an animal having four feet)*.

-free, *suffix.* from Old English, used after nouns to form adjectives meaning "not containing (the noun mentioned); without": *sugar + -free → sugar-free (= not containing sugar); trouble + -free → trouble-free (= without trouble)*.

-ful, *suffix.* from Old English, used **1.** after nouns to form adjectives meaning "full of; characterized by": *beauty + -ful → beautiful (= full of beauty); care + -ful → careful (= characterized by care)*. **2.** after verbs to form adjectives meaning "tending to; able to": *harm + -ful → harmful (= tending to harm); wake + -ful → wakeful (= tending to stay awake)*. **3.** after nouns to form nouns meaning "as much as will fill": *spoon + -ful → spoonful (= as much as will fill a spoon); cup + -ful → cupful (= as much as will fill a cup)*.

-fy, *suffix.* ultimately from Latin, used **1.** after roots to form verbs meaning "to make; cause to be; render": *pure + -fy → purify (= to make pure); simple + -fy → simplify (= make simple); liquid + -fy → liquefy (= to make into a liquid)*. **2.** to mean "cause to conform to": *citify (= cause to conform to city ways)*. Compare -IFY.

-gate, *suffix.* derived from *Watergate,* originally the name of a hotel complex where officials of the Republican party were caught trying to burglarize Democratic party headquarters. *Watergate* then came to be associated with "a political cover-up and scandal." The suffix is used after some nouns to form nouns that refer to scandals resulting from concealed crime in government or business: *Iran + -gate → Irangate (= a scandal involving arms sales to Iran)*.

-gon, *suffix.* from Greek, meaning "side; angle." This suffix is used after roots to form nouns that refer to plane figures having the number of sides mentioned: *poly- (= many) + -gon → polygon (= a many-sided figure)*.

-gram, *suffix.* from Greek, meaning "what is written." It is used after roots to form nouns that refer to something written or drawn, either by hand or machine: *cardio- (= of or relating to the heart) + -gram → cardiogram (= a recording and diagram of a heartbeat, drawn by a machine)*. Compare -GRAPH-.

-hearted, *suffix.* from Middle English, used after adjectives to form adjectives meaning "having the character or personality of (the adjective mentioned)": *cold + -hearted → coldhearted (= having a cold heart; unkind or mean); light + -hearted → lighthearted (= feeling light and happy)*.

-holic, *suffix.* another form of -AHOLIC: *choco(late) + -holic → chocoholic (= person addicted to chocolate)*.

-hood, *suffix.* from Old English, used to form nouns meaning **1.** "the state or condition of": *likely + -hood → likelihood (= the state or condition of being likely); child + -hood → childhood (= the state or period of time of being a child)*. **2.** "a body or group of persons of a particular character or class": *priest + -hood → priesthood (= a body of priests)*.

-ian, *suffix.* from Latin, used to form nouns and adjectives with the meanings of -AN: *Orwell + -ian → Orwellian (= interested in, or relating to, the writing of*

George Orwell); Washington + -ian → Washingtonian (= a person who lives in Washington).

-iatrics, *suffix.* from Greek, used after some roots to form nouns meaning "healing; the medical practice of": *ger- (= old people) + -iatrics → geriatrics (= the healing of older people); ped- (= child) + -iatrics → pediatrics (= medical practice involving children).*

-iatry, *suffix.* from Greek, used after some roots to form nouns meaning "healing; the medical practice of": *pod- (= foot) + -iatry → podiatry (= the healing of the foot); psych- (= the mind) + -iatry → psychiatry (= the medical practice dealing with the mind).*

-ibility, *suffix.* from Latin, used to form nouns from adjectives that end in *-ible: reducible (adjective) → reducibility (= the state or condition of being reducible, of being able to be reduced); flexible (adjective) → flexibility (= the state or condition of being able to move smoothly)* See -ABILITY, -ABLE, -IBLE.

-ible, *suffix.* a variant form of -ABLE, used after roots, mostly of verbs, to form adjectives meaning "capable of, fit for, tending to": *cred- (= believe) + -ible → credible (= that can be believed); vis- (= see) + -ible → visible (= that can be seen); reduce + -ible → reducible (= that can be reduced).* See -ABILITY, -ABLE, -IBILITY.

-ic, *suffix.* from Middle English, used after nouns to form adjectives meaning "of or relating to": *metal + -ic → metallic; poet + -ic → poetic.* This suffix is also used after nouns to form adjectives meaning "having some characteristics of; in the style of": *ballet + -ic → balletic; sophomore + -ic → sophomoric; Byron + -ic → Byronic (= in the style of the writer Byron).*

-ical, *suffix.* a combination of -IC and -AL[1], used after roots to form adjectives meaning "of or relating to": *rhetor- + -ical → rhetorical.* This suffix originally provided synonyms to adjectives that ended in -IC: *poet + -ic → poetic; poet + -ical → poetical.* But some of these pairs of words or formations are now different in meaning: *econom- + -ic → economic (= of or relating to economics); econom- + -ical → economical (= being careful in spending money); histor- + -ic → historic (= having a long history; important); histor- + -ical → historical (= happening in the past).*

-ician, *suffix.* extracted from physician, musician, etc., used after nouns or roots to form nouns meaning "the person having the occupation or work of": *beauty + -ician → beautician (= person who works in a beauty shop); mort- (= death) + -ician → mortician (= person working to prepare dead people for burial).*

-ics, *suffix.* from Latin, used after roots to form nouns meaning "a body of facts, knowledge, or principles." Such nouns usually correspond to adjectives ending in IC or-ICAL: *eth- (= custom; character) + -ics → ethics (= the principles of good character); phys- (= body) + -ics → physics (= the principles of bodies in motion and at rest).*

-ier, *suffix.* from French, used after nouns or roots to form nouns meaning "person or thing that does (the action of the word mentioned); person or thing in charge of (the word mentioned)": *finance + -ier → financier (= person doing finance); cour- (= run) + -ier → courier (= messenger); hotel + -ier → hotelier (= person in charge of hotels).* Compare -ER[1].

-ify, *suffix.* from French, used to form verbs meaning "cause to be in (a stated condition); to make or cause to become (a certain condition)": *intense + -ify → intensify (= cause to be intense); speechify (= make speeches).* See -FY.

-in, *suffix.* extracted from *sit-in,* used after some verbs to form nouns that refer to organized protests through, using, or in support of the named activity: *pray + -in → pray-in (= a protest in which participants engage in passive resistance and prayer).*

-ine¹, *suffix.* from Latin, used after some roots or nouns to form adjectives meaning "of, relating to, or characteristic of; of the nature of; made of": *crystal + -ine → crystalline (= of, like, or made of crystal); equ- (= horse) + -ine → equine (= of or relating to horses).*

-ine², *suffix.* from French, used after some roots to form nouns that name chemical substances and elements: *caffe- (= coffee) + -ine → caffeine (= a chemical substance found in coffee); chlor- + -ine → chlorine.*

-ing¹, *suffix.* **1.** from Old English, used after verbs to form nouns that express the action of the verb or its result, product, material, etc.: *build + -ing → building: the art of building; a new building.* **2.** after roots (other than verb roots) to form nouns: *off + -ing → offing.*

-ing², *suffix.* from Middle English, used after verbs to form the present participle of verbs: *walk + -ing → walking: Is the baby walking yet?* These participles are often used as adjectives: *war + -ing → warring: warring factions.* Some adjectives ending in *-ing* are formed by combining a prefix with a verb. Thus *outgoing* is formed from *out-* + the present participle form of the verb *go (= going).* Other examples: *uplifting, outstanding, incoming.*

-ion, *suffix.* ultimately from Latin, used after some roots to form nouns that refer to action or condition: *uni- (= one) + -ion → union (= condition of being one).* Compare -TION.

-ious, *suffix.* from Latin, a variant form of -OUS, used after roots to form adjectives: *hilar- (= cheerful) + -ious → hilarious (= very funny).*

-ise, *suffix. Chiefly British.* See -IZE.

-ish, *suffix.* from Old English, used **1.** after nouns or roots to form adjectives meaning **a.** relating to; in the same manner of; having the characteristics of: *brute + -ish → brutish.* **b.** of or relating to the people or language of: *Brit- + -ish → British; Swede + -ish → Swedish.* **c.** like; similar to: *baby + -ish → babyish; mule + -ish → mulish; girl + -ish → girlish.* **d.** addicted to; inclined or tending to: *book + -ish → bookish (= tending to read books a great deal).* **e.** near or about: *fifty + -ish → fiftyish (nearly fifty years old).* **2.** after adjectives to form adjectives meaning "somewhat, rather": *old + -ish → oldish (= somewhat old); red + -ish → reddish (= somewhat red); sweet + -ish → sweetish.*

-ism, *suffix.* from Greek, used **1.** after verb roots to form action nouns: *baptize → bapt- + -ism → baptism.* **2.** to form nouns showing action or practice: *adventure + -ism → adventurism (= the action or practice of taking risks in intervening in international affairs).* **3.** used to form nouns showing state or condition: *alcoholism (= disease or condition in which alcohol is involved).* **4.** after roots to form nouns showing the names of principles or doctrines: *Darwinism (= principles of Darwin's theory of evolution); despotism.* **5.** to form nouns showing an example of a use: *witticism (= example of something witty); Africanism (= word from Africa or from an African language).* Compare -IST, -IZE.

-ist, *suffix.* from French and Latin, forms nouns usually corresponding to verbs ending in *-ize* and nouns ending in *-ism,* and referring to a person who practices or is concerned with something: *novel + -ist → novelist (= someone writing a novel); terrorist (= one who practices terrorism, one who terrorizes).*

-ite, *suffix.* from Latin, used after nouns and roots to form nouns meaning: **1.** a person associated with or living in a place; a person connected with a tribe, leader, set of beliefs, system, etc.: *Manhattan + -ite → Manhattanite; Israel + -ite → Israelite; Labor + -ite → Laborite (= someone following the Labor Party).* **2.** mineral or fossil; explosive; chemical compound or drug product: *anthracite; cordite; dynamite; sulfite.*

-itis, *suffix.* ultimately from Greek, used **1.** after roots that refer to an inflammation or disease affecting a certain part of the body: *appendix + -itis → appendicitis; bronchi (= part of the lungs) + -itis → bronchitis.* **2.** to form nouns made up for a particular occasion to refer to something comparable in a funny way to a disease: *The teenagers seem to be suffering from telephonitis (= excessive use of the telephone, as if using it were a disease).*

-ive, *suffix.* from French and Latin, used after roots or nouns to form adjectives meaning "having a tendency or connection with; like": *act(ion) + -ive → active (= tending to be full of action or activity); sport + -ive → sportive (= like sports).*

-ize, *suffix.* ultimately from Greek, used to form verbs meaning **1.** "to make; cause to become": *fossil + -ize → fossilize (= to make something into a fossil); sterile + -ize → sterilize (= to make something sterile).* **2.** "to convert into, give a specified character or form to; change to a state of": *computer + -ize → computerize (= make an office use computers); dramat- + -ize → dramatize (= give the form of a drama to some other piece of work); American + -ize → Americanize (= convert to an American character).* **3.** "to subject to; cause to undergo or suffer from (an emotion or a process, sometimes named after its originator)": *hospital + -ize → hospitalize (= cause to undergo treatment in a hospital); terror + -ize → terrorize (= cause to suffer terror); galvan- + -ize → galvanize (= to coat metal or stimulate electrically, as by the experiments of L. Galvani, Italian physicist).* Also, *chiefly British,* **-ise.**

-less, *suffix.* from Old English, used **1.** after nouns to form adjectives meaning "without, not having (the thing or quality named by the noun)": *care + -less → careless; shame + -less → shameless* **2.** after verbs to form adjectives meaning "that cannot be" plus the *-ed/en* form of the verb; or "that never" plus the *-s* form of the verb: *tire + -less → tireless (= that never tires); count + -less → countless (= that cannot be counted).*

-let, *suffix.* from Middle English, used **1.** after a noun to form a noun that is a smaller version of the original noun or root: *book + -let → booklet (= a smaller book); pig + -let → piglet (= a smaller pig).* **2.** after a noun to form a noun that is a band, ornament, or article of clothing worn on the part of the body mentioned: *ankle + -let → anklet (= piece of clothing like a sock worn on* *the ankle); wrist + -let → wristlet (= ornament like a bracelet worn on the wrist).*

-like, *suffix.* from Middle English, used after nouns to form adjectives meaning "of or resembling (the noun base)": *child + -like → childlike; life + -like → life-like.*

-ling, *suffix.* from Old English, used **1.** to form a noun that indicates a feeling of distaste or disgust for the person or thing named: *hire + -ling → hireling (= someone hired to do menial or distasteful tasks); under + -ling → underling.* **2.** to form a noun that is a smaller version or example of the base word: *prince + -ling; duck + -ling → duckling.*

-logy, *suffix.* from Greek, meaning "word." It is used after roots to form nouns meaning "field of study, discipline; list of": *astro- (= star) + -logy → astrology (= study of the influence of stars or events); bio- (= life) + -logy → biology (= study of living things).*

-ly, *suffix.* from Middle English, used **1.** after adjectives to form adverbs: *glad + -ly → gladly; gradual + -ly → gradually.* **2.** after nouns that refer to units of time, to form adjectives and adverbs meaning "at or for every (such unit of time)": *hour + -ly → hourly (= at every hour); day + -ly → daily (= on or for every day).* **3.** after nouns to form adjectives meaning "like (the noun mentioned):" *saint + -ly → saintly; coward + -ly → cowardly.*

-man, *suffix.* from Old English, used to form nouns meaning "person, or man, who is or does (something connected with the noun base)": *mail + -man → mailman (= person who delivers mail).*

-mania, *suffix.* from Greek, used after roots to form nouns meaning "great or strong enthusiasm for (the element of the root)": *biblio- (= book) + -mania → bibliomania (= excessive or strong interest or enthusiasm for books).*

-ment, *suffix.* from French and Latin, used **1.** after verbs to form nouns that refer to the action of the verb: *govern + -ment → government.* **2.** after verbs to form nouns that refer to a state or condition resulting from the action of a verb: *refresh + -ment → refreshment.* **3.** after verbs to form nouns that refer to a product resulting from the action of a verb: *frag- + -ment → fragment (= a piece resulting from the breaking off of something).*

-ness, *suffix.* from Old English, used after adjectives and verbs ending in *-ing* or *-ed/-en* to form nouns that refer to the quality or state of the adjective or verb: *dark + -ness → darkness; prepared + -ness → preparedness (= a state of being prepared).*

-o, *suffix.* derived from Romance nouns ending in -o, used **1.** as the final element in certain nouns that are shortened from longer nouns: *ammo* (from "ammunition"); *combo* (from "combination"); *promo* (from "promotion"). **2.** after certain adjectives and nouns to form nouns that have an unfavorable or insulting meaning: *weird + -o → weirdo (= a very weird person); wine + -o → wino (= someone who drinks too much wine).* **3.** after certain nouns and adjectives to form informal nouns or adjectives; these are often used when speaking directly to another: *kid + -o → kiddo (= a kid or person); neat + -o*

→ *neato (= an informal use of "neat"); right + -o → righto (= an informal use of "right").*

-off, *suffix.* from Old English, used to form nouns that name or refer to a competition or contest, esp. between finalists or to break a tie: *cook + -off → cookoff (= a cooking contest); runoff (= a deciding final contest).*

-oid, *suffix.* from Greek, used to form adjectives and nouns meaning "resembling, like," with the suggestion of an incomplete or imperfect similarity to the root element: *human + -oid → humanoid (= resembling a human, but not quite the same).*

-onym, *suffix.* from Greek, meaning "word, name." This meaning is found in such words as: *pseudonym, homonym.*

-or, *suffix.* from French, used to form nouns that are agents, or that do or perform a function: *debtor; tailor; traitor; projector; repressor; sensor; tractor.*

-ory¹, *suffix.* **1.** from Middle English, used after nouns and verbs that end in *-e* to form adjectives meaning "of or relating to (the noun or verb mentioned)": *excrete + -ory → excretory (= of or relating to excreting); sense + -ory → sensory (= of or relating to the senses).* **2.** after certain roots to form adjectives meaning "providing or giving": *satisfact- + -ory → satisfactory (= giving satisfaction).*

-ory², *suffix.* from Latin, used after roots to form nouns that refer to places or things that hold (the root), or places that are used for (the root): *cremat- + -ory → crematory (= a place where bodies are cremated); observat(ion) + -ory → observatory (= place where observations of the heavens are made).*

-ose¹, *suffix.* from Latin, used after roots to form adjectives meaning "full of, abounding in, given to, or like (the root)": *verb- (= word) + -ose → verbose (= full of words); bellic- (= war) + -ose → bellicose (= eager for fighting or war).*

-ose², *suffix.* extracted from *glucose,* used after roots to form nouns that name sugars, carbohydrates, and substances that are formed from proteins: *fruct- + -ose → fructose (= a fruit sugar); lact- + -ose → lactose (= a milk sugar); prote- + ose → proteose (= a compound made from protein).*

-ous, *suffix.* from French, used **1.** after roots to form adjectives meaning "possessing, full of (a given quality)": *glory + -ous → glorious; wonder + ous → wondrous; covet + -ous → covetous; nerve + -ous → nervous.* **2.** after roots to form adjectives referring to the names of chemical elements: *stannous chloride,* $SnCl_2$.

-person, *suffix.* from Latin, used to replace some paired, sex-specific suffixes such as -MAN and -WOMAN or -ER¹ and -ESS: *salesman/saleswoman* are replaced by *sales + -person → salesperson; waiter/waitress* are replaced by *wait + -person → waitperson.*

-phile, *suffix.* from Greek, used **1.** after roots and sometimes words to form nouns meaning "lover of, enthusiast for (a given object)": *biblio- + -phile → bibliophile (= lover of books); Franco- + -phile → Francophile (= lover of France or French things).* **2.** after roots to form nouns meaning "a person sexually attracted to or overly interested in (a given object)": *pedo- + -phile → pedophile (= someone with a sexual attraction for children).*

-phobe, *suffix.* from Greek, used after roots and sometimes words to form nouns that refer to persons who have a fear of something named by the root or preceding word: *Anglo- + phobe → Anglophobe (= fear of English-speakers or of England)*.

-phobia, *suffix.* from Greek, used after roots and sometimes words to form nouns with the meaning "dread of, unreasonable hatred toward (a given object)": *agora- (= open space) + phobia → agoraphobia (= fear of open spaces); xeno- (= foreign) + -phobia → xenophobia (= hatred toward foreigners)*.

-phobic, *suffix.* from Greek, used after roots and words to form adjectives or nouns meaning "(a person) having a continuous, irrational fear or hatred toward" the object named in the root or preceding word: *xeno- (= foreign) + -phobic → xenophobic (= (a person) having a fear or hatred of foreigners)*.

-proof, *suffix.* ultimately from Latin, used to form adjectives meaning "resistant; not allowing through" the word mentioned: *child + -proof → childproof (= resistant to a child's opening it); water + proof → waterproof (= not allowing water through)*.

-ry, *suffix.* See -ERY.

-s¹ (or **-es**), (s, z, iz), *suffix.* from Old English, used after the root form of verbs and marks the third person singular present indicative form, agreeing with a subject that is singular: *He walks. She runs. The wind rushes through the trees.*

-s² (or **-es**), *suffix.* from Old English, used after count nouns and marks the plural form: *weeks; days; bushes; taxes; ladies; pianos; potatoes.*

-ship, *suffix.* from Old English, used to form nouns meaning **1.** "state or condition of": *friend + -ship → friendship; kin + -ship → kinship.* **2.** "the skill or ability of": *statesman + -ship → statesmanship; apprentice + -ship → apprenticeship.* **3.** "the relation of": *fellow + -ship → fellowship.*

-sick, *suffix.* from Old English, used to form adjectives meaning "sick or ill of or from (the noun of the root)": *car + -sick → carsick (= sick from traveling in a car); air + -sick → airsick (= sick from flying in a plane).*

-some¹, *suffix.* from Old English, used to form adjectives meaning "like; tending to": *burden + -some → burdensome (= like a burden); quarrel + -some → quarrelsome (= tending to quarrel).*

-some², *suffix.* from Old English, used to form nouns meaning "a collection (of the number mentioned) of objects": *threesome (= a group of three).*

-speak, *suffix.* from Old English, used after the ends of words and sometimes roots to form compound nouns that name the style or vocabulary of a certain field of work, interest, time period, etc., that is mentioned in the first word or root: *ad(vertising) + -speak → adspeak (= the jargon of advertising); art + -speak → artspeak (= the language used in discussing art); future + -speak → futurespeak.*

-ster, *suffix.* from Old English, used at the ends of words to form nouns, often implying a bad or negative sense, and referring esp. to one's occupation, habit, or association: *game + ster → gamester (= one greatly interested in games); trick + -ster → trickster (= one who uses or enjoys dishonest tricks).*

-th, *suffix.* ultimately from Greek, used after words that refer to numbers to form adjectives referring to the number mentioned: *(four + -th →) fourth; tenth.*

-tion, *suffix.* from Latin, used after verbs to form nouns that refer to actions or states of the verb: *relate + -tion → relation; sect- + -tion → section; abbreviate + -tion → abbreviation.* Compare -ION.

-tious, *suffix.* from Latin, used after roots to form adjectives, some of which are related to nouns: *fiction: fictitious; ambition: ambitious; caution: cautious; rambunctious, propitious.*

-tude, *suffix.* from Latin, used after roots, especially adjectives, to form nouns that refer to abstract ideas: *exact + -tude → exactitude; apt + -tude → aptitude; gratitude; altitude.*

-ty, *suffix.* from French, used after adjectives to form nouns that name or refer to a state or condition: *able + -ty → ability; certain + -ty → certainty; chaste + -ty → chastity.*

-ure, *suffix.* from French, used after roots and verbs to form abstract nouns that refer to action, result, and instrument or use: *press- + -ure → pressure; legislate + -ure → legislature; fract- + ure → fracture.*

-ville, *suffix.* from French, used **1.** in place names, where it meant "city, town": *Charlottesville.* **2.** after roots or words to form informal words, not all of them long-lasting, that characterize a condition, place, person, group, or situation: *dulls + -ville (= a dull, boring situation); gloomsville.*

-ward, *suffix.* from Old English, used to form adjectives or adverbs meaning "in or toward a certain direction in space or time": *backward.* Also, **-wards.**

-ways, *suffix.* from Middle English, used to form adjectives or adverbs meaning "in a certain direction, manner, or position": *sideways.*

-wide, *suffix.* from Old English, used to form adjectives meaning "extending or applying throughout a certain, given space," as mentioned by the noun: *community + -wide → communitywide (= applying to or throughout the community); countrywide; worldwide.*

-wise, *suffix.* from Old English, used **1.** to form adjectives and adverbs meaning "in a particular manner, position, or direction": *clockwise (= moving in a direction like the hands of a clock).* **2.** to form adverbs meaning "with reference to": *Timewise we can finish the work, but qualitywise, I'm not so sure.*

-woman, *suffix.* from Middle English, used to form nouns meaning "involving a woman; a woman in the role of": *chairwoman; spokeswoman.*

-worthy, *suffix.* from Old English, used to form adjectives meaning **1.** "deserving of, fit for": *news + -worthy → newsworthy (= fit for the news); trust + -worthy → trustworthy.* **2.** "capable of travel in or on": *road + -worthy → roadworthy (= capable of traveling on the road); seaworthy.*

-y[1], *suffix.* from Old English, used to form adjectives meaning "having, showing, or similar to (the substance or action of the word or stem)": *blood + -y → bloody; cloud + -y → cloudy; sexy; squeaky.*

-y[2] (or **-ie**), *suffix.* from Middle English, used **1.a.** to form nouns that bring or add a meaning of dearness or familiarity to the noun or adjective root, such as proper names, names of pets, or in baby talk: *Bill + -y → Billy; Susan + -*

ie → *Susie; bird* + *-ie* → *birdie; sweetie.* **b.** to form nouns that are informal, new, or intended to be new; sometimes these have slightly unpleasant meanings or associations: *boondocks* → *boon-* + *-ies* → *boonies; group* + *-ie* → *groupie; Okie (a person from Oklahoma); preemie (= a premature baby); rookie.* **2.** after adjectives to form nouns, often with the meaning that the noun is an extreme (good or bad) example of the adjective or quality: *bad* + *-ie* → *baddie; big* + *-ie* → *biggie; toughie; sharpie; sickie; whitey.* Compare -o.

-y,³ *suffix.* from Latin, used after verbs to form nouns of action, and certain other abstract nouns: *inquire* + *-y* → *inquiry; in* + *fame* + *-y* → *infamy.*

C. Important Roots to Know

-acr-, *root.* from Latin, meaning "sharp." This meaning is found in such words as: *acerbic, acrid, acrimonious, exacerbate.*

-acro- *root.* from Greek, meaning "high." This meaning is found in such words as: *acrobat, acronym, acrophobia.*

-act-, *root.* from Latin, meaning "to do; move." It is related to the root -AG-. This meaning is found in such words as: *act, action, exact, transact.*

-ag-, *root.* from Latin and Greek, meaning "to move, go, do." This meaning is found in such words as: *agent, agenda, agile, agitate.*

-agon-, *root.* from Greek, meaning "struggle, fight." This meaning is found in such words as: *agony, antagonist, protagonist.*

-agr-, *root.* from Latin, meaning "farming; field." This meaning is found in such words as: *agriculture, agronomy.*

-alesc-, *root.* from Latin, meaning "grow, develop." This meaning is found in such words as: *adolescence, adolescent, coalesce.*

-alg-, *root.* from Greek, meaning "pain." This meaning is found in such words as: *analgesic, neuralgia, nostalgia.*

-ali-, *root.* from Latin, meaning "other, different." This meaning is found in such words as: *alias, alibi, alien, alienate.*

-alte-, *root.* from Latin, meaning "other, different." This meaning is found in such words as: *alter, alternate, alternative, alternator, altruism, altruist.*

-alti-, *root.* from Latin, meaning "high; height." This meaning is found in such words as: *altimeter, altitude, alto, exalt.*

-am-¹ *root.* from Latin, meaning "love, like." This meaning is found in such words as: *amiable, amorous, amour, paramour.*

-am-² *root.* from Latin, meaning "take out; come out." This meaning is found in such words as: *example, sample.*

-ambl-, *root.* from Latin, meaning "walk." This meaning is found in such words as: *amble, ambulance, ambulate, perambulator, circumambulate.*

-ampl-, *root.* from Latin, meaning "enough; enlarge." This meaning is found in such words as: *ample, amplify, amplitude.*

-andro-, *root.* from Greek, meaning "male; man." This meaning is found in such words as: *androgynous, android, polyandry.*

-anima-, *root.* from Latin, meaning "spirit, soul." This meaning is found in such words as: *animate, animosity, animus, equanimity, inanimate.*

-ann-, *root.* from Latin, meaning "year." This meaning is found in such words as: *annals, anniversary, annual, annuity, biannual, semiannual, superannuated.*

-anthro-, *root.* from Greek, meaning "man; human." This meaning is found in such words as: *anthropocentric, anthropoid, anthropology, anthropomorphism, misanthrope.* See -ANDRO-.

-apt-, *root.* from Latin, meaning "fit, proper." This meaning is found in such words as: *adapt, apt, aptitude, inept.*

-arch-, *root.* **1.** from Greek, meaning "chief; leader, ruler." This meaning is found in such words as: *archbishop, archdiocese, archpriest, monarch, matriarch, patriarch, anarchy, hierarchy, monarchy.* **2.** also used to form nouns that refer to persons who are the most important, most notable, or the most extreme examples of (the following noun): *archenemy (= the most important enemy); archconservative (= the most extreme example of a conservative).* **3.** also appears with the meaning "first, earliest, original, oldest in time." This meaning is found in such words as: *archaeology, archaism, archaic, archetype.*

-arm-, *root.* from Latin, meaning "weapon." This meaning is found in such words as: *armada, armament, arms, disarmament.*

-astro- (or **-aster-**), *root.* from Greek, meaning "star; heavenly body; outer space." These meanings are found in such words as: *aster, asterisk, asteroid, astrology, astronomy, astronaut, disaster.*

-athl-, *root.* from Greek, meaning "contest, prize." This meaning is found in such words as: *athlete, athletics, pentathlon.*

-aud-, *root.* from Latin, meaning "hear." This meaning is found in such words as: *audible, audience, audio, audit, audition, auditorium.*

-bat-, *root.* from Latin, meaning "beat, fight." This meaning is found in such words as: *battalion, batten, batter, battle, combat.*

-bell-, *root.* from Latin, meaning "war." This meaning is found in such words as: *antebellum, bellicose, belligerence, belligerent.*

-bene-, *root.* from Latin, meaning "well." This meaning is found in such words as: *benediction, benefactor, beneficial, benefit, benevolent, beneficent.*

-biblio-, *root.* from Greek, meaning "book." This meaning is found in such words as: *bible, bibliography, bibliophile.*

-botan-, *root.* from Greek, meaning "plant, herb." This meaning is found in such words as: *botanical, botany.*

-brev-, *root.* from Latin, meaning "short." This meaning is found in such words as: *abbreviate, abridge, brevity, brief.*

-cad- (or **-cas-**), *root.* from Latin, meaning "fall." This meaning is found in such words as: *cadence, cadenza, decadent.* See -CIDE-².

-cap-, *root.* from Latin, meaning "take, hold." This meaning is found in such words as: *capacious, captures, caption.*

-caut-, *root.* from Latin, meaning "care; careful." This meaning is found in such words as: *caution, cautious, caveat, precaution.*

-cede-, *root.* from Latin, meaning "go away from; withdraw; yield." This meaning is found in such words as: *accede, antecedent, cede, concede, precede, precedent, recede, secede.* See -CEED-, -CESS-.

-ceed-, *root.* from Latin, meaning "go; move; yield." It is related to -CEDE-. This meaning is found in such words as: *proceed, succeed.*

-ceive-, *root.* from Latin, meaning "get, receive." This meaning is found in such words as: *conceive, deceive, misconceive, perceive, receive, transceiver.*

-celer-, *root.* from Latin, meaning "swift, quick." This meaning is found in such words as: *accelerate, celerity, decelerate.*

-cent-, *root.* from Latin, meaning "one hundred." This meaning is found in such words as: *cent, centavo, centigrade, centimeter, centennial, centipede, century, percent.*

-cep-, *root.* from Latin, meaning "get, receive, take." This meaning is found in such words as: *accept, anticipate, perception, reception.* See -CEIVE-.

-cern-, *root.* from Latin, meaning "separate; decide." These meanings are found in such words as: *concern, discern.*

-cert-, *root.* from Latin, meaning "certain; sure; true." This meaning is found in such words as: *ascertain, certain, certificate, certify, concert, disconcerted.*

-cess-, *root.* from Latin, meaning "move, yield." It is related to -CEDE-. This meaning is found in such words as: *access, accessible, accessory, cession, process, procession, recess, recession, success, succession.*

-chor-, *root.* from Greek, meaning "sing; dance." This meaning is found in such words as: *choir, choral, chord, chorus, choreograph, chorister.*

-chrom-, *root.* from Greek, meaning "color." This meaning is found in such words as: *chromatic, chromosome, lipochrome, monochrome, polychromatic.*

-chron-, *root.* from Greek, meaning "time." This meaning is found in such words as: *anachronism, chronic, chronicle, chronology, synchronize.*

-cide-[1], *root.* from Latin, meaning "kill; cut down." This meaning is found in such words as: *biocide, genocide, germicide, herbicide, homicide, insecticide, matricide, patricide, suicide.*

-cide-[2], *root.* from Latin, meaning "fall; happen." It is related to -CAD-. This meaning is found in such words as: *accident, incident.*

-cise-, *root.* from Latin, meaning "cut (down)." It is related to -CIDE-[2]. This meaning is found in such words as: *circumcise, decisive, incision, incisor, incisive, precise, scissors.*

-claim-, *root.* from Latin, meaning "call out; talk; shout." This meaning is found in such words as: *acclaim, claim, clamor, exclaim, proclaim.*

-clos-, *root.* from Latin, meaning "close." This meaning is found in such words as: *cloister, close, closet, disclose, enclose.*

-clud- (or **-clus-**), *root.* from Latin, meaning "to close, shut." This meaning is found in such words as: *include, seclude, inclusion, seclusion.*

-cord-, *root.* from Latin, meaning "heart." This meaning is found in such words as: *accord, concord, concordance, cordial, discord.*

-corp-, *root.* from Latin, meaning "body." This meaning is found in such words as: *corpora, corporal, corporation, corps, corpse, corpus, corpuscle, incorporate.*

-cosm-, *root.* from Greek, meaning "world, universe; order, arrangement." This meaning is found in such words as: *cosmetic, cosmic, cosmopolitan, cosmos, microcosm.*

-cour-, *root.* ultimately from Latin where it has the meaning "run; happen." It is related to -CUR-. This meaning is found in such words as: *concourse, courier, course, discourse, recourse.*

-cred-, *root.* from Latin, meaning "believe." This meaning is found in such words as: *credence, credential, credible, credit, credo, credulous, creed, incredible.*

-cres-, *root.* from Latin, meaning "grow." This meaning is found in such words as: *crescendo, crescent, decrease, increase.*

-culp-, *root.* from Latin, meaning "blame." This meaning is found in such words as: *culpable, culprit, exculpate.*

-cum-, *root.* from Latin, meaning "with." It is used between two words to mean "with; combined with; along with": *a garage-cum-workshop (= a garage that is combined with a workshop).*

-cur-, *root.* from Latin, meanings "run; happen." These meanings are found in such words as: *concur, concurrent, currency, current, curriculum, cursive, cursor, cursory, occur, occurrence, recur, recurrence.* See -COUR-.

-cura-, *root.* from Latin, meaning "help; care." This meaning is found in such words as: *accurate, curable, curate, curator, curative, cure, manicure, pedicure, secure, sinecure.*

-cycle-, *root.* from Greek, meaning "cycle; circle; wheel." This meaning is found in such words as: *bicycle, cycle, cyclo, cyclone, cyclotron, recycle, tricycle.*

-dece- *root.* from Latin, meaning "correct, proper." This meaning is found in such words as: *decent, indecent.*

-dent-, *root.* from Latin, meaning "tooth." This meaning is found in such words as: *dental, dentifrice, dentist, dentistry, denture.*

-derm-, *root.* from Greek, meaning "skin." This meaning is found in such words as: *dermatitis, dermatology, dermis, epidermis, hypodermic, pachyderm, taxidermy.*

-dict-, *root.* from Latin, meaning "say, speak." This meaning is found in such words as: *benediction, contradict, Dictaphone, dictate, dictator, diction, dictionary, dictum, edict, predict.*

-doc-, *root.* from Latin, meaning "to teach." This meaning is found in such words as: *docile, doctor, doctrine, document.*

-dox-, *root.* from Greek, meaning "opinion, idea, belief." This meaning is found in such words as: *doxology, orthodox.*

-drom-, *root.* from Greek, meaning "run; a course for running." This meaning is found in such words as: *aerodrome, dromedary, hippodrome, palindrome, syndrome, velodrome.*

-du-, *root.* from Latin, meaning "two." This meaning is found in such words as: *dual, duel, duet, duo, duplex, duplicity.*

-duc-, *root.* from Latin, meaning "to lead." This meaning is found in such words as: *abduct, abduction, adduce, aqueduct, conducive, conduct, deduce, deduct, ducal, duct, duke, educate, induce, induction, introduce, oviduct, produce, production, reduce, reduction, seduce, seduction, viaduct.*

-dur-, *root.* from Latin, meaning "hard; strong; lasting." These meanings are found in such words as: *durable, duration, duress, during, endure.*

-dyn-, *root.* from Greek, meaning "power." This meaning is found in such words as: *dynamic, dynamism, dynamite, dynamo, dynasty.*

-equa- (or **-equi-**), *root.* from Latin, meaning "equal; the same." This meaning is found in such words as: *equable, equal, equanimity, equilibrium, equity, equivocal, inequality, inequity, unequal.*

-fac-, *root.* from Latin, meaning "do; make." This meaning is found in such words as: *benefactor, de facto, facsimile, fact, faction, faculty, manufacture.* See -FEC-, -FIC-.

-face-, *root.* from Latin, meaning "form; face; make." It is related to -FAC-. This meaning is found in such words as: *deface, efface, facade, face, facet, facial, surface.*

-fec-, *root.* from Latin, meaning "do; make." It is related to the root -FAC-. This meaning is found in such words as: *affect, defecate, defect, effect, infect.*

-fed-, *root.* from Latin, meaning "group; league; trust." This meaning is found in such words as: *confederate, federal, federalize, federation.*

-fend-, *root.* from Latin, meaning "strike." This meaning is found in such words as: *defend, defense, defensive, fend, forfend, indefensible, offend, offense, offensive.*

-fer-, *root.* from Latin, meaning "carry." This meaning is found in such words as: *confer, defer, differ, efferent, ferrous, ferry, infer, pestiferous, prefer, transfer.*

-fess-, *root.* from Latin, meaning "declare; acknowledge." This meaning is found in such words as: *confess, confession, confessional, profess, profession, professional, professor.*

-fic-, *root.* from Latin, meaning "make, do." It is related to -FAC- and -FEC-. This meaning is found in such words as: *beneficial, certificate, efficacy, fiction, honorific, horrific, pacific, prolific, simplification.*

-fid-, *root.* Latin, meaning "faith; trust." This meaning is found in such words as: *confide, confidence, fidelity, fiduciary.*

-fin-, *root.* from Latin, meaning "end; complete; limit." This meaning is found in such words as: *confine, define, definite, definition, final, finale, finance, fine, finish, finite.*

-fix-, *root.* from Latin, meaning "fastened; put; placed." This meaning is found in such words as: *affix, fixation, infix, prefix, suffix.*

-flat-, *root.* from Latin, meaning "blow; wind." This meaning is found in such words as: *conflate, deflate, flatulence, inflate.*

-flect-, *root.* from Latin, meaning "bend." It is related to -FLEX-. This meaning is found in such words as: *deflect, inflect, genuflect, reflect.*

-flex-, *root.* from Latin, meaning "bend." It is related to -FLECT-. This meaning is found in such words as: *circumflex, flex, flexible, reflex, reflexive.*

-flor-, *root.* from Latin, meaning "flower." This meaning is found in such words as: *efflorescence, flora, floral, florescence, florid, florist, flour, flourish, flower.*

-flu-, *root.* from Latin, meaning "flow." This meaning is found in such words as: *affluence, affluent, confluence, effluence, effluent, flu, flue, fluctuate, fluent, fluid, flume, fluoride, flux, influence, influenza.*

-foli-, *root.* from Latin, meaning "leaf." This meaning is found in such words as: *defoliate, foil, foliage, folio, portfolio.*

-form-, *root.* from Latin, meaning "form, shape." This meaning is found in such words as: *conform, deform, formalize, format, formula, malformed, multiform, nonconformist, perform, platform, reform, transform, uniform.*

-fort-, *root.* from Latin, meaning "strong; strength." This meaning is found in such words as: *comfort, discomfort, effort, fort, forte, fortify, fortitude, fortress, uncomfortable.*

-fortun-, *root.* from Latin, meaning "by chance; luck." This meaning is found in such words as: *fortuitous, fortunate, fortune, misfortune, unfortunate.*

-frac-, *root.* Latin, meaning "break; broken." This meaning is found in such words as: *fractious, fracture, fragile, fragment, frail, infraction, refraction.*

-frat-, *root.* from Latin, meaning "brother." This meaning is found in such words as: *fraternal, fraternity, fratricide.*

-fug-, *root.* from Latin, meaning "flee; move; run." This meaning is found in such words as: *centrifugal, centrifuge, fugitive, fugue, refuge, subterfuge.*

-funct-, *root.* from Latin, meaning "perform, execute; purpose, use." This meaning is found in such words as: *defunct, disfunction, function, functional, malfunction, perfunctory.*

-fus-, *root.* from Latin, meaning "pour, cast; join; blend." This meaning is found in such words as: *confuse, defuse, diffuse, effusive, fuse, fusion, infuse, profuse, suffuse, transfusion.*

-gam-, *root.* from Greek, meaning "marriage." This meaning is found in such words as: *bigamy, bigamist, gamete, misogamist, polygamy.*

-gen-, *root.* from Greek and Latin, meaning "race; birth; born; produced." These meanings are found in such words as: *antigen, carcinogen, congenital, degenerate, engender, erogenous, eugenics, gender, gene, generate, genus, homogenize.*

-geo-, *root.* from Greek, meaning "the earth; ground." This meaning is found in such words as: *apogee, geography, geology, geopolitics, perigee.*

-gest-, *root.* from Latin, meaning "carry; bear." This meaning is found in such words as: *congestion, digest, gestation, gesticulate, gesture, ingest, suggest.*

-glot-, *root.* from Greek, meaning "tongue." This meaning is found in such words as: *diglossia, epiglottis, gloss, glossary, glossolalia, glottis, isogloss, polyglot.*

-gnos-, *root.* from Greek and Latin, meaning "knowledge." This meaning is found in such words as: *agnostic, cognition, cognizant, diagnosis, diagnostic, incognito, precognition, prognosis, recognize.*

-grad-, *root.* from Latin, meaning "step; degree; rank." This meaning is found in such words as: *biodegradable, centrigrade, degrade, grad, gradation, gradient, gradual, graduate, retrograde, undergraduate, upgrade.* See -GRESS-.

-graph-, *root.* from Greek, meaning "written down, printed, drawn." This meaning is found in such words as: *autograph, bibliography, biography, calligraphy, cartography, choreography, cinematography, cryptography, demographic, digraph, epigraph, ethnography, geography, graph, graphic, graphite, hagiography, holography, homograph, ideograph, lexicography, lithography, mimeograph, monograph, oceanography, orthography, paragraph, phonograph, photograph, pictograph, polygraph, pornography, seismograph, telegraph, typography.* See -GRAM.

-grat-, *root.* from Latin, meaning "pleasing; thankful; favorable." This meaning is found in such words as: *congratulate, grateful, gratify, gratis, gratitude, gratuitous, gratuity, ingrate, ingratiate, ingratitude.*

-greg-, *root.* from Latin, meaning "group; flock." This meaning is found in such words as: *aggregate, congregate, desegregate, egregious, gregarious, segregate.*

-gress- *root.* from Latin, meaning "step; move." It is related to -GRAD-. This meaning is found in such words as: *aggression, congress, digress, egress, ingress, progress, regress, transgress.*

-gyn-, *root.* from Greek, meaning "wife; woman." This meaning is found in such words as: *androgyny, gynecology, misogyny.*

-hab-, *root.* from Latin, meaning "live, reside." This meaning is found in such words as: *cohabit, habitant, habitable, habitat, habitation, inhabit.*

-habil-, *root.* from Latin, meaning "handy; apt; able." These meanings are found in such words as: *ability, able, habilitate, rehabilitate.*

-hale-, *root.* from Latin, meaning "breathe." This meaning is found in such words as: *exhale, halitosis, inhale.*

-hap-, *root.* from Old Norse, meaning "luck; chance." This meaning is found in such words as: *haphazard, hapless, happen, mishap, perhaps.*

-helio-, *root.* from Greek, meaning "sun." This meaning is found in such words as: *aphelion, heliocentric, helium, perihelion.*

-here-, *root.* from Latin, meaning "cling, stick tight." It is related to -HES-. This meaning is found in such words as: *adhere, adherent, cohere, coherence, coherent.* See -HES-.

-hes-, *root.* Latin, meaning "cling, stick to." It is related to -HERE-. This meaning is found in such words as: *adhesive, cohesive, hesitate.*

-hetero-, *root.* from Greek, meaning "the other of two; different." This meaning is found in such words as: *heterogeneous, heterosexual.*

-hexa-, *root.* from Greek, meaning "six." This meaning is found in such words as: *hexagon, hexameter.*

-homo-, *root.* from Greek, meaning "same, identical." This meaning is found in such words as: *homogeneous, homogenize, homonym.*

-horr-, *root.* from Latin, meaning "shake, tremble." This meaning is found in such words as: *abhor, abhorrent, horrendous, horrible, horrify, horror.*

-hum-, *root.* from Latin, meaning "ground." This meaning is found in such words as: *exhume, humble, humiliate, humility, humus, posthumous.*

-hydr-, *root.* from Greek, meaning "water." This meaning is found in such words as: *anhydrous, carbohydrate, dehydration, hydrant, hydrate, hydraulic, hydrocarbon, hydroelectric, hydrofoil, hydrogen, hydrophobia, hydroplane, hydroponics, hydrotherapy.*

-jec-, *root.* from Latin, meaning "throw; be near; place." This meaning is found in such words as: *eject, adjacent, adjective, ejaculate, abject, dejection, conjecture, object, reject, inject, project, interject, trajectory, subject.*

-jour-, *root.* from French and ultimately from Latin, meaning "daily; of or relating to one day." This meaning is found in such words as: *adjourn, journal, journey, sojourn.*

-jud-, *root.* from Latin, meaning "judge." It is related to -JUR- and -JUS-. This meaning is found in such words as: *adjudge, adjudicate, injudicious, judge, judicial, misjudge, nonjudgmental, prejudgment, prejudice.*

-junc-, *root.* from Latin, meaning "join; connect." This meaning is found in such words as: *adjoin, adjunct, conjunction, disjointed, disjunctive, enjoin, injunction, join(t), rejoinder, subjunctive.*

-jur-, *root.* from Latin, meaning "swear." It is related to the root -JUS-, meaning "law; rule." This meaning is found in such words as: *abjure, conjure, injure, juridical, jurisdiction, jury, perjure.*

-jus-, *root.* from Latin, meaning "law; rule; fair; just." It is related to the root -JUR-. This meaning is found in such words as: *adjust, just, justice, maladjusted, readjust, unjust.*

-lab-, *root.* from Latin, meaning "work." This meaning is found in such words as: *belabor, collaborate, elaborate, labor, laborious.*

-laps-, *root.* from Latin, meaning "slip; slide; fall; make an error." This meaning is found in such words as: *collapse, elapse, lapse, prolapse, relapse.*

-lat-^{1}, *root.* from Latin, meaning "carried." This meaning is found in such words as: *ablative, collate, correlate, dilatory, elated, oblate, prelate, prolate, relate, relative.*

-lat-^{2}, *root.* from Latin, meaning "line; side." This meaning is found in such words as: *bilateral, collateral, dilate, equilateral, lateral, latitude, unilateral, vasodilator.*

-lax-, *root.* from Latin, meaning "loose, slack." This meaning is found in such words as: *lax, laxative, relax.*

-lec-, *root.* from Latin (and sometimes Greek), meaning "gather; choose" and also "read." This meaning is found in such words as: *collect, eclectic, eligible, elite, ineligible, election, lectern, lector, lecture, recollect, select.* See -LEG-.

-leg-, *root.* from Latin, meaning "law" and "to gather," also "to read." It is related to -LEC-. These meanings are found in such words as: *delegate, eclectic, illegal, illegible, intellect, intelligent, legacy, legal, legate, legend, legible, legion, legitimate, legislate, paralegal, privilege, relegate, sacrilege.*

-lev-, *root.* from Latin, meaning "lift; be light." This meaning is found in such words as: *alleviate, cantilever, elevate, elevator, levee, lever, leverage, levitate, levity, levy, relevant, relieve.*

-liber-, *root.* from Latin, meaning "free." This meaning is found in such words as: *deliver, liberal, liberate, libertine, liberty, livery.*

-libr-, *root.* from Latin, meaning "book." This meaning is found in such words as: *libel, library, libretto.*

-libra-, *root.* from Latin, where it has the meaning "balance; weigh." This meaning is found in such words as: *deliberate, equilibrium, librate.*

-lig-, *root.* from Latin, meaning "to tie; bind." This meaning is found in such words as: *ligament, ligature, obligate, oblige, religion.*

-lim-, *root.* from Latin, meaning "line; boundary; edge; threshold." This meaning is found in such words as: *eliminate, illimitable, limbic, limbo, liminal, limit, preliminary, sublime, subliminal.* See -LIN-.

-lin-, *root.* from Latin, meaning "string; line." This meaning is found in such words as: *crinoline, colinear, curvilinear, delineate, line, lineage, lineal, linea-*

ment, linear, linen, lingerie, matrilinear, patrilineal, rectilinear. The meaning is also found in many compound words with *line* as the last part, such as *baseline, guideline, hairline, pipeline, sideline, underline.* See -LIM-.

-ling-, *root.* from Latin, meaning "tongue." This meaning is found in such words as: *bilingual, interlingual, language, lingo, linguine, linguistic, monolingual.*

-lit-, *root.* from Latin, meaning "letter; read; word." This meaning is found in such words as: *alliteration, illiterate, letter, literacy, literal, literary, obliterate, transliteration.*

-lith-, *root.* from Greek, meaning "stone." This meaning is found in such words as: *lithium, lithography, megalith, microlith, monolith, neolithic, paleolithic.*

-loc-, *root.* from Latin, meaning "location; place." This meaning is found in such words as: *allocate, collocation, dislocate, echolocation, local, locale, locate, locative, locomotive, locus, relocate.*

-log-, *root.* from Greek, meaning "speak; word; speech." This meaning is found in such words as: *analog, apology, chronology, decalogue, dialogue, doxology, epilogue, eulogy, ideology, homologous, illogical, logarithm, logic, logo, monologue, neologism, philology, syllogism, tautology, terminology.*

-loq- (or **-loc-**), *root.* from Latin, meaning "speak; say." This meaning is found in such words as: *circumlocution, elocution, eloquent, grandiloquent, interlocutor, locution, loquacious, magniloquent, soliloquy, ventriloquist.*

-lu- (or **-lav-**), *root.* from Latin, meaning "wash." This meaning is found in words as: *dilute, lavatory, ablution.*

-luc-, *root.* from Latin, meaning "light." This meaning is found in such words as: *elucidate, lucid, Lucite, lucubrate, pellucid, relucent, translucent.*

-lud- (or **-lus-**), *root.* from Latin, meaning "to play." This meaning is found in such words as: *allude, allusion, collusion, delude, elusive, illusion, illusory, interlude, ludicrous, prelude.*

-lys-, *root.* from Greek and Latin, meaning "to break down, loosen, dissolve." This meaning is found in such words as: *analysis, catalyst, dialysis, electrolysis, electrolyte, hydrolysis, paralysis, paralytic, palsy, urinalysis.*

-man-[1], *root.* from Latin, meaning "hand." This meaning is found in such words as: *amanuensis, legerdemain, maintain, manacle, manage, manual, maneuver, manufacture, manure, manuscript.*

-man-[2], *root.* -man- comes from Latin, meaning "stay; to last or remain." This meaning is found in such words as: *immanent, impermanent, permanent, remain.*

-mand-, *root.* from Latin, meaning "order." This meaning is found in such words as: *command, countermand, demand, mandate, mandatory, remand.*

-mater-, *root.* from Latin, meaning "mother." This meaning is found in such words as: *maternal, maternity, matriarch, matricide, matrimony, matrix, matron.*

-mech-, *root.* from Greek (but for some words comes through Latin), meaning "machine," and therefore "instrument or tool." This meaning is found in such words as: *machination, machine, machinery, mechanic, mechanical, mechanize.*

-medi-, *root.* from Latin, meaning "middle." This meaning is found in such words as: *immediate, intermediate, media, medial, median, mediate, mediator, medieval, mediocre, medium, multimedia.*

-mem-, *root.* from Latin, meaning "mind; memory." This meaning is found in such words as: *commemorate, immemorial, memento, memo, memorandum, memoir, memorabilia, memorial, memory, remember, remembrance.*

-men-, *root.* from Latin, meaning "mind." This meaning is found in such words as: *commentary, mental, mentality, mention, reminiscent.*

-merc-, *root.* from Latin, meaning "trade." This meaning is found in such words as: *commerce, commercial, infomercial, mercantile, mercenary, merchant.*

-merg-, *root.* from Latin, meaning "plunge; dip; mix." This meaning is found in such words as: *emerge, emergency, immerse, immersion, merge, merger, submerge.*

-meter-, *root.* from Greek, where it has the meaning "measure." This meaning is found in such words as: *anemometer, barometer, centimeter, chronometer, diameter, geometry, kilometer, meter, metric, metronome, nanometer, odometer, parameter, pedometer, perimeter, symmetry.*

-migr-, *root.* from Latin, meaning "move to a new place; migrate." This meaning is found in such words as: *emigrant, emigrate, immigrate, migrant, migrate, transmigration.*

-min-, *root.* from Latin, meaning "least; smallest." This meaning is found in such words as: *diminish, diminution, diminutive, miniature, minimal, minimum, minor, minority, minuend, minus, minute.*

-mir-, *root.* from Latin, meaning "look at." This meaning is found in such words as: *admirable, admire, admiration, miracle, miraculous, mirage, mirror.*

-mis-, *root.* from Latin, meaning "send." It is related to -MIT-. This meaning is found in such words as: *admission, commissar, commissary, commission, compromise, demise, dismiss, emissary, impermissible, intermission, missal, missile, mission, missionary, missive, omission, permission, permissive, promise, promissory, remiss, submission, surmise, transmission.*

-misc-, *root.* from Latin, meaning "mix." This meaning is found in such words as: *miscegenation, miscellaneous, miscellany, miscible, promiscuous.*

-miser-, *root.* from Latin, meaning "wretched." This meaning is found in such words as: *commiserate, miser, miserable, miserly, misery.*

-mit-, *root.* from Latin, meaning "send." It is related to -MIS-. This meaning is found in such words as: *admit, commit, committee, emit, intermittent, noncommittal, omit, permit, remit, remittance, submit, transmit.*

-mne-, *root.* from Greek, meaning "mind; remembering." This meaning is found in such words as: *amnesia, amnesty, mnemonic.*

-mob-, *root.* from Latin, meaning "move." It is related to -MOT- and -MOV-. This meaning is found in such words as: *automobile, mobile, mobility, mobilize.*

-mod-, *root.* from Latin, meaning "manner; kind; measured amount." This meaning is found in such words as: *accommodate, commodious, immoderate, immodest, modal, mode, model, modern, modicum, module, mood, outmoded, remodel.*

-mon-, *root.* from Latin, meaning "warn." This meaning is found in such words as: *admonish, admonitory, admonition, monitor, monitory, monition, monster, monstrous, monument, premonition, summon.*

-monstr-, *root.* from Latin, meaning "show; display." This meaning is found in such words as: *demonstrate, monstrance, muster, remonstrate.*

-mor-, *root.* from Latin, meaning "custom; proper." This meaning is found in such words as: *amoral, demoralize, immoral, moral, morale, morality, mores.*

-morph-, *root.* from Greek, meaning "form; shape." This meaning is found in such words as: *allomorph, amorphous, anthropomorphism, metamorphic, metamorphosis, morph, morpheme, morphine.*

-mort-, *root.* from Latin, meaning "death." This meaning is found in such words as: *amortize, immortal, immortality, immortalize, morgue, mortal, mortality, mortgage.*

-mot-, *root.* from Latin, meaning "move." It is related to -MOV-. This meaning is found in such words as: *automotive, commotion, demote, emote, emotion, immotile, locomotive, motif, motion, motive, motivate, motor, promote, remote.*

-mov-, *root.* from Latin, meaning "move." It is related to -MOT-. This meaning is found in such words as: *movable, move, movement, removal, remove, unmoving.*

-mut-, *root.* from Latin, meaning "change." This meaning is found in such words as: *commute, commutation, immutable, mutate, mutation, mutual, pari-mutuel, permutation, permute, transmute.*

-nat- (or **-nasc-**), *root.* from Latin, meaning "born; birth." This meaning is found in such words as: *cognate, denatured, innate, naive, nascent, natal, nativity, nation, national, native, nature, naturalize, supernatural.*

-naut-, *root.* from Greek, meaning "sailor." It has become generalized to mean "traveler." These meanings are found in such words as: *aeronautic, astronaut, cosmonaut, nautical, nautilus.*

-nav-, *root.* from Latin, meaning "boat, ship." It is related to -NAUT-. This meaning is found in such words as: *circumnavigate, naval, nave, navicular, navigable, navigate, navy.*

-nec- (or **-nex-**), *root.* from Latin, meaning "tie; weave; bind together." This meaning is found in such words as: *annex, connect, disconnect, interconnect, nexus, unconnected.*

-neg-, *root.* from Latin, meaning "deny; nothing." This meaning is found in such words as: *abnegate, negate, negation, negative, neglect, negligee, negligence, negligible, renegade, renege.*

-noc- (or **-nox-**), *root.* from Latin, meaning "harm; kill." This meaning is found in such words as: *innocent, innocuous, nocuous, noxious, obnoxious.*

-noct-, *root.* from Latin, meaning "night." This meaning is found in such words as: *equinoctial, noctambulism, nocturnal, nocturne.*

-nom-¹, *root.* from Greek, meaning "custom; law; manage; control." This meaning is found in such words as: *agronomy, anomalous, anomaly, anomie, astronomy, autonomic, autonomous, autonomy, economy, gastronome, gastronomy, taxonomy.*

-nom-², *root.* from Latin and from Greek, meaning "name." This meaning is found in such words as: *binomial, cognomen, denomination, ignominious, ignominy, monomial, nomen, nomenclature, misnomer, nominal, nominate, nominative, noun, onomastic, onomatopoeia, polynomial, pronominal.*

-norm-, *root.* from Latin, meaning "a carpenter's square; a rule or pattern." This meaning is found in such words as: *abnormal, enormous, enormity, norm, normal, normalcy, normalize, paranormal, subnormal.*

-nota-, *root.* from Latin, meaning "note." This meaning is found in such words as: *annotate, connotation, denote, notable, notary, notarize, notation, note, notorious, notoriety.*

-nounce-, *root.* from Latin, meaning "call; say." It is related to -NUNC-. This meaning is found in such words as: *announce, denounce, mispronounce, pronounce, renounce.*

-nov-, *root.* from Latin, meaning "new." This meaning is found in such words as: *innovate, innovation, nova, novel, novella, novelette, novelist, novelty, novice, novitiate, renovate, renovation.*

-null-, *root.* from Latin, meaning "none; not one." This meaning is found in such words as: *annul, null, nullify.*

-num-, *root.* from Latin, meaning "number." This meaning is found in such words as: *enumerate, innumerable, number, numeral, numerator, numerous, outnumber, supernumerary.*

-nunc-, *root.* from Latin, meaning "call; say." It is related to -NOUNCE-. This meaning is found in such words as: *annunciation, denunciation, enunciate, mispronunciation, nuncio, renunciation.*

-ocul-, *root.* from Latin, meaning "eye." This meaning is found in such words as: *binocular, monocle, ocular, oculist.*

-oper-, *root.* from Latin, meaning "work." This meaning is found in such words as: *cooperate, inoperative, opera, operate, opus.*

-opt-, *root.* from Latin, meaning "choose; choice." This meaning is found in such words as: *adopt, co-opt, opt, option, optional.*

-opti-, *root.* from Greek, meaning "light; sight." This meaning is found in such words as: *autopsy, biopsy, myopia, myopic, ophthalmology, optic, optical, optician, optometrist, optometry, synoptic.*

-ord-, *root.* from Latin, meaning "order; fit." This meaning is found in such words as: *coordinate, extraordinary, inordinate, insubordinate, ordain, order, ordinance, ordinal, ordinary, ordination, subordinate.*

-orga-, *root.* from Greek, meanings "tool; body organ; musical instrument." These meanings are found in such words as: *disorganize, homorganic, inorganic, microorganism, organ, organize, reorganize.*

-ori-, *root.* from Latin, meaning "rise; begin; appear." This meaning is found in such words as: *aboriginal, aborigine, abort, abortion, disorient, orient, orientation, origin, original.*

-pac-, *root.* from Latin, meaning "peace." This meaning is found in such words as: *pacific, pacify, pact.*

-pact-, *root.* from Latin, meaning "fasten." This meaning is found in such words as: *compact, impact, impacted, subcompact.*

-pand-, *root.* from Latin, meaning "spread; get larger." This meaning is found in such words as: *expand, expansion, expanse, expansive, spandrel.*

-par-, *root.* from Latin, meaning "equal; a piece." This meaning is found in such words as: *apart, apartheid, bipartisan, comparable, compare, compartment,* *counterpart, depart, department, departure, disparage, impart, incomparable, pair, par, parenthesis, part, partial, participle, particle, particular, partisan, partition, party, repartee.*

-pare-[1], *root.* from Latin, meaning "prepare." This meaning is found in such words as: *apparatus, disparate, pare, prepare, preparation, rampart, repair, separate.*

-pare-[2], *root.* from Latin, meaning "to bring forth; breed." This meaning is found in such words as: *multiparous, parent, postpartum, parturition, vivaparous.*

-pass-[1], *root.* from Latin, meaning "step; pace." This meaning is found in such words as: *bypass, compass, encompass, impasse, pass, passable, passage, passageway, passport, surpass, trespass, underpass.*

-pass-[2], *root.* from Latin, meaning "suffer; experience." It is related to -PAT-. This meaning is found in such words as: *compassion, compassionate, dispassionate, impassioned, impassive, passion, passive.*

-pat-, *root.* from Latin, meaning "suffer; experience." It is related to -PASS-[2]. This meaning is found in such words as: *compatible, impatience, impatient, incompatible, patience, patient, simpatico.*

-path-, *root.* from Greek, meaning "suffering; disease; feeling." This meaning is found in such words as: *antipathy, apathetic, apathy, empathy, homeopathy, osteopath, pathetic, pathology, pathos, psychopath, sympathetic, sympathize, sympathy, telepathy.*

-patr-, *root.* from Latin, meaning "father." This meaning is found in such words as: *compatriot, expatriate, paterfamilias, paternal, paternity, patriarch, patrician, patricide, patriot, patron, patroon, patronymic.*

-ped-[1], *root.* from Latin, meaning "foot." This meaning is found in such words as: *biped, centipede, expedient, expedite, expedition, impede, impediment, millipede, moped, pedal, pedicure, pedestal, pedestrian, pedometer, quadruped.*

-ped-[2], *root.* from Greek, meaning "child." This meaning is found in such words as: *encyclopedia, orthopedic, pedagogue, pedagogy, pederasty, pediatrics, pediatrician, pedophile.*

-pel-, *root.* from Latin, meaning "drive; push." It is related to the root -PULS-. This meaning is found in such words as: *compel, dispel, expel, impel, propel, propeller, repel, repellant.*

-pen- *root.* from Latin and Greek, meaning "penalty; wrong," and hence "repent." These meanings are found in such words as: *impenitent, penal, penalize, penitence, penology, repent, repentance, subpoena.*

-pend-, *root.* from Latin, meaning "hang; be suspended or weighed." This meaning is found in such words as: *append, appendage, appendix, compendium, depend, expend, impending, independent, pending, pendant, pendulum, pendulous, spend, stipend, suspend.*

-pet-, *root.* from Latin, meaning "seek; strive for." This meaning is found in such words as: *appetite, centripetal, compete, competition, competence, competent, impetigo, impetuous, impetus, perpetual, petition, petulant, repeat, repetition.*

-phil-, *root.* from Greek, meaning "love; loving." This meaning is found in such words as: *hemophilia, necrophilia, philander, philanthropic, philanthropy, philharmonic, philodendron, philology, philosophy.*

-phon-, *root.* from Greek, meaning "sound; voice." This meaning is found in such words as: *cacophony, euphony, homophone, microphone, megaphone, phoneme, phonetic, phonics, phonograph, phonology, polyphony, saxophone, stereophonic, symphony, telephone, xylophone.*

-phys-, *root.* from Greek, meaning "origin; form; nature; natural order." This meaning is found in such words as: *geophysics, metaphysics, physic, physician, physics, physiognomy, physiology, physique.*

-plac-, *root.* from Latin, meaning "to please." This meaning is found in such words as: *complacent, implacable, placate, placebo, placid.*

-plaud-, *root.* from Latin, meaning "clap; noise." It is related to the root -PLOD-. This meaning is found in such words as: *applaud, plaudit, plausible.*

-plen-, *root.* from Latin, meaning "full." It is related to the root -PLET-. This meaning is found in such words as: *plenary, plenipotentiary, plenitude, plenteous, plenty, plenum, replenish.*

-plet-, *root.* from Latin and Greek, meaning "full." This meaning is found in such words as: *complete, deplete, plethora, replete.* See -PLEN-.

-plex-, *root.* from Latin, meaning "fold." It is related to the root -PLIC-. This meaning is found in such words as: *complex, duplex, multiplex, perplex, Plexiglas, plexus.*

-plic-, *root.* from Latin, meaning "fold, bend." This meaning is found in such words as: *accomplice, application, complicate, complicity, duplicate, duplicity, explicable, explicate, explicit, implicate, implicit, inexplicable, multiplication, replica, replicate, supplicant.* See -PLEX-

-plod-, *root.* from Latin, meaning "noise." This meaning is found in such words as: *explode, implode.* See -PLAUD-.

-ploy-, *root.* from French and ultimately from Latin, meaning "bend; fold; use; involve." It is related to -PLIC-. This meaning is found in such words as: *deploy, employ, employee, employer, employment, ploy.*

-pod-, *root.* from Greek, meaning "foot." This meaning is found in such words as: *antipode, arthropod, chiropodist, podiatrist, podiatry, podium, pseudopod, tripod.*

-point-, *root.* from French and ultimately from Latin, meaning "point, prick, pierce." It is related to the root -PUNCT-. This meaning is found in such words as: *appoint, disappoint, midpoint, pinpoint, point, pointless, viewpoint.*

-poli-, *root.* from Latin, meaning "polish, smooth." This meaning is found in such words as: *impolite, polish, polite.*

-polis-, *root.* from Greek, meaning "city." This meaning is found in such words as: *cosmopolitan, geopolitical, impolitic, megalopolis, metropolis, metropolitan, necropolis, police, policy, politicize, political, politico, politics, polity.*

-pon-, *root.* from Latin, meaning "put, place." It is related to the root -POSIT-. This meaning is found in such words as: *component, deponent, exponent, opponent, postpone, proponent.*

-pop-, *root.* from Latin, meaning "people." This meaning is found in such words as: *populace, popular, popularity, popularize, populate, populous.*

-port-, *root.* from Latin, meaning "carry; bring." This meaning is found in such words as: *comport, comportment, deport, export, import, importance, important, opportune, opportunity, portable, portage, portfolio, porter, portmanteau, purport, rapport, report, support, transport, transportation.*

-posit-, *root.* from Latin, meaning "to put, place." It is related to the root -PON-. This meaning is found in such words as *deposit, position, postpone.*

-pot-, *root.* from Latin, meaning "power; ability." This meaning is found in such words as: *impotence, impotent, omnipotent, plenipotentiary, potent, potential, potency.*

-pound-, *root.* from French and ultimately from Latin, meaning "put; place." It is related to the root -PON-. This meaning is found in such words as: *compound, expound, impound, propound.*

-preci-, *root.* from Latin, meaning "value; worth; price." This meaning is found in such words as: *appreciate, depreciate, precious, price, semiprecious.*

-prehend-, *root.* from Latin, meaning "seize; grasp hold of; hold on to." This meaning is found in such words as: *apprehend, comprehend, misapprehend, prehensile.* See -PRIS-.

-press-, *root.* from Latin, meaning "squeeze; press (down)." This meaning is found in such words as: *acupressure, compress, compression, decompress, decompression, depress, depression, express, impress, impressive, irrepressible, oppress, press, pressure, repress, suppress.*

-prim-, *root.* from Latin, meaning "first." This meaning is found in such words as: *primacy, primary, primal, primeval, primate, prime, primitive, primo, primogeniture, primordial, prince, principal, principle, unprincipled.*

-pris-, *root.* from French and ultimately from Latin, meaning "grasp; take hold; seize." It is related to the root -PREHEND-. This meaning is found in such words as: *apprise, comprise, enterprise, prison, prize, reprisal, reprise, surprise.*

-priv-, *root.* from Latin, meaning "separated; apart; restricted." This meaning is found in such words as: *deprivation, deprive, privacy, private, privation, privatize, privilege, privy, underprivileged.*

-prob-, *root.* from Latin, meaning "prove." This meaning is found in such words as: *approbation, improbable, opprobrious, opprobrium, probable, probability, probate, probation, probe, probity, reprobate.* See -PROV-.

-propr-, *root.* from Latin, meaning "one's own." This meaning is found in such words as: *appropriate, expropriate, improper, impropriety, misappropriate, proper, property, proprietary, proprietor, propriety.*

-prov-, *root.* from French and ultimately from Latin, meaning "prove." It is related to the root -PROB-. This meaning is found in such words as: *approve, approval, disapprove, disprove, improve, proof, prove, proven.*

-prox-, *root.* from Latin, meaning "close; near." This meaning is found in such words as: *approximate, approximation, proximity.*

-pter-, *root.* from Greek, meaning "wing; feather." This meaning is found in such words as: *archaeopteryx, dipterous, helicopter, monopterous, pterodactyl.*

-pugn-, *root.* from Latin, meaning "fight; fist." This meaning is found in such words as: *impugn, pugilism, pugnacious, repugnant.*

-puls-, *root.* from Latin, meaning "push; drive." This meaning is found in such words as: *compulsion, expulsion, impulse, impulsive, propulsion, pulsar, pulsation, pulse, repulse, repulsive.* See -PEL-.

-punct-, *root.* from Latin, meaning "point; prick; pierce." This meaning is found in such words as: *acupuncture, compunction, expunge, punctilious, punctual, punctuality, punctuation, puncture, pungent.* See -POINT-.

-pur-, *root.* from Latin, meaning "pure." This meaning is found in such words as: *expurgate, impure, impurity, pure, purée, purgative, purgatory, purge, purify, puritan, purity.*

-pute-, *root.* from Latin, meaning "to clean, prune; consider; think." This meaning is found in such words as: *amputate, compute, computation, deputy, dispute, disreputable, impute, indisputable, putative, reputable, reputation.*

-quad-, *root.* from Latin, meaning "four, fourth." This meaning is found in such words as: *quad, quadrangle, quadrant, quadriplegic, quadruped, quadruplet.*

-quer-, *root.* from Latin, meaning "seek; look for; ask." This meaning is found in such words as: *conquer, query.* See -QUIR-, -QUES-, -QUIS-.

-ques-, *root.* from Latin, meaning "seek; look for; ask." This meaning is found in such words as: *conquest, inquest, quest, question, request.*

-quie-, *root.* from Latin, meaning "quiet, still." This meaning is found in such words as: *acquiesce, acquiescent, disquieting, quiescent, quiet, quietude.*

-quir-, *root.* from Latin, meaning "seek; look for." This meaning is found in such words as: *acquire, enquiry, inquire, inquiry, require, requirement.* See -QUIS-, -QUER-.

-quis-, *root.* from Latin, meaning "seek; look for." This meaning is found in such words as: *acquisition, exquisite, inquisitive, inquisition, perquisite, prerequisite, requisite.* See -QUIR-.

-quit-, *root.* from Latin, meaning "release; discharge; let go." This meaning is found in such words as: *acquit, quit, quite, requite, unrequited.*

-quot-, *root.* from Latin, meaning "how many; divided." This meaning is found in such words as: *quota, quotation, quote, quotidian, quotient.*

-rape-, *root.* from Latin, meaning "carry off by force." This meaning is found in such words as: *enrapture, rape, rapid, rapine, rapt, rapture.*

-rase-, *root.* from Latin, meaning "rub; scrape." This meaning is found in such words as: *abrasion, erase, raze, razor.*

-ratio-, *root.* from Latin, meaning "logic; reason; judgment." This meaning is found in such words as: *irrational, overrated, rate, ratify, ratio, ration, rational.*

-real-, *root.* from Latin, meaning "in fact; in reality." This meaning is found in such words as: *real, reality, realistic, realize, really, surreal.*

-rect-, *root.* from Latin, meaning "guide; rule; right; straight." This meaning is found in such words as: *correct, direct, erect, indirect, insurrection, misdirect, resurrection, rectangle, rectify, rectitude, rector, rectum.*

-reg-, *root.* from Latin, meaning "rule; direct; control." This meaning is found in such words as: *deregulate, interregnum, irregular, regal, regalia, regency, regular, regicide, regime, regimen, regiment, region, regional.*

-rend-, *root.* from Latin, meaning "give." This meaning is found in such words as: *render, rendition, surrender.*

-roga-, *root.* from Latin, meaning "ask; demand." This meaning is found in such words as: *abrogate, arrogant, derogatory, interrogate, prerogative, surrogate.*

-rota-, *root.* from Latin, meaning "round." This meaning is found in such words as: *orotund, rotary, rotate, rotation, rotogravure, rotor, rotund, rotunda.*

-rupt-, *root.* from Latin, meaning "break." This meaning is found in such words as: *abrupt, corrupt, disrupt, erupt, eruption, incorruptible, interrupt, rupture.*

-salv-, *root.* from Latin, meaning "save." This meaning is found in such words as: *salvation, salvage, salver, salvo.*

-san-, *root.* from Latin, meaning "health." This meaning is found in such words as: *insane, insanitary, sanatorium, sane, sanitary, sanitize.*

-sanct-, *root.* from Latin, meaning "holy." This meaning is found in such words as: *sacrosanct, sanctify, sanction, sanctity, sanctuary.*

-sat-, *root.* from Latin, meaning "full, enough, sufficient." This meaning is found in such words as: *dissatisfy, dissatisfaction, insatiable, sate, satiated, satire, satisfy, satisfaction, saturate, unsatisfied.*

-scend-, *root.* from Latin, meaning "climb." This meaning is found in such words as: *ascend, condescend, descend, transcend, transcendent.*

-schol-, *root.* from Latin, meaning "school." This meaning is found in such words as: *scholar, scholastic, school, unschooled.*

-sci-, *root.* from Latin, meaning "to know." This meaning is found in such words as: *conscience, conscious, omniscient, omniscience, prescient, prescience, science, scientific.*

-scope-, *root.* from Greek, meaning "see." This meaning is found in such words as: *fluoroscope, gyroscope, horoscope, microscope, microscopic, oscilloscope, periscope, radioscopy, spectroscope, stethoscope, telescope, telescopic.*

-scrib-, *root.* from Latin, meaning "write." This meaning is found in such words as: *ascribe, circumscribe, conscribe, describe, indescribable, inscribe, prescribe, proscribe, scribble, scribe, subscribe, transcribe.*

-script-, *root.* from Latin, meaning "writing." This meaning is found in such words as: *description, inscription, scripture.*

-sect-, *root.* from Latin, meaning "cut." This meaning is found in such words as: *bisect, dissect, intersect, resection, section, sector, vivisection.*

-semble-, *root.* from Latin, meaning "seem; appear(ance)." This meaning is found in such words as: *assemble, assembly, dissemble, ensemble, resemblance, resemble, semblance.*

-sene-, *root.* from Latin, meaning "old." This meaning is found in such words as: *senate, senescence, senescent, senile, senior.*

-sens-, *root.* from Latin, meaning "sense; feel." This meaning is found in such words as: *consensus, dissension, extrasensory, insensible, insensitive, nonsense, sensation, sensational, sense, senseless, sensitive, sensor, sensory, sensual, sensuous.* See -SENT-.

-sent-, *root.* from Latin, meaning "feel." It is related to the root -SENS-. This meaning is found in such words as: *assent, consent, dissent, presentiment, resent, resentful, resentment, scent, sentence, sentient, sentiment.*

-seq-, *root.* from Latin, meaning "follow." This meaning is found in such words as: *consequence, consequent, consequential, inconsequential, obsequious, sequel, sequence, sequential, subsequent.*

-serv-¹, *root.* from Latin, meaning "slave." This meaning is found in such words as: *deserve, disservice, servant, serve, service, servile, servitude, subservient.*

-serv-², *root.* from Latin, meaning "save." This meaning is found in such words as: *conserve, conservation, observe, observation, preserve, preservation, reserve, reservation, reservoir, unreserved.*

-sess-, *root.* from Latin, meaning "sit; stay." It is related to the root -SID-. This meaning is found in such words as: *assess, assessor, dispossess, intersession, obsession, possession, repossession, session.*

-sid-, *root.* from Latin, meaning "sit; stay; live in a place." This meaning is found in such words as: *assiduous, dissident, insidious, preside, president, presidium, presidio, reside, residual, residue, siege, subside, subsidiary, subsidy, subsidize.* See -SESS-.

-sign-, *root.* from Latin, meaning "sign; have meaning." This meaning is found in such words as: *assign, assignation, consign, cosign, design, designate, ensign, insignia, insignificant, resign, signal, signature, signet, significant, signify.*

-simil-, *root.* from Latin, meaning "alike, similar." This meaning is found in such words as: *assimilate, assimilation, dissimilar, dissimulate, facsimile, similar, simile, simulcast, simulate, simultaneous, verisimilitude.*

-sist-, *root.* from Latin, meaning "remain; stand; stay." This meaning is found in such words as: *assist, consist, desist, inconsistent, insist, irresistible, persist, resist, subsist, subsistence.*

-soc-, *root.* from Latin, meaning "partner; comrade." This meaning is found in such words as: *associate, association, disassociate, disassociation, social, socialize, society, socio-, unsociable.*

-sola-, *root.* from Latin, meaning "soothe." This meaning is found in such words as: *console, consolation, disconsolate, inconsolable, solace.*

-sole-, *root.* from Latin, meaning "only; alone." This meaning is found in such words as: *desolate, desolation, sole, soliloquy, solipsism, solitaire, solitary, solitude, solo.*

-solv-, *root.* from Latin, meaning "loosen; release; dissolve." This meaning is found in such words as: *absolve, dissolve, insolvent, resolve, solve.*

-som-, *root.* from Greek, meaning "body." This meaning is found in such words as: *chromosome, psychosomatic, ribosome, somatic.*

-son-, *root.* from Latin, meaning "sound." This meaning is found in such words as: *consonant, dissonant, dissonance, resonant, resonance, resonate, resound, sonar, sonata, sonic, sonnet, sonogram, sound, supersonic, ultrasonic, unison.*

-soph-, *root.* from Greek, meaning "wise." This meaning is found in such words as: *philosopher, philosophy, sophism, sophistry, sophisticated, sophomore, theosophical, theosophy, unsophisticated.*

-sort-, *root.* from Latin, meaning "kind; type; part." This meaning is found in such words as: *assorted, consort, consortium, resort, sort.*

-spec-, *root.* from Latin, meaning "look at; examine." This meaning is found in such words as: *aspect, expect, inspect, inspector, inspection, introspection, irrespective, perspective, prospect, prospective, prospectus, respect, respectable, retrospect, special, specialty, specialize, specie, species, specific, specify, specimen, specious, spectacle, spectacular, spectrum, speculate, suspect.*

-sper-, *root.* from Latin, meaning "hope; hope for; expect." This meaning is found in such words as: *desperado, desperate, prosper, prosperity, prosperous.*

-spir-, *root.* from Latin, meaning "breathe; have a longing for." This meaning is found in such words as: *aspire, conspire, expire, inspire, perspire, respiration, respiratory, respire, spiracle, spirit, transpire.*

-spond-, *root.* from Latin, meaning "pledge; promise." This meaning is found in such words as: *correspond, correspondent, correspondence, despondent, respond, transponder.*

-stab-, *root.* from Latin, meaning "stand." This meaning is found in such words as: *establish, instability, stabilize, stable, unstable.*

-stan-, *root.* from Latin, meaning "stand; remain." This meaning is found in such words as: *constant, circumstance, distance, distant, happenstance, inconstant, inconstancy, insubstantial, stance, stanch, stanchion, stand, stanza, stanch, substance, substantial, substantive, transubstantiation.*

-stat-, *root.* from Latin (and in some cases from Greek), meaning "stand; remain." This meaning is found in such words as: *hemostat, instate, interstate, misstate, overstate, photostat, prostate, reinstate, rheostat, state, static, station, statistics, stative, statute, status, statutory, thermostat, understate.*

-stin-, *root.* from Latin, meaning "separate; mark by pricking." This meaning is found in such words as: *distinct, distinguish, indistinct, indistinguishable, instinct.*

-stit-, *root.* from Latin, meaning "remain; stand." This meaning is found in such words as: *constitute, constitution, destitute, institute, prostitute, prostitution, reconstitute, restitution, substitute, superstition, unconstitutional.*

-strain-, *root.* from French and ultimately from Latin, meaning "stretch; tighten; bind." It is related to the root -strict-. This meaning is found in such words as: *constrain, restrain, strain, strait, straiten, unrestrained.*

-strat-, *root.* from Latin, meaning "cover; throw over" and "level." These meanings are found in such words as: *prostrate, strata, stratify, stratosphere, stratum, substrate.*

-strict-, *root.* from Latin, meaning "draw tight; bind; tighten." This meaning is found in such words as: *constrict, district, redistrict, restrict, strict, stricture, vasoconstrictor.*

-stroph-, *root.* from Greek, meaning "turn; twist." This meaning is found in such words as: *apostrophe, catastrophe, strophe.*

-stru-, *root.* from Latin, meaning "build, as by making layers; spread." This meaning is found in such words as: *construct, construction, construe, destruct, destruction, indestructible, infrastructure, instruct, instruction, instrument, instrumentation, misconstrue, obstruct, reconstruct, structure.*

-stud-, *root.* from Latin, meaning "be busy with; devote oneself to." This meaning is found in such words as: *student, studio, study, understudy.*

-suade-, *root.* from Latin, meaning "recommend; urge as being agreeable or sweet." This meaning is found in such words as: *dissuade, persuade.*

-sum-, *root.* from Latin, meaning "take up; pick up." This meaning is found in such words as: *assume, assumption, consume, consumption, presume, presumption, presumptuous, resume, resumé, resumption, subsume, sumptuous.*

-tact- (or **-tang-**), *root.* from Latin, meaning "touch." This meaning is found in such words as: *contact, intact, tact, tactile, tangent, tangible.*

-tail-, *root.* from French and ultimately from Latin, meaning "cut." This meaning is found in such words as: *curtail, detail, entail, retail, tailor.*

-tain-, *root.* from French and ultimately from Latin, meaning "hold." It is related to the root -TEN-. This meaning is found in such words as: *abstain, attain, contain, detain, entertain, maintain, obtain, pertain, rein, retain, retinue, sustain.*

-tech-, *root.* from Greek, meaning "skill; ability." This meaning is found in such words as: *polytechnic, pyrotechnic, tech, technical, technician, technique, technology.*

-temp-, *root.* from Latin, meaning "time." This meaning is found in such words as: *contemporary, contretemps, extemporaneous, tempo, temporary, temporize.*

-ten-, *root.* from Latin, meaning "hold." This meaning is found in such words as: *abstinence, content, continent, countenance, incontinent, impertinent, incontinence, lieutenant, pertinent, retentive, sustenance, tenable, tenacious, tenant, untenable.* See -TAIN-.

-tend-, *root.* from Latin, meaning "stretch; stretch out; extend; proceed." This meaning is found in such words as: *attend, contend, distend, extend, intend, portend, pretend, superintend, tend, tender, tendency, tendon.*

-term-, *root.* from Latin, meaning "end; boundary; limit." This meaning is found in such words as: *determine, exterminate, indeterminate, interminable, predetermine, term, terminal, terminate, terminology, terminus.*

-terr-, *root.* from Latin, meaning "earth; land." This meaning is found in such words as: *extraterrestrial, extraterritorial, subterranean, terrace, terrain, terrarium, terrestrial, terrier, territory.*

-test-, *root.* from Latin, meaning "witness." This meaning is found in such words as: *attest, contest, detest, incontestable, intestate, pretest, protest, protestation, Protestant, test, testament, testate, testify, testimonial, testimony.*

-theo-, *root.* from Greek, meaning "god." This meaning is found in such words as: *atheism, atheist, monotheism, pantheon, polytheism, theocracy, theology, theosophy.*

-therm-, *root.* from Greek, meaning "heat." This meaning is found in such words as: *hypothermia, thermal, thermodynamics, thermometer, thermostat.*

-thes-, *root.* from Greek, meaning "put together; set down." This meaning is found in such words as: *antithesis, epenthesis, hypothesis, parenthesis, photosynthesis, prosthesis, synthesis, synthetic, thesis.*

-tom-, *root.* from Greek, meaning "cut." This meaning is found in such words as: *anatomy, appendectomy, atom, diatom, dichotomy, hysterectomy, lobotomy, mastectomy, tome, tomography, tonsilectomy, vasectomy.*

-ton-, *root.* from Greek, meaning "sound." This meaning is found in such words as: *atonal, baritone, detonate, intonation, intone, monotone, monotonous, overtone, semitone, tonal, tone, tonic, undertone.*

-tort-, *root.* from Latin, meaning "twist." This meaning is found in such words as: *contort, distort, extort, retort, tort, torte, tortilla, tortuous, torture.*

-tox-, *root.* from Latin, meaning "poison." This meaning is found in such words as: *antitoxin, detoxify, intoxicated, intoxication, toxic, toxin.*

-trac-, *root.* from Latin, meaning "pull." This meaning is found in such words as:

abstract, attract, attraction, contract, contraction, detract, distract, extract, extractor, intractable, protracted, protractor, retract, subcontract, subtract, tract, tractable, traction, tractor.

-troph-, *root.* from Greek, meaning "food, nourishment." This meaning is found in such words as: *atrophy, isotrophy, phototrophic, trophic.*

-trude-, *root.* from Latin, meaning "thrust, push." This meaning is found in such words as: *extrude, intrude, obtrude, protrude.*

-turb-, *root.* from Latin, meaning "stir up." This meaning is found in such words as: *disturb, disturbance, imperturbable, masturbate, perturb, perturbation, turbid, turbine, turbo, turbulent.*

-type-, *root.* from Greek, meaning "impression." This meaning is found in such words as: *archetype, atypical, prototype, stereotype, type, typical, typify, typography.*

-ult-, *root.* from Latin, meaning "beyond; farther." This meaning is found in such words as: *antepenultimate, penultimate, ulterior, ultimatum, ultimate, ultra-.*

-uni-, *root.* from Latin, meaning "one." This meaning is found in such words as: *reunion, reunite, unicameral, unicorn, unicycle, uniform, unify, unilateral, union, unique, unisex, unit, unitary, unite, university.*

-urb-, *root.* from Latin, meaning "city." This meaning is found in such words as: *conurbation, suburb, suburban, suburbanite, suburbia, urb, urban, urbane.*

-vac-, *root.* from Latin, meaning "empty." This meaning is found in such words as: *evacuate, vacancy, vacant, vacate, vacation, vacuous, vacuum.*

-vade-, *root.* from Latin, meaning "go." This meaning is found in such words as: *evade, invade, pervade.*

-val-, *root.* from Latin, meaning "value; worth; health; be strong." This meaning is found in such words as: *devalue, equivalent, evaluate, prevalent, undervalue, value, valiant, valid, validate, valor.*

-var-, *root.* from Latin, meaning "change." This meaning is found in such words as: *invariable, variable, variance, variant, variation, varied, variegate, variety, variform, various, vary.*

-vec-, *root.* from Latin, meaning "drive; convey." This meaning is found in such words as: *convection, invective, vector.*

-ven-, *root.* from Latin, meaning "come." This meaning is found in such words as: *advent, adventure, avenue, circumvent, contravene, convene, convention, convenience, convent, covenant, event, eventual, inconvenience, inconvenient, intervene, invent, invention, inventory, misadventure, prevent, provenance, revenue, souvenir, unconventional, uneventful, venture, venturesome, venue.*

-venge-, *root.* from Latin, meaning "protect, avenge, punish." This meaning is found in such words as: *avenge, revenge, vengeance.*

-ver-, *root.* from Latin, meaning "true; truth." This meaning is found in such words as: *veracious, veracity, verily, verify, verisimilitude, veritably, verity.*

-verb-, *root.* from Latin, meaning "word." This meaning is found in such words as: *adverb, adverbial, proverb, proverbial, verb, verbal, verbalize, verbatim, verbiage, verbose.*

-verg-, *root.* from Latin, meaning "turn; bend." This meaning is found in such words as: *converge, diverge, verge.* See -VERT-.

-vert- (or **-vers-**), *root.* from Latin, meaning "turn; change." This meaning is found in such words as: *adversary, adverse, advertise, advertisement, aversion, avert, controversial, controversy, conversation, conversant, converse, conversion, convert, diverse, diversion, divert, extrovert, extroversion, inadvertent, incontrovertible, introvert, invert, inversion, irreversible, obverse, perverse, perversion, pervert, reversal, reverse, revert, subversive, subversion, subvert, transverse, traverse, universal, universe, versatile, verse, versed, version, versus, vertebra, vertebrate, vertex, vertical, vertiginous, vertigo.*

-via-, *root.* from Latin, meaning "way; route; a going." This meaning is found in such words as: *deviant, devious, obviate, trivial, via, viaduct.*

-vict-, *root.* from Latin, meaning "conquer." It is related to the root -VINC-. This meaning is found in such words as: *convict, evict, victor, victorious, victory.*

-vide-, *root.* from Latin, meaning "see." It is related to the root -VIS-. This meaning is found in such words as: *evidence, evident, provide, providence, providential, video, videodisc, videocassette, videotape.*

-vinc-, *root.* from Latin, meaning "conquer; defeat." This meaning is found in such words as: *convince, evince, invincible, vincible. See -VICT-.*

-vis-, *root.* from Latin, meaning "see." This meaning is found in such words as: *advice, advisable, advise, envisage, envision, inadvisable, invisible, provision, proviso, revise, revision, supervise, supervision, supervisor, television, visa, visage, vis-à-vis, visible, vision, visit, visor, vista, visual.* See -VIDE-.

-vit-, *root.* from Latin, meaning "life; living." It is related to the root -VIV-. This meaning is found in such words as: *aqua vitae, curriculum vitae, revitalize, vita, vital, vitalize, vitamin.*

-viv-, *root.* from Latin, meaning "life; alive; lively." This meaning is found in such words as: *convivial, revival, revive, survival, survive, survivor, viva, vivacious, vivid, viviparous, vivisection.*

-voc-, *root.* from Latin, meaning "call." This meaning is found in such words as: *advocate, avocation, convocation, convoke, equivocal, evocative, evoke, invocation, invoke, irrevocable, provocation, provocative, provoke, revocation, revoke, unequivocal, unprovoked, vocabulary, vocal, vocation, vociferous.*

-vol-, *root.* from Latin, meaning "wish; will." This meaning is found in such words as: *benevolent, involuntary, malevolent, volition, voluntary, volunteer.*

-volv- (or **-volut-**), *root.* from Latin, meaning "turn, roll." This meaning is found in words such as: *evolve, revolve, evolution, revolution.*

-vor-, *root.* from Latin, meaning "eat." This meaning is found in such words as: *carnivore, carnivorous, devour, herbivore, omnivore, omnivorous, voracious.*

-vot-, *root.* from Latin, meaning "vow." This meaning is found in such words as: *devote, devotee, devout, vote.*

-voy-, *root.* from French, ultimately from Latin VIA, meaning "way; send." This meaning is found in such words as: *envoy, invoice, voyage.*

Tips for Further Study

Random House Webster's College Dictionary, Newly Revised and Updated. Random House, Inc. © 1998. One of America's best general dictionaries. It is especially strong in its coverage of new words. Definitions are clear and easy to understand.

Webster's New World College Dictionary, Third College Edition, Revised and Updated. Macmillan, © 1997. One of America's best dictionaries, *Webster's New World* features extremely clear definitions and labels.

Random House Unabridged Electronic Dictionary, CD-ROM, Version 3.0 for Windows™ 95 and higher versions. It features over 120,000 recorded pronunciations. The print version of this dictionary has a New-Words Section in the front.

30 Days to a More Powerful Vocabulary. Dr. Wilfred Funk & Norman Lewis. Pocket Books, © 1970. The most widely used manual of its kind, this book shows how to acquire a larger, more effective vocabulary in one month by studying 15 minutes a day.

Jesse's Word of the Day. Jesse Sheidlower. Random House, Inc. © 1998. Fascinating questions and answers from the Internet's hottest language site: www.jessesword.com.

Merriam-Webster's Collegiate Dictionary, Tenth Edition. Merriam-Webster, © 1996. CD-ROM of dictionary and thesaurus is available.

Index